Gender in Scottish History since 1700

Gender in Scottish History since 1700

Edited by
Lynn Abrams, Eleanor Gordon,
Deborah Simonton and Eileen Janes Yeo

Edinburgh University Press

Edinburgh University Press Ltd
22 George Square, Edinburgh

Typeset in 10.5/13 Sabon
by Servis Filmsetting Ltd, Manchester

A CIP record for this book is available from the British Library

ISBN 0 7486 1760 4 (hardback)
ISBN 0 7486 1761 2 (paperback)

The right of the several authors to be identified as authors of this work has been
asserted in accordance with the Copyright, Designs and Patents Act 1988.

Published with the support of the
Edinburgh University Scholarly Publishing Initiatives Fund.

Contents

Preface and Acknowledgements

The impetus for this collection was a lengthy lunch date between Lynn Abrams and Elizabeth Ewan in an Edinburgh wine bar in 2000. The wine bar subsequently burned down but the ideas and enthusiasm for this book survived, culminating in a Scottish Women's History Network (now renamed Women's History Scotland) project to apply theories of gender to the writing of modern Scottish history. From the start, we agreed that gendering Scottish history was rather different from writing a history of Scotland that was inclusive of women's experience. Hence, Women's History Scotland adopted a two-pronged strategy. The production of *The Biographical Dictionary of Scottish Women* (Edinburgh, 2006) is our ambitious solution to redress the relative absence of women as historical actors in the writing of Scotland's past. Containing more than 800 entries, the *Dictionary* has brought about an inestimable improvement in our knowledge of the women who contributed to this country's identity and history. It is, in a sense, a companion volume to this one in that biographies of many of the women mentioned in the following chapters appear in the *Dictionary*. *Gender in Scottish History*, on the other hand, represents the intellectual and ideological foundations of our engagement with Scottish history. By viewing the past through the lens of gender, we have endeavoured to question some of the more entrenched myths of the historical narrative and to produce some alternative readings of those myths. By adding women to the story, we have produced a more complex mix of ingredients, and by problematising men's experiences we have decentred elements of the story. The result constitutes a stretching of the boundaries of what constitutes the narrative of Scottish history in the modern period.

From the start, this project has been a collective endeavour which owes its completion to many individuals. The members of Women's History Scotland have made practical and intellectual contributions to the project. Women's History Scotland is a diverse community of individuals researching and writing on women's and gender history, many of whom learned their craft in a different national historical tradition but find themselves in the stimulating and lively community of women's historians in Scotland. We would like to thank all the participants in the Scottish Women's History Network workshop in May 2001 on the theme of 'Gender in Scottish History', especially the leaders and summarisers of the workshop sessions. In addition to the editors, these were Callum Brown, Yvonne Brown, Paul Burton, Elizabeth Ewan, Sue Innes, Sarah Smith and Perry Willson. Participants in subsequent conferences on 'Writing Biography', 'Gender, Families and Relationships' and 'Gender at Work' also helped us to develop and hone our ideas. The Steering Committee of Women's History Scotland has been a steady source of practical and intellectual support to the editors, and Rose Pipes in particular has played a key role in keeping us all focused. John Davey of Edinburgh University Press believed in the project from the beginning. Our families and friends have lived with this project for too long; we thank them for their patience. We also owe a huge debt to the wider international community of women's historians whose work has informed and stimulated our own. Sue Innes was a key instigator and champion of this project within the Scottish Women's History Network. Her enthusiasm for women's and gender history was infectious, and her networking abilities were legendary. We think she would have approved of this book.

1

Introduction: Gendering the Agenda

Lynn Abrams

This book was conceived at the start of the new millennium, in the wake of Scottish devolution and the opening of the new Scottish parliament.[1] These events stimulated new interest and investment in Scotland's past, and Scottish historians rose to the occasion, producing a series of new national histories – studies claiming to present a fresh, inclusive, recognisable and usable narrative of the past.[2] The election of a record number of women members to the first Scottish parliament in 1999 also excited comment; but this incursion of women into the Scottish political landscape was not paralleled by a similar recognition of women's place in Scotland's past.

As historians, we all understand the importance of national histories: they act to reaffirm a sense of identity, they have a place in nation-building and they serve to fix particular narratives as representative of the nation's past in popular memory. Histories like this have great resonance. Siân Reynolds has noted that, in France, history is a 'lieu de mémoire', a site of memory which possesses tremendous power, to be used (and maybe abused) by those who construct and pass on the sense of the past.[3] Moreover, national histories or textbook histories create the illusion of 'transmitting a "universal" and synthetic image of history'. Yet, as we know, they can only do this by selecting and excluding certain voices and experiences.[4] No textbook can be neutral. Such texts reveal much about the preoccupations of those who write them and to some extent of their audience too. Thus we should be concerned about how such narratives are written, about what they include and exclude.

National histories written in any country tend to be weighty, immobile and usually conservative in their content and method. But they should be alive to new developments, not only in history-writing but also in respect of contemporary concerns. Scotland at the start of the twenty-first century is a culturally diverse country, where gender equality is high on the political agenda and where women regard themselves as equal participants in the national story. Historians of women have been especially concerned to reveal the partiality of most national histories in their silencing of women's voices, their marginalisation of women's experiences and their elision of women's pasts. Informing this concern is the knowledge that history informs, empowers and liberates, and thus it should offer everyone the possibility of a recognisable and usable past.

The aim of this book is to engage with and expand the Scottish historical narrative, by adding women's experience and by applying gender as a category of analysis. We have endeavoured to stretch concepts, to question, reassess and reinterpret some dominant narratives and, where appropriate, to punch holes in some of the long-standing myths of Scottish history. In short, we suggest new ways of looking at the story of Scotland's past from different angles and through different lenses.

Women's history and a history informed by understandings of gender are two different enterprises, though they are connected. The history of women seeks to explore the experiences of women in the past, since 'we may assume that time as lived by the female part of humanity does not pass according to the same rhythms and that it is not perceived in the same way as that of men'; in short, that women have a history of their own.[5] Of course, women's historians aimed first to achieve visibility for women in the past, but today in the developed world their aim is to identify women as historical subjects or as social actors and to integrate their stories into the historical landscape. Gender history developed out of women's history when historians of women realised that, in order to understand women's position in the past in relation to that of men, they needed a theoretical framework that did not rest upon biological explanations or upon the rather static concept of patriarchy.[6] As Sheila Rowbotham put it, historians required a framework that helped them to understand 'the kaleidoscope of forms within which women and men have encountered one another'.[7] Using gender as a category of analysis enables a re-evaluation of some of the ways in which Scotland's past is imagined. This means thinking about gender as discourse; as socially constructed and not immutable. It means considering the ways in which ideas about gendered attributes and roles were constructed and experienced by both men and women in different social, economic and political contexts. It helps us to understand relations between men and women and how power is constituted. Applying a gendered analysis, though, does not simply mean adding women's experience to the mix, although sometimes this is a necessary first step. It also means thinking more deeply about the male experience and accepting that men as much as women lived their lives within a framework of ideals and injunctions about proper modes of behaviour which might be no less constraining than those imposed on women.

Historians of women and gender in Scotland have been disappointed at the marginalisation of women's experience in much of the writing of the Scottish past. Despite more than two decades of research into Scottish women's history,[8] and the existence of theories of gender relations which offer frameworks for thinking about male and female roles in the past, the 'right of women to exist historically' in the Scottish narrative, not to mention the need to problematise men's roles and experience through the lens of gender, is still a battle to be fought.[9] The presence of women in the grand narratives of Scottish history is fragile and partial.[10] In Scotland, we have not yet reached the stage where 'there is a comfort with, and support of, the empirical contribution women's history has made to historical writing'.[11] Women's experience, it seems, is difficult to integrate into the dominant narrative of Scotland. Hence women are often divorced from the weighty histories of nation and money-making, and are placed analytically within the family and community and are associated with matters sexual and corporeal.[12] This is despite copious evidence from beyond Scotland that women played a crucial role in capital accumulation, informal political engagement and industrial production, to name just a few examples.[13] To be fair, however, some analyses have positioned women firmly within the narrative, and not only as wives and mothers but as workers and campaigners too.[14] The texture of women's lives is now beginning to be revealed, as is its complexity and heterogeneity. But gender as a category of analysis, the conceptual leap that underpins historical understandings of culture, society, identity and experience in scholarship elsewhere in the world, has failed to penetrate the foundations of Scotland's community of historians.

There are a number of explanations for the exclusion of women's experience from dominant narratives of the Scottish past. The first concerns the general representation of Scotland as a 'man-made' and patriarchal country from the earliest times, a picture which past historians felt needed no explanation or comment.[15] Focus on military exploits, political struggles and the institutions identified as the heart of a distinctive Scottish identity and past (the church, law and education) privileged the male story (albeit the story of only some men). The subordination of women within the political and religious structures of the nation removed them from view, at least until the early modern period.[16] Today, the breadth of research into medieval and early modern women's and gender history in Scotland makes such elisions unsustainable.[17]

A second explanation concerns the hegemony of the political story over the social, particularly in the modern period. Notwithstanding the strength and depth of Scottish economic and social history, recent

national narratives and the associated preoccupation with national identity (defined almost invariably in political and sectarian terms) have
charted a story marked by significant political and intellectual moments:
the 1707 Act of Union, the Scottish Enlightenment and the rise of the
labour movement. Yet, as Joan Scott has reminded us, 'gender is one of
the recurrent references by which political power has been conceived,
legitimised, and criticised', and thus the absence of women from the narrative, and their positioning as objects outside the national project or as
passive objects – usually mothers – to be utilised by promoters of the
nation state, perpetuates a separate-spheres model which confines
women to the private sphere and delegitimises or silences their political
involvement.[18] We have little insight into the meaning of a national identity for women and the ways in which women intersected with the discourses on nationalism and nation-state formation. In Scottish historical
writing on national identity and culture, there has been virtually no
acknowledgement of the notion of gendered identities,[19] and women are
almost entirely missing from the analysis despite the fact that citizenship
was implicitly gendered in that it was defined as the domain of men.[20]
Because women appear not to have been present or to have engaged
in political debates, their voices are silenced and their interests are
overlooked, while the national destiny is by default associated with male
actors.

Thirdly, the legacy of the nineteenth-century ideology of separate
spheres encompassing the public sphere of work, commerce and politics
and the private sphere of home and family has had a noticeable influence
on the ways in which women and men are situated within the historical
narrative. This universal framework was not just seen to underpin the
activities of men and women in the past, but also it supported 'a general
identification of women with domestic life and of men with public life'.[21]
Defined in this rigid sense, separate spheres was a convenient framework
used to justify the exclusion of women's experience from narratives dominated by what went on in public life. For feminist historians, the identification of a discursive world which assigned understandings of sexual
difference to culture rather than nature was beneficial in that it focused
attention on the aspects of women's lives that are distinctive but which
were hitherto deemed ahistorical or simply undeserving of historical
enquiry. One approach then was to recapture and celebrate women's
experience that had been hidden from view.[22] More recently, though, the
use of separate spheres as shorthand to describe lived experience has
been challenged and superseded by the understanding that it was a historically contingent ideology, which took on multiple shapes in different

contexts.[23] The discourses of separate spheres were undeniably powerful but not deterministic.[24] Moving beyond the public–private dyad allows us to see gender as a pervasive organising principle, implicit in most – if not all – social processes.

It remains an anomaly that women's experience should be set aside in national narratives in view of the quality and depth of the research into women's lives in Scotland. Far from concentrating on women's role within the private sphere of home and family (an area ironically under-researched in the Scottish context), historians of women have mapped out the complexities of women's engagement in the labour market from medieval to modern times, their role within the labour movement and politics more generally, the fight for women's rights in the public sphere, as well as their engagement with intellectual movements and their place in the religious, social and economic order.[25] There is no need for national narratives to consign women to the domestic sphere for want of material or analytical rigour. The reason they so often do this must lie in the assumptions of the writers.

However, much of the early research into women's experience in the workplace, in politics and even in the kirk utilised structuralist models of domination to explain women's exclusion from the key institutions of national life.[26] And this mapping of the structures of patriarchy tended to cast women as subordinated by those patriarchal mechanisms that denied them parity of representation, of wages and of respect. For historians whose prime focus was not women, this approach fitted with a more general acceptance of structuralist explanations for historical developments, at least in the modern period. Hence the national story that has emerged is of a misogynist Scotland, a man-made history where women were oppressed, symbolised by the archetypes of the female victim: the witch, the adulteress, the prostitute, the wage-worker. Feminist historians have uncovered women's agency in a variety of contexts from the factory floor to the kirk session, but the new perspective on women's active engagement in historical process did not substantially alter the dominant narratives.

It has not always been so. T. C. Smout's *History of the Scottish People 1560–1830* (1969) and the sequel *A Century of the Scottish People 1830–1950* treated the intimate and everyday elements of life as an intrinsic part of the national story.[27] Mirroring the great explosion in social history at that time, Smout's analysis of Scottish culture in the broadest sense (including the family, sexual relations, superstition and education) was inclusive not only of women's experience but also of personal relationships, anticipating the gendered approach advocated in this collection. However, many of those who went on to research these fields in greater depth interpreted their material within structuralist models; hence the history of the family largely became a demographic project, and the history of sexuality was subjugated to quantitative analysis and the patriarchal model.[28] And when the important social and economic history series *People and Society in Scotland* appeared in the 1980s and 1990s, women were included but largely contained within a separate chapter.[29] It is only now, with the shift to poststructuralist and cultural approaches to the past, that women (and men) might be liberated from this rigid framework, anticipating a partial return to the more inclusive narrative initiated by Smout and permitting the foregrounding of identity and experience.[30]

It was one of the aims of the pioneers of women's history to do more than merely place women on the historical agenda. They wanted to force a change to the historical landscape. This ambition was epitomised by Joan Kelly's *cri de cœur*, 'Did women have a Renaissance?'[31] Kelly's research into the history of the Italian Renaissance, and specifically her discovery that men and women did not experience it equally, led her to argue that if this was the case for what had been hitherto regarded as a major turning point in European history then it was legitimate to interrogate other so-called turning points for their impact upon women's position and status (and consequently to question traditional periodisation as resting upon male progress and achievement). Along with Kelly, many women's historians hoped, perhaps naively, that once we knew enough about women in the past, once we had reclaimed enough women from the archives, then the canvas upon which we all write our histories – the periodisation, the turning points, the assumptions and categories of analysis – would be irrevocably altered. Today, few of us remain so optimistic. In Scotland at least, the details of the picture might have changed somewhat but the framework has remained the same. It is not sufficient just to add women on as decoration, what one gender historian has described as 'tinsel they can hang on their old tree'.[32]

A gendering of Scottish history means the use of gender as a primary category of analysis. This is especially needed in those areas traditionally regarded as gender-free such as state formation and nation-building, but also in those research fields more self-evidently gendered such as religion, education and the family. We should challenge these dominant narratives of history, not only to demand that they include women's voices and experiences but also more fundamentally to question the façade of gender neutrality which is so often implicit in national histories. Interpreted here as 'knowledge about sexual difference and the ways in which it establishes meanings for bodily difference', the potential of theories of gender to explain how 'gender hierarchies are constructed, legitimated, challenged and maintained' has been largely passed by in favour of class and ethnicity within the Scottish historical tradition.[33] Giving birth should feature just as prominently in a national history as signing a treaty.[34] Most historians would no longer accept the view that we do not need to think or write about gender because it is natural and thus ahistorical. Rather, it is precisely because gender is always present that, to quote Marilyn Lake, 'the interaction of masculinity and femininity is the dynamic force in history', that a project to write a gendered history of Scotland assumes some urgency at this point in Scotland's history.[35]

Historians of women have a head start in this project. We are used to reading against the grain, interpreting silences and utilising ephemeral sources. We are also practised in adopting a consciously critical stance when reading texts and interpreting our material within theoretical frameworks which help us to understand the relationship between, for example, the discursive construction of women and women's actual or lived experience. The history of men and of masculinity, in contrast, is in its infancy in Scotland. Despite popular conceptions of Scotland as a hard man's country, epitomised by the Highland clansman, the military hero and the manual industrial worker, few have attempted to understand conceptions and experiences of masculinity in specific temporal and geographical contexts. John Dwyer's work on the virtuous discourses of the Enlightenment stands as one of few analyses in Scotland of changing constructs of masculinity within the intellectual classes.[36] We are beginning to gain a more complex picture of gender relations and men's experiences among the industrial working class in the nineteenth and twentieth centuries with research addressing issues such as domestic strife, fatherhood, unemployment and industrial health.[37] The history of men and of constructions and experiences of masculinity is of heightened importance at the start of the twenty-first century in the light of massive changes in the Scottish labour market and contemporary concerns about men's health.[38]

Although there have been numerous textbooks on women's or gender history which are written 'with unavoidable partiality' – both within Scotland and beyond – there have been few attempts to write national or synthetic histories which prioritise gender as the key category of analysis.[39] One of the most controversial is the challenge to the representation of Australia's national history, *Creating a Nation, 1788–1990*, co-written by a team of Australia's leading women's historians.[40]

Creating a Nation offered to challenge 'the conventional view of Australia's past as a creation of white men of British descent'. The authors' starting point was the understanding that 'gender is integral to the processes that comprise the history of Australia – that political and economic as well as social and cultural history are constituted in gendered terms'.[41] The narrative departs from traditional national histories by not merely adding in women but also integrating gender with other issues such as race, war, nationalism, politics and the state. Similarly, Susan Kingsley Kent's *Gender and Power in Britain, 1640–1990* offers some new insights into 'how the various political regimes in Britain from 1640 to the present both constituted and were constituted by gender'.[42]

Gender in Scottish History is not such a text in that we do not aim to be comprehensive or to provide a competing meta-narrative of the modern Scottish past. Indeed, we are suspicious of totalising accounts precisely because they must exclude as much as they include. This book does contain an exploration of the ways in which the modern Scottish past might be reconfigured by adding women and by looking through a gendered lens. We have chosen to interrogate a number of prominent themes common to most Scottish histories of the modern period. We have been selective rather than comprehensive. We are conscious of the complexity of the story of Scotland's past and are aware that in this short collection we are unable to do sufficient justice to regional and local difference, the Highland and especially the Gaelic experience, and the sheer nitty-gritty of everyday life experienced by men and women in this period.[43] We have also, perhaps inevitably, given greater attention to women's experiences than to men's, partly to redress the imbalance in existing histories and partly to reflect new research. We have chosen what we consider as some of the more long-standing of themes within the modern narrative as opportunities to demonstrate how the application of a gendered perspective and the inclusion of new material on women's experience might shift some of the shibboleths. The 'gender agenda' for Scottish history has the potential to show how universal histories are partial and to contribute to a more inclusive reading of Scotland's history.

One does not have to try very hard to imagine ways in which ideas about gender and gender roles have shaped the Scottish past. In the field of work and labour relations, ideas about appropriate masculine and feminine behaviour and spheres had different ways of manifesting themselves in the work relations of the Highlands and the Western Isles, the agricultural lowlands and the industrial heartland. An understanding of Scotland's industrial growth is incomplete without an analysis of the contribution of female labour and the definition of that labour as unskilled, temporary and unorganised.[44] However, masculine identities, particularly in urban parts of Scotland, were created and reinforced not only through work but also through male-dominated organisations such as the Masonic and Orange Lodges, trade unions and leisure associations.[45] Notions of prescribed gendered behaviour were central to the kirk's power in much of Scotland until the early nineteenth century and had an impact on the differential treatment of men and women concerning issues around sexual behaviour.[46] The regulation of family life in Scotland has been profoundly affected by gendered constructions of appropriate or acceptable behaviour and the disciplining of sexuality.[47] Ideas about motherhood and fatherhood have had important repercussions for the ways in which the family has been understood by the state.[48] The representation of men and women in the civil and criminal courts cannot be explained without an understanding of dominant gendered constructions of masculinity and femininity and the ways these notions were complicated by class.[49] All of these issues are part of Scotland's story. Ideas about masculinity and femininity are not limited to the social or private sphere; they affect all social relationships and thus impact upon all economic, political and cultural processes. Many of these applications are to be found within this collection.

The following contributions aim to stimulate research and new thinking by approaching themes from unusual angles, by pushing at the boundaries of accepted interpretations and by synthesising and analysing material which has existed on the margins of the standard interpretations. In order to include women's experiences, some authors have had to stretch traditional definitions and frameworks, thus reshaping the landscape in which our characters act. Sue Innes and Jane Rendall have redefined what constitutes 'the political' to include civil society and expressions of citizenship which allow for a more inclusive and expansive consideration of Scottish political life, ranging from the political influence of aristocratic women to the grassroots activities of the late twentieth-century women's movement. In their exploration of Scottish identity, Esther Breitenbach and Lynn Abrams have looked beyond the accepted expressions of national identity to alternative sites – the foreign mission, the creative arts – as well as looking critically at how women used national symbols and rhetoric in ways different from and sometimes similar to their male counterparts. The boundaries of what constitute religion are also stretched by Callum Brown, who eschews a history of the kirk as an institution and replaces it with a wide-ranging survey of how the experience of religious life in Scotland has been riddled with gendered assumptions and instructions to men and women about how they should behave. In the arena of culture, Siân Reynolds suggest that we expand our analysis to what Bourdieu describes as the 'cultural field', a 'structured space of relations' in which the participants relate to one another competitively and where gender as much as class defines one's place in the rankings. In respect of the family, Eleanor Gordon argues that a redefinition of what constitutes the family (beyond the immediate nuclear core) and work (to include all productive labour) opens up a narrative history of the Scottish family characterised by continuity across the pre-industrial and industrial periods.

In some cases, it has been necessary to rotate the kaleidoscope in order to reveal how particular institutions and fields of experience have been shaped by gendered understandings and assumptions. The story of Scottish education, for instance, as Lindy Moore makes plain, was riddled with gender inequalities at all levels, from the administration and policy to the teaching and learning experience. It is simply not sufficient merely to point out women's exclusion or subordinate position, as in 'entry to university was open to anyone (but not women or girls)'. The historian must interrogate the reasons for this situation and try to understand the gendered discourses which informed educational policy in this country. In the workplace too, as Deborah Simonton describes, gendered definitions of work, of work practices and of the value placed on men's and women's work permeated the work experience at every level and throughout the period. And in the realm of science and medicine, as Eileen Janes Yeo explains, ideas about gender permeated not only practice but also the very nature of what constituted scientific and medical progress and how it was conceived.

Finally, we have questioned some of the more persistent myths of Scottish historical writing – myths in the sense of widely accepted totalising interpretations or stories: the myth of a unitary Scottish identity, of the democratic intellect, of a civilising society, of almost seamless scientific progress. Looking at these afresh reveals much more contest and conflict than has been indicated hitherto. We do not suggest that the inclusion of women's experience alone upsets these myths. Indeed, there are instances where women collude with them or at least find elements of them with which they identify, as in the case of female missionaries who exported the same values, forms and practices from the homeland as their menfolk. Rather, we argue that the use of gender as an analytical concept forces one to see how the construction of ideal types of masculinity and femininity and of male and female roles informed structures, policies, actions and experience. We offer some new knowledge, some new ways of thinking and some new interpretations of the more recent Scottish past, and in doing so have started on the road to creating a usable, inclusive and recognisable history.

FURTHER READING

Alberti, J., *Gender and the Historian* (Harlow: Longman, 2002).

Brotherstone, T., D. Simonton and O. Walsh (eds), *Gendering Scottish History: An International Approach* (Glasgow: Cruithne Press, 1999).

Damousi, J., 'Writing gender into history and history into gender: *Creating a Nation* and Australian historiography', *Gender & History* 11 (1999), 612–24.

Downs, L. L., *Writing Gender History* (London: Hodder Arnold, 2004).

Ewan, E. and M. M. Meikle (eds), *Women in Scotland c.1100–c.1750* (East Linton: Tuckwell, 1999).

Grimshaw, P., M. Lake, A. McGrath and M. Quartly, *Creating a Nation, 1788–1990* (London: Penguin, 1996).

Kent, S. K., *Gender and Power in Britain, 1640–1990* (London: Routledge, 1999).

Reynolds, S., *France Between the Wars: Gender and Politics* (London: Routledge, 1996).

Scott, J. W., *Gender and the Politics of History* (New York: Columbia University Press, 1988).

Shoemaker, R. and M. Vincent (eds), *Gender and History in Western Europe* (London: Arnold, 1998).

www2.uoguelph.ca/eewan – bibliography on Scottish women's history.

NOTES

I would like to thank Elizabeth Ewan and Callum Brown for their thoughtful comments on earlier versions of this chapter.

1. An earlier version of this introduction was published as L. Abrams, 'Gendering Scottish history: an agenda for change', in *Women's History Magazine* 40 (2002), 11–14.

2. T. M. Devine, *The Scottish Nation: 1700–2000* (London: Allen Lane, 1999); R. A. Houston and W. W. J. Knox (eds), *The New Penguin History of Scotland: From the Earliest Times to the Present Day* (London: Penguin, 2001); M. Lynch, *Scotland: A New History* (London: Pimlico, 1991); M. Lynch (ed.), *The Oxford Companion to Scottish History* (Oxford: Oxford University Press, 2001); M. G. H. Pittock, *A New History of Scotland* (Stroud: Sutton, 2003).

3. S. Reynolds, *France Between the Wars: Gender and Politics* (London: Routledge, 1996), p. 4. Here she refers to 'the cultural power of the textbook'.

4. G. Pomata, 'History particular and universal: on reading some recent women's history textbooks', *Feminist Studies* 19 (1993), 7–50.
5. G. Bock citing M. Albistur, 'Women's history and gender history: aspects of an international debate', in R. Shoemaker and M. Vincent (eds), *Gender and History in Western Europe* (London: Arnold, 1998), p. 85.
6. For a survey of developments in women's and gender history generally, see J. Alberti, *Gender and the Historian* (Harlow: Longman, 2002).
7. S. Rowbotham, 'The trouble with patriarchy', *New Statesman* (December 1979), here cited in Alberti, *Gender and the Historian*, p. 43.
8. For an extensive bibliography on Scottish women's history, see www2. uoguelph.ca/eewan
9. There are several overviews of this state of affairs: see, for example, E. Ewan and M. M. Meikle, 'A monstrous regiment of women', in E. Ewan and M. M. Meikle (eds), *Women in Scotland c.1100–c.1750* (East Linton: Tuckwell, 1999), pp. xix–xxx; S. Reynolds, 'Historiography and gender: Scottish and international dimensions', J. McDermid, 'Missing persons? Women in modern Scottish history' and T. Brotherstone, 'Women's history, Scottish history, historical theory', all in T. Brotherstone, D. Simonton and O. Walsh (eds), *Gendering Scottish History: An International Approach* (Glasgow: Cruithne Press, 1999), pp. 1–18, 37–45 and 251–69. On gender as a category of analysis for historians, the key text is J. W. Scott, *Gender and the Politics of History* (New York: Columbia University Press, 1988).
10. One prominent Scottish historian has remarked that 'women's history is in fact what you would call passé': 'Writing women back into history books', *Scotsman*, 19 January 2005.
11. J. Damousi, 'Writing gender into history and history into gender: *Creating a Nation* and Australian historiography', *Gender & History* 11 (1999), 612–24, here p. 613.
12. See Devine, *Scottish Nation*, chapter on women. J. F. McCaffrey, *Scotland in the Nineteenth Century* (Basingstoke: Macmillan, 1998), pays limited lip service to women's presence. Lynch (ed.), *Oxford Companion to Scottish History*, contains a separate entry on women, but elsewhere they are few and far between, the entry on 'culture' being a case in point.
13. See, for example, L. Davidoff and C. Hall, *Family Fortunes: Men and Women of the English Middle Class 1780–1850* (London: Routledge, 1987); H. Barker and E. Chalus (eds), *Gender in Eighteenth-Century England: Roles, Representations and Responsibilities* (London: Longman, 1997); A. Vickery (ed.) *Women, Privilege and Power: British Politics, 1750 to the Present*, (Stanford, CA: Stanford University Press, 2001); M. Berg, 'What difference did women's work make to the industrial revolution?', *History Workshop Journal* 35 (1993), 22–44.
14. R. A. Houston and W. W. Knox (eds), *The New Penguin History of Scotland: From the Earliest Times to the Present Day* (London: Penguin, 2001) has a much better record on this score, with women's experience

highlighted in several chapters; but the index is enlightening, with women appearing in the context of birth control, breastfeeding, domesticity, education and literacy, to name just the first few entries. See also C. Harvie, *Scotland: A Short History* (Oxford: Oxford University Press, 2002), which contains some choice anecdotes and examples of the female experience; C. A. Whatley, *Scottish Society 1707–1830: Beyond Jacobitism, Towards Industrialisation* (Manchester: Manchester University Press, 2000); W. W. Knox, *Industrial Nation: Work, Culture and Society in Scotland, 1800–Present* (Edinburgh: Edinburgh University Press, 1999).

15. See J. Hendry, 'Snug in the asylum of taciturnity: women's history in Scotland', in I. Donnachie and C. Whatley (eds), *The Manufacture of Scottish History* (Edinburgh: Polygon, 1992), pp. 125–42.

16. Women are not explicitly identified in Lynch's *Scotland: A New History* until page 176, when they appear as economic actors.

17. For a representative sample of this work, see Ewan and Meikle (eds), *Women in Scotland*.

18. Scott, *Gender and the Politics of History*, p. 48. On motherhood as a prime duty of citizenship, see G. Bock and P. Thane (eds), *Maternity and Gender Policies: Women and the Rise of European Welfare States 1880s–1950s* (London: Routledge, 1989); S. Koven and S. Michel (eds), *Mothers of a New World: Maternalist Politics and the Origins of Welfare States* (London: Routledge, 1993). I have made this point elsewhere: see L. Abrams, 'Feminists – Citizens – Mothers: debates about citizenship, national identity and motherhood in nineteenth-century Germany', in T. Brotherstone et al. and (eds), *Gendering Scottish History*, pp. 186–98.

19. D. McCrone, in *Understanding Scotland: The Sociology of a Stateless Nation* (London: Routledge, 1992), only acknowledges in passing that the archetypal Scottish identity is based on a masculine identity associated with the military and manual work (p. 190).

20. 'We allow a woman to sway our sceptre, but by law and custom we debar her from every other government but that of her own family . . .', W. Alexander, *The History of Women from the Earliest Antiquity to the Present Time* (1779), cited in L. Colley, *Britons: Forging the Nation 1707–1837* (London: Vintage, 1996), p. 253.

21. M. Rosaldo, 'A theoretical overview', in M. Rosaldo and L. Lamphere (eds), *Women, Culture and Society* (Stanford, CA: Stanford University Press, 1974), pp. 23–4.

22. The classic study here is C. Smith-Rosenberg, 'The female world of love and ritual', *Signs* 1 (1975), 1–30; but studies of childbirth, domesticity and so on also fall into this category.

23. On the role of this ideology in class-formation, see Davidoff and Hall, *Family Fortunes*.

24. See E. Gordon and G. Nair, *Public Lives: Women, Family and Society in Victorian Britain* (London: Yale University Press, 2003) for an analysis of

the workings of separate spheres among the Glasgow middle classes. Also E. J. Yeo, 'The "creation" of motherhood and women's responses in Britain and France, 1759–1914', *Women's History Review* 8:2 (1999), 201–18.

25. See, for example, E. Sanderson, *Women and Work in Eighteenth-Century Edinburgh* (London: Macmillan, 1996); E. Gordon and E. Breitenbach (eds), *The World is Ill-Divided: Women's Work in Scotland in the Nineteenth and Early Twentieth Centuries* (Edinburgh: Edinburgh University Press, 1990); E. Breitenbach and E. Gordon (eds), *Out of Bounds: Women in Scottish Society 1800–1945* (Edinburgh: Edinburgh University Press, 1992); E. Gordon, *Women and the Labour Movement in Scotland, 1850–1914* (Oxford: Clarendon Press, 1991); M. K. Smitley, ' "Woman's Mission": The Temperance and Women's Suffrage Movements in Scotland, c.1870–1914', Ph.D. thesis, University of Glasgow, 2002; L. Orr Macdonald, *A Unique and Glorious Mission: Women and Presbyterianism in Scotland 1830–1930* (Edinburgh: John Donald, 2000).

26. For example, C. Larner, *Enemies of God: The Witch-hunt in Scotland* (London: Chatto and Windus, 1981); Gordon, *Women and the Labour Movement*.

27. T. C. Smout, *History of the Scottish People 1560–1830* (London: Collins, 1969) and *A Century of the Scottish People 1830–1950* (London: Collins, 1986).

28. M. Anderson, 'Why was Scottish nuptuality depressed for so long?', in I. Devos and L. Kennedy (eds), *Marriage and Rural Economy: Western Europe since 1400* (Turnhout: Brepos, 1999), pp. 49–54; A. Blaikie, *Illegitimacy, Sex and Society: Northeast Scotland 1750–1900* (Oxford: Oxford University Press, 1993); L. Leneman and R. Mitchison, *Sexuality and Social Control: Scotland, 1660–1780* (Oxford: Blackwell, 1989).

29. T. M. Devine and R. Mitchison (eds), *People and Society in Scotland, Vol. I, 1760–1830* (Edinburgh: John Donald, 1988), contains only passing references to women's experience. See also W. H. Fraser and R. J. Morris (eds), *People and Society in Scotland, Vol. II, 1830–1914* (Edinburgh: John Donald, 1990), which contains E. Gordon, 'Women's spheres' and a fair sprinkling of references to women; and A. Dickson and J. H. Treble (eds), *People and Society in Scotland, Vol. III, 1914–1990* (Edinburgh: John Donald, 1992), containing A. J. McIvor, 'Women and work in twentieth-century Scotland' (pp. 138–73).

30. Examples include D. A. Symonds, *Weep Not for Me: Women, Ballads and Infanticide in Early Modern Scotland* (University Park, PA: Pennsylvania State University Press, 1997); L. Abrams, *Myth and Materiality in a Woman's World: Shetland 1800–2000* (Manchester: Manchester University Press, 2005).

31. J. Kelly, 'Did women have a Renaissance?', in R. Bridenthal and C. Koonz (eds), *Becoming Visible: Women in European History* (Boston, MA: Houghton Mifflin, 1977), pp. 175–202. See the discussion of this agenda in

L. L. Downs, *Writing Gender History* (London: Hodder Arnold, 2004), pp. 20–9.

32. I. Hull, 'Feminist and gender history through the looking glass: German historiography in postmodern times', *Central European History* 22 (1989), 283.

33. Scott, *Gender and the Politics of History*, p. 3.

34. This is made crystal clear in Reynolds, *France Between the Wars*, ch. 1, 'Demography and its Discontents', when she cites Clemenceau in 1919: 'If France stops producing large families, you can put the grandest clauses in the treaty [of Versailles] . . . and it will be to no purpose: France will be lost, because there will be no more Frenchmen' (p. 8). On the wider implications of the gendering of the nation, see N. Yuval-Davis, *Gender and Nation* (London: Sage, 1997).

35. M. Lake, quoted in Damousi, 'Writing gender into history', p. 618.

36. J. Dwyer, *Virtuous Discourse: Sensibility and Community in Late Eighteenth-century Scotland* (Edinburgh: John Donald, 1987). See also M. C. Moran, 'From Rudeness to Refinement: Gender, Genre and Scottish Enlightenment Discourse', Ph.D. thesis, The John Hopkins University, Baltimore, MD, 1999.

37. A. Clark, *The Struggle for the Breeches: Gender and the Making of the British Working Class* (London: Rivers Oram Press, 1995); L. Abrams, ' "There was nobody like my Daddy": fathers, the family and the marginalisation of men in modern Scotland', *Scottish Historical Review* 78:2 (1999), 219–42; D. Wight, *Workers not Wasters: Masculine Respectability, Consumption and Employment in Central Scotland* (Edinburgh: Edinburgh University Press, 1993); R. Johnston and A. McIvor, 'Dangerous work, hard men and broken bodies: masculinity in the Clydeside heavy industries, c. 1930–1970s', *Labour History Review* 69:2 (2004), 135–51.

38. For example, C. Emslie, K. Hunt and R. O'Brien, 'Masculinities in older men: a qualitative study in the West of Scotland', *Journal of Men's Studies* 12 (2004), 207–26. See also the MRC Social and Public Health Sciences Unit, University of Glasgow research programme 'The West of Scotland Twenty-07 Study: Health in the Community'.

39. Pomata, 'History particular and universal', p. 43. See Reynolds, *France Between the Wars*; M. L. Roberts, *A Civilisation without Sexes? Reconstructing Gender in Postwar France 1917–27* (Chicago: University of Chicago Press, 1994); L. Abrams and E. Harvey (eds), *Gender Relations in German History: Power, Agency and Experience from the Sixteenth to the Twentieth Century* (London: UCL Press, 1996); and S. K. Kent, *Gender and Power in Britain, 1640–1990* (London: Routledge, 1999).

40. P. Grimshaw, M. Lake, A. McGrath and M. Quartly, *Creating a Nation, 1788–1990* (London: Penguin 1996).

41. Ibid., p. 4.

42. Kent, *Gender and Power in Britain*, p. xi.

43. A forthcoming series of books on *The History of Everyday Life in Scotland* (4 vols, Edinburgh University Press) will, it is hoped, fill some of these lacunae.

44. See S. Reynolds, *Britannica's Typesetters* (Edinburgh: Edinburgh University Press, 1989); Gordon, *Women and the Labour Movement*; and C. A. Whatley, 'Women and the economic transformation of Scotland, c.1740–1830', *Scottish Economic and Social History* 14 (1994), 19–40.

45. On the identity of the working-class man, see Wight, *Workers not Wasters*. On Orangeism, see G. Walker, 'The Orange Order in Scotland between the wars', *International Review of Social History* 37 (1992), 177–206.

46. See R. Mitchison and L. Leneman, *Girls in Trouble: Sexuality and Social Control in Rural Scotland 1660–1780* (Edinburgh: Scottish Cultural Press, 1998); and R. Mitchison and L. Leneman, *Sin in the City: Sexuality and Social Control in Urban Scotland 1660–1780* (Edinburgh: Scottish Cultural Press, 1998).

47. On the family life of the Glasgow middle classes, see Gordon and Nair, *Public Lives*, and on the working classes see L. Mahood, *Policing Gender, Class and Family: Britain, 1850–1940* (London: UCL Press, 1995).

48. See Abrams, ' "There was nobody like my Daddy" '.

49. See L. Leneman, *Alienated Affections: The Scottish Experience of Divorce and Separation, 1684–1830* (Edinburgh: Edinburgh University Press, 1998); Y. G. Brown and R. Ferguson (eds), *Twisted Sisters: Women, Crime and Deviance in Scotland since 1400* (East Linton: Tuckwell, 2002).

2

Gender and Scottish Identity

Esther Breitenbach and Lynn Abrams

INTRODUCTION

It has often been pointed out that representations of Scottish identity privilege masculinity, just as it has been argued that the marginalisation of female experience in Scottish history denies women the possibility of a recognisable gendered past.[1] Though there is historical evidence that Scotland, as elsewhere, was represented as a female figure, for example as 'Dame Scotia' in the sixteenth and seventeenth centuries,[2] and in seventeenth-century masques,[3] such figures do not seem to have typically personified Scotland as Britannia, Marianne and Germania have personified Britain, France and Germany respectively.[4] Nor has a discourse of 'motherland' been prominent in Scotland, though the twentieth-century Scottish writer Willa Muir, for example, designated Scotland as mother: 'Scotland as a nation has been for so long a "puir auld mither" that Scottish mothers are likely to have a fellow feeling for her', suggesting that women's identity was predicated more upon an association of their own oppression (by men) with that of their country (by England) than upon any sense of pride and association with a glorious past.[5]

Though some evidence of female imagery and iconography of Scotland exists, the privileging of masculinity in imagery and symbols of Scottish national identity is notable. The militarism of nineteenth-century Scotland and popular enthusiasm for it has been frequently remarked upon, and within the context of the British Empire in particular the image of the Highland soldier became emblematic of Scottishness.[6] The majority of popular icons of Scottishness are male – for example, Wallace, Bruce, Burns, Scott – though Mary, Queen of Scots and Flora Macdonald have been prominent female alternatives. A great deal has been written about Mary, and different interpretations of her life offered, though how she has served to symbolise and represent Scottishness, and who has promoted her as doing so, is a subject that itself merits investigation. Of Flora Macdonald, it has been commented that her myth was dissonant from the historical reality of her years as part of the slave-owning society of North Carolina, a reality which undercuts the epithets of 'honour', 'courage' and 'dignity in adversity' which she was said to symbolise.[7] In his deconstruction of the myth of Macdonald, McArthur underlines the active process of its construction, exemplified by a campaign in Inverness to erect a statue to 'the heroic maiden'.[8] What part women themselves may have played in this process is an interesting question.

Much discussion of Scottish national myths was prompted, not surprisingly, by the release of the film *Braveheart* in 1995. Edensor, in his discussion of responses to *Braveheart* in Scotland, comments on the gendered themes which were present in it.[9] He notes that some critics have maintained that films such as *Braveheart* and *Rob Roy* (1995) have been shaped for international audiences by 're-situating the ethos of the western in a Scottish setting', and that central to such films is the 'fantasy of male control, and empowerment through physical engagement', with 'the heterosexual love story' also being 'a staple ingredient'.[10] He further argues that 'In *Braveheart* these gendered themes are transcoded in an imaginary Scottish landscape populated by the "wild charismatic men" and "the fey elusive women" cited in *Scotch Reels*'.[11] The debate in Scotland about such representations raised the question of the appropriation of heroes and underlines the point that such images are not passively consumed. Moreover, Edensor claims that motifs in the film such as 'independence', 'freedom', 'equality' and 'democracy' were 'reclaimed to re-enchant contemporary political narratives'.[12] Despite his comments on the 'hyper-masculine qualities' of Wallace as depicted in the film, however, Edensor makes no comment on how responses to such images may have been gendered, and to what extent women as well as men may have reclaimed a concept of equality from it.

Imagery of Scotland is not only presented and consumed in a Scottish context. It may also be presented in other countries as part of a process of strengthening economic and political links, such as the representations of Scotland which were central to the creation of National Tartan Day (6 April) in the USA in 1998.[13] Many critics dismissed this as presenting outdated stereotypes of Scottishness and the kind of kitsch that Tom Nairn has so comprehensively denounced as 'vulgar tartanry'.[14] The establishment of National Tartan Day, however, also drew on Scottish historical traditions through arguing that the Declaration of Arbroath of 1320 was the model for the American Declaration of Independence, a view which, according to Hague, has no historical authenticity. He argues that one of the functions of the use of this historical symbolism is the 'centring of masculinity', which is indicated by the use of gendered language, and the emphasis on the military and 'soldierly masculinity'.[15]

Both the discussions of *Braveheart* and of National Tartan Day raise the question of historical authenticity and underline how this is subordinated to the mythical and the symbolic as well as emphasising the masculine character of such myths and symbols. Finlay has discussed 'the cults of Burns, Wallace, and the Jacobites', and their enduring popularity, though he does not comment on the masculinity of such icons.[16] He makes the important point, however, that 'Scotland has many historical myths and they have played a significant role in the political, social and cultural development of the nation, either as vehicles of change or to express dominant political ideologies'.[17] Historians, he argues, need to engage with the myths, and not just disparage them. We might add that one form of engagement with such myths would be the investigation of how women have used and responded to them, and to what extent this might be differentiated from men's appropriation of them.

GENDER AND NATIONAL IDENTITY

The growing recognition of the gendered character of representations of Scottish identity indicated by the work cited above is welcome, and much needed in debates on national identity, where gender has been relatively neglected. Though it has come to be widely acknowledged that identities are complex, many-sided and fluid, and that, among other facets of identity, nationality and gender are likely to be significant, in discussions of national identity in Scotland its relationship to gender seldom gets more than a passing mention.

There is of course a distinction to be made between the ways in which women and men express their gender identity, and the ways in which they express other facets of identity, such as regional or local, class, or national identities. In the case of the former, given the ways in which gender roles are constructed and negotiated, it is to be expected that systematic differences would be apparent in how women expressed their identity as women and men as men. However, with respect to other facets of identity, gender differences in how these are articulated may be much less salient. And indeed, in respect of some of the key themes in debates about nationalism and national identity, a gender analysis may have little to offer, for example questions such as: whether nations and nationalism are purely modern phenomena; whether national identity draws on premodern antecedents; what sort of thing national identity is; or in Scotland, in particular, debates on when Scotland became a nation or

Scots developed a national consciousness; why political nationalism in the form of a demand for an independent state failed to emerge in nineteenth-century Scotland; the relationship of Scottish to British identities, and which was dominant when.

If gender and national identity is a relatively neglected theme, there is a growing body of feminist work on nations and nationalism; and yet this often seems to have little application to the Scottish case, since it is concerned on the one hand with ethnic nationalisms and on the other with nation states.[18] In essence, the key concerns of feminist writers have been: the regulation and control of women through nationalist ideologies which posit subordinate roles for women or give them particular symbolic values; the position of women within nationalist struggles and the capacity for these to also deliver gender equality; women's role in cultural reproduction; and gendered access to the rights of citizenship (which conflates the nation with the state).[19] It is largely twentieth-century nationalism that has attracted the attention of feminist scholars, whether anti-colonial nationalist struggles or recent ethnic nationalist conflicts; and on the whole this work does not ask the question as to how women themselves articulate national identity, apart from the generalisation that women are reproducers of culture (as, of course, are men, albeit in different ways), nor does it ask about their commitment to nationalist aims.[20]

It has been argued, however, that there are many nationalisms, and in particular that there is a distinction to be made between ethnic and civic nationalism, with Scotland, Catalunya and Quebec, for example, being representative of the latter.[21] As a political movement, nationalism attracted limited support in nineteenth-century Scotland, but a nationalist consciousness was expressed in other ways, in particular through civil society and urban governance.[22] In the twentieth century, nationalism in Scotland has been notable for the prominence of women as leading figures, and the Scottish National Party (SNP) currently supports a civic nationalism with gender equality as an integral part of this, even if the party itself has not fully supported measures for gender equity in political representation.[23]

Anthony Smith has argued that, of all collective identities, national identity is the 'most fundamental and inclusive', and that today national identity exerts 'a more potent and durable influence than other collective cultural identities'.[24] Other forms of collective identity, such as class, gender, race and religion, 'may overlap or combine with national identity but they rarely succeed in undermining its hold, though they may influence its direction'.[25] Of gender in particular, Smith comments that 'the very universality and all-encompassing nature of gender differentiation makes it a less cohesive and potent base for collective identification and mobilization'.[26] In his view, 'gender cleavages' must ally themselves to other more cohesive identities, such as nationalism or socialism, 'if they are to inspire collective consciousness and action'.[27]

Christopher Smout, drawing on Smith's ideas of concentric identities and loyalties, makes a similar point, albeit somewhat dismissively, about the lack of capacity of other collective identities to overcome national loyalties: 'There is an international workers' movement and an international women's movement, but the workers of the world famously did not unite and the women of the world are equally unlikely to do so'.[28] International solidarity, however, does not necessarily mean the suppression of other forms of identity. As Alice Brown has commented, feminists have expressed both a common identity and their differences simultaneously, and in claiming 'Welshness or Irishness or Scottishness, they are not forced to deny their feminist, class, colour, or other identities'.[29]

In Smout's view, women are likely to identify themselves as Scottish as readily as men, though the 'potent' images of Scottishness which he cites are stereotypically gendered: the 'Wee Hard Man' and 'Grannie's Hieland Hame'.[30] Whether or not these images evoke a strong response nowadays, he is surely generally correct in this view. Indeed, sociological evidence would bear this out. McCrone has noted that the tendency observable in recent decades for more Scots to identify themselves as Scottish rather than British holds across gender, age, region, religion and class.[31]

Like other writers, McCrone acknowledges that, among crucial markers in the 'social processing of the self', gender, social class and ethnicity are among the more important ones, along with national identity, which is both pervasive and usually implicit.[32] Paterson writes that 'multiple identities are an accepted fact of politics' in Scotland, and suggests that 'national identity is now not so much an allegiance to some overarching collective project, but rather a way of "presenting the self" (Goffman 1973), with roughly the same function as identities based on gender, ethnicity or – even – social class'.[33] Both McCrone and Paterson then suggest the capacity for choice in privileging particular identities, and that there is a changing relationship in the articulation of gender and national identities, with Paterson in particular arguing that national identity does not function above the others. The writers cited above share the view that national and gender identities play an important role in individual identity, but appear to differ in the precedence of one over the other, and in the capacity that they have for generating collective consciousness and action. Historical research into processes of identity construction, as well as contemporary sociological research, might be able to put such views to the test.

If some of the more obvious symbols of Scottish national identity are masculine and invite easy confirmation of the view that representations of Scottish national identity privilege the masculine, in fact researching and analysing national identity from a gender perspective is a complex task. A fundamental challenge is that representations and discourses of national identity are everywhere present, in the language of everyday life as well as in political or patriotic rhetoric,[34] and in cultural forms of all kinds. They are not unitary, and they change over time. Identifying particular representations and discourses of national identity is in itself not sufficient to substantiate claims about how Scots in general represented their identity, nor how Scotsmen or Scotswomen did so. To establish which representations or discourses of national identity had a wide currency or came to be hegemonic requires evidence of their collective reproduction and consumption, not simply of their production. Public life, such as political or civil society associational activity and institutional life, offers a rich source for investigation of this theme, since it entails conscious, deliberate, collective activity, appeals for public support, and public endorsement. It provides a range of source material – for example, ephemeral and periodical literature, reports in contemporary newspapers and journals and so on – together with evidence of participation in organisations and institutions, from which can be inferred the extent to which particular representations of national identity were actively consumed and reaffirmed. Literary and artistic productions are also rich sources of representations of national identity, though they present a greater challenge in assessing their currency or popularity, since such representations are not only produced by individual authors but may be read in very different ways, as Siân Reynolds shows, in Chapter 7 of this volume, in her discussion of readings of MacDiarmid. Literary representations are of course much more easily accessible than other types of source material relevant to the question of national identity, but it may be harder to judge their impact.

With the complexity of this theme and the challenge of researching it in mind, the remaining part of this chapter illustrates by three case studies some of the ways in which gender and Scottish national identity intersect: the political sphere where women engaged both intellectually and practically with the politics of nation; the foreign-mission movement, a sphere of institutional religious life in which women articulated a Scottish identity in counterpoint to the identity of colonial 'others'; and finally the cultural arena, which has arguably offered women the most freedom to explore their identity as Scots through self-expression in oral or written performance.

WOMEN AND NATIONAL IDENTITY IN THE SPHERE OF FORMAL POLITICS

The political realm might be considered a problematic space in which to identify women's expression of a national identity, since, as Sue Innes and Jane Rendall point out in Chapter 3 of this volume, formal politics was gendered male until fairly recently. Exclusion from elected office or from the franchise, however, did not prevent women from holding political opinions, or from participating in political campaigns such as the Chartist movement, or from organising their own political movement in the form of the campaign for women's suffrage. In all these contexts, there is some evidence of the articulation of a Scottish identity.

In 1706, Katherine Hamilton, Duchess of Atholl, remarked in a personal note shortly before the passing of the Act of Union: '[God will] bring to pass the good of this land and put a stop to uniting of it on such monstrous ill terms . . . yet he may open peoples eyes . . . yet they may have no hand in the ruin and distruction of their native country'.[35] Katherine was deeply troubled about the fate of her country and her religion around the time that union with England was being debated. For her, Presbyterianism and Scottish nationhood went hand in hand, and her own identity as a Scotswoman and a Presbyterian could not be separated.[36] It has been commonly assumed that politics in the eighteenth century was men's business. In the formal sphere of Scottish politics, it was of course. Moreover, the 'production of the nation' and the development of concepts of national membership were explicitly masculinist.[37] Men's national agency was founded upon their ability to defend their nation, and this in turn came to define their masculinity within the nation.[38] However, as Katherine Hamilton's remarks show, her Scottish identity was integral to her interest in politics. Katherine's husband was a member of the Scottish parliament and regularly corresponded with his wife on political matters. Although not able to engage in high politics, women of the aristocracy were likely to be knowledgeable and interested in the politics of the day and could use their influence. The debate about the union provided a backdrop for women as well as men to express their loyalties, albeit more likely in private correspondence than in open debate.[39]

It is at these moments of political turmoil that we might expect to find the gendered politics of identity. Just as in France during the 1789

Revolution, when women who lacked citizenship rights nevertheless demonstrated their loyalties to the new political entity by wearing revolutionary symbols such as the cap of liberty, in Scotland women's exclusion from the formal political sphere forced them to find other means of expressing their political and national loyalties. In Chapter 3, Sue Innes and Jane Rendall examine women's engagement in political life and the language of citizenship in the Scottish context. Here, we are concerned with whether expressions of national identity were part and parcel of women's forays into the political sphere. At the time of Union, the politics of nation was explicit. In the nineteenth century, however, the nature of political debate had shifted, with democratic reform and labour politics dominating the agenda: that is, other collective identities such as class superseded or sat alongside national affiliation. This is not to say that radicalism eschewed nationalist concerns altogether. The announcement in April 1820 by West of Scotland radicals of a provisional government of Scotland – known as the Scottish Insurrection – following some years of popular unrest and violence may suggest a separatist strand of thought within Scottish radicalism. Radical meetings were punctuated by orchestral renditions of 'Scots Wha Hae', and speeches made references to Scots heroes and historical events.[40] Thus, though Scottish radicals drawn from the ranks of the impoverished and threatened labouring classes may not have been motivated by or even concerned with nationalist political aims, they articulated their Scottish identity within the context of demands being made of the British state. The grievances of the men and women involved in the unrest were common to all working families in Britain at this time: poverty, oppression and a lack of political representation. Class solidarity with others elsewhere in Britain was emphasised by the prominent use by male and more often female radicals of the universalist symbol of liberty and democracy – the cap of liberty.[41] Female Chartists, such as those from Dunfermline in 1838, emphasised their solidarity with other working-class women across the British Isles rather than as Scots:

> WOMEN OF THE POLITICAL UNION OF BIRMINGHAM!
> We, the Women of the Political Union of Dunfermline, Congratulate you for the noble and patriotic spirit which has induced you to come forward in a united body, to aid and assist in the great contest now going forward between the working men of Britain and their heartless rulers. You know as well as we do, what it is to be the Wives and Daughters of working men . . . We fondly hope that your example and ours will be followed in every town in Britain. With perseverance, we have every thing to hope for, but without that we will remain in our chains. No right-thinking woman can submit patiently, day

after day, and year after year, and see her children pining in want, and covered with rags, while her oppressors are rioting in luxury and debauchery, enjoying the fruits of their oppression. If there is a woman in Britain can tamely submit to such usage – if her soul does not rise in arms against her oppressors, she deserves not the name of woman![42]

By the later nineteenth century, familiar symbols of Scottishness were commonly being used for a variety of reasons – sometimes playful, sometimes mocking and sometimes strategic and political – by campaigners for democratic reform. Since the French Revolution, visual symbols had assumed some importance; and, in the age of mass marches and public events by Chartists, trade unionists, temperance campaigners and suffragists, such events provided opportunities to present one's national identity in public. In 1840, a deputation of Chartist women from Calton and Mile-end in Glasgow led by Agnes Muir, present at a ceremony to celebrate the release from jail of three male Chartist heroes, decorated these men with medals and Scots plaid. On presenting Mr Collins, Agnes Muir

hoped when he looked at those gifts he would think of Scotland – the plaided forefathers of the people of Scotland – who, by their sufferings, bequeathed the liberty of meeting to demand their rights – when he looked at them she hoped he would think of

Scotland's woods and Scotland's floods,
Her mountains, glens and passes,
Her noble sons, but boon them a'
Think o'er her bonny lasses.   (Enthusiastic cheering)[43]

Another of the heroes was decorated with 'a handsome blue Glengarry bonnet'.

Symbols and motifs representing Scotland were widely used by all manner of Scottish organisations throughout the century, including women's associations. Scottish temperance women decorated their banners with thistles and the saltire colours of blue and white. The elaborate banners created and carried by Scottish branches of the National Union of Women's Suffrage Societies (NUWSS) at marches in Edinburgh and in London often bore symbols of Scotland and slogans in Scots. The banner for the 1908 Edinburgh march was designed by Ann Macbeth, who was head of Glasgow School of Art's embroidery department. Scottish marches were often accompanied by woman pipers, suggesting not merely the appropriation of a nineteenth-century symbol of Scottishness but also perhaps a challenge to the masculine and military identification with the pipes by this time.[44] The special Women's Social and Political Union's

(WSPU) china was emblazoned with a thistle. The thistle also became a sign of the Scottish women's determination to achieve their goal, with the slogan 'You maunna tramp on the Scots thistle, laddie' taken up by the suffragettes as their 'war cry'.[45] In view of the tensions that existed between the Scottish associations for women's suffrage and the London-based leadership, the tendency for English suffrage campaigners to incorporate Scotswomen in a sisterhood defined and run from London, and the representation of Scottish women as 'sisters' by their English comrades, thus downplaying national differences and conflicts, it is perhaps not surprising that when Scottish women travelled to London they were keen to express their distinctive identity.[46]

This kind of evidence is hard to interpret. Was the use of imagery and symbolism a means of demonstrating or expressing a Scots identity in opposition to the Englishness or Britishness that characterised the suffrage campaign? Or were Scottish suffragists expressing what Smith calls 'concentric loyalty',[47] unafraid of identifying with Britain but *equally* proud of their Scottish heritage which incorporated progressive laws (on marriage, divorce and property) and the first call for female enfranchisement in 1843, by Marion Kirkland Reid, a Scotswoman.[48] In the case of suffrage campaigners, Megan Smitley argues, Scotswomen regarded themselves as part of a wider cause; the shared British 'national' struggle overshadowed a discussion of Scottish difference and focused on the agitation of 'sisters'.[49] But, at the same time, Scottish feminists highlighted the special contribution of Scotland as a partner in the British women's movement.

In addition to this kind of generic imagery utilised by men and women, there were the references to Scots heroes and symbolic events in Scottish history, not necessarily to emphasise separateness but to motivate and stimulate identification with the cause and its antecedents. The 1908 Edinburgh suffrage march incorporated a pageant of representations of great Scottish female historical figures including the Covenanting martyrs, Jenny Geddes, Grisel Baillie and Flora Macdonald.[50] The masculine icons we discussed earlier are less prominent, suggesting that women found little to identify with in military heroes like Wallace and Bruce. However, this example of a poetic tribute written for the Scottish Co-operative Women's Guild at the end of the nineteenth century inserted the guildswomen into a familiar narrative, that of the victory of Bruce at the Battle of Bannockburn; but it is notable that the poem was penned by a man.

> We have read in that olden time story,
> Of the 'Scots wham Bruce aften had led'
> When the Bannock burn red was and gory

With the blood of its dying and dead.
Proud Edward well knew that resistance
Was vain, when his dark eyes beheld
A host on the heights in the distance,
The first Women's Co-operative Guild.

[. . .]

Have we now no more need for such women?
Are we less in the balance than they?
Ah no! sorely pressed by the foemen,
Men still need their helpmeets today
To bear up their arms, and remind them,
As they fight like the Bruce in the field,
Of the host that is gathered behind them,
The Mothers and Maids of the Guild.[51]

Let us return to Katherine Hamilton at the start of the eighteenth century. Her identity rested upon her Presbyterian faith and her nation; the two were intertwined. But it was her sex that informed the way she expressed her identity outwith the formal political sphere. Within the sphere of political action, the extent to which a Scottish identity was articulated depended a great deal on context. It is, however, notable that, even in the context of demands being made of the British state, such as democratic reform, women's suffrage and the alleviation of poverty, women (and men) drew upon the various symbols and leitmotifs of Scottishness as a means of collective identification.

INSTITUTIONS AS SITES OF CONSTRUCTION OF NATIONAL IDENTITY

It has become a commonplace to say that Scottishness is typically embodied in major institutions such as the law, the church and the education system. These key institutions, together with other civil society organisations, have been identified as important sites for the construction of national and other identities, such as class, professional and religious identities. Morton, for example, has argued that the middle-class governance of urban Scotland through such institutions and organisations in the mid-nineteenth century sustained a strong sense of Scottish national identity, simultaneously with support for the Union, and indeed that the symbolic figures of Wallace and Bruce were reconstructed in a Unionist mode.[52] This represented a process of collective mobilisation and claim-making, and suggests that these forms of organisation are significant sites for investigation of both national identity and gendered engagement in its construction. The campaigns for national monuments to Scott and to Wallace can be construed as representing constructions of masculinity as well as of national identity. It is apparent, however, that women participated in fund-raising activities such as the Waverley Balls organised to raise funds for the Scott Monument, and at the public openings of these monuments.[53]

Though this theme is as yet little investigated, there are examples of recent research that have addressed it in the context of the education system and of the kirk, both institutions which, as noted, are seen as central to Scottish identity. As Anderson has commented, 'education has become a marker of Scottish identity, associated with various supposed qualities of the Scottish character such as individualism, social ambition, respect for talent above birth, or "metaphysical" rationalism'.[54] He notes that the scrutiny of the myth of the 'lad of parts' by historians and sociologists has led to the conclusion that it corresponded to 'some underlying reality, albeit idealized', which allowed for 'individual social mobility', and to some extent 'challenged class barriers' though 'hardly acknowledged those of gender'.[55]

As Lindy Moore shows in Chapter 5, gender inequalities in education have historically been a feature of Scottish society, in terms of access and levels of achievement until very recently. The value of education has, however, long been appreciated by women, as the campaign for access to higher education in the nineteenth century and increasing participation in the twentieth century show. Thus, even within a system that was patriarchal, as Jane McDermid has argued of the late nineteenth century, 'the myths of universality and the meritocratic ideal were not static' and could be reshaped to include women to a greater extent than previously.[56] McDermid outlines how gender, class and national identity came into play in the debates around educational reform and 'anglicisation' in the latter part of the nineteenth century. She argues that Unionist support for anglicisation, and middle-class feminists' support for a separate domestic curriculum for working-class girls, were resisted by teachers and parents, who defended the tradition of intellectual education for girls as well as boys. This national tradition was of course male-centred, 'revolving around the talented boy (the lad of parts) and the male graduate teacher (the dominie)',[57] and initially the presence of women in the profession created anxiety about national identity being undermined. Women, however, came to be 'recognised as junior partners in preserving the educational tradition'.[58] She notes Anderson's argument that Scottish women 'adopted the classic "lad of parts to dominie" route both to improve their own education and to become respectably self-supporting'. McDermid concludes that

> Women contributed not simply to the preservation of the educational myth, but also to the reshaping of it, so that it included girls and women, thus giving substance to the claim of universality, and allowing at least a minority of working-class girls to benefit from the meritocracy.[59]

Her study illustrates the ways in which national identity was invoked to protect a particular vision of education in the context of class and political divisions, and that different groups of women took different positions in this debate. In particular, she shows that, notwithstanding gender inequalities, many women subscribed to the same views as men when it came to asserting the centrality of the system of education to Scottish national identity. In this context, then, gender inequalities could co-exist with a shared identity between women and men.

The Scottish Presbyterian Kirk is also commonly seen as a carrier of national identity.[60] While it is acknowledged that this marginalises the experience of Scottish Catholics, such claims appear to be well-founded, even in the light of the divisions between Presbyterians in the nineteenth century. Lesley Orr has written that, in the earlier part of the nineteenth century, 'Religious belief and practice dominated the aspirations and fears of ordinary Scots', and that consequently 'There was an identifiable Scottish presbyterian ethos which seemed to give the nation its distinctive character'.[61] Though the kirk remained a patriarchal institution throughout the nineteenth and twentieth centuries, a theme addressed by Callum Brown in Chapter 4 of this volume, women managed to extend their sphere of action in the churches and through their involvement in church organisations became active in public life.

Further confirmation of women's enlargement of their role is offered by recent research on the foreign-mission movement.[62] Not only does investigation of this sphere of civil society organisation illustrate the opportunities that were created by voluntary and paid work for women as missionaries and as activists at home and women's entry thereby into the public domain, it also provides an abundant source of representations of identity, constructed both by missionaries and by their supporters at home. Analysis of the discourses of missionary literature – pamphlets, sermons, addresses, periodicals, memoirs and biographies – underlines the relational character of identity, where it is manifested both in the context of the 'others' of empire and of 'others' closer to home. Thus there is a constant interplay between the idea of European Christian civilisation, in contrast to less civilised believers in other religions in

India or uncivilised 'heathens' in Africa, and between appeals to Scottish, British and English collectivities.

Analysis of this literature also makes clear that a central concern of the missionary enterprise was the organisation of gender relations in colonial territories, and that missionaries sought to impose monogamy, sexual modesty and a view of gender roles derived from their own societies, however inappropriate these might have been to the circumstances in which other peoples lived. Women were crucially involved in this as missionary practitioners, and as supporters at home. Though, as Orr has noted, women's attempts to extend their sphere of action sometimes led to conflict,[63] in the literature produced on women's missionary work an idealised version of woman as 'helpmeet', equal but different, continued to be presented and contrasted with the position of women in India and Africa, generally characterised as 'degraded'. This view of gender relations, however, was not characterised as specifically Scottish, but rather as representative of European civilisation.

Scottish identity as such was manifested through a number of modes of expression. These included recalling the homeland in routine accounts of everyday life, and the symbolic reproduction of the homeland through naming of colonised places and through the introduction to 'native' peoples of cultural forms from the homeland, such as songs. Institutional forms and practices of the homeland were introduced, such as Presbyterian forms of religious worship and organisation and an educational system based on the Scottish model, with pride in the tradition of achievement and openness being stressed. Scottish identity among mission workers was also nurtured through the creation of a Scottish missionary tradition fulfilling the aims of the Reformed kirk, with individuals being located in a missionary lineage, especially after Livingstone's death where he typically became the reference point; and claims of Scottish leadership, including with reference to women's work with women. Through these modes of expression, women often expressed a Scottish identity in much the same way as men, though with some differences in tone. Recalling the homeland was for women more likely to have an emotional timbre, expressing attachment to landscapes, family and friends, and women were less likely to be situated in Scottish historical traditions, both these differences reflecting differences in gender roles. Women, however, clearly subscribed to the same values as their male counterparts – a Presbyterian religion, with all that this implies, and self-improvement through education.

If there were similarities in the ways in which women and men articulated their Scottish identity, and a sense of shared values with respect to education, morality and belief in the superiority of their civilisation, there was an asymmetry in representations of female and male missionaries. Most biographers of the time were male (including Mary Slessor's first biographer, W. P. Livingstone), and male subjects were more likely to be situated in the traditions of the Reformed Kirk, and to be claimed as making a contribution to empire. Similarly, there was more emphasis on scientific and professional achievements in relation to men. Though Slessor too was acclaimed for her contribution to the expansion of imperial territories and to their administration, and though there was an overlap in the characterisations of female and male missionaries, as for example in terms of bravery and courage, there were also differences, with the maternal and caring aspects of women's work and characters being emphasised.[64] In biographies of Mrs Sutherland and Mary Slessor, their bravery and courage is acclaimed at the same time as their feminity or capacity to serve.[65] In John Wilson's memoir of his wife Margaret, her intellectual capacities and achievements are emphasised, as well as her capacity through her educational work with girls in India to be a 'mother to hundreds'. To a large extent, this reflected the actual differences in men's and women's roles. The secular appropriation of missionary icons, in contemporary newspapers and journals, emphasised even more the role of the contribution to empire, the 'civilising mission' and scientific and professional achievements, which provided a more masculinised version of the missionary enterprise than missionary literature itself did. Again, this reflects male dominance of public life, of newspapers and of civil society organisations.

Towards the end of the nineteenth century, in the period when imperialism was at its height, the missionary enterprise came to be increasingly claimed as a Scottish contribution to empire, embodied above all in the myth of Livingstone. Though yet again a male icon was to predominantly represent this Scottish identity, it is notable that a female icon was also constructed in the person of Mary Slessor. This was symbolic confirmation of the part that women played in the missionary enterprise, even if they continued to be overshadowed by men. However, it is apparent that women were inspired not only by women but also by men, and might seek in some ways to emulate them and to use icons such as Livingstone in order to express their own national identity. Comparisons were drawn between Mrs Sutherland and Livingstone in terms of their humble origins for example, and Mary Slessor was inspired by Livingstone, as well as being compared to him in her determined attitude and strong faith.[66] This analysis suggests, overall, that there were many similarities in the ways in which women and men articulated a Scottish identity in the context of the missionary enterprise, and that women and men responded to both male and female icons of the missionary movement. In their participation in the movement, and in their representations of it, women actively supported and shaped this construction of Scottish national identity together with men. The evidence drawn from the institutions of education and the kirk thus confirms both that these institutions were carriers of Scottish national identity, and that, despite being characterised by gender inequalities, they provided a vehicle for women to express a sense of national identity similar in many respects to that expressed by men.

WOMEN'S VOICES

Finally, we turn to the field of literature and oral culture, an arena in which frequent and explicit expressions of a Scottish identity are more easily accessible than in political and institutional life, although at the same time we are confronted with considerable complexity regarding interpretation. Scholars of Scottish literature have advanced further than historians in the quest to problematise and understand the construction of national and gendered identity. In terms of critique (of the 'Scottish canon'), discovery (of women writers) and analysis, literary scholars have effectively questioned any residual notion of a unitary or homogenous Scottish identity in view of the evident decentred or plural identities adopted by the writers whom they study.[67] To take just two examples – Mrs J. L. Story (Janet Leith Maughan, 1828–1926), a Victorian novelist and memoirist, and Jackie Kay (b. 1961), a contemporary dramatist, poet and novelist – the complex issues implicit in trying to think about gender and identity are easy to see.

In 1911, at the age of 83, Mrs Story began her *Early Reminiscences* by situating herself as a Scottish writer, while at the same time acknowledging the plurality of her identity:

> I am thoroughly cosmopolitan as regards my birth and parentage, for my father was an Englishman, my mother a Scotswoman, I was born in India, and the greater part of my life has been passed in Scotland; so I have always considered myself as Scotch, though I have been told that the nationality of the father determined that of the children.[68]

For Jackie Kay, identity is no less complex. As a black lesbian woman adopted as a child by white communist parents in Glasgow, her identity as a Scot is palpable in her writing, as in 'In My Country':[69]

> Walking down by the waters
> Down where an honest river

Shakes hand with the sea, a woman passed round me
In a slow watchful circle,
as if I were a superstition;

or the worst dregs of her imagination,
so when she finally spoke
her words spliced into bars
of an old wheel. A segment of air.
Where do you come from?
'Here,' I said, 'Here. These parts.'[70]

Yet, Kay has been determined to be seen first and foremost as a writer, because 'it's through your writing that people should get a sense of who you are. Because I write directly from my own experience, people do get a sense of the multiplicity of who I am.'[71] Late twentieth-century women writers have perhaps been less likely to ascribe to themselves a singular or unified identity (female or Scottish or lesbian or whatever) which could be seen as a constraint on what they write and, more importantly, how they are read. Ellen Galford (b. 1947) expressed this powerfully in 1993:

'What can I call myself?' . . . coming in as a sort of inward immigrant, having been here most of my adult life, and yet still having the accent from there, and then of course the Jewish thing and where does that stand inside the Scottish thing, and the lesbian thing inside the rest . . .[72]

A. L. Kennedy recently wrote that 'I am a woman, I am heterosexual, I am more Scottish than anything else and I write. But I don't know how these things interrelate.'[73] Modern published writers, then, have agonised about the issue of identity in ways in which their predecessors – the female storytellers, poets and ballad-singers – did not. This is in part on account of the cultural (and political) weight that modern Scottish writers are asked to bear by those who seek to bolster a distinct Scottish identity through the nation's cultural output. But their responses, as we have seen, have more often than not been equivocal. The writer Dot Allan (1892–1964), whose novel *The Syrens* (1921) was set on the Clyde, was uncomfortable with being pigeonholed as a 'Glasgow' writer or even a Scottish writer for, as she explained, 'I don't believe in the localisation of a writer's talent. One ought to take the world as one's field if one wants to.'[74] And, as Willa Muir remarked in 1931 with reference to a forthcoming novel, 'you needn't look for Nationalism with a big N in it. None the less, I think I shall be "doing my bit" for Scotland.'[75]

Female writers and performers of the premodern era, and especially those who practised their craft within the ballad tradition, were not themselves explicitly concerned with expressing a national identity, but they and their songs have been used subsequently to define a Scottish cultural identity. The ballad, like all forms of oral culture, was a fluid and flexible form, and thus it was socially and historically contingent. Female balladeers and storytellers were able to use these forms to tell stories that reflected their own experiences. Kerrigan goes further in arguing that 'in its power to tell a story, in providing a place for unrecorded experience, the ballad became for many women poets the home of their history'.[76] In this sense, then, the ballad may be a prime medium for the expression of a Scottish female identity. Yet, few of the ballads or songs composed or performed by women contain explicit national sentiment. Certainly, the subject matter drew on the everyday, on the banal life-cycle events affecting most women and men in rural Scotland, but it is this very groundedness in the Scottish everyday that gave them such a resonance, especially for those who had migrated far from their homes. One mid-nineteenth-century writer nicely summed up the emotional power of the Scottish song.

> Scotch songs are not 'pretty' . . . they are yet born of the people . . . they were the growth of simple taste, of true feeling, often of intense passion: Love, joy and patriotism are their inspiration; not an *affected* feeling of things, but real, earnest, genuine feeling. Their power seizes hold of you.[77]

But it was the listeners perhaps, more than the balladeers, who saw in this medium a pure expression of Scottish identity.

The ballad and the song were indigenous cultural forms which, through performance in the community, were means by which people (and perhaps especially women) could shape a sense of themselves and their place in Scotland's past and in the present. Others, of course, used these traditional forms (as well as folktales, fairy stories, superstitions and so on) to make a statement about difference and identity. The act of collection and publication of ballads, songs and folktales by antiquarians in the eighteenth and nineteenth centuries might be interpreted as a means of exploiting one manifestation of Scottish culture for nationalist purposes. Certainly, Daiches has argued that this fashion for collecting and publication of collections of songs was an acceptable form of nationalism, whereas open protests against the Union of 1707 were unacceptable expressions of Scottish identity.[78] But it is more likely that collectors saw their work as having a cultural rather than a political purpose. In the case of oral culture, the relationship between gender and Scottish identity may have been identifiable at the point of performance; but, once the songs were collected and published, these productions were incorporated into a more banal and undifferentiated cultural context, and the gendered nature of the original performance disappeared.

A. L. Kennedy recently wrote that Scottish identity is created by telling stories.[79] In the past, as Siân Reynolds demonstrates in Chapter 7, attributes of Scottishness have been deduced from the work of mainly male writers – Walter Scott pre-eminently in the nineteenth century, but also more recently in the work of West of Scotland male novelists. But, as Christianson argues with reference to Elspeth Barker's *O Caledonia* and Kelman's *How Late It Was, How Late*, 'why should the intensely imagined girlhood in the North East of a heroine who is murdered in a castle aged 16 be any less emblematic of nationhood than a man who wakes up blind in a prison cell in the West of Scotland?'[80] There is no reason why narratives from the female perspective may not express Scottishness; but they may differ from the construction of Scottishness present within the narratives which foreground male experience.

CONCLUSION

From the evidence cited above, a number of conclusions may be drawn. The examples of politics, education and the kirk suggest women's agency in repositioning themselves in institutional and public life, and that they created a public space where they could act alongside men, sometimes in separate organisations and sometimes together with men. In the process, women often articulated values and aspirations in similar ways to men, especially in subscribing to values associated with Scottishness. The use of such imagery and symbols served to legitimise claims for greater equality, just as women drew on evangelical and imperialist discourses 'to sanction their entry into the public sphere'.[81] While gender difference remained inscribed in and regulated by such institutions, they also provided a location for the expression of a shared national identity, and it was through appeals to this that women could enlarge their sphere of action.

The evidence also suggests that, in certain contexts, women positioned themselves in terms of class, religion and nation, in much the same way as men did, and the identities that men and women shared in such groups were often more important than the identity they might share with other women. Or, shared identity functioned as a means of expression of class or 'national' power, as in the efforts of middle-class women to control working-class women and Indian and African women in colonial territories. Women's work with women in the mission field was premised on a notion of gender identity, but this was structured by relations of class and empire, rather than the basis of a collective solidarity of women. Elsewhere though, as in the suffrage campaign, Scottish women consciously articulated their identity as members of the Scottish nation in order to stress their special contribution to the cause of women's rights without undermining their membership of the suffrage sisterhood.

In the sphere of culture, older traditions of ballad and song have provided a vehicle for the expression of identity, and of gender and national identities among others. These forms have also been appropriated as typifying Scottishness at particular times. Creative literature in particular provides evidence of the plurality and multi-faceted nature of identity, though this has also been evident elsewhere, as in the literature produced about foreign missions, where the imperial context brought into play a range of markers of identity. However, the former also provides evidence that national identity is not necessarily prioritised as a facet of identity, or may be regarded with ambiguity. Gender differences in the expression of Scottish identity may be more marked in literature and other forms of cultural production than they are in collective and institutional constructions of identity. These differences underline, however, that representations of Scottish identity should not be taken as universal and unitary in any context, since such representations always express the interests of particular individuals or groups.

In the voices heard in the historical record, and in the gendered character of representations of Scottish national identity, there remains of course an asymmetry. Though women are not wholly absent, men (and maleness) are much more obviously present. Iconic figures have always been important to representations of national identity – not just in Scotland – but also everywhere else. In Scotland over the centuries, the figures of Wallace and Bruce have been reinterpreted to symbolise Scottish national identity in a manner fitting the political circumstances of the time – for example, both as the harbingers of the Union of 1707 and as symbols of separatism – and new iconic figures have also been constructed such as Burns, Scott, Livingstone and the heroes of Red Clydeside. The deconstruction of such myths helps to identify whose interests they served; and examination of the uses to which masculine icons are put, as in the works cited above, has underlined that imagery of Scottishness can be appropriated not just for domestic purposes but also furth[82] of Scotland to reassert and 'centre' masculinity. Yet, such icons are not necessarily always used for such purposes, and the question of the extent to which they are used by men to reinforce male hegemony, or the extent to which they may serve to symbolise abstract ideals of democracy and freedom, or indeed the extent to which women have appropriated them in the cause of gender equality, merits further investigation.

We suggest, then, that continuing the investigation into gender and Scottish national identity will help in understanding to what extent the construction of this was itself the site of consensus or contest between women and men, or between different groups of women and different groups of men. To test this, circumstances in which gender roles have been actively contested, or circumstances in which Scottish national identity has been actively contested, or both simultaneously, may be particularly fruitful to investigate: the women's suffrage movement; campaigns for access to higher education; campaigns around women's status in the churches; and the second-wave women's movement. Since the later decades of the twentieth century, feminists have explicitly challenged constructions of Scottish national identity and historical narratives that have privileged the masculine or have promulgated stereotypes of masculinity and femininity, and have sought to research women's experience and to construct historical narratives which include this. Beyond any intellectual or academic contribution that such work is making, valuable in itself, it contributes to the process of claiming equality that has generated collective action in recent decades on the basis of a gender identity. As in the case of many previous political movements, women are doing this in the name of creating a more egalitarian and democratic society, both calling upon dominant myths of Scottish national identity and finding them wanting. To what extent Scottish identity was similarly called upon and challenged by previous women's campaigns and movements remains a matter for investigation – but it would be surprising indeed if no examples were to be found.

FURTHER READING

National identity

Anderson, B., *Imagined Communities: Reflections on the Origin and Spread of Nationalism* (London: Verso, 1991).

Colley, L., *Britons: Forging the Nation 1707–1837* (New Haven: Yale University Press, 1992).

Crick, B., 'Essay on Britishness', *Scottish Affairs* 2 (1993), 71–83.

Di Domenico, C., A. Law, J. Skinner and M. Smith (eds), *Boundaries and Identities: Nation, Politics and Culture in Scotland* (Dundee: University of Abertay Press, 2001).

McCrone, D., *The Sociology of Nationalism* (London: Routledge, 1998).

Morton, G., *Unionist Nationalism: Governing Urban Scotland, 1830–1860* (East Linton: Tuckwell Press, 1999).

Smith, A., *National Identity* (London: Penguin, 1991).

Gender and identity/gender and nationalism

Blom, I., K. Hagemann and C. Hall (eds), *Gendered Nations: Nationalisms and Gender Order in the Long Nineteenth Century* (Oxford: Berg, 2000).

Gifford, D. and D. McMillan (eds), *A History of Scottish Women's Writing* (Edinburgh: Edinburgh University Press, 1997).

Whyte, C. (ed.), *Gendering the Nation: Studies in Modern Scottish Literature* (Edinburgh: Edinburgh University Press, 1995).

Yuval-Davis, N., *Gender and Nation* (London: Sage Publications 1997).

NOTES

1. See, for example, E. Breitenbach, ' "Curiously rare": Scottish women of interest or the suppression of the female in the construction of national identity', *Scottish Affairs* 18 (1997), 82–94; A. Howson, No gods and precious few women: gender and cultural identity in Scotland, *Scottish Affairs* 2 (1993), 37–49.

2. Michael Lynch has noted how 'Dame Scotia' was initially the 'metaphor of a Catholic priest for the beleaguered homeland' in the 1540s, but had become a Protestant icon by the 1630s, identified with the kirk itself, 'the suffering bride of Christ'. See M. Lynch, 'A nation born again? Scottish identity in the sixteenth and seventeenth centuries', in D. Broun, R. J. Finlay and M. Lynch (eds), *Image and Identity: The Making and Re-making of Scotland through the Ages* (Edinburgh: John Donald, 1998), pp. 143–56.

3. See, for example, the discussion of female figures representing Scotland and other countries and continents in seventeenth-century masques, including on the occasion of Charles I's state entry into Edinburgh in 1633, in C. Withers, *Geography, Science and National Identity: Scotland since 1520* (Cambridge: Cambridge University Press, 2001), pp. 62–5.

4. See W. Webster, 'Representing nation: women, obituaries and national biography', in A.-M. Gallagher, C. Lubelska and L. Ryan (eds), *Re-presenting the Past: Women and History* (London: Longman, 2001), pp. 124–41, here p. 136.

5. Willa Muir, 'Women in Scotland', *Left Review* Nov. (1936), in M. Palmer McCulloch (ed.), *Modernism and Nationalism: Literature and Society in Scotland 1918–1939* (Glasgow: ASLS, 2004), pp. 215–18, here p. 218.

6. See, for example, R. Finlay, *A Partnership for Good? Scottish Politics and the Union since 1880* (Edinburgh: John Donald, 1997), and T. M. Devine, *Scotland's Empire* (London: Allen Lane, 2003).

7. C. McArthur, 'Culloden: a pre-emptive strike', *Scottish Affairs* 9 (1994), 97–126. Sue Innes and Jane Rendall, in Chapter 3 of this volume, note how the mythologisation of the Jacobite past, including its heroines, has exaggerated the attractiveness of Jacobitism as a form of political opposition.

8. McArthur, 'Culloden', p. 113.

9. T. Edensor, 'Reading Braveheart: representing and contesting Scottish identity', *Scottish Affairs* 21 (1997), 135–58.

10. Ibid., p. 138.

11. Ibid., p. 138. *Scotch Reels* offered a critique of representations of Scottishness in cinema and television. See C. McArthur (ed.), *Scotch Reels: Scotland in Cinema and Television* (London: British Film Institute, 1982).

12. Ibid., p. 155.

13. See E. Hague, 'National Tartan Day: rewriting history in the United States', *Scottish Affairs* 38 (2002), 94–124.

14. See T. Nairn, *The Break-up of Britain* (London: Verso, 1981).

15. Hague, 'National Tartan Day', p. 112.

16. R. J. Finlay, 'Heroes, myths, and anniversaries in modern Scotland', *Scottish Affairs* 18 (1997), 108–25.

17. Ibid., p. 123.

18. See, for example, N. Yuval-Davis, *Gender and Nation* (London: Sage Publications, 1997); S. Walby, 'Woman and nation', in G. Balakrishnan (ed.), *Mapping the Nation* (London: Verso, 1996), pp. 235–54.

19. See, for example, the contributions in I. Blom, K. Hagemann and C. Hall (eds), *Gendered Nations: Nationalisms and Gender Order in the Long Nineteenth Century* (Oxford: Berg, 2000); and, for a synopsis of the European literature, see L. Abrams, *The Making of Modern Woman: Europe 1789–1918* (London: Longman, 2002), pp. 223–41.

20. There are some exceptions; for example, see L. Ryan, 'Splendidly silent: representing Irish Republican women, 1919–23', in Gallagher, et al. (eds), *Re-presenting the Past*, pp. 23–43.

21. See, for example, D. McCrone, *The Sociology of Nationalism* (London: Routledge, 1998); L. Paterson, *The Autonomy of Modern Scotland* (Edinburgh: Edinburgh University Press, 1994).

22. See G. Morton, *Unionist Nationalism: Governing Urban Scotland, 1830–1860* (East Linton: Tuckwell Press, 1999).

23. See F. Mackay, 'Women and the 2003 elections: keeping up the momentum', *Scottish Affairs* 44 (2003), 74–90.

24. A. Smith, *National Identity*, (London: Penguin, 1991), p. 174.

25. Ibid., p. 143.

26. Ibid., p. 4.

27. Ibid., p. 4.

28. T. C. Smout, 'Perspectives on the Scottish identity', *Scottish Affairs* 6 (1994), 101–13, here p. 104.

29. A. Brown, 'Introduction: gender and national identity', *Scottish Affairs* 18 (1997), 41–4, here p. 44.

30. Smout, 'Perspectives on the Scottish identity', p. 104.

31. D. McCrone, 'National identity', in J. Crowther, I. Martin and M. Shaw (eds), *Renewing Democracy in Scotland* (Leicester: NIACE, 2003), pp. 5–8.

32. Ibid., p. 5.

33. L. Paterson, 'Conclusion: does nationalism matter?', *Scottish Affairs* 17 (1996), 112–19. The quote from Goffman refers to E. Goffman, *The Presentation of the Self in Everyday Life* (New York: Overview Press, 1973).

34. See, for example, M. Billig, *Banal Nationalism* (London: Sage, 1995); McCrone, 'National identity'.

35. Blair Castle, Duke of Atholl MSS, 29 (2) 4, 'My Wifes Meditations Concerning the Union, Dunkeld, 13th October, 1706'.

36. R. Carr, ' ". . . this nation is so deluded". Gendering the Union of 1707', unpublished paper, 13th Annual Women's History Network Conference, Hull, September 2004.

37. T. Mayer, 'Gender ironies of nationalism: setting the stage', in T. Mayer (ed.), *Gender Ironies of Nationalism: Sexing the Nation* (London: Routledge, 2000), p. 14.

38. I. Blom, 'Gender and nation in international comparison', in Blom et al. (eds), *Gendered Nations*, pp. 10–15.

39. Carr, ' ". . . this nation is so deluded" '.

40. C. A. Whatley, *Scottish Society 1707–1830* (Manchester: Manchester University Press, 2000), p. 315.

41. E. King, 'The Scottish women's suffrage movement', in E. Breitenbach and E. Gordon (eds), *Out of Bounds: Women in Scottish Society 1800–1945* (Edinburgh: Edinburgh University Press, 1992), pp. 121–50, here pp. 124–5. Whatley, *Scottish Society*, p. 312.

42. *True Scotsman*, 17 November 1838.

43. *Scots Times*, 30 September 1840. See also A. Clark, *The Struggle for the Breeches: Gender and the Making of the British Working Class* (London: Rivers Oram, 1995), pp. 227–31.

44. R. J. Morris, 'Victorian values in Scotland and England', in T. C. Smout (ed.), *Victorian Values* (Oxford: Oxford University Press, 1992), pp. 31–48, here pp. 37–8.

45. King, 'Scottish women's suffrage movement', p. 140.

46. M. K. Smitley, ' "Woman's Mission": The Temperance and Women's Suffrage Movements in Scotland, c.1870–1914', Ph.D. thesis, University of Glasgow, 2002, pp. 241–8; M. K. Smitley, 'Feminist Anglo-Saxonism?: representations of "Scotch" women in the English women's press in the late nineteenth century', *Social and Cultural History*, forthcoming.

47. J. Hutchinson and A. D. Smith (eds), *Nationalism* (Oxford: Oxford University Press, 1994); L. Leneman, *A Guid Cause: The Women's Suffrage Movement in Scotland* (Edinburgh: Edinburgh University Press, 1991), p. 219.

48. M. K. Reid, *A Plea for Woman* (Edinburgh: W. Tait, 1843).

49. Smitley, 'Feminist Anglo-Saxonism?'.

50. Leneman, *A Guid Cause*, pp. 80–1. Sue Innes and Jane Rendall also note, in Chapter 3, a similar use of Scottish women's history and iconography in the suffragette pageant and procession in Edinburgh in 1909.

51. Inspector Aitken, 'Fitting tribute to the "mother branch" ', in A. Buchan,

History of the Scottish Co-operative Women's Guild (Scottish Co-operative Women's Guild, 1913), p. 27.

52. Morton, *Unionist Nationalism*.

53. Ibid., ch. 7.

54. R. D. Anderson, *Scottish Education since the Reformation* (Edinburgh: Economic and Social History Society of Scotland, 1997), p. 2.

55. Ibid., p. 54.

56. J. H. McDermid, 'The Schooling of Working-Class Girls in Nineteenth-Century Scotland: The Interaction of Nationality, Class, and Gender' Ph.D. thesis, University of London Institute of Education, 2000, p. 9.

57. Ibid., p. 155.

58. Ibid., p. 189.

59. Ibid., p. 209.

60. See, for example, Paterson, *The Autonomy of Modern Scotland*; D. Forrester, 'The church', in Crowther et al. (eds), *Renewing Democracy in Scotland*, pp. 56–9; C. Kidd, 'Race, empire, and the limits of nineteenth-century Scottish nationhood', *The Historical Journal* 46 (2003), 873–92.

61. L. Orr Macdonald, *A Unique and Glorious Mission: Women and Presbyterianism in Scotland 1830–1930* (Edinburgh: John Donald, 2000), p. 17.

62. E. Breitenbach, 'Empire, Religion and National Identity: Scottish Christian Imperialism in the Nineteenth and Early Twentieth Centuries', Ph.D. thesis, University of Edinburgh, 2005. This research set out to examine the impact of participation in the British Empire on constructions of Scottish national identity, using as case studies civil society organisations which were concerned with empire or aspects of imperial experience. Of these, missionary societies and the churches furnished the most significant examples. An analysis of a range of forms of 'missionary literature' produced in the period from the 1820s to the 1910s was conducted in order to identify the dominant markers of identity expressed in this context. A brief summary of the findings on gender and national identity is given here.

63. See Orr Macdonald, *A Unique and Glorious Mission*.

64. Agnes Waddel, *Memorials of Mrs Sutherland of Old Calabar* (Paisley: J. and R. Parlane, 1883); W. P. Livingstone, *Mary Slessor of Calabar, Pioneer Missionary* (London: Hodder and Stoughton, 1916); John Wilson, *Memoir of Mrs Margaret Wilson* (Edinburgh: John Johnstone, 1838).

65. Mrs Sutherland (c.1820–81) was a predecessor of Mary Slessor at Old Calabar in West Africa. Born Euphemia Miller in Culross, she was in domestic service in Glasgow before training as a missionary with the support of the United Secession Church.

66. See Waddel, *Mrs Sutherland*; Livingstone, *Mary Slessor*. Women's periodicals enjoined their readers to read books on, for example, Livingstone, Duff, Chalmers and Paton. See, for example, Church of Scotland, *News of Female Missions*, New Series no. 6 (February 1903).

67. For example, see C. Whyte (ed.), *Gendering the Nation: Studies in*

Modern Scottish Literature (Edinburgh: Edinburgh University Press, 1995); D. Gifford and D. McMillan (eds), *A History of Scottish Women's Writing* (Edinburgh: Edinburgh University Press, 1997); A. Christianson, 'Imagined corners to debatable land: passable boundaries', *Scottish Affairs* 17 (1996), 120–34. See also Siân Reynolds' contribution to this volume (Chapter 7).

68. Mrs Story, *Early Reminiscences* (1911), quoted in Gifford and McMillan (eds), *History of Scottish Women's Writing*, p. xiii.

69. See also Kay's poem 'So You Think I'm a Mule?', discussed in S. Hagemann, 'Women and nation', and in D. McMillan, 'Twentieth-century poetry II', both in Gifford and McMillan (eds), *History of Scottish Women's Writing*, pp. 316–28 and 570–3.

70. J. Kay, 'In My Country', in J. Kay, *Other Lovers* (Newcastle: Bloodaxe, 1993).

71. Quoted in C. Gonda, 'An other country: mapping Scottish/lesbian/writing', in Whyte (ed.), *Gendering the Nation*, p. 11.

72. Quoted in ibid., p. 7.

73. A. L. Kennedy, 'Not the changing world', in I. A. Bell (ed.), *Peripheral Visions* (Cardiff: University of Cardiff Press, 1995), p. 100.

74. E. Kyle, 'Modern women authors', *Scots Observer* (June 1931), in Palmer McCulloch (ed.), *Modernism and Nationalism*, p. 206.

75. Willa Muir, letter to F. Marian McNeill (July 1931), in Palmer McCulloch (ed.), *Modernism and Nationalism*, p. 209.

76. C. Kerrigan (ed.), *An Anthology of Scottish Women Poets* (Edinburgh: Edinburgh University Press, 1991), p. 5.

77. Eliza Cook (1852), quoted in K. McCue, 'Women and song 1750–1850', in Gifford and McMillan (eds), *History of Scottish Women's Writing*, p. 67.

78. D. Daiches, *The Paradox of Scottish Culture: The Eighteenth-Century Experience* (Oxford: Oxford University Press, 1964), p. 28.

79. A. L. Kennedy, 'The role of notable silences in Scottish history', in *Night Geometry and the Garscadden Trains: Short Stories* (London: Vintage, 1990).

80. Christianson, 'Imagined corners', p. 125.

81. E. Gordon and G. Nair, *Public Lives: Women, Family and Society in Victorian Britain* (New Haven and London: Yale University Press, 2003), p. 4.

82. 'Furth' is a Scots word meaning 'forth', 'outside of'. See *The Online Scots Dictionary*, www.scots-online.org

3

Women, Gender and Politics

Sue Innes and Jane Rendall

INTRODUCTION

This chapter focuses primarily on writing the political history of Scottish women, in relation to shifting discourses of masculinity and citizenship. It seeks to recover that political history but also to focus on the meaning of the political, taking into account feminist redefinitions and wider visions of 'the political'.[1] So far, the only areas of women's political activism in Scotland which have been studied at all extensively are anti-slavery movements, suffrage campaigns and the labour movement; much more needs to be done even in these areas.[2] Political history in Scotland has been dominated by the labour movement and, more recently, by work on the 'growth of the nation', both of which have tended to marginalise women's and gender history.[3] Politics in Scotland has been gendered in that it has been almost exclusively defined as a 'male game' via the exclusion of women (as well as other exclusions). It has continued to be gendered in that women's political participation has been understood as joining formal institutions, or oppositional movements, and learning to play by their rules.[4]

Simply 'adding women' does not address the history of the gendered boundaries of both formal and informal institutions that still has to be written. Clear distinctions between private/public boundaries have often been taken for granted, yet are now widely questioned. Jürgen Habermas identified in the eighteenth and nineteenth centuries what he called a bourgeois public sphere, the institutions of a reasoning public, its urban culture, voluntary societies, press and periodicals. Though criticised by feminists for its gender-blindness, his approach has encouraged the study of women's participation in print culture and in associations such as clubs, salons and philanthropic societies.[5] Our definitions of the political will include not only these but also the political influence and expression centred in the family, and the writing of the political through the ballad or the novel. This chapter aims to illustrate different understandings of what is political and the consequences for Scottish women's political history. We pay particular attention to women's approaches to civil society and to citizenship.

Civil society has particular significance for the history of Scotland from 1707 after the loss of the Scottish parliament; Scots were distinctive and pioneering theorists of civil society in the eighteenth century, and Scottish identity has been bound up with its distinctive civil society within the Union.[6] This is particularly important for Scottish women's political history. If Scottish women's history suffers from a double deficit, less visible for the reasons that women everywhere have been, but also because Scottish history has been marginalised, there is a third layer of deficit for women's political history, since so many of the ways in which women have acted politically and much of the work of autonomous women's organisations do not come within conventional definitions of the political. Definitions that focus on state government intensify that deficit in Scotland.[7]

The meanings of citizenship are also gendered. Different definitions from the eighteenth century onwards reflect the varied discourses of masculine citizenship, whether achieved or demanded, employed by, among others, the middle-class professional man, the skilled artisan, the respectable shopkeeper and the trade unionist. All claimed the right to formal citizenship, a goal that most – though not all – men had achieved before 1918; in Glasgow in 1911, only 54 per cent of adult males were enfranchised.[8] Women's political history in the late nineteenth and twentieth centuries is frequently written around access to formal citizenship. Yet, long before their acquisition of the vote, some Scotswomen were active in areas that are now not contested as the subject of political decision-making – anti-slavery, child protection and child care, social work and public health, in today's terminology – although such work was not described as 'political'. Through such activity, women made a claim to influence in public life and to a role as citizens that did not depend on formal voting rights.

This chapter also seeks to relate the history of the organised women's movement in Scotland to a broader, gendered political history. It is possible to draw tentative links from the founding of the Edinburgh National Society for Women's Suffrage in 1867 to the campaign for gender balance in representation in the Scottish parliament in the 1990s. In 1918, members of that society set up the Edinburgh Women Citizens' Association. Towards the end of its active life, that association, with the Scottish Council of Women Citizens' Associations, contributed to Scottish activities for International Women's Year in 1975, and to the establishment in 1977 of the Scottish Convention of Women, which was among the organisations pressing for gender parity in the Scottish parliament.[9] There is one intriguing reference to links between women's suffrage and the campaign for home rule; in her will, the suffragist Mary Burton in 1909 left a legacy to the Edinburgh society, to support its campaign 'for the admission of women to sit as members of parliament either at Westminster or in a Scottish Parliament'.[10] However, we do not suggest any simple continuous narrative of progress towards one particular end. We recognise the many differences within Scottish women's political history and their varied and changing claims to citizenship, though we also note where cross-class connections and degrees of unity existed.

Nevertheless, in May 1999, when the first Scottish parliament met in Edinburgh, 37 per cent of its members were women, an inclusiveness which for many Scots symbolised the renewal of democracy in Scotland. Gendering the history of Scottish politics can help to explain the significance of that moment, as also what has followed and will continue to follow from it.

THE POLITICS OF INFLUENCE: CONFLICTS AND CHALLENGES, 1707–89

Bruce Lenman has suggested that one interpretation of eighteenth-century Scottish politics might be of 'little more than a froth floating on the surface', barely disturbing the unchanging structures of power, though he qualifies this by emphasising the significance of discontinuities and challenges.[11] Certainly, the masculine elite of landowners and gentry, who after the Union of 1707 controlled the Scottish electoral system, composed the effective Scottish political nation throughout this period. The formal political order, after as before 1707, depended upon customary forms of landed power. The tiny minority of men who participated in that electoral system qualified, in the counties, through complex landowning rights dependent on different forms of feudal tenure, including the provision that husbands might qualify through freeholds held by their wives. In the sixty-six burghs, grouped into fourteen constituencies, only members of the burgh councils could vote, a system which allowed local landowners overwhelming influence. Throughout the eighteenth century, politics was mainly an informal matter, a question of patronage, faction and influence, conducted by landowning networks bound together by family connections and dynastic marriage alliances.

Elaine Chalus has demonstrated, primarily for England, how a minority of aristocratic women, usually widows or heiresses, could through the influence of their rank and family participate to some degree in eighteenth-century politics. The consequences for women's political influence in Scotland have not been systematically investigated. Rosalind Carr has shown that, even in the debates around the Union of 1707, individual aristocratic women engaged actively with the issues. Some, like Katherine Hamilton, Duchess of Atholl, expressed their hostility: 'as for the Treaty I am still of the same mind, but more and more against it'.[12] Throughout the eighteenth century, aristocratic Scottish women could and did approach government ministers based in London, knowing the importance of their influence in maintaining support in Scotland. Chalus's study of the female correspondents of the Duke of Newcastle includes Katherine, Duchess of Gordon. A young widow with four children, she had assumed control of the large Gordon estates in 1752 and was a committed Whig. When asking for a paid office for her second husband, or for £400 for herself, she promised to exert the Gordon interest for the government in the next election, and reported her success in raising the first Gordon regiment.[13]

The correspondence of the political managers of Scotland was equally dominated by patronage and questions of management, and here too women's influence was acknowledged. In the Angus election of 1795–6, Henry Dundas reminded the widowed Lady Dalhousie to make her personal support for him known, against the wishes of her husband's brother, to swing the votes towards his favoured candidate.[14] There is certainly evidence of such propertied women exerting their own influence also in the electoral system, though the extent of this is still unknown. In the election of 1731, the burgh of Irvine was controlled by the widowed Countess of Eglinton together with Lord Milton, the political agent of the Duke of Argyll, as joint guardians of the young Lord Eglinton.[15] And, as late as 1820, Lady Ann Grant intervened in an exceptionally riotous election at Elgin, calling out 700 of her tenants to march on the town to support her candidate, deterred only by the intervention of the Sheriff of Moray and local ministers.[16]

Exceptionally, great wealth could allow a woman to exercise an unprecedented combination of economic and political influence throughout this period. At the beginning of the eighteenth century, the long career of Anne, the third Duchess of Hamilton, was drawing to a close, but she continued to control and improve the Hamilton estates.[17] As hereditary sheriff of Lanarkshire in her own right, she possessed often decisive influence in the county of Lanarkshire and in the constituency of Linlithgow. In the latter in 1713, she even found herself in conflict with her daughter-in-law, the fourth Duchess, over the candidate to be elected.[18] In 1785,

Elizabeth, Countess of Sutherland heiress to the great Sutherland estate since 1766, married an English aristocrat, George Leveson Gower, later Marquess of Stafford, heir to a massive industrial fortune. The Countess's personal energy and immense wealth allowed her to maintain a 'virtually impregnable' hold on the political representation of the county of Sutherland as well as the burgh of Dornoch, and, notoriously, to clear much of its population from the land.[19] Of course, for the great majority even of aristocratic and gentry women in Scotland, such influence was exercised mainly by their fathers, husbands and brothers.

The most direct challenge to the management of Scotland in the Hanoverian interest came of course from the cause of Jacobitism, which in the failed invasions of 1708 and 1719, and the risings of 1715 and 1745, presented a major threat to political stability. Though the movement drew much of its major military strength from the Highlands, Jacobite support could be found almost everywhere across Scotland. It was most closely associated with Catholic and Episcopalian religious communities, notably in the Highlands and in north-eastern Scotland, though there were also many instances of Presbyterian Jacobitism. In this conflict, the aristocracy and gentry were the leading players, linked on both sides by marriage alliances and by family and religious loyalties.[20] Most seriously, in 1715 in the Highlands, twenty-eight clans out of fifty rose in support. In such a conflict, powerful women could find a major role. The Catholic and Jacobite Penelope Mackenzie, Lady Clanranald, controlled the family influence after her husband's death at the Battle of Sheriffmuir in 1715, regained its forfeited estate in 1727 and helped to sustain Catholic clergy and the Catholic faith throughout the western Gaelic-speaking region.[21] The appeal of a young prince in 1745 certainly added some attractiveness to Jacobite political opposition for women, but the extent of this – in what was in the main a brutal and ruthless conflict – has been exaggerated by the nostalgia of later generations and the mythic status of Jacobite heroines.

Jacobite women of rank – like their Hanoverian counterparts – undoubtedly expressed in these years a political support legitimated through family loyalty, and influenced events in the absence, death or exile of husbands, fathers and brothers. Poorer women might also express their loyalty, and their attachment to clan chiefs, as did, quite exceptionally, Margaret Maclean (Mairearad nighean Lachlainn) in her 'Cry of the Mull Women', an elegy to Sir John Maclean of Duart, who died in 1716 shortly after the battle of Sheriffmuir, and a passionate lament for clan and family.[22] Support for the Jacobite movement was greatly reduced by 1745. Though its military heart remained in the

Highlands, many clans, won over by the material rewards of union, did not support it. Again, as others had done before them, after the call to arms in the summer of 1745, women expressed their loyalties, as Jean Cameron of Glendessary led 300 Cameron men to Glenfinnan, and 'Colonel' Anne Mackintosh raised a regiment for the cause.[23] The distinctive structure of the clans was clearly identified by the British government as central to Jacobite survival, and the defeat at Culloden in 1746 brought a destructive onslaught on all aspects of clan life. High-ranking Jacobite women were imprisoned briefly, or went into exile; poorer women took their chances.

Challenges to political stability also came from civil disorders not obviously associated with Jacobitism. The level of popular disturbances in Scotland in the 1720s and 1730s was high, and Christopher Whatley suggests that the combination of increasing commercialism, dissatisfaction with the Union, and serious food shortages, helped to bring about extensive food rioting in Angus, Fife and Perthshire in 1720, often directed against customs and excise officers. A high proportion of women in these crowds was noted, as in other popular disturbances in early eighteenth-century Scotland. Observers commented that women involved in such collective activity tended to use force, especially against the representatives of authority, as in Edinburgh in 1740 when a magistrate had to be protected from the women in the crowd.[24] It has been suggested that they participated in such actions partly through their own responsibility for family survival, partly through identifying with the collective action of their communities. However, recent evidence that two-thirds of those prosecuted in south-west Scotland were single suggests that we should look to the latter explanation and to personal circumstances.[25]

Women's participation in such collective action can be identified in many contexts throughout the eighteenth century and beyond. They took part in actions directed against the presentation of new ministers imposed by patrons, as on the Lovat estate in 1766 or in Assynt in 1813.[26] In 1782 in Letterfinlay, Lochaber, a group of women attacked a prospective sheep farmer and beat him up, foreshadowing many decades of conflict over the clearance of land in the Highlands. Women actively opposed military recruitment and the activities of press gangs.[27] The exact level of women's participation in such activities remains very difficult to calculate, and is probably frequently under-recorded. But the evidence we have suggests that both urban and rural women identified with the moral economies of their communities and united with them against external threats.

The political and social stability of Scotland was enhanced rather than threatened by new cultural developments. After the Union, reforms in the universities of Edinburgh, Glasgow and Aberdeen and the appearance of a more liberal though still Presbyterian theology in the Church of Scotland began to allow a questioning of older orthodoxies. The expansion of polite culture in Scotland, including the growth of printing and publishing and the newspaper and periodical press, and the appearance of libraries, clubs and societies, pointed towards a commitment to improvement. By the early 1750s, the men of letters of the Scottish Enlightenment were developing a coherent programme of intellectual enquiry into human nature, civil society and the nature of political and economic science, alongside related scientific and medical investigations. The Scottish Enlightenment was a part of the British and European Enlightenments, but it had its own distinctive characteristics, both in its fields of enquiry and as a social movement.[28]

One of its outstanding achievements lay in its theorisation of civil society and its progress, and of the discourses of masculinity and femininity in that progress. Moral philosophers Francis Hutcheson and David Hume, together with historians Adam Ferguson, John Millar, Lord Kames and William Robertson, were interested in tracing the development of society – by which they meant the totality of human custom and experience – through a series of economic stages towards the highest state, commercial civilisation. The term 'civilisation' drew upon Scottish civil law and was used in opposition to the 'savagery' and 'barbarism' of earlier stages of development, in both contemporary and historical societies.[29] In this narrative, gender relations were historically relative, related to stages of development, not divinely ordained and unchanging. The history of progress towards that civilisation could be told in terms of the history of women's condition, in terms of marriage and family relations, and of manners and customs. In John Millar's *Observations concerning the Distinction of Ranks* (1771), he foresaw the place of women in a modern commercial society within a domesticated family, divided by labour but united by 'esteem and affection' and 'neither the slaves, nor the idols of the other sex, but the friends and companions'.[30] The company of women also encouraged the growth of masculine refinement; for, as David Hume wrote, 'What better school for manners than the company of virtuous women, where the mutual endeavour to please must insensibly polish the mind . . . ?'[31] For William Alexander, author of *The History of Women* (1778), the condition of women in any country indicated 'the exact point in the scale of civil society to which the people of such country have arrived'.[32] These themes were to become commonplaces in progressive narratives of historical change by the end of the eighteenth century.

In spite of the intellectual concerns of the literati, the Scottish Enlightenment was, comparatively, a conservative movement. Margaret Jacob and others have argued that the bourgeois public sphere of the European Enlightenment as defined by Habermas contained institutions and practices – an expanding print culture, a new world of sociability and voluntary associations – which could be open to women. In Scotland, new sites of mixed sociability – such as, in Edinburgh, the Assembly Rooms, St Cecilia's Hall, the theatre, Leith racecourse and the wide streets of the New Town – certainly flourished after the 1760s. Some women – Alison Cockburn, Jane, Duchess of Gordon, Elizabeth Rose of Kilravock – were frequent correspondents of and lively hostesses for leading figures in the Enlightenment in Scotland.[33] But the social context of the Scottish Enlightenment was very different from and much less diverse than the Enlightenments of London, Paris or Amsterdam, deriving much of its coherence from its narrow base in the clerical and academic worlds of the universities of Edinburgh, Glasgow and Aberdeen, in alliance with an improving gentry and landlord class. Intellectual debate and exchange were rooted in masculine societies – the Select Society, the Poker Club – arising from the shared and homosocial experiences of university education, academic life, and participation in the General Assembly of the Church of Scotland as well as city taverns.[34] No equivalents of the blue-stocking gatherings or female debating societies of London, the salonnières of Paris or the female masonic lodges and scientific societies of the Netherlands have yet been identified in Scotland.

That absence is perhaps not so surprising, for the theorists of civil society in the Scottish Enlightenment wrote of it in terms not so much of a world observed as of a state to which they aspired. Their works were intended to educate, as the characteristics assigned to women in a polite, commercial society became the goals of aspiration and the subject of instruction. In John Gregory's *A Father's Legacy to His Daughters* (1774), James Fordyce's *Sermons to Young Women* (1764) and Henry Mackenzie's periodicals, the *Mirror* and the *Lounger*, the ideals of refinement and propriety for young women participating in the mixed sociability of such a society were elaborated. Young men were similarly, though less frequently, encouraged towards the polite masculinity appropriate to this commercial, though still hierarchical, world. As Mary Catherine Moran has argued, such authors sought to create an enlightened female reader, capable of drawing upon the lessons of moral philosophy and, especially, of history, to help influence the civil society of the future. The politics of middle-class women were in the future to draw upon that rhetoric of civilisation and enlightenment.[35]

REVOLUTION AND REFORM, 1789–1867

In the American and French Revolutions, new concepts of citizenship were defined in radical and republican terms, as the framers of both the Declaration of Independence and the Declaration of the Rights of Man associated citizenship with a masculine 'independence' and a civic virtue dependent on ability to defend the new nation. Though such concepts, as expressed by Tom Paine in the *Rights of Man* (1791–2), could potentially extend the political nation to all men, the major challenge to the *ancien régime* in the following decades was to come from the politics of the reforming middle classes, a politics which could be associated with models of gender relations rather different from those of the aristocratic dynasty or the polite, fashionable world. These could include more sharply defined and separate gender roles, but also ideas of women's potentially civilising influence and of middle-class men's domestic responsibilities. Reforming men tended to stress the values of rational and moral improvement and religious freedom, in opposition to the power of the aristocracy, its moral and political corruption and its luxury. These values were also adopted by some working-class campaigners, though by no means all.

The outbreak of the Revolution in France in 1789, and, even more, war between Britain and France from 1793, polarised Scottish political opinion to an unprecedented degree, and challenged for a time even the political management of Henry Dundas. The debate about the French Revolution has been christened by Marilyn Butler the 'war of ideas' because it was a debate not only about citizenship and political change but also about changes in the family and society, expressed in novels and poetry as well as in political pamphlets.[36] From 1789 and especially from 1792, Scottish opinion was divided between those who associated themselves with the conservative government response to events in France, and the positions of Whigs, liberals and radicals who in different degrees welcomed the idea of a fairer representative system for Scotland, or even more radical visions. Some radical emigrant Scots – like James Mackintosh and Thomas Christie – responded to Edmund Burke's conservative *Reflections on the Revolution in France* (1790). Christie founded the *Analytical Review*, for which Mary Wollstonecraft wrote. A few leading figures of the Enlightenment, like John Millar, welcomed the news from France, though most supported the government. Women from Whig and radical middle-class families shared their hopes for the future. The autobiographer Eliza Fletcher, married to the burgh reformer Archibald Fletcher, wrote of her great friend Robina Millar, married to

John Millar's son, John Craig Millar, a member of the Edinburgh Society of the Friends of the People, that the 'sympathy we had in the political feelings and principles of our husbands was a strong bond between us'.[37]

There could be a clear association between the principles of the rights of men and the education of women, as Lord Buchan's essays in *The Bee* in 1791, under the pseudonym 'Sophia', suggested:

> The rights of men begin now to be everywhere felt, understood, and vindicated; by and bye, I would fain hope the rights of our sex will be equally understood, and established upon the basis of a new code of education, suited to the dignity and importance of our state in society . . .[38]

The impact of Mary Wollstonecraft's writing, and of the challenge to gender relations implicit in events in France, was clearly felt in Scotland during the 1790s. From Glasgow in 1794, Anne Grant wrote of the *Vindication of the Rights of Woman* as 'so run after here, that there is no keeping it long enough to read it leisurely', though she herself disapproved of Wollstonecraft.[39]

But loyalist opinion was also mobilising, especially after the outbreak of war. Eliza Fletcher described the suspicions that surrounded her foundation of a Female Benefit Society in Edinburgh by a 'group of ladies suspected of democratic principles'. She found the conservative atmosphere in Edinburgh equally hostile to a reforming politics and to any modest changes in the condition of women.[40] Elizabeth Hamilton's novel, *Memoirs of Modern Philosophers* (1800), overtly a critical and anti-Jacobin satire on the radical ideas of William Godwin and Mary Wollstonecraft, in practice attempted to steer a middling route through the extremes of radical and loyalist politics. She sought to recover Wollstonecraft's educational ideas for a more stable society, best exemplified in her text in an idealised vision of the harmonious relations of a rural Scottish parish.[41]

Poor women shared opposition to the government in the King's Birthday Riots in Edinburgh in 1792, demonstrating especially outside the house of Lady Arniston, Henry Dundas's mother, with an effigy of her son. In 1797 at Tranent, they were at the forefront of opposition to the Militia Act.[42] But no historian has yet found women participating in the radical societies of male artisans founded in Scotland from 1792 onwards. Only after the end of war in 1815 were working-class women in Scotland engaged in a politics of mass action, when they were called upon to boycott articles like tea, whisky, ale and tobacco, so they would no longer pay taxes to a corrupt government. In the reform meetings organised in the textile communities around Glasgow, men and women carried banners and caps of liberty to signify their identification with the politics of reform. The women who marched in 1819 from the weaving village of Anderston towards Glasgow did so in the cause of manhood suffrage. They were still attacked by the conservative paper *Reformer* as 'women, Scottish Women! introduced on a stage to mimic the most degrading fooleries of the Poissards [fishwives] of Paris, during the maddest moments of revolutionary frenzy'.[43]

It was in the years after 1800 that a form of bourgeois public sphere – or critical public opinion – appeared, and became, inconspicuously, a site of gender conflict. The foundation of the Whig *Edinburgh Review* in 1802 was followed by the Tory *Quarterly Review* in 1809, and by *Blackwood's Edinburgh Magazine*, also in the Tory interest, in 1817. The contests between these journals built upon the shared inheritance of the Scottish Enlightenment and the lively Edinburgh culture of the last years of that Enlightenment, and they provided the intellectual vanguard for party conflicts across Britain in these years. These reviewers deliberately redefined the republic of letters as a space for gentlemen, identifying with a mainly though not entirely upper middle-class reading public. In this, they strove to erect barriers against unwelcome intruders, like women writers, who ventured beyond their appropriate territory.[44] Intellectually ambitious women – like Joanna Baillie or Frances Wright – were likely to be savaged, though a few reviewers, like Sydney Smith, were more sympathetic. At the same time, these reviewers enjoyed the hospitality and sociability of women like Eliza Fletcher, Elizabeth Hamilton and Anne Grant, who entertained Edinburgh's cultural elite. In 1819, the *Blackwood's* reviewer John Gibson Lockhart signalled the presence of blue-stocking aspirations in the claims of Edinburgh ladies 'to be able to talk with fluency about the Politics and Belles Lettres of the day'.[45] The gendered boundaries of sociability, as of political opinion, were here both flexible and contested.

By 1833, the political climate had been radically transformed, as the Reform Act for Scotland promised to create what was welcomed by the Whigs as a 'Scotch millennium'. Some women shared in these hopes. Eliza Fletcher wrote of it as 'nothing short of a revolution for Scotland'.[46] Margaret Mylne, very young in 1832, later recalled that 'the new, and, as it seemed to us, splendid idea of "a hustings at the Cross of Edinburgh", drove its inhabitants, both male and female, half frantic with delight' and that she began at that point to think it unfair that women householders should not also gain the £10 franchise.[47] The Reform Act transformed the parliamentary franchise and initiated the lengthy period of Liberal political dominance in Scotland which gave

Scottish politics 'a unique air of permanence' before 1885 and lasted in many respects until 1914.[48] It also introduced new and uniform burgh constitutions. Between the 1830s and 1860s, as Graeme Morton has argued, it was this local level of self-government in Scotland which allowed the urban middle classes to dominate and structure Scottish civil society.[49] It did so only partly through formal local government, since this was also the period of the extensive growth of voluntary societies.

The associational culture developing from as early as the 1790s gave new means of access to public life. Voluntary organisation allowed excluded groups to affirm their position before entering the wider public arena. In Scotland, because of the enhanced role of civil society and limited access to formal channels of power, that arena was arguably even more important for women, offering routes into public life and opportunities to learn skills and to experiment with new forms of social action. To some extent, this drew on the expansion of philanthropic action which had begun in the 1790s, including Bible Societies, Friendly Societies, Societies for the Suppression of Beggars and Magdalen Asylums. Much women's public work drew on the concept of 'woman's mission', both in a religious context and in taking and reshaping Christian duty in more secular arenas. Though inspired by the late eighteenth-century evangelical impetus and contributing to a confining domestic ideology, even 'woman's mission' could become a language of agency.[50]

The anti-slavery movement exemplified how both evangelical inspiration and reformers' commitment to enlightened progress allowed women as well as men to enter a form of associational politics, although it also illustrates the tensions that could result. There is little evidence of women's participation in anti-slavery activity in Scotland before 1814; once campaigning was revived, however, petitions from Inverkeithing and Hawick were the only two female ones from nearly 800 presented to the British government in 1814, calling other nations' commitment to end the slave trade to be inserted into the peace treaty.[51] When campaigners focused on the abolition of slavery itself in the early 1820s, ladies' associations appeared from 1825 onwards. The Quaker Jane Smeal, whose family was to play a leading part in abolitionist campaigning, was already before 1833 secretary of the Glasgow Ladies' Emancipation Society. The Edinburgh Female Anti-Slavery Society actively promoted a policy of abstention from slave-grown products.[52] Scottish women were active in signing anti-slavery petitions in the period before emancipation, 1830–3. In Edinburgh, the petition of May 1833 was signed by around a quarter of female adults in the town.[53]

The anti-slavery movement was very rapidly transformed in Scotland into a transatlantic abolitionism. The Glasgow and Edinburgh Emancipation Societies, founded in 1833, were both accompanied by active Ladies' Emancipation Societies, and between 1833 and 1868 there were sixteen female abolitionist and freedmen's aid societies in Scotland.[54] The Scottish societies were particularly affected by the splits in the American movement, evident at the World Anti-Slavery Convention held in London in 1840. There, the contrast between the radical abolitionists led by William Lloyd Garrison, who supported women's rights, and the evangelical wing of the movement, was apparent. The British society refused to accept women delegates in the convention. Following their exclusion, US women delegates toured Britain, and Lucretia Mott, a Quaker from Philadelphia, later one of the founders of the US women's movement, preached from a Unitarian pulpit in Glasgow in 1840. In Glasgow, the Ladies' Emancipation Society remained conservative, and a new, Garrisonian Ladies' Emancipation Society was founded, though it failed to take a positive stand on women's rights. In Edinburgh, the Quaker Eliza Smeal Wigham attempted to steer the society on an independent course, sympathetic to Garrisonianism.[55] Women active in mid-nineteenth-century abolitionism came from a wide range of social backgrounds, though the leaders were clearly middle-class. Jane Smeal wrote of Glasgow in 1836 that it was not the wealthiest women who were most involved, for 'our subscribers and most efficient members are all in the middling and working classes'. That society was open to working women, with no minimum subscription and many members paying only 1s. In Perth, too, most members were working women.[56]

The leadership of the anti-slavery movement was part of a wider reforming culture within the urban middle classes. The interests of women like Eliza Wigham and Agnes Renton illustrate that culture. Wigham, a Quaker minister, supported a wide variety of reforming associations, including the peace movement, temperance, savings banks, mothers' meetings and a home for destitute young girls. Agnes Renton, also from a prominent Edinburgh Liberal family, an anti-slavery activist though not a supporter of women's rights, worked for the temperance and peace movements, the redemption of prostitutes and female prisoners, and was interested in political reform and in the voluntary controversy, the movement among dissenting Presbyterians to challenge the establishment of the Church of Scotland. Although the Scottish societies varied in their radicalism and were weakened by schisms, as Orr Macdonald comments, 'abolitionism at least exposed women to a theory of justice which was understood in terms of equal value and human rights'.[57]

The history of the liberal and radical middle-class elites of mid-nineteenth-century Scotland suggests some means of understanding the different ways in which women from such locations, and also some men, came to question the gender relations of their society as they participated in the dynamism of campaigning associational movements and religious dissent in these years. It is possible to see that dynamism as encouraged by the Disruption, the schism within the Church of Scotland leading to the establishment of the Free Church of Scotland in 1843. Though Graeme Morton and R. J. Morris have written of this as 'an aggressively male event', they have also observed that a similar 'sense of self-direction and escape from hierarchy lay behind the entry of many women into both secular and religious areas of public life in the second half of the century'.[58]

It was from this reforming culture that the most significant calls for women's rights from Scotland in this period came, from Margaret Mylne and Marion Reid. Present at the Edinburgh hustings in 1832, Mylne, writing in 1841 in the *Westminster Review*, called for women who exercised the duties of citizens to enjoy the right to vote, and demanded the reform of the laws affecting married women.[59] Reid, who is thought to have attended the World Anti-Slavery Convention of 1840, published her influential text, *A Plea for Woman*, in 1843. It has been suggested that this was the first work in Britain or the USA to give priority to achieving civil and political rights for women, in addition to reforming the laws of marriage. Both women shared the assumption, expressed in the language of the Enlightenment, that women participated in the progressive development of an improving civilisation, though that progress had not gone far enough.[60]

However, among the Scottish working classes, disappointment with the consequences of the reforms of 1832 were soon apparent. Industrial organisations – like that, for instance, of the Glasgow powerloom weavers from 1833 and the Aberdeen weavers and spinners from 1834 – provided a different form of association to working women by the 1830s. Robert Owen's utopian socialism, and especially its emphasis on education and improvement, provided another form of community action, with women lecturers like the 20-year-old Agnes Walker of Glasgow speaking publicly of female emancipation. Both Owenism and industrial action, as well as the politics of democratic radicalism, contributed to the growth of the Chartist movement and its goals of universal male suffrage and political reform. In 1839, the *Scottish Chartist Circular* used the language of the Enlightenment to appeal to women to join in Chartist activities: 'By *politics* we mean *the science of human progression*; and this requires the elevation of woman as well as man in the scale of society'.[61]

There were at least twenty-three female Chartist associations in Scotland, flourishing especially in the textile districts of Glasgow and Aberdeen, but also in Kirriemuir, Stirling, Perth, Dunfermline and Forfar.[62] Even after 1842, new societies, like that in Perth, were being established, and there was a revival of female associations in major Scottish cities in the late 1840s. They participated in most major activities, including the writing and distribution of Chartist literature petitioning on behalf of the Charter and for political prisoners, attending major demonstrations and encouraging exclusive dealings with favourable tradesmen. In 1840, at one Glasgow soirée with 1,200 guests, female Chartists read the address of welcome to three released prisoners. One of them, Miss Muir, recalled the glorious history of the defence of Scottish freedoms by 'the plaided forefathers of the people of Scotland'. In the Glasgow Chartist Church, lectures were regularly given on women's rights, education and union activity.[63]

Male and female Chartists did not always, however, pursue the same goals. Trade-union objectives in these years frequently drew upon the language of domesticity and the representation of the sufferings of factory women to campaign for breadwinners' wages and factory reforms which excluded or limited the work of women and children. Chartist women, too, shared the desire to reconstruct family lives disrupted by industrialisation. But Anna Clark has argued that their self-image as mothers, wives and activists differed significantly from male Chartist representations and was less melodramatic, less passive. For some, the campaign led to the demand for a more active role and for rights of their own. 'A plain working woman' of Glasgow, a weaver, argued in 1838 that women deserved the vote, and in 1839 the Gorbals Female Universal Suffrage Society was formed, with female officers. In Glasgow in 1840, a Miss M'Kay asserted: 'the sex to which I belong has rights, and . . . these rights have been unlawfully taken from us as from the other sex'.[64]

By the 1850s, after the decline of Chartism, a form of radical liberal politics was cutting across class boundaries in Scotland, supporting causes which could include peace and support for European nationalism, sometimes linked to anti-Catholicism, temperance and abolitionism. A number of male radical Liberals – Duncan McLaren and David Masson in Edinburgh, H. W. Crosskey in Glasgow – were sympathetic to women's rights.[65] On a visit to Edinburgh in 1857, the English Unitarian Bessie Parkes met Isa Craig, a poet and contributor to the *Scotsman*, and together they noticed the Glasgow-based periodical, the *Waverley Journal*, published by 'ladies'. They wrote for it, eventually purchased it, and in 1858 relaunched it in London as the *English Woman's Journal*, the first journal of the British women's movement.[66] But only in 1865 did the revival of a general campaign for parliamentary reform allow the emergence of the issue of women's suffrage in a broader political arena, supported especially by women activists and radical liberal sympathisers.

ORGANISATION AND ENFRANCHISEMENT, 1867–1918

In mid-nineteenth-century Scotland, the terms of the relationship between civil society and the imperial state were shifting as the boundaries of citizenship expanded. The Reform Acts of 1867–8, which created new urban electorates including skilled and semi-skilled working men, marked a significant extension of the male franchise, which was expanded again to include all male householders in 1884. In the political campaigns organised by the skilled male trades in 1866 and 1884, both Scottish national identity and British patriotism were linked to the call for male enfranchisement, though women's claims for political rights were barely mentioned. In these years, work, independence and respectability all qualified men to be counted as citizens; the poor and the unskilled male labourers, both urban and rural, including a high proportion of Catholics, whose numbers had greatly increased since the Irish famine of the 1840s, remained without the parliamentary franchise.[67] The distinctive nature of Scottish politics in the nineteenth century depended on the institutions of its civil society, its church, its legal and educational system, its local government and wealth of voluntary societies. But an increasingly powerful British state, responsible both for a complex industrial society and for the administration of an empire, required a greater level of regulation. Yet the Scottish Office, founded in 1885 to meet such centralised needs, originally based in Whitehall, also symbolised the separate place of Scotland within the United Kingdom. The full implications of such devolution for gender relations in politics and civil society await further research.[68]

The relationship between women's claims, initially for single and householding women, and the goal of full adult suffrage – whose defenders might see women's claims as a diversion – was a complex one. Although formal citizenship of the nation was denied them, Scotswomen, mainly but not only from the middle and upper classes, were increasingly active in areas defined by contemporaries in religious or philanthropic terms, in voluntary associations of all kinds and, for a very few middle- and upper-class women, in different levels of local government. They exercised influence in public life as citizens without formal parliamentary voting rights, though the absence of such rights appeared increasingly anomalous. The dominance of Liberal politics in Scotland, especially in the burghs, perhaps encouraged support for women's claims by an active male minority. The debate could not be ignored, by sympathisers or opponents; gender conventions and restraints had been brought to light and the privileges of masculinity made visible across class divisions.[69] At the same time, in political parties as in women's organisations, Scottish women shared the assumptions of an imperial culture, identifying with the language of cultural superiority and the mission of 'civilisation'.

Women's public work and role in the church, and the language of mission, contributed to the development of an organised women's movement in Scotland, most apparent from the 1860s.[70] Many such societies were church-based or facilitated, and took the church's educational and welfare roles in new directions. Eleanor Gordon and Gwyneth Nair make clear the access to public roles that middle-class women in Glasgow negotiated.[71] A gendered exercise of philanthropy, in such associations as the Dorcas Societies, Mothers' Meetings, Temperance Societies and Zenana Missions, certainly lay within the boundaries of acceptability. The powerful Scottish Union of the British Women's Temperance Association, with twenty-one branches in 1879, was an 'important training ground' for women interested in a wider role. Quoting Lady Frances Balfour's abhorrence of 'the class of woman who could not look beyond the top of their bonnet', Gordon and Nair comment that engagement with the public world 'was no longer merely a privilege: it had become a requirement for the middle-class woman'.[72] The rapid growth of the Scottish Co-operative Women's Guild (SCWG), founded in 1892, suggests that this movement was not confined to the middle classes. The 1910 Annual Report encouraged each Guildswoman to see herself as 'a missionary for the cause of women's progress'. The SCWG modelled its style of organisation on churchwomen's meetings. Guildswomen rapidly learnt to organise and conduct meetings 'in thoroughly business-like fashion'.[73]

The designation of education, social care, health care and moral guidance as female spheres of influence became an opportunity for some women to develop public, if voluntary, careers in those areas, and a language of female duty and service, drawing on Christian ideals. As social organisations and, later, the state found a role in many areas of social welfare, woman's mission was repositioned in relation to public welfare. Women were neither challenging contemporary gender ideologies nor competing for power in a male sphere, but extending their familial responsibilities within civil society towards the broader terrain of social and national welfare.

Women's first formal political participation, in local government, reflected this view of their distinctive responsibilities. The timetable of their admission broadly followed that for England and Wales.[74] The first woman to be elected to public office in Scotland appears to have been Jane Arthur, an active local philanthropist elected to the Paisley School Board in 1873, a year after the passing of the Scottish Education Act in 1872 made it possible for any woman to stand; only qualified women ratepayers could, however, vote.[75] From the school boards, women moved into other areas of local government, in parishes, burghs and counties. The *Englishwoman's Review* recorded the election of Margaret Foulton in 1876 to the managing committee of the Inverkeithing Parochial Board.[76] Scottish women ratepayers were granted burgh enfranchisement in 1881, thirteen years later than in England and Wales, votes for county councils in 1889 (though they could not stand as representatives), and for parish councils – to which they could be elected – in 1894. Mary Lily Walker, of Dundee Social Union, and Agnes Husband of the Independent Labour Party (ILP), were the first women elected to Dundee Parish Council, in 1901; by 1902 there were thirty-seven women parish councillors in Scotland, including three chairs. Women were admitted as town councillors in 1907, and county councillors in 1914, though subject to certain restrictions. Lavinia Malcolm, a prominent member of the Women's Liberal Federation and a suffragist, was elected Scotland's first woman town councillor in 1907, and first woman provost in 1913. As Megan Smitley has argued, the small minority of elite women able to participate in local government actively contributed to the shaping of middle-class public life and civic identity through their view of the woman citizen's responsibilities. [77]

For many women committed to public service, their welfare role had an evangelical zeal. They presented themselves as pursuing womanly ends, not as self-seeking but as serving others. These values were embodied in the Edinburgh Ladies' Debating Society, originally formed as the Edinburgh Essay Society in 1865, which met continuously for seventy years. Sarah Mair's 'perfect self-possession and poise of manner and address' and 'gracious womanliness' indicate the qualities in public life aspired to within this group. The list of members includes women who campaigned for girls' education, university admission, local-government education and parochial work, the Scottish Women's Hospitals, and suffrage. Mair recalled that, when the society began,

[T]here were no School Boards, no University Education for Women, no women doctors, no Jubilee Nurses . . . no women sat on Town Councils and no women voted in the Parliamentary election or sat in Parliament. All these activities have been reflected in our Debating Society.[78]

The case for women's suffrage was also suffused with a sense of 'woman's mission', a concept malleable enough to be used by anti-suffrage as well as several strands of pro-suffrage campaigners.[79] The Edinburgh National Society for Women's Suffrage, founded in November 1867, was the first women's suffrage society in Scotland, and one of the first three in Britain to be formed, following the defeat of John Stuart Mill's women's suffrage amendment to the 1867 Reform Act for England and Wales. In its first years, the movement sought to enfranchise women on the same terms as men, limiting its objectives to single householding women for tactical reasons. In Scotland, as elsewhere, there was a direct link between the emerging women's movement, anti-slavery work and the culture of reform. The Edinburgh Society, like the Ladies' Debating Society, was embedded in the reform culture of the city, with the McLaren and Wigham families prominent in supporting women's suffrage.[80] The degree of support gained in the early years of the movement, especially among Liberals, including crowded meetings in Edinburgh, runs contrary to the dominant image of suffrage campaigning as oppositional.[81] The first women's suffrage society in Glasgow was formed in March 1870, and in the following year societies were formed in Aberdeen, St Andrews and Galloway. Meetings were held throughout Scotland, with the itinerant suffrage speaker, Jessie Craigen, attracting large working-class audiences throughout the country, and Jane Taylor from Stranraer undertaking extensive tours of the Highlands and islands.[82]

By 1874, there were twenty-four women's suffrage societies in Scotland; but, in spite of increasing support and municipal enfranchisement, the Third Reform Act of 1884 made no concessions to women. Increasingly, divisions on policy within the women's suffrage movement were apparent. Jessie Craigen and Priscilla Bright Maclaren shared a radical perspective, calling for the enfranchisement of married women, and the ultimate goal of adult suffrage, as did two radical groups with similar goals, the Women's Franchise League and the Women's Emancipation Union, active in Scotland in the 1890s.[83]

By the end of the nineteenth century, Liberal dominance in Scottish politics was challenged from several directions. Older issues formerly dominating Scottish politics – especially disestablishment and temperance – were receding in importance. After the Reform Acts of 1867–8, political parties across the United Kingdom needed to appeal to a much wider electorate. The Scottish Liberal Association was founded in 1881, and the National Union of Conservative Associations of Scotland in 1882.[84] But the introduction of William Gladstone's Home Rule Bill for Ireland in 1886 and the secession of Liberal Unionists was a serious blow to Scottish Liberalism.[85] Mobilising the Protestant Orange Order, most powerful in Glasgow and the West of Scotland, in defence of the Union would provide one route for the Conservatives to build mass support. Among some Liberals, Irish Home Rule inspired the pursuit of Scottish Home Rule; a Scottish Home Rule Association was founded in 1886. But Liberal indifference to social and economic issues helped to alienate working-class voters, as the growth of the ILP and the Scottish labour movement offered more attractive options to working-class women and men.

By the late nineteenth century, the major political parties were seeking to attract women in Scotland as elsewhere, though this remains an under-researched field. The Corrupt Practices Act of 1883 and the Reform Act of 1884 meant that party organisers had to reconsider their electoral tactics, recognising a role, if a subsidiary one, for women. Though excluded from Liberal, Conservative and Unionist party organisations until 1918, women were welcomed into subsidiary associations in significant numbers, and had an important supportive role, especially during elections and in canvassing and registration. This new prominence clearly interacted with the increasingly visible demand for women to have the parliamentary franchise.[86]

The first Women's Liberal Associations appeared in England about 1880, and the Women's Liberal Federation (WLF) was formed in 1887. In Scotland, this development appears to have been stimulated by the Home Rule controversy, with simultaneous organisation among Liberal and Liberal Unionist women. In 1888, Women's Liberal Unionist Associations in the east of Scotland affiliated their branches to the East and North of Scotland Liberal Unionist Association, to be followed in 1889 by branches in the west. In that year, the first Scottish branch of the WLF was founded in Glasgow, and a Scottish section of the Federation set up in 1890, with a brief to pay special attention to working-class women. The Scottish WLF included among its objectives from the beginning 'the removal of all legal disabilities on account of sex'. Its numbers grew until 1914, when it had 25,000 members in 174 branches. Increasingly, Liberal women were more interested in questions of social policy and women's suffrage than in the older issues of free trade and temperance.[87] Eastern Scottish Liberal Unionists appointed their own 'Lady

Organiser' in 1897, and in 1906 the East of Scotland Women's Unionist Association dropped the word 'Liberal' and increasingly attracted Conservative women, with numbers by 1910 reaching around 30,000.[88]

The Scottish branch of the Conservative and imperialist Primrose League was formed in 1885, and from its beginning there was some active support within it for a women's suffrage bill, especially one enfranchising single propertied women. Although a large membership (100,476 women in 1908) was claimed, it seems that membership was ebbing to the growing numbers of Women's Unionist Associations, which continued their active recruitment drive into the 1920s.[89] The only mainly female imperial propaganda society, the small Victoria League, established in 1901, was avowedly apolitical and philanthropic in outlook; many members also belonged to the Primrose League, although the Victoria League did include many Liberal Imperialists. The Edinburgh branch was founded in 1906, by six aristocratic women, with others in St Andrews and Nairn. The Scottish leadership accepted the desirability of London dominance, which suited their own political views and the social and parliamentary Season there.[90]

The Primrose League was much less robust in its popular organisation than the expanding Protestant Orange Order, growing in strength among the Protestant Irish working class in the west of Scotland since the 1860s. Although originally organised as a secret society through all-male lodges, by the twentieth century it also had an important social role for members and their families. Orange women's lodges were first set up in Scotland in 1909 as a result of women's pressure on male officials and proved very successful, although at the same time the Order also continued to encourage young men's sectarian street politics and violence.[91]

The working-class political culture developing in Scotland in the late nineteenth and early twentieth centuries had many facets. The organised trade-union movement tended to draw upon the traditions of male craft organisations; though it attempted to extend trade unionism to the unskilled, male trade-union leaders worked to exclude female competition from male trades, without denying the need for appropriate, separate, forms of women's work. After 1890, more women were drawn into trade unions, at first through organisations led by middle-class philanthropists, including the Women's Protective and Provident League and the Scottish Council for Women's Trades, the latter led by Margaret Irwin for forty-four years. The English-based Women's Trade Union League, also with its middle-class activists, was more clearly committed to labour politics, and built up a significant base in Scotland. In 1903, Mary Macarthur from Ayr, President of the Shop Assistants' Union, became its

Secretary, and in 1906 founded both the National Federation of Women Workers (NFWW), for women workers not admitted to the appropriate trade union, and its newspaper, the *Woman Worker*. Macarthur and the NFWW supported full adult suffrage.[92]

Many working-class organisations supported women's political participation as comrades, going far beyond the admission of women to formal membership. The co-operative movement, a number of left-wing groups and parties – of which the ILP was the most influential and the most encouraging of women – and wider, social and family-based activities all attempted to create an effective form of 'cultural politics'. The SCWG, with the largest women's membership within the labour movement, had by 1913 157 branches and 12,420 members, largely from the better-off sections of the working class.[93] It aimed to spread the principles of co-operation, but it also had social and educational purposes and a growing campaigning role on social issues including housing, temperance, the female franchise and women's working conditions. Though developing women's domestic roles and skills, it also encouraged women's influence in the labour movement and expressed political opinions, petitioning for the vote in 1893 and calling for the female franchise at subsequent Annual General Meetings. In 1905, it explicitly rejected the policy of the Labour Party, to which it was by then affiliated, on priority for adult suffrage.[94]

The Scottish Labour Party (SLP) had soon after its foundation established a separate 'Scottish Women's Party', which survived until 1898, consistently raising the question of votes for women at party conferences. Keir Hardie's amendment at the 1895 annual conference, committing the ILP, with which the SLP had merged in 1895, to extending electoral rights 'to both men and women', was partly a consequence of pressure exerted by the Glasgow Women's Labour Party and its representative Isabella Pearce (the journalist 'Lily Bell'). Alone of the socialist groups, the ILP, which was particularly strong in Scotland, supported the extension of the franchise to women on the same basis as men. Keir Hardie was an unwavering supporter of women's suffrage, as was Tom Johnston, editor of the Glasgow newspaper *Forward*. It has been suggested that the ILP saw women not as a political problem but as political assets, an approach which drew many more women into the ambit of political activity than formally joined the organisation. Like the SCWG, it emphasised the value and political salience of women's knowledge and skills as wives and mothers, and placed a greater stress on social and political struggles in the locality around housing, rents and education, than on industrial struggles in the workplace. However, growing links with trade unionism, before and after the formation of the Labour Representation Committee of 1900, later the Labour Party, were to bring a stronger emphasis on the economic basis of socialism, and ambivalence towards campaigns which gave priority to women's suffrage rather than adult suffrage.[95]

The ILP did not have a separate section for women, but many women members joined the Women's Labour League, the first Scottish branch of which was set up in Glasgow in 1908. It was active throughout Scotland from 1910, especially at elections, and like other left groups established political education classes.[96] Women played both local and leadership roles in the social organisations of the Labour movement, including the Clarion movement and Socialist Sunday Schools, rambling clubs, socialist orchestras and choirs.[97] Such a culture offered new ways for women and men to work together politically and to build more equal relationships. It could provide a stepping stone into formal political activity; from this world came Marion McNab Shaw, national president of the Socialist Sunday Schools, a Women's Labour League activist, member of the Labour Party Scottish Executive, School Board member, councillor and later MP.

The established and largely middle-class Scottish women's suffrage movement continued to grow. In 1902, the new Glasgow and West of Scotland Association for Women's Suffrage (GWSAWS) brought together Unionist and Liberal women, and the SCWG, and affiliated to the National Union of Women's Suffrage Societies (NUWSS). But the foundation, in 1903, of the Women's Social and Political Union (WSPU) in Manchester spurred new campaigning in Scotland, and led to many defections to the WSPU when its Scottish branch was formed in 1906, with Teresa Billington-Greig and Helen Fraser as organisers. This was short-lived because of the foundation by Billington-Greig and others who rejected the increasingly autocratic control of the Pankhursts of the militant but non-violent Women's Freedom League (WFL), which was particularly strong in Scotland.[98]

Scotland, as a Liberal stronghold, was a particular focus for militant campaigning because of its policy of attacking the government. Key by-elections were a focus of high-profile WSPU campaigns, as in 1907 in Aberdeen; Lindy Moore has stressed the extent to which militancy co-existed in this election with middle-class campaigners' assumptions of their womanly and philanthropic responsibility for working-class women. Scottish women went on hunger strike, marched in London and were imprisoned in Holloway. Militant actions, including attacks on pillar-boxes and arson against empty properties, spread to Scotland in the spring of 1913.[99] Although there was tension between militant and constitutionalist organisations, they also often worked together, as on 9 October 1909 in the grand suffrage pageant and procession in Edinburgh, which used women's history and Scottish iconography to show 'what women have done, can do and will do'.[100] A Scottish branch of the Men's League for Women's Suffrage was started in 1907 by actor and playwright Graham Moffat. Later, the Northern Men's Federation for Women's Suffrage was set up, following a deputation in July 1913 of eminent, mainly Liberal Scottish men to Asquith, who refused to see them.[101]

The Scottish Churches League for Woman Suffrage, founded in 1912, was another organisation where women and men worked together, arguing that the principle of political equality followed from 'the spiritual equality of the sexes'. But the conservative Church of Scotland as an institution was resistant to pressure from its suffrage-supporting members, many of whom were disillusioned by its refusal to engage with the issue. Many ministers were active in the Scottish National Anti-Suffrage League, led by the wealthy and philanthropic Duchess of Montrose, founded in April 1910, an organisation in need of further research.[102] There was still considerable and in some cases organised opposition to the movement within Scotland.

Women's suffrage continued to receive support from a wide political spectrum, but especially from the Labour Party, to which the NUWSS was allied and many WSPU members had close links. Affiliations with Liberalism remained very strong, especially in GWSAWS, which opposed the alliance with the Labour Party.[103] And, by 1914, all Scottish suffrage organisations, except the WSPU, had also come to focus on the possibilities of Scottish Home Rule. The NUWSS nationally supported the inclusion of women's suffrage clauses into Home Rule Bills for Scotland and Wales, and in Ireland. Two women, Provost Lavina Malcolm of Dollar and Councillor Annie Barlaw of Callander, participated in the meeting of 400 burgh representatives at the Convention of Royal and Parliamentary Burghs in April 1914, which, after Annie Barlaw's intervention, successfully called for the inclusion of a women's suffrage clause. The debate which followed was dominated by the issue of women's suffrage, and, partly as a result, the Bill was talked out.[104]

Two prominent aspects of Scottish women's campaigning in the early twentieth century – the case for the women graduates' vote, taken to the House of Lords in 1908, and the Glasgow rent strikes of 1915 – illustrate how diverse that movement could be. The universities of Edinburgh and St Andrews together elected an MP. In 1906, five female Edinburgh and St Andrews graduates, led by Chrystal Macmillan, claimed the right to vote for the university MP. The women argued that, as graduates who were members of the General Council of each university, they were entitled to vote and that the university franchise was unique, as 'a franchise of education, of intellect'.[105] When the registrar refused their claim, they took the case to the Court of Session, unsuccessfully. When their appeal in November 1907 also failed, they went to the House of Lords, in November 1908, in what became a *cause célèbre*. Macmillan, who was acting as senior counsel, was described as a 'modern Portia'. The appeal was dismissed, but generated much press coverage and sympathetic support.

Rather different, but equally illustrative of the organisational energy of the suffrage movement, were the rent strikes in Glasgow, which have become one of the iconic narratives of Red Clydeside. After the outbreak of war in 1914, as labour moved in to work in munitions and shipbuilding, landlords threatened steep rent rises. The Glasgow Women's Housing Association was formed in 1915 to organise resistance to rent increases, and to ensure, with the support of the Glasgow Labour Party, that housing became a major issue in local politics. The Kinning Park Co-operative Women's Guild may have been the first association to suggest a rent strike. Tenants' committees met to gather information on impending evictions. By ringing handbells and 'ricketies', they alerted women who came out onto the streets to drive off the sheriff's officers. Meetings took place in women's homes, or in public places at times designed to suit housewives. The leaders of the Glasgow Women's Housing Association included Helen Crawfurd, a member of GWSAWS, later of the WSPU, and later still of the Communist Party, and Mary Barbour, later the first woman Labour councillor in Glasgow. On 17 November 1915, the strike culminated in a huge demonstration when thousands of women, supported by engineers and shipyard workers, marched to the sheriff court in George Square. Their action resulted in the Rent Restrictions Act of 1915.[106]

Several of the women active in the rent strikes later founded the Women's Peace Crusade in Glasgow in June 1916, which similarly developed its own activities, street meetings and demonstrations. Chrystal Macmillan was committed to the international women's peace movement; after attending the International Woman Suffrage Alliance in Stockholm in place of Millicent Fawcett in 1911, she became honorary secretary from 1913 to 1923. It was at her suggestion that an International Peace Conference was held in The Hague in 1915.[107] However, after 1914, most Scottish women's suffrage societies rapidly became involved in committees and organisations to relieve distress caused by the war, and supported the Scottish Women's Hospitals for Foreign Service initiative, led by the suffragist Dr Elsie Inglis. They continued to press their case after 1916, and celebrated the Representation of the People Act of 1918, which brought full adult suffrage for men and for women householders and wives of householders over 30, and tripled the Scottish electorate. In 1918, women were admitted to a qualified citizenship, limited in ways which reflected not so much the achievements of women as war workers, but rather the qualities of independence and respectability expected of male citizens throughout this period.

THE MEANINGS OF CITIZENSHIP, 1918–2000

The Act of 1918 transformed the electorate in Scotland even more dramatically than that of England and Wales, given its lower levels of male enfranchisement before 1918. By 1921, 94 per cent of Scottish men had the vote, compared to about 60 per cent in 1911, and 79 per cent of Scottish women over 30; women were 40.5 per cent of the electorate, and, when given the equal franchise in 1928, 53 per cent.[108] In the changing political circumstances after the war, a realignment in Scottish politics saw an increasingly class-based polarisation of political parties, while demobilisation appeared to offer the prospect of a return to prewar gender roles. The weakness and eventual collapse of Scottish Liberalism allowed the growth of a reinvigorated Unionism. The ILP, drawing on its wartime strength, increased working-class enfranchisement and expanding trade-union membership, greatly enlarged its base, returning thirty members to the House of Commons in 1922.

For women, there were continuing tensions between the formal and the informal practice of politics, between participating in party politics as insiders and remaining in radical opposition. The exercise of women's informal influence continued, though in a wider variety of settings. As Siân Reynolds has shown, Ishbel Gordon, Lady Aberdeen, was in 1919 able to lobby the statesmen and diplomats of Versailles, and to influence the rules of the new League of Nations, partly because of her position within the Scottish aristocratic elite, though explicitly because she was President of the International Council of Women.[109]

By 1924, it was clear that the political scene in Scotland had been transformed. Liberal strength had crumbled away, with the Unionist party enjoying its most favourable position since 1832. Its growth was aided by the increasing conservatism of the Church of Scotland, the Scottish legal system, the university sector and the Scottish press, but also by the effectiveness of its party organisation and its deliberate appeal to new women voters. Each constituency association was required to have a woman as one of the two vice-presidents, and the constitution provided that women take up one-third of the places on national and regional councils. By 1924, there were around 400 women's sections, with women's organisers and a programme of political education.[110] However, this was an issue not only of organisation but also of policy. The aim was to win the former Liberal vote, both by an anti-socialist politics and by an emphasis on the Liberal Unionist inheritance, suggesting a greater interest in social and economic issues, and in public-sector provision, than English Conservatives. The first Scottish woman MP, Katharine, Duchess of Atholl, elected in 1923, had opposed women's suffrage and has been described as an 'accidental trailblazer', though in her views and her background in public service she also illustrated some of these trends. As Parliamentary Secretary to the Board of Education, 1924–9, she was also the first female Conservative government minister. However, after 1929, her humanitarian interest in the welfare of women and children – including the controversial issue of African female circumcision, and anxiety for the treatment of girls and women in India – began to marginalise her within her party.[111]

There were a number of reasons for the decline of Liberalism: the internal divisions created by the war, the party's financial crisis and the apparent irrelevance of Liberal policies. Asquith's opposition to women's suffrage also had its effect. Large numbers of new women voters in East Fife voted against him for this reason.[112] The new Scottish Liberal Federation, formed in 1918, was anxious to draw women into the party, but no Liberal woman secured a Scottish seat in the interwar years.[113] The growth of Labour was of course a major factor. In addition to the increased electorate, Labour drew upon the Irish Catholic vote, and at the same time, to some extent, the Orange working-class vote, no longer necessarily identified with the Unionists. Co-operation was also more influential in Scotland than in England, and both men's and women's co-operative guilds worked for the Labour Party. In Dunfermline in 1922, the Labour candidate deliberately appealed to women co-operators. In recognition of the importance of appealing to women's votes, Agnes Hardie was appointed Scottish Women's Organiser in 1919, a new Scottish Labour Women's Conference was established and constitutional provision made for women's representation. Annmarie Hughes has written of the ILP's 'politics of the kitchen' on interwar Clydeside, its attempt to create a policy which reflected the everyday lives of working-class women, identified with the needs of housewives and mothers. Labour women defied their leadership, notably on the promotion of birth control. But the Labour movement was diverse, also drawing heavily on male-led trade unions, which rested on masculine solidarities and culture, especially from the Clydeside heavy industries, and was preoccupied with countering Communist growth in the early 1920s. It was unable to develop an efficient organisational structure which appealed to women members in the interwar period.[114] Some women involved in wartime rent strikes chose to join the Communist Party of Great Britain, notably Helen Crawfurd in 1920. She rapidly became a member of the executive committee, and concentrated on increasing female membership.

Hughes has argued that former middle-class Glasgow suffragists failed to take up the opportunities for a potential rapprochement with the ILP in the 1920s, preferring class-based Liberal or Unionist policies to the municipal socialism and social welfare policies of the labour movement.[115] Helen Fraser stood against Labour as a National Liberal candidate in Govan in 1922 before offering herself to the Unionists as a candidate. The first Labour woman MP for a Scottish seat, for North Lanark from February 1929, was the 24-year-old Jennie Lee, who, dismissing feminism as for middle-class women, told a woman friend: 'You are concerned with the problems of humanity; I am concerned with the needs and greeds of my class'.[116] She was joined by only one other, Agnes Hardie, before 1945. Between 1918 and 1945, thirty-three women stood as candidates in Scottish seats but only eight individual women were returned as MPs.[117]

Party managers were for the most part more concerned to win women's votes than to offer them women candidates. The fear of a Woman's Party certainly existed in Scotland. The *Scotsman* noted with relief in December 1918: 'There is no appearance of anything like a tendency towards a block vote'.[118] We know relatively little about how women voted. Dyer has noted the bias of the electorate against single working-class women before 1928, hypothesising that the women's vote may have strengthened the Unionist bias of suburban and rural areas. Norman Watson has suggested that in Dundee women twice voted as a block, electing the only British Prohibition Party MP, Edwin Scrymgeour in 1922, against Churchill, with the local press viewing women's votes as crucial to Scrymgeour's success and the Dundee Women Citizens' Association (WCA) campaigning for him. He won the seat again in 1929 with the support of an expanded female electorate, which also helped to elect the city's first woman MP, the Conservative Florence Horsbrugh in 1931.[119]

The important question, however, is 'what difference did the vote make?'[120] One answer is that it made very little difference, as women followed their class interest at a time of pressure to conform to primarily domestic roles as the women's movement after 1918 went into decline. Clearly, more detailed voting studies are needed. But a longer view needs to be taken. Though many women joined political parties, even more belonged to non-party political organisations. They began to work as political insiders, aiming to influence the legislative process and to support women standing as MPs and councillors. The untold story is the role the women's movement played in building political support for what became the postwar 'welfare state', even as women politicians and women's organisations continued to meet prejudice, opposition and marginalisation.

The only woman parliamentary candidate to stand in Scotland in 1918, Eunice Murray, a WFL activist, stood as an independent candidate, focusing on the need for social reform, especially in housing. Such independence from party was reflected in the work of the fifteen WCAs formed during 1918 and 1919. They came together to set up the Scottish Council of Women Citizens' Associations in December 1919; by 1934, it had twenty-one member associations. The history of the WCAs in Scotland supports an account of the period after 1918 as one of considerable political activity, even if outside party politics. There was no sense that the campaign was over, but rather that they were embarking on a new and complex agenda for political and social reform, in alliance with numerous other women's organisations active in interwar Scotland. Women's politics in the interwar period and the political differences between organisations can usefully be understood as a continuum organised around shared broad goals of women's empowerment and representation and social reform, in which 'citizenship' as an organising concept could stretch across political representation, equal legal and employment rights, participation in civil society and social and welfare campaigning.[121] There was no sharp division between the goal of political and civil equality, and a 'new feminism' concerned with social and welfare issues. In Edinburgh, the WCA adopted as its objectives education for citizenship, work for women's representation and the securing of 'a real equality of liberties, status and opportunities between men and women'. In their approach to political participation after 1918, they were functioning as 'insiders', seeing active citizenship as central to democracy.[122]

Tom Johnston's administration as Secretary of State for Scotland, 1941–5, helped to ensure Labour strength in Scotland from 1945 and support for a postwar reconstruction which incorporated a clearly defined sexual division of labour within the family. But, from the election of 1959 onwards, Scottish electoral politics began to deviate quite sharply from the pattern in the rest of Britain, as Scottish Conservatism began its steady decline. The initial beneficiary was the Labour Party, which emerged with an overwhelming majority in the 1960s and 1970s. The most dramatic change, however, came with the successes of the Scottish National Party. In the interwar period, any hope that Home Rule for Scotland might be achieved through alliance with existing parties had receded, and the National Party of Scotland was founded in 1928 and renamed the Scottish National Party in 1934, though it remained small and without parliamentary representation before 1945. From 1929 onwards, it attempted to appeal directly to women voters, and founded a Women's Section. The Greenock teacher Elma Campbell, 'one of our most brilliant speakers', was the only nationalist woman parliamentary candidate in the interwar years. Only in the 1960s did the SNP become a more effective political force, with the decline of Unionism and the erosion of the Labour vote. In 1967, there was a startling success for Winifred Ewing at the Hamilton by-election, followed by the high point of the election of 1974, when it achieved 30 per cent of the popular vote. The elections of Margo Macdonald in 1973 and Margaret Bain in 1974 helped to associate the SNP with women representatives in the public mind, though they also, as young married women, attracted much sexist comment.[123] After the referendum of 1979, and the failure to achieve a vote of 40 per cent of the Scottish electorate in favour of devolution, Labour reasserted its electoral strength.

'Second-wave' feminism emerged, in Scotland as elsewhere in Europe, from the late 1960s, with a dual aspect: women's trade unionism and the Women's Liberation Movement (WLM). The latter saw a move away from the politics of 'insiders' and a swing to radical opposition and defining politics differently (the personal is political). The Women's Liberation Movement was very much in opposition to what it considered the reformism of earlier feminism, and saw itself as part of the left in Scotland. It contained rapidly diverging emphases and analyses, as radical and socialist feminisms vied with each other. Its varied activities included WLM workshops in Edinburgh and St Andrews, and the Glasgow Women's Centre from 1975. Their campaigns included, among others, support for lesbian politics and for anti-pornography campaigns, the development of Women's Aid and Rape Crisis Centres in Scotland, and participation in environmental and anti-nuclear protests.[124] In relation to devolution, in 1979 many feminists were hostile to participation in parliamentary politics and ambivalent as to the character of a future

Scottish Assembly, fearing that it would not be sympathetic to women's rights, though a minority actively campaigned in favour.

Scottish feminism survived the Thatcher years from 1979 to 1990 as an eroded but identifiable movement, part of Scotland's oppositional culture, in a way that was not true in the South.[125] Municipal feminism was significant, with women's and equality committees supporting initiatives such as the *Zero Tolerance* campaign, and instituting International Women's Day on 8 March as an annual celebration. And, in the 1980s and 1990s, the development of a Scottish identity and perspective became increasingly important to the movement. In the early 1990s, new groups, Engender and the Scottish Women's Forum, were founded, and witnessed a swing back to insider politics with the prospect of a new Scottish parliament. The women's movement began to engage (again) with the state, and the campaign for equal representation in the proposed parliament brought together women from most political parties and from a wide range of women's groups. There was a ground-breaking agreement in Scotland, followed in Wales, that at the first elections to the new parliaments in 1999 the dominant Labour Party would adopt a twinning arrangement, with a male and a female candidate adopted in two constituency seats. That agreement led to the breakthrough of 37 per cent female membership for the new Scottish parliament in 1999 (compared to 18 per cent at Westminster in 1997).

It is tempting to see that breakthrough as distinctively rooted in Scottish experience, though it is important to remember that a 40 per cent figure was achieved in the Welsh National Assembly. Clearly, the major impetus to such an effective intervention towards gender parity was the proposed constitutional change, 'a catalyst for a more radical and assertive response to the issue of women's representation in public life'.[126] It was an opportunity seized by activists in Scotland. The women's committee of the Scottish Trades Union Congress proposed that there should be gender equity in the new parliament, and the campaign for increasing representation came to be known as the 50:50 campaign. The increased number of women candidates adopted for the Scottish parliament came to symbolise a renewal of democracy in Scotland.

Reflection on the achievements of the campaign for gender balance in the Scottish parliament reminds us of the progress achieved in a short time. Debate on equality in Scotland since has also been concerned with what has not been achieved. The absence of any real effort to ensure that women and men from ethnic minority groups participate more fully in political life is a problem that there seems little apparent will to remedy. There remains a continuing tension in women's political activity, a tension which has been evident throughout this chapter, between insider roles and radical opposition, between women playing the masculine game of politics, using its shifting rules, and women defining politics very differently, drawing on their different orientation to civil society. The experience of the Scottish campaign for gender balance in the new parliament shows the value of alliances between women working inside and outside formal political structures. A conscious strategy to achieve this will be needed if progress is to be sustained in Scotland. As Esther Breitenbach and Fiona Mackay have written, 'Communication, dialogue, support and alliances are all crucial to ensuring that those on the inside and on the outside, and on the threshold, can sustain the transformative project of feminism.'[127]

FURTHER READING

Burness, C., 'The long slow march: Scottish women MPs, 1918–45', in E. Breitenbach and E. Gordon (eds), *Out of Bounds: Women in Scottish Society 1800–1945* (Edinburgh: Edinburgh University Press, 1992), pp. 151–73.

Burness, C., 'Drunk women don't look at thistles: women and the SNP, 1934–1994', *Scotlands* 2 (1994), 131–54.

Burness, C., 'Tracing women in Scottish politics since 1880 and the case of an accidental trailblazer: Katharine, Duchess of Atholl, and member of Parliament for Kinross and West Perthshire, 1923 to 1938', *Scottish Archives* 4 (1998), 63–75.

Duncan Rice, C., *The Scots Abolitionists 1833–1861* (Baton Rouge, LA: Louisiana State University Press, 1981).

Gordon, E., *Women and the Labour Movement in Scotland, 1850–1914* (Oxford: Clarendon Press, 1991).

Innes, S., 'Constructing women's citizenship in the inter-war period: the Edinburgh Women Citizens' Association', *Women's History Review* 13 no. 4 (2004), 621–47.

King, E., *The Hidden History of Glasgow's Women: The Thenew Factor* (Edinburgh: Mainstream, 1993).

Leneman, L., *A Guid Cause: The Women's Suffrage Movement in Scotland* (Edinburgh: Mercat Press, 1995).

Orr Macdonald, L., *A Unique and Glorious Mission: Women and Presbyterianism in Scotland 1830–1930* (Edinburgh: John Donald, 2000).

Rendall, J., ' "Women that would plague me with rational conversation": aspiring women and Scottish Whigs, c. 1790–1830', in S. Knott and B. Taylor (eds), *Feminism and the Enlightenment* (London: Palgrave, 2005), pp. 326–47.

Smyth, J., *Labour in Glasgow, 1896–1936: Socialism, Suffrage, Sectarianism* (East Linton: Tuckwell Press, 2000).

NOTES

Jane Rendall would like to thank Esther Breitenbach for her thoughtful reading of this chapter. Sue Innes wished to acknowledge the support of the Lipman-Miliband Trust and the Carnegie Trust towards her research for this chapter.

1. V. Randall, 'Feminism and political analysis', *Political Studies* 39 (1991), 513–32; G. Eley, 'Rethinking the political: social history and political culture in eighteenth- and nineteenth-century Britain', *Archiv für Sozialgeschichte* 21 (1981), 427–57; A. Vickery (ed.), *Women, Privilege and Power: British Politics, 1750 to the Present*, 'Introduction' (Stanford, CA: Stanford University Press, 2001), pp. 1–56.

2. See C. Burness, 'The long slow march: Scottish women MPs, 1918–45', in E. Breitenbach and E. Gordon (eds), *Out of Bounds: Women in Scottish Society 1800–1945* (Edinburgh: Edinburgh University Press, 1992), pp. 151–73; E. Gordon, *Women and the Labour Movement in Scotland, 1850–1914* (Oxford: Clarendon Press, 1991); S. Holton, *Feminism and Democracy: Women's Suffrage and Reform Politics in Britain* (Cambridge: Cambridge University Press, 1986); E. King, *The Scottish Women's Suffrage Movement* (Glasgow: People's Palace Museum 1978), 'The Scottish women's suffrage movement', in Breitenbach and Gordon (eds), *Out of Bounds*, pp. 121–50, and *The Hidden History of Glasgow's Women: The Thenew Factor* (Edinburgh: Mainstream, 1993); L. Leneman, *A Guid Cause: The Women's Suffrage Movement in Scotland* (Edinburgh: Mercat Press, 1995); J. Smyth, *Labour in Glasgow, 1896–1936: Socialism, Suffrage, Sectarianism* (East Linton: Tuckwell Press, 2000).

3. E. Breitenbach, ' "Curiously rare"?: Scottish women of interest or the suppression of the female in the construction of national identity', *Scottish Affairs* 19 (1997), 82–4; articles by S. Reynolds, E. Ewan and J. McDermid in T. Brotherstone, D. Simonton and O. Walsh (eds), *Gendering Scottish History: An International Approach* (Glasgow: Cruithne Press, 1999), pp. 1–45.

4. Recent histories of the Scottish nation have paid more attention to women's history, though much less to the gendered nature of Scottish politics. See T. M. Devine, *The Scottish Nation 1700–2000* (Harmondsworth: Allen Lane, 1999), ch. 22 and throughout. *The New Penguin History of Scotland*, ed. R. A. Houston and W. W. J. Knox (London: Penguin, 2001), p. xlviii, acknowledges the need for a broader conception of politics, though this promise is not entirely fulfilled.

5. J. Habermas, *The Structural Transformation of the Public Sphere* (Oxford: Polity, 1962, tr. 1989); M. Jacob, 'The mental landscape of the public sphere: a European perspective', *Eighteenth-Century Studies* 28, no. 1 (1994), 95–113.

6. G. Morton, *Unionist Nationalism: Governing Urban Scotland 1830–1860*

(East Linton: Tuckwell Press, 1999), pp. 1–8; D. McCrone, *Understanding Scotland: The Sociology of a Stateless Nation* (London: Routledge, 1992), ch. 1.

7. E. Breitenbach and E. Gordon (eds), *The World is Ill-Divided: Women's Work in Scotland in the Nineteenth and Early Twentieth Centuries* (Edinburgh: Edinburgh University Press, 1990), p. 1; S. Innes, quoted in R. J. Morris and G. Morton, 'Where was nineteenth-century Scotland?', *Scottish Historical Review* 73 (1994), 88–99, here pp. 98–9.

8. Smyth, *Labour in Glasgow*, p. 12.

9. Scottish Convention of Women MSS, National Library of Scotland (NLS), Acc. 9395, Boxes 4/1 and 6/1.

10. Will of Mary Burton, National Archives of Scotland (NAS), SC70/4/406 ff. 229–34.

11. B. Lenman, 'From the Union of 1707 to the franchise reform of 1832', in Houston and Knox (eds), *New Penguin History of Scotland*, pp. 276–354, here pp. 316–17.

12. R. Carr, 'Gender and the nation: women and nationalist discourse in the eighteenth century', unpublished paper presented to Scottish Women's History Network Workshop, March 2004.

13. E. Chalus, ' "To serve my friends": women and political patronage in eighteenth-century England', in Vickery (ed.), *Women, Privilege and Power*, pp. 57–88, here p. 72.

14. R. M. Sunter, *Patronage and Politics in Scotland, 1707–1832* (Edinburgh: John Donald, 1986), p. 136.

15. J. S. Shaw, *The Management of Scottish Society 1707–1764: Power, Nobles, Edinburgh Agents and English Influences* (Edinburgh: John Donald, 1983), p. 96.

16. Ibid., p. 189.

17. R. Marshall, *The Days of Duchess Anne: Life in the Household of the Duchess of Hamilton 1656–1716* (London: Collins, 1973), pp. 226–8.

18. E. Cruickshanks, S. Handley and D. W. Hayton, *The House of Commons 1690–1715*, 5 vols (Cambridge: Cambridge University Press, 2002), vol. 2, pp. 862–5, 923–6.

19. L. Namier and J. Brooke, *The House of Commons 1754–90*, 2 vols (London: HMSO, 1964), vol. 1, pp. 497, 510–12; R. G. Thorne, *The House of Commons 1790–1820*, 5 vols (London: Secker and Warburg, 1986), vol. 2, pp. 585–6, 619–22.

20. B. Lenman, *The Jacobite Risings in Britain 1689–1746* (London: Eyre Methuen, 1980), ch. 6; P. Monod, 'The politics of matrimony: Jacobitism and marriage in eighteenth-century England', in E. Cruickshanks and J. Black (eds), *The Jacobite Challenge* (Edinburgh: John Donald, 1988), pp. 24–41.

21. D. U. Stiùbhart, 'Women and gender in the early modern western Gàidhealtachd', in E. Ewan and M. M. Meikle (eds), *Women in Scotland c.1100– c.1750* (East Linton: Tuckwell Press, 1999), pp. 232–49, here p. 240.

22. R. Black (ed.), *An Lasair: Anthology of 18th-Century Scottish Gaelic Verse* (Edinburgh: Birlinn, 2001), pp. 61–72.

23. See M. Craig, *Damn' Rebel Bitches: The Women of the '45* (Edinburgh: Mainstream, 1997).

24. C. Whatley, *Scottish Society 1707–1830: Beyond Jacobitism, Towards Industrialisation* (Manchester: Manchester University Press, 2000), p. 198.

25. A.-M. Kilday, 'Women and Crime in South-west Scotland: A Study of the Justiciary Court Records, 1750–1815', unpublished Ph.D. thesis, University of Strathclyde, 1998, cited in Whatley, *Scottish Society*, p. 199.

26. Whatley, *Scottish Society*, p. 199; K. Logue, *Popular Disturbances in Scotland 1780–1815* (Edinburgh: John Donald, 1979), p. 200.

27. Logue, *Popular Disturbances*, pp. 55–6, 200–3.

28. See D. Daiches, P. Jones and J. Jones (eds), *A Hotbed of Genius: The Scottish Enlightenment 1730–1790* (Edinburgh: Edinburgh University Press, 1986); R. B. Sher, *Church and University in the Scottish Enlightenment* (Princeton, NJ: Princeton University Press, 1985); J. Buchan, *Capital of the Mind: How Edinburgh Changed the World* (London: John Murray, 2003).

29. G. Caffentzis, 'On the Scottish origin of "civilization" and its implications for "western civilization"', in S. Federici (ed.), *Enduring Western Civilization: The Construction of the Concept of Western Civilization and its 'Others'* (Westport, CT: Praeger, 1995), pp. 13–36, here pp. 14–15, cited in M. C. Moran, 'From Rudeness to Refinement: Gender, Genre and Scottish Enlightenment Discourse', D.Phil, thesis, Johns Hopkins University, 1999, pp. 45–6.

30. J. Millar, *Origins of the Distinction of Ranks*, 3rd edn (London: John Murray, 1779), repr. in W. C. Lehmann, *John Millar of Glasgow 1735–1801* (Cambridge: Cambridge University Press, 1960), p. 219.

31. D. Hume, *Essays Moral, Political and Literary* (London: Oxford University Press, 1963), p. 278, quoted in G. Kelly, 'Bluestocking feminism', in E. Eger et al. (eds), *Women, Writing and the Public Sphere 1700–1830* (Cambridge: Cambridge University Press, 2001), pp. 163–80, here p. 166.

32. W. Alexander, *The History of Women, from the Earliest Antiquity to the Present Time*, 2 vols (1782 edn, repr. Bath: Thoemmes Press, 1995), vol. 1, p. 151.

33. Jacob, 'The mental landscape of the public sphere'; A. Vickery, *The Gentleman's Daughter: Women's Lives in Georgian England* (London: Yale University Press, 1998); for biographical details on Scottish women mentioned here and throughout, see E. Ewan, S. Innes and S. Reynolds (eds), *Biographical Dictionary of Scottish Women* (Edinburgh: Edinburgh University Press, 2006).

34. N. T. Phillipson, 'Politics, politeness and the anglicisation of early eighteenth-century Scottish culture', in R. Mason (ed.), *Scotland and England 1286–1815* (Edinburgh: John Donald, 1987), pp. 226–46; Sher, *Church and University*.

35. J. Dwyer, *Virtuous Discourse: Sensibility and Community in Late Eighteenth-Century Scotland* (Edinburgh: John Donald, 1987); Moran, 'From Rudeness to Refinement'.

36. M. Butler, *Jane Austen and the War of Ideas* (Oxford: Oxford University Press, 1975, repr. 1988).

37. J. Rendall, ' "Women that would plague me with rational conversation": aspiring women and Scottish Whigs, c. 1790–1830', S. Knott and B. Taylor (eds), in *Feminism and the Enlightenment* (London: Palgrave, 2005), pp. 326–47, here p. 328.

38. [Lord Buchan], *The Anonymous and Fugitive Essays of the Earl of Buchan . . .* (Edinburgh: J. Ruthven, 1812), pp. 26–47.

39. A. Grant, *Letters from the Mountains; being the real correspondence of a lady between the years 1773 and 1807*, 3 vols, 4th edn (London: Longman, Hurst, Rees & Orme, 1809), vol. 2, pp. 268–77.

40. E. Fletcher, *Autobiography of Mrs Fletcher with Letters and Other Family Memorials*, edited by the survivor of her family [M. Richardson] (Edinburgh: Edmonston and Douglas, 1875), p. 76.

41. E. Hamilton, *Memoirs of Modern Philosophers* (1800), ed. Claire Grogan (Peterborough, Ontario: Broadview Press, 2000), pp. 110–17.

42. Logue, *Popular Disturbances*, pp. 133–45, 200–3.

43. A. Clark, *The Struggle for the Breeches: Gender and the Making of the British Working Class* (Berkeley, CA: University of California Press), p. 161; King, *Hidden History*, p. 64.

44. J. Rendall, 'Bluestockings and reviewers: gender, power and culture in Britain, c. 1800–1830', *Nineteenth-Century Contexts* 26 no. 4 (December 2004), 355–74; I. Ferris, *The Achievement of Literary Authority: Gender, History, and the Waverley Novels* (Ithaca, NY: Cornell University Press, 1991), chs 1–2.

45. J. G. Lockhart, *Peter's Letters to His Kinsfolk*, 2nd edn, 3 vols (Edinburgh: William Blackwood, 1819), vol. 1, p. 293; Rendall, 'Bluestockings and reviewers', pp. 359–61.

46. For the use and significance of the term 'Scotch Millennium', see K. Miller, *Cockburn's Millennium* (London: Duckworth, 1975), pp. 28, 105; Eliza Fletcher to Matilda Tone Wilson, 24 May 1831, NLS MS Acc. 4278.

47. M. Mylne, *Woman and Her Social Position: An article reprinted from the Westminster Review, No. LXVIII, 1841* (London: C. Green and Son, 1872), p. iii.

48. H. J. Hanham, *Elections and Party Management: Politics in the Time of Disraeli and Gladstone* (Hassocks, Sussex: Harvester, 1978), p. 156.

49. Morton, *Unionist Nationalism*.

50. R. J. Morris, 'Voluntary societies and British urban elites, 1780–1850: an analysis', *Historical Journal* 26 (1983), 95–118; L. Orr Macdonald, *A Unique and Glorious Mission: Women and Presbyterianism in Scotland 1830–1930* (Edinburgh: John Donald, 2000), pp. 41–7.

51. C. Midgley, *Women Against Slavery: The British Campaigns 1780–1870* (London: Routledge, 1992), p. 24.

52. Ibid., pp. 61, 206.

53. Ibid., p. 68.

54. Ibid., pp. 206–7.

55. C. Duncan Rice, *The Scots Abolitionists 1833–1861* (Baton Rouge, LA: Louisiana State University Press, 1981), ch. 4; L. Billington and R. Billington, ' "A burning zeal for righteousness": women in the British anti-slavery movement, 1820–1860', in J. Rendall (ed.), *Equal or Different: Women's Politics 1800–1914* (Oxford: Basil Blackwell, 1987), pp. 82–111, here pp. 97, 100, 105; Midgley, *Women Against Slavery*, pp. 131–7, 158–65, 169; F. N. Tolles (ed.), *Slavery and 'The Woman Question': Lucretia Mott's Diary of Her Visit to Great Britain to attend the World's Anti-Slavery Convention of 1840*, *Journal of the Friends' Historical Society*, supp. 23 (1952), p. 69.

56. Midgley, *Women Against Slavery*, pp. 85, 151.

57. Orr Macdonald, *A Unique and Glorious Mission*, pp. 59–61, 243–5.

58. G. Morton and R. J. Morris, 'Civil society, governance and nation, 1832–1914', in Houston and Knox (eds), *New Penguin History of Scotland*, pp. 355–416, here p. 359; see also P. R. McCleave, 'Family, friends and feminism: a mid-Victorian retrospect', *Scottish Archives* 4 (1998), 77–84.

59. M. Mylne, 'Woman and her social position', *Westminster Review* 35 (1841), 24–52.

60. M. Reid, *A Plea for Woman* (Edinburgh: W. Tait, 1843); S. Ferguson, 'Foreword' to M. Reid, *A Plea for Woman* (Edinburgh, Polygon, 1988).

61. Quoted in D. Thompson, *The Chartists* (Aldershot: Wildwood House, 1986), p. 125.

62. Clark, *Struggle for the Breeches*, p. 228; L. C. Wright, *Scottish Chartism* (Edinburgh: Oliver and Boyd, 1953), p. 43; R. Duncan, 'Artisans and proletarians: Chartism and working-class allegiance in Aberdeen', *Northern Scotland* 4 (1981), 51–68, here pp. 57–8, 64–5.

63. *Scots Times*, 30 September 1840; *Northern Star*, 24 April 1841, cited in Thompson, *The Chartists*, p. 125.

64. Clark, *Struggle for the Breeches*, p. 230; see also King, *Hidden History*, p. 66.

65. W. H. Fraser, *Scottish Popular Politics: From Radicalism to Labour* (Edinburgh: Polygon, 2000), ch. 4.

66. J. Rendall, 'Friendship and politics: Barbara Leigh Smith Bodichon (1827–1891) and Bessie Rayner Parkes (1829–1925)', in S. Mendus and J. Rendall (eds), *Sexuality and Subordination* (London: Routledge, 1989), pp. 136–70.

67. M. Dyer, *Capable Citizens and Improvident Democrats: The Scottish Electoral System 1884–1929* (Aberdeen: Aberdeen University Press, 1996), ch. 2; Smyth, *Labour in Glasgow*, pp. 10–23; Morton and Morris, 'Civil society, governance and nation, 1832–1914', pp. 391–3.

68. Morris and Morton, 'Where was nineteenth-century Scotland?', pp. 95–9.

69. J. Tosh, 'The making of masculinities: the middle class in late nineteenth-century Britain', in A. V. John and C. Eustance (eds), *The Men's Share: Masculinities, Male Support and Women's Suffrage in Britain 1890–1920* (London: Routledge, 1997), pp. 38–61.

70. We entirely reject J. Young's view that there was no distinctive women's movement in Scotland. Young, *Women and Popular Struggles: A History of British Working-class Women* (Edinburgh: Mainstream, 1985), p. 71.

71. E. Gordon and G. Nair, *Public Lives: Women, Family and Society in Victorian Britain* (New Haven, CT:Yale University Press, 2003), p. 201.

72. Ibid., p. 208; Orr Macdonald, *A Unique and Glorious Mission*, p. 257; M. Smitley, ' "Inebriates", "Heathens", Templars and Suffragists: Scotland and imperial feminism c. 1870–1914', *Women's History Review* 11 (2002), 455–80.

73. A. Buchan, *History of the Scottish Co-operative Women's Guild, 1892–1913* (Glasgow: Scottish Co-operative Wholesale Society, 1913), pp. 5, 64, 268.

74. M. Smitley, 'Women and local government in Scotland, 1881–1914', forthcoming, *Journal of Scottish Historical Studies*; C. Hall, K. McClelland and J. Rendall, *Defining the Victorian Nation: Class, Race, Gender and the British Reform Act of 1867* (Cambridge: Cambridge University Press, 2000), pp. 157–60.

75. Leneman, *A Guid Cause*, pp. 17, 254.

76. *Englishwoman's Review (EWR)* 36 (May 1876), 228.

77. Smitley, 'Women and local government'; N. Watson, 'Daughters of Dundee. Gender and Politics in Dundee: The Representation of Women 1870–1997', Ph.D. thesis, Open University, 2000; *EWR*, 15 April and 15 October 1902.

78. L. M. Rae (ed.), *Ladies in Debate: Being a History of the Ladies' Edinburgh Debating Society 1865–1935* (Edinburgh: Oliver and Boyd, 1936), pp. 8–9, 22, 32–3.

79. Orr Macdonald, *A Unique and Glorious Mission*, pp. 290–1.

80. Leneman, *A Guid Cause*, p. 12.

81. Ibid., pp. 12–14, 19; Hall et al., *Defining the Victorian Nation*, pp. 146–7; *EWR* 2 n.s. (April 1870), 91–7.

82. Leneman, *A Guid Cause*, pp. 20–4; on Jessie Craigen, see S. Holton, *Suffrage Days: Stories from the Women's Suffrage Movement* (London: Routledge, 1996), ch. 3.

83. Holton, *Suffrage Days*, pp. 60–4; Leneman, *A Guid Cause*, pp. 23–7.

84. I. G. C. Hutchison, *A Political History of Scotland 1832–1924: Parties, Elections and Issues* (Edinburgh: John Donald, 1986), pp. 145–9, 192.

85. Ibid., p. 193.

86. L. Walker, 'Party political women: a comparative study of Liberal women and the Primrose League, 1890–1914', in Rendall (ed.), *Equal or Different*, pp. 165–91, here pp. 165–6; for an excellent guide to further research on women and Scottish political parties, see C. Burness, 'Tracing women in

Scottish politics since 1880 and the case of an accidental trailblazer: Katharine, Duchess of Atholl, and member of Parliament for Kinross and West Perthshire, 1923 to 1938', *Scottish Archives* 4 (1998), 63–75.

87. Hutchison, *Political History of Scotland*, pp. 170, 232, 237; Leneman, *A Guid Cause*, p. 35.

88. C. Burness, *'Strange Associations': The Irish Question and the Making of Scottish Unionism, 1886–1918* (East Linton: Tuckwell Press, 2003), pp. 199–200.

89. Burness, *'Strange Associations'*, pp. 78, 82, 141, and 'The long slow march: Scottish women MPs, 1918–45', in Breitenbach and Gordon (eds), *Out of Bounds*, pp. 154–5; Leneman, *A Guid Cause*, p. 34; M. Pugh, *The Tories and the People 1880–1935* (Oxford: Basil Blackwell, 1985), pp. 48–51, 128–33; Hutchison, *Political History of Scotland*, pp. 222–3.

90. J. Bush, *Edwardian Ladies and Imperial Power* (London: Leicester University Press, 2000), pp. 7–9; E. Riedi, 'Women, gender and the promotion of Empire: the Victoria League, 1901–14', *Historical Journal* 45 no. 3 (2002), 569–99, here p. 576; Lady Wallace, *The Story of the Victoria League in Scotland 1907–57* (n.p., 1957), p. 4.

91. G. Walker, 'The Orange Order in Scotland between the wars', *International Review of Social History* 36 (1992) 177–206, here pp. 203–5; E. McFarland, ' "Outposts of the Loyalists of Ireland": the Orangemen's Unionist vision', in C. Macdonald (ed.), *Unionist Scotland, 1800–1997* (Edinburgh: John Donald, 1998), pp. 27–52.

92. Gordon, *Women and the Labour Movement*, ch. 6.

93. Ibid., p. 266.

94. Buchan, *History of the Scottish Women's Co-operative Guild*, p. 68; Smyth, *Labour in Glasgow*, pp. 172–3; Gordon, *Women and the Labour Movement*, pp. 266–7.

95. Gordon, *Women and the Labour Movement*, pp. 159–61; L. Ugolini, ' "It is only justice to grant women's suffrage": Independent Labour Party men and women's suffrage, 1893–5', in C. Eustance, J. Ryan and L. Ugolini (eds), *A Suffrage Reader: Charting Directions in British Suffrage History* (London: Leicester University Press, 2000), pp. 126–44, here p. 128.

96. Gordon, *Women and the Labour Movement*, pp. 263–5; Smyth, *Labour in Glasgow*, pp. 60–4.

97. King, *Hidden History*, p. 140.

98. Leneman, *A Guid Cause*, pp. 38–42, 50–2; on the Women's Freedom League in Scotland, see also C. Eustance, ' "Daring to be Free": the evolution of women's political identities in the Women's Freedom League 1907–30', D.Phil. thesis, University of York, 1998.

99. Leneman, *A Guid Cause*, pp. 87–8, 109–12, 131ff., 184–7.

100. L. Moore, 'Feminists and femininity: a case-study of WSPU propaganda and local response at a Scottish by-election', *Women's Studies International Forum* 5 no. 6 (1982), 675–84; Leneman, *A Guid Cause*, pp. 80–1.

101. Leneman, *A Guid Cause*, pp. 48–9, 148–51, 156, 212–13; C. Eustance, 'Citizens, Scotsmen, "bairns": manly politics and women's suffrage in the Northern Men's Federation, 1913–20', in John and Eustance (eds), *The Men's Share*, pp. 182–204.

102. Orr Macdonald, *A Unique and Glorious Mission*, pp. 297–9; Leneman, *A Guid Cause*, pp. 94, 164, 266; B. Harrison, *Separate Spheres: The Opposition to Women's Suffrage in Britain* (London: Croom Helm, 1978), pp. 121–2.

103. Holton, *Feminism and Democracy*, pp. 107–8; Leneman, *A Guid Cause*, pp. 188–9.

104. Leneman, *A Guid Cause*, p. 192; I. Fletcher, ' "Women of the Nations, Unite!": Transnational suffragism in the United Kingdom, 1912–1914', in I. Fletcher, L. Mayhall and P. Levine (eds), *Women's Suffrage in the British Empire: Citizenship, Nation and Race* (London: Routledge, 2000), pp. 103–20.

105. *Glasgow Herald*, 11 November 1908.

106. Smyth, *Labour in Glasgow*, pp. 174–6; J. Melling, *Rent Strikes: People's Struggles for Housing in West Scotland 1890–1916* (Edinburgh: Polygon, 1983).

107. Smyth, *Labour in Glasgow*, pp. 176–8; A. Wiltsher, *Most Dangerous Women: Feminist Peace Campaigners of the Great War* (London: Pandora, 1985); J. Liddington, *The Long Road to Greenham: Feminism and Anti-Militarism in Britain since 1820* (London: Virago, 1989).

108. H. C. G. Matthew et al., 'The franchise factor in the rise of the Labour Party', *English Historical Review* 91 (1976), 723–52, here pp. 727–32; Dyer, *Capable Citizens*, pp. 113–22.

109. S. Reynolds, 'Historiography and gender: Scottish and international dimensions', in T. Brotherstone et al. (eds), *Gendering Scottish History*, pp. 1–18.

110. I. G. C. Hutchison, *Scottish Politics in the Twentieth Century* (Basingstoke: Palgrave, 2001), p. 43; Burness, 'The long slow march', pp. 154–6.

111. Burness, 'Tracing women in Scottish politics'; S. Hetherington, *Katharine Atholl, 1874–1960: Against the Tide* (Aberdeen: Aberdeen University Press, 1989), pp. 120–1.

112. S. Ball, 'Asquith's decline and the general election of 1918', *Scottish Historical Review* 61 (1982), 44–61, here p. 60.

113. Burness, 'The long slow march', pp. 152–4.

114. A. Hughes, ' "The politics of the kitchen" and the dissenting domestics: the ILP, labour women, and the female "citizens" of inter-war Clydeside', *Scottish Labour History* 34 (1999), 34–51; Hutchison, *Scottish Politics*, pp. 56–66, and *Political History of Scotland*, p. 288; Burness, 'The long slow march', pp. 156–8; R. Johnston and A. McIvor, 'Dangerous work, hard men and broken bodies: masculinity in the Clydeside heavy industries, c. 1930–1970s', *Labour History Review* 69: 2 (2004), 135–51.

115. A. Hughes, 'Fragmented feminists? The influence of class and political identity in relations between the Glasgow and West of Scotland Suffrage Society and the Independent Labour Party in the West of Scotland, c. 1919–1932', *Women's History Review* 14 no. 1 (2005), 7–31.

116. P. Hollis, *Jennie Lee: A Life* (New York: Oxford University Press, 1997), p. 46.

117. Burness, 'The long slow march', p. 151.

118. Ibid., p. 159.

119. Dyer, *Capable Citizens*, p. 115; Watson, 'Daughters of Dundee', pp. 91–9.

120. P. Thane, 'What difference did the vote make?', in Vickery (ed.), *Women, Privilege and Power*, pp. 253–88.

121. C. Law, *Suffrage and Power: The Women's Movement, 1918–1928* (London: I. B. Taurus, 1998), pp. 224–31.

122. S. Innes, 'Constructing women's citizenship in the inter-war period: the Edinburgh Women Citizens' Association', *Women's History Review* 13 no. 4 (2004), 621–47, and 'Love and Work: Feminism, Family and Ideas of Equality and Citizenship, Britain 1900–1939', Ph.D. thesis, University of Edinburgh, 1998.

123. C. Burness, 'Drunk women don't look at thistles: women and the SNP, 1934–1994', *Scotlands* 2 (1994), 131–54, here pp. 135, 141; M Bain, 'Scottish women in politics', *Chapman* 27/28 (Summer 1980), 4–9.

124. S. Henderson and A. Mackay (eds), *Grit and Diamonds* (Edinburgh: Stramullion, 1990).

125. See J. Lovenduski and V. Randall, *Contemporary Feminist Politics: Women and Power in Britain* (Oxford: Oxford University Press, 1993); E. Breitenbach, *The Women's Movement in Scotland in the 1990s*, New Waverley Papers (Edinburgh: University of Edinburgh, 1996).

126. I. Lindsay, 'Constitutional change and the gender deficit', in Woman's Claim of Right Group (ed.), *A Woman's Claim of Right in Scotland: Women, Representation and Politics* (Edinburgh: Polygon, 1991), pp. 7–13, here p. 8.

127. E. Breitenbach and A. Mackay, *Women and Contemporary Scottish Politics: An Anthology* (Edinburgh: Edinburgh University Press, 2001), p. 20.

4

Religion

Callum G. Brown

FIRST WORDS

In 2001, marginally more Scots women (82.1 per cent) than men (79.6 per cent) claimed to have a religious tradition. Women outnumbered men in nearly all Christian traditions, and only in Islam, Hinduism, Sikhism and Judaism were men reported as more numerous. But, with non-Christian religions accounting for only 1.6 per cent of the population, women in Scotland claim an overall dominance of religious belonging.[1] This conforms with evidence from all other countries and from the past that women have been more prominent in Christian belonging and practice than men, creating the view that Christianity is a 'woman's religion'.

But Scotland is a Christian country in which male dominance of the kirk has long been accepted as a truism. The myth of the Calvinist misogynism of this country has been widely acknowledged in both popular and academic culture. The historian seems confronted with Scotland as an empire of patriarchy, in which theology legitimated the disparagement of women, and ecclesiastical structures forged female subordination. Undoubtedly, the Scottish churches were important agents of male domination; and this chapter will review the arguments concerning this – especially in the period from the Reformation to around 1800. But gender history as a discipline is not merely concerned with patriarchy and subordination. One of the ironies emerging from gender historians in recent decades has been that idealised Christian goodness at certain points in the past was identified in womanhood (and especially motherhood), while manhood was vilified (in spite of patriarchal subordination of women). Women were idolised as the epitome of Christian piety, notably in the nineteenth and early twentieth centuries, while men were demonised for their innate tendencies to drink and dissipation.

This apparent contradiction – between men's dominance of church institutions at the same time as women's dominance of Christian ideals – is a perspective emerging as many historians move between social history and cultural history. This may be described as the drift from the study of the gendered *structures* of society to study of the gendered *representations* of culture. Each approach is important, because they both reveal things about the religious experience of both men and women. Conversely, to study gender in the past, before the great de-Christianisation of Scotland in the second half of the twentieth century, the historian must look at the religious contribution. Religion was a vital agent in defining the nature of male and female experience and the construction of masculine and feminine identities. And towards the end of our period, the de-Christianisation (or secularisation as it is often called) of Scotland since the 1960s has involved important gender dimensions. Religion matters to gender history, and gender matters to religious history.

This chapter reflects upon the main strands of historical interpretation of religion and gender in Scotland, while examining some of the types of historical evidence upon which those strands have rested. It looks at the conceptual use of patriarchy, followed by revisionist arguments against patriarchal analysis, then the cultural historians' drift to the study of gendered religious discourse, and finally to issues of gender in the confusing religious trends of the late twentieth century.

PATRIARCHY 1: THE NORMALITY OF THE MAN'S KIRK

The earliest histories of Scottish Christianity accepted that the kirk was a man's business, and that patriarchy was 'normal'. This has moulded Scottish history-writing in ways which still cast a shadow.

Scotland has stood in the historical narrative of Christian religion as an exemplar of patriarchy at the extremes. For a story of religious men's domination of women, Scotland has provided great examples. In the Scottish Reformation of the sixteenth century, there was an immense struggle of wills between John Knox, the leading clergyman of the Scottish Protestant Reformation, and Mary Stuart, the Roman Catholic Queen of Scots. This stands out in the nation's historical record, and has been represented frequently in book and film. From the same period, the Scottish parish was developed by Knox and the Protestant Reformers as a system to impose strict moral supervision on the people, and especially upon women and their sexual behaviour, with the parish minister and his lay male elders supervising conduct on a weekly basis. Scotland seemed to exceed Calvin's Geneva and the Protestant Netherlands as a society controlled by religious men for the subjugation of women. This has provided Scotland with a powerful myth upon which rises so much of the narrative of the nation's submersion into darkness and the struggle to come out of it.

Scotland seemed to perfect the demonisation of women. They were portrayed in Scottish culture as having many failings of biology and character. Such representations in books, sermons, daily speech and court cases encouraged the widespread notion of women as having bad characteristics. There was already a widespread European representation or discourse on women as 'disorderly' – as disruptive, foul-mouthed, violent and careless, and who challenged men to manage them by taming the unruly heart of the female 'shrew'. But the Scottish Reformation of the sixteenth century and the Second Reformation of the seventeenth century transformed this discourse on 'the disorderly women' into something even more abominable and unacceptable. John Knox set the tone in a tract of 1558, entitled *First Blast of the Trumpet against the Monstrous Regiment of Women*. In this, he condemned as 'monstrous' any 'commonwealth where a woman beareth empire' and 'every realm and nation where a woman beareth dominion'. A nation may exalt a woman as head, he said:

> But impossible it is to man and angel to give unto her the properties and perfect offices of a lawful head. For the same God that hath denied power to the hand to speak, to the belly to hear and the feet to see, hath denied to woman power to command man and hath taken away wisdom to consider and providence to foresee things that he profitable to the commonwealth; yea, finally, He hath denied to her in any case to be head to man, but plainly hath pronounced that man is head to woman, even as Christ is head to all man.[2]

This was an extreme broadside at the character of women. However, John Knox said his comments were aimed at Queen Elizabeth of England, while Queen Mary of Scotland thought that they were aimed at her.[3] But it was a third interpretation that was more influential – that he aimed the remarks at women in general. Indeed, it is hard to imagine these remarks being about a single woman without a more general disrespect for women generally. The way in which he expressed his views seemed to convey a strong discourse on the weakness of female piety, the fragility of the female mind, the danger of women to good moral and social order, and the desirability for the strict control of female sensibility and sexuality. Moreover, the injunction that his writings gave to men was clear:

> the authority of a woman is a corrupted fountain and therefore from her can never spring any lawful officer. She is not born to rule over men, and therefore she can appoint none by her gift nor by her power (which she hath not) to the place of a lawful magistrate. And therefore whosoever receiveth of a woman office or authority are adulterous and bastard officers before God.[4]

No man should stand for female command, and a man was clearly to be judged on his ability to control the unruly and disorderly women in his realm (be it a nation or the humblest household).

So, in Scots tradition, the thesis of 'the monstrous regiment' put forward here has been understood for centuries to be about *the entire gender*, not about two women. The way it has been 'read' (irrespective of the author's intention) is as a representation of a deep vein of women-hating in Scottish culture – one that has been nurtured and refined by the Presbyterian Christianity that Knox initiated in the 1550s and 1560s. Scots culture came to understood Presbyterianism as the culprit for this sexism, and Knox as its prime architect. Whether right or not, this rendering of the story of the Scottish past was one that was current in Scottish education in the twentieth century in two clashing narratives told separately in the religiously segregated state schools of Scotland – with the non-denominational schools upholding Knox as hero, and Catholic schools denigrating him as villain. However, come more liberal and questioning times at the end of the twentieth century, Knox came to answer to at least three groups – Catholics, women and liberals. Sympathetic portrayals of Knox declined after the 1950s, and he became widely (though not universally) vilified.

Knox's concept that a man was 'adulterous' by receiving office from a woman is important. He termed such action a sexual offence. This raises another aspect of the late modern heritage of patriarchy. From Knox's Reformation of the 1560s sprang what developed in the 1590s and the first half of the seventeenth century into the Presbyterian system of church government – the system that appeared to establish a patriarchal democracy. The kirk session was a parish committee, chaired by the minister, on which sat male elders who each took responsibility for supervising the moral habits of the people in a small part of the parish. This imposed religious and moral conformity, giving a vigorous role for the kirk in local life, and made the church intrusive in the lives of the citizens. The way in which it operated has, for many historians, seemed intensely patriarchal. The centre of its interest was undoubtedly the sexual behaviour of citizens, especially in the later seventeenth and eighteenth centuries. This invariably involved a focus upon women and their sexual behaviour. This arose for two reasons. Firstly, in purely functional terms, the way in which extreme sexual behaviour was most easily detected was via women. Secondly, women were the object of intense 'discursive' commentary regarding what was appropriate sexuality and appropriate behaviour. Let us examine these in turn.

First, it was through women that sexual misdemeanour was most often discovered by the Scottish kirk. Moral crime was usually revealed when a woman became pregnant – or became the object of rumour that she was pregnant. The result was that women's sexual misdemeanours were prioritised over those of men's, and a woman's body was regarded as the site of sin requiring intrusive investigation. An unmarried woman could be quizzed and interrogated during childbirth about the name of the man with whom she had had sex. But if she was suspected of concealing a birth, she might have her breasts milked for 'evidence'. Since a good proportion of single women did not reveal the fathers of their children, they were subjected to repeat summonses before kirk sessions and presbytery (a higher court to which difficult cases were passed), especially if they refused to name the father or if a man denied being the father. Women kept being called back to appear before church courts, where there was a seemingly constant presence of women whose bodies were needing to be policed.[5] This applied to both established and dissenting Presbyterian congregations. A good example is that of Margaret Littlejohn from Muckhart in Fife, who, in April 1773, was charged by the Antiburgher Seceder presbytery of Stirling with bearing the child of her master, then aborting it, and thus being guilty of child murder. As was typical, the case started in a church court, not a civil one. Her father David Littlejohn was an elder, and was inexplicably permitted to investigate his own daughter. He cleared her of the offences after her sister used the standard Presbyterian method of enquiry – trying to milk breasts for evidence of pregnancy – and reportedly failed to produce the evidence. The Church believed not a word of it, suspended David from the eldership, and found Margaret guilty of uncleanness, lying and murder, excommunicating her from the Church. But she fled Muckhart amid warnings to Church members to 'beware of this woman'. Eight years later, it was discovered that Margaret had assumed the new identity of Margaret Smith, joining the Kilwinning congregation in Ayrshire. But when she was unmasked there, she moved to Perth, where she was clearly informed upon and was imprisoned by the civil authorities on suspicion of child murder. But no evidence was produced, and she was freed by the civil authorities after a few days with no legal action. She then sought readmission to church membership through her home presbytery.[6] Throughout, the running in this matter was made by church authorities, and, what is more, by dissenters.

This reflected the significance of kirk justice in society at large, and the significance of sexual policing of women. This was to continue in much of Scotland until the 1850s and 1860s. Despite industrial revolution and urban growth, sexual misdemeanour became even more important in church courts. To make a comparison, in the early seventeenth century, during a single year in each of three sample parishes, only 29 per cent of church legal cases (78 out of 268 cases) concerned sexual misdemeanour or marriage irregularity, compared with 56 per cent (50 cases) concerning profanation or violation of the Sabbath.[7] But in the following two centuries, in one parish between 1755 and 1841, 67 per cent of cases (64 out of 96) concerned fornication, a further 25 per cent (twenty-four cases) concerned adultery, but only 8 per cent (eight cases) concerned Sabbath profanation.[8] This reflected how church justice was narrowing to be almost exclusively concerned with sexual misdemeanour; and, though this sexual control was waning in the larger cities from the 1780s, in most of the rest of Scotland it was only gradually between the 1830s and 1870s that kirk control of non-marital sex effectively disappeared.

A second reason for the prominence of women in the church justice system was what a cultural historian would call 'discursive'. Women from the sixteenth to the early nineteenth centuries were represented in culture as the major cause of disorder in both kirk and society. This was especially the case in the sixteenth century, when witchcraft trials tended to target women much more than men. But women were also the object of prosecution for crimes of tale-bearing and evil-speaking – crimes for which a woman was liable to be punished by the distinctive imprisoning in the *branks*, or metal head-clamps that stopped her tongue from moving.[9] This was both a literal and a symbolic punishment. Even after that form of punishment died out in the early eighteenth century, women were still the object of special attention. In the parish of Sandwick in Shetland in 1756, a woman and her male neighbour were called before the kirk session after a shouting match between them was heard 'at a good distance' by an elder and others. Margaret Jamesdaughter at first denied, and then on evidence being given, admitted swearing at and scolding Magnus Magnuson. The session deliberated and found 'it was a grave sin against God, and had given scandel & offence in the neighbourhood, and if such wickedness went unpunished woud be of very bad consequence by emboldening others in like sins'. She was sentenced to stand before the congregation on Sunday to be rebuked by the minister, but she refused, and the session requested the local magistrate to compel her submission.[10] This type of case remained a kirk matter in many parts of Scotland; and, though men were not immune from punishment for similar offences, women tended to outnumber them and to be pursued with greater venom (including, as in this case, using the civil magistrate when necessary). Women were represented in both official and popular culture as the 'problem' of society, and were pursued accordingly. This perceived 'problem' stemmed from a discourse on women's inferior religious piety. The solution was portrayed in Scottish culture as being the vigorous and strong family man. Men were judged on their ability to control the wayward behaviour of their womenfolk. John Knox reflected this common pre-1800 discourse when he presented the angel as being male (or at least not-female): 'impossible it is to man and angel to give unto her [woman] . . .'

In this way, the patriarchal system of the pre-1800 Scottish church was underpinned by a culture that perceived piety as a male thing, not a female thing. In the twentieth century, Scottish culture came to understand patriarchy through clergy-written history taught in universities and schools in which the gender division of Christianity was taken as God-given, Christ-endorsed, and not susceptible to any sensible criticism. The apostles were male, leaving no room for female admission to the clergy. This understanding was implicitly accepted by church historians between the 1880s and the 1970s, who, in writing of the seventeenth and eighteenth centuries, were rather blind to the prioritisation of the male over the female. The historians shared in the 'normality' of the idea that patriarchy was justified (usually by biblical sanction), and therefore tended not to comment upon it in the post-Reformation kirk.

The consequence was that patriarchy in Scottish Christianity was seen as not so much peculiar in its *existence* but only in its *extremeness*. Scottish historians applauded the eighteenth-century Enlightenment for its liberal ideas and its churchmen for encouraging the rise of reason and high learning. But women's bodies were being prodded and abused by the church, and Scottish church historians ignored this. Even in many standard textbooks of today, there is no acknowledgement of ecclesiastical sexism in the past. There remains a tendency to avoid the church's manifest ills to women. In one lengthy book on the early modern period, just over one page is devoted to witches and the church's treatment of women, of which the authors state that the most barbaric story 'is best left untold'.[11] Similarly, the treatment of women under the witchcraft laws until 1735, and the exploration and control of the female body down to the mid-nineteenth century, are ignored. Little is allowed to get in the way of presenting Scotland in the age of the glorious Enlightenment and presenting the kirk in a commensurate 'age of the Moderates'. Kirk and national historians contrived together to bolster the sense of Scottish churchmen promoting intellectual and social development – a good example being Stewart Mechie, who sought in 1960 to insert 'the place of the Church in that social development'.[12]

But, with an avowedly male-dominated understanding of Christianity –
a patriarchy of historiography that understood and, by its common
silence, legitimated the patriarchy of the gendered kirk in the past –
the question remains open for engaged debate as to whether women
had an Enlightenment in eighteenth-century Scotland (for which see
Chapter 3 of this volume). The church was the principal institution which
wrested from women agency over their own bodies. For Scottish church
history, the understanding of religion in Scotland took patriarchy as
normal and was unremarked upon. It was 'naturally' a man's kirk in post-
Reformation Scotland.

PATRIARCHY 2: CRITIQUING THE SEXIST KIRK

The earliest revision to the Scottish religious story was from historians
who saw the churches as sexist. This attack was made mainly in the
1960s, 1970s and 1980s by anti-authoritarian, mostly anti-religious historians who were drawn inexorably to pinpoint the Presbyterian kirk of
the past as one of the key flaws – if not *the key flaw* – in the whole of
Scottish civil society.

The first revisionism was by socialist and left-wing historians who
espied in the kirk the bulwark to the elite authoritarianism that underpinned class politics in Scotland. The patriarchal nature of the kirk
became seen as an embedded authoritarian quality in Scottish civil life,
making sexism a mere rehearsal for modern classism and the class struggle. These historians argued that the churches – including dissenting
and even the Roman Catholic churches – were institutions that mod-
ernised their operations and outlooks in order to support the industrial-
capitalist system. They viewed the churches as providing business
entrepreneurs with a trained, disciplined, compliant and sober labour
force, dominated by men. At the same time, they viewed the churches as
encouraging women to adhere to a stay-at-home ideal of femininity and
motherhood that bred a fit and willing labour force for the future. Babies
were born in profusion, procreating a cheap labour supply for the long-
term good of rapid business growth, and flexible and mobile workers.

In this way, Marxist historians and commentators fell upon the evidence of the masculine kirks with glee. Leading among these was the
work of Allan MacLaren, whose studies of Aberdeen helped to inaug-
urate a Scottish Marxist front against kirk tyranny. Of course, historical
scholarship in England had already created an agenda and schema for
this work,[13] and in Scotland a suitable sentiment was already being
broadcast by left-wing intellectuals like Tom Nairn, who in the 1960s

wrote that 'Scotland will only be free when the last Church of Scotland Minister has been strangled with the last copy of the *Sunday Post*'.[14] MacLaren developed a distinctively focused study of the church system itself at the time of the Disruption of 1843, when a third of the clergy and perhaps 40 per cent of the members left the Church of Scotland to create the Free Church. He argued, using social-stratification analysis of kirk elders and a study of the kirk-session discipline system in Aberdeen, how the Church of Scotland's control by a patrician and gentrified middle class was the object of revolt by a *nouveau* middle class which defected to the Free Church and to the city's west-end suburbs. This left the working classes even more excluded than they had previously been from church and organised religion.[15] MacLaren's work set a tone for the Scottish Marxist historical encounter with Presbyterianism – most of it tangential to wider studies of class and power in industrial, rural and Highland society.[16] In a sense, a bit of a blindness developed among Marxist scholars as to the meaning and significance of the gender question. The sexism was obvious – so obvious that it was taken for granted. They tended to regard the 'real' subjugation as being of working people, not of women.

Yet, the beginnings of a women's-history agenda infiltrated new writings of the 1980s. Early second-wave feminist scholarship in Scottish historical writing produced one classic study of religious patriarchy in the early modern period. In Christina Larner's sociology of the seventeenth-century witch-hunt, we find an exploration of the operation of a deep oppression that, by targeting more than 80 per cent of the victims as female, was only, as Larner observed, 'one degree removed from an attack on women as such'. This revealed a particular concern for the dangers to which the female body was exposed, and expressed the state's concern for its control and regulation.[17] This was innovative historical research, of a calibre that put Scottish history onto an international stage – yet it presented no real opening for a more subtle consideration of female subordination in Scottish Presbyterian experience. There were limitations upon what might emerge from studies based solely on patriarchy as an analytical category. There were in Scotland deep issues about women's position in Calvinism and the kirk to be scrutinised; and much work – including that of the present author – was restricted in the 1980s by what might be described as an obsession with *the structures of patriarchy*.[18] If women's experience of religion was presented as self-evidently the product of patriarchy, then it limited what could 'usefully' be said of the issue and removed the reason for exploring further. To break out required new directions that opened boundaries beyond these limits.

REVISIONISM: THE COMPASSIONATE GENDERED KIRK

The break-out to new understandings of gender and religion in Scotland came in a variety of ways in the 1980s and 1990s. One was structuralist analysis of Scottish religious institutions that relied less on the concept of patriarchy, and another was the study of masculinity.

In relation to the second of these, there emerged in the 1980s a new softer, apologist approach to the masculinity of the Scottish Kirk. This was represented especially by the work of Rosalind Mitchison and Leah Leneman. Though their positions on the sexism of the Scottish Kirk shifted in the course of the 1990s and early 2000s, still their work represents a departure from the largely crude patriarchal analysis of Scottish left-wing historians. What emerged was, of course, deeply ironic. Mitchison and Leneman were two of the leading women's historians of Scottish society researching and writing in the late twentieth century, and they were coming forward with an approach that seemed to let the male-dominated kirk off the hook for misdemeanours of sexism in the past for which it had long been found guilty by the political left.

The argument put forward by Leneman and Mitchison was that the system of the kirk session (the parish court of the Church of Scotland) was essentially designed not to oppress and subjugate women, but to protect them and their children.[19] These historians subjected kirk-session and poor-relief sources to a minute examination that opened up what was for the radical wing of Scottish social historiography a quite stunning possibility: that the kirk session's interest in the close examination of women, their sexual reproduction and disciplining of their bodies, was designed for – and succeeded in being for – their own good. In essence, kirk justice became re-evaluated as good for women. The Leneman–Mitchison argument became that the kirk elders' primary concern in single pregnant women was twofold. First, the concern was for the reduction in the cost to the local taxpayers and churchgoers in maintaining the poor fund from which single mothers would receive handouts because of the absence of support from fathers. The second concern was based on legitimate moral and family grounds (with which we might identify) that interrogation of the mother – even by means of a midwife's questioning in the pains of childbirth – would be to the benefit of both child and mother. This was because the identity of a father would lead to him being compelled to take monetary responsibility for raising a child, and, by exerting pressure on a single man to marry, would lead to the creation of a family unit to nurture the child and protect the mother. The thesis emerged that the kirks' brutality towards the female body was a system operated by a well-meaning church establishment which, in each parish, had to balance the financial means of the community against the economic needs of the poor. The poor were disproportionately the women and children left bereft of fathers, sometimes by death, but often by sexual misdemeanour. Thus, Leneman argued that the kirk was so fierce in its interrogation of women precisely because they held the key to financial salvation for themselves and financial relief for the parish as a whole. Clearly, this latter cause of interrogation was not entirely altruistic. The financial burdens of the parish fell upon the rich – or at least, a failure to secure the provisions for women and children would be an inconvenience and blow to the self-esteem of the elites in the parish, and might undermine authority in the long term. Yet, a major thesis emerged in Scottish religious history-writing that patriarchal systems worked to the benefit of women.

The church as a friend to woman was an approach that in the 1990s found favour among other historians tackling different issues. Michael F. Graham noted in Scottish towns of the early seventeenth century that women turned to the kirk for support in defence of their position in relation to husbands and suitors. He concluded that 'it does appear that women, particularly those without close ties to burgh authorities, found kirk sessions much more approachable and responsive to their needs for justice, support and protection'.[20] Deborah Symonds argued in her study of infanticide in early modern Scotland that kirk sessions offered a protection to single mothers by exposing them and their children before the danger of child murder arose.[21] In a similar vein, Anna Clark was also much more sympathetic to the kirk in her pioneering study of marital relations (and wife-beating in particular) in Glasgow in the late eighteenth and early nineteenth centuries. She showed how women turned to the kirk sessions for protection from men, and how they were willing to use the system to humiliate men as a defensive strategy against marital violence. The perpetrators of domestic violence in the period of early industrialisation in the city, she demonstrated, were more likely to be artisans whose status in class and gender terms was the most vulnerable to trade cycles. And, as the work of Hillis has shown, this was the very social group that was the largest single component of the Presbyterian churches (certainly by the 1840s, and there seems little reason to doubt the wider applicability of this finding).[22]

Despite the importance of this evidence of the compassionate kirk, it only adds to, rather than displaces, the more conventional understanding of the kirk's subjugation of women. Recent work of other scholars, some of it already referred to, continues to show how many women found themselves brutalised in their relations with one or other of Scotland's Christian denominations in the eighteenth and early nineteenth centuries. After about 1800, brutal punishment diminished, but women and men continued to be treated differently.

By 1800, men were coming before kirk sessions more and more for drunkenness. Their poor behaviour in relation to temptations of alcohol, gambling and Sabbath-breaking created family problems and made them clearly the object of suspicion. Women, on the other hand, seemed to stand alone accused of serious crimes. Child murder remained a special concern of the churches. Up to 1800, the kirk was part of the mechanism of law enforcement that heard gossip, sought witnesses and interrogated suspected infant-murdering women before they were passed to the civil courts, where they might expect severe punishment. But after 1809, there was a very dramatic turnaround in the treatment of this crime, with women being the object of considerable court sympathy, and mild sentences being imposed.[23] Yet, the kirk did not lose its interest. Evidence shows that, in those places where after 1800 the Church of Scotland remained a hegemonic moral force in the community, the role of the ministers and elders continued in the collection of gossip, interrogation of suspected women, and passing such cases to sheriff courts for civil prosecution by the procurator fiscal. In 1854, for instance, Agnes Hawick of Northmavine in Shetland, described in court as 'a very quiet and apparently pious girl', was investigated by her minister, elders and the local doctor for having given birth and then allegedly murdering her child. Typically in these cases, the kirk session had first heard the matter and gained what it considered confessions from Agnes. However, she withdrew these confessions at a final hearing, and the case was passed to Lerwick Sheriff Court, where the evidence of elders and minister was heard.[24]

This type of case could not continue long in the modern civil state. A clearer idea of the demarcation between civil and religious offences developed slowly between 1780 and 1860, and church justice declined. One reason for this was the rise of many new religious groups and traditions who did not accept these notions of kirk justice. Large-scale immigration from Ireland brought Roman Catholics as well as Episcopalians and Methodists who would not in any way submit to these types of church courts. But one short-term consequence was intensification of moral justice *within church groups*. In many places, the rise of dissenting churches (which made up as much as two-thirds of the churchgoers in many Lowland communities, and as much as 90 per cent in some Highland parishes) led to the enforcement of extremely strict moral censure on their flocks between the 1740s and the 1880s. But this censure moved by the 1870s from a judicial-enforcement model into a more 'club-membership' concept; instead of the kirk representing the community, it represented the club's members, and instead of enforcing court justice, it suspended or ejected the culprit. So, church courts no longer acted for society as a whole, and the state no longer recognised the powers of the churches to act in the name of government. The state found it more appropriate to develop civil courts and, more importantly, civil police forces after 1850 – each of which took a declining interest in policing sexual behaviour.

But all of this occurred against the background of a much bigger cultural trend. The power of moral enforcement was passing in modern culture from the state (including the state church) to the moral censure of public discourse. The period from 1780 to 1830 in Scotland, as perhaps in most of Europe, was when (as Foucault described it) the moral power of the *ancien régime* passed to the individual as s/he internalised the discourse of modern moral behaviour.[25] Woman (and men) became pressed by the extreme power of moral convention in a new puritan age, as families and communities pressed individuals to obey very strict conventions of behaviour. These conventions were circulated and enforced in published media, community gossip and family familiarity. Moreover, as we shall see shortly, women became after 1800 less the object of religious criticism and more its apotheosis.

Despite the liberalisation in the churches' treatment of women after 1800, they remained the object of special religious attention for moral offences. Whether angel or harlot, the Scottish churches had in place a special system and sense of responsibility for the moral regulation of women and their bodies, and this did not automatically disappear with Enlightenment sensibilities in the late eighteenth century. Women were watched, scrutinised and objectified as the embodiment of community morality; and, if the patriarchal structure of the kirk became less involved as gatekeeping, its legacy lingered in the moral regimen of Victorianism.

REVISIONISM AND ITS LIMITS

The patriarchal structures of Scottish religion have been approached in another way – through exploration of women's role as Christian leaders, preachers, missionaries and assistants. This historiography has been an essential task in Scottish culture of re-remembering the place of women.

Women who aspired to be religious leaders and preachers were invariably constructed in popular and ecclesiastical discourse as 'strange'.

Elspeth Buchan (c.1738–91) started a sect in 1781 in Glasgow, then Irvine, whose members accepted her as 'the woman clothed with the sun' (Revelations 12). They were much mocked then and after. Robert Burns, who some said had a female admirer in the sect, hinted at sexual perversion and lesbianism, writing that Elspeth 'pretends to give them the Holy Ghost by breathing on them which she does with postures and practices that are scandalously indecent', and they 'lye and lodge all together, and hold likewise a community of women, as it is another of their tenets that they can commit no mortal sin'.[26] Though mocked for her claims to religious leadership and biblical authority, Elspeth exposed a strain of female religiosity in the decade when the romantic and idealised female Christian piety of the future century and a half was emerging.

Indeed, from the 1790s there emerged a significant feminisation of Scottish Presbyterianism – what historian Lesley Orr has described in her pioneering study of women and Presbyterianism as a feminisation of service rather than of status or authority.[27] Starting with the rise of women's auxiliaries for mission fund-raising, there was from the 1830s a more sustained growth of the role of women as assistants to their husbands' overseas mission work, and as agents in the home mission where they worked as Bible women, temperance reformers and tract distributors. Women took on key roles in the anti-slavery movement, in the drive for prohibition and in campaigning for an increasing range of moral and women's issues. By the 1850s and 1860s, female preachers were challenging as preachers in some of the smaller evangelical denominations like the Brethren, but even there a reaction set in during the last quarter of the century. By then, a more sustained campaign for 'moderate' female recognition in areas of religious and moral work was gaining widespread acceptance in Scotland as in England, leading to the formation of the Woman's Guild in 1883 and the expansion of the female diaconate in the Church of Scotland. The social question of the 1890s and 1900s brought together issues about the unionisation of women workers, the churches' role in ethics of female subordination, and the suffrage question, propelling the disturbance of the patriarchal institutions of Scottish mainstream Presbyterianism. In 1926, Elizabeth Hewat was the first female divinity graduate from Edinburgh New College, to be followed by the first ordination of women (in the Congregational and United Free churches) in the 1920s and 1930s. It took until 1968 for women to be admitted as elders and ministers of the Church of Scotland, and from that point the process of feminisation of the professional Christian Protestant church started in earnest, so that, by the end of the twentieth century, more than 10 per cent of ministers and almost half of the divinity students were female. In 2004, the supreme court of the Church of Scotland, the General Assembly, appointed the first woman as moderator, Dr Alison Elliot.[28] The 'monstrous regiment' was now in control of the kirk.

The timing, nature and scale of the patriarchy of the institutions of Scottish Christian churches are thus better understood. But herein lies a problem. The study of patriarchy is essentially a study of women's history – of women's subordination and exclusion. It is less a study of men (in this case in the Church). Studying patriarchy tends to tilt only slightly at the agenda of traditional historical scholarship, as it takes as 'read' that the history being confronted is that of a male institution. The maleness of religion and religiosity is actually elided in this approach. Consequently, in large part, the rise of *gender* history comes from a change in method. One way in which this has happened is in the shift from the study of the structures (in this case, of patriarchy) as the category of analysis to assembling a collage of the cultural representations and experiences of men and women in the past.

GENDERING RELIGIOUS DISCOURSE

The ways in which the institutions of the kirk (or more precisely the kirks) from 1700 to 2000 dealt with women and gender relations are only one element of the story in the gendering of Scottish religious historiography. Much of the recent work in the vast expansion of religious social history and women's history has been in the area of discourse analysis. Across North America, Europe and into the developing world, there has been a new 'reading' of gender into the past. Still controversial in Scotland, where gender as a category of analysis is itself but poorly understood among many Scottish historians, the reading of discourse has become an elemental tool in vast swathes of the academy. For understanding religious experience on a gendered basis, discourse analysis provides the essential grounding for any understanding of the cultural breadth of religion in society.

In the development of Christendom in Europe from 800 to about 1780, the literature that I have read on religion and gender has suggested a growing rift across time in the constructions of gender. This means that the nature of manhood and womanhood each changed.[29] There is a sense in the literature that, in the late centuries of the first millennium of the Common Era (600–1000), there was a remarkable tradition of approaching the religious dimension of identity in a similar way for women and for men. Women's place in the developing agencies of the Christian church, and in the rituals and the architecture of the early European Christian church, rested on a gendered representation of piety that was quite balanced between masculine and feminine qualities. But, from the twelfth and more especially the thirteenth centuries, there was an increasing privileging given to male religious identity, to the importance of the masculine qualities in the religiosity of both men and women, and an increasing representation of male religious heroes and male architectural styles in the church. Women's religious identity became increasingly portrayed in the discourse of religious culture as something troublesome, something potentially at variance to good order, and something that needed to be expressed more and more in discreet places and ways. This was reflected in how religious women became increasingly marginalised out of sight, in closed religious houses (or convents), representing a mounting victory for male virtue in religious identity. This trend continued and gathered pace from the fourteenth to the sixteenth centuries, within the Reformation as well as outwith it. Women's religious rituals became suppressed, and a woman's religiosity became attached in discourse to her 'troublesome nature' – her irascibility, bad-temperedness and ability to create a chaotic household and church. It was represented in the concept of the taming of the shrew – that a man's religious and civil credentials were established by his ability to control a wife, and thus his household. In other words, he established the virtue of his household by his exemplary expression of masculine abilities to enjoin submission from a wife. It was further exemplified in the European witch-hunt of 1450 to 1730, which was perhaps the high point in the Christian demonisation of women. Female religiosity required submission and absorption of male qualities – seen in the representation of the maleness of Joan of Arc, for instance – and in the increasing tendency in many parts of Europe to portray the Virgin Mary in statues as something non-European or strange – the prevalence of the black madonnas across central France, in Poland and Greece. Putting either a maleness or a racial 'otherness' to the forefront of representing female piety decentred the female qualities to women's Christianity. In Europe as in Scotland, from the Reformation to the end of the eighteenth century, women suffered from having female religiosity portrayed as the problem, and male religiosity as the solution.

But things changed. From around 1790 onwards, this gendered identity to religious ideals was reversed. The reversal was perhaps heralded by the decriminalisation of witchcraft in 1735 (though it sustained a discourse against women by criminalising the mostly female *claims* to witchcraft). There were also movements in eighteenth-century philosophical thought, mirrored strongly in Scotland (as the historian John Dwyer showed), towards the representation of femininity as the basis of Christian piety.[30] But it is in the last two decades of the century that male religiosity became inverted from object for praise to object of doubt – the big problem of European society, the problem that needed to be controlled, investigated, probed and curtailed. Men became portrayed in post-1800 discourse as innately susceptible to temptation – to drinking alcohol to excess and to drunkenness, to gambling, to womanising, to being disorderly and bad fathers, and to be, in short, the problem of urban industrial society. During the next 150 years, Scots men became portrayed as the major religious and social problem of the nation. One example comes from 1878, when the *British Messenger* religious newspaper from the Stirling-based Drummond Tract Enterprise ran a series asking 'Are you a man?':

> My friend, are men – real, downright, genuine men – men that would meet God's high purpose, plentiful now? Has our boasted civilization largely produced them? Do they congregate in our towns and great commercial cities? Have our political schemes and parties, even our numerous churches and chapels, evoked them? Is the crop really good? We fear that as heaven looks down upon us, and compares its standards with what, even so-called, Christian nations can supply, it would find it hard to discover what in God's sight would be accounted a man . . . [T]o be a man, a true and real man, we must keep the 'body in subjection', put a rein upon the appetites, and a bridle on the passions. So far as anyone fails in this, he ceases to be a man, and takes level with the brutes. Even the pagan poets perceived this; picturing vice as half man and half goat, a wild capering satyr in fact . . . Is the drunkard, with brain soddened in strong drink, a man? Is the unclean person? Is anyone who 'lives after the flesh', and whose false love turns from the corruption of the senses, and takes no lustre from the soul? No![31]

The 'home heathen' of the nineteenth and early twentieth centuries was invariably represented as a man. Even the male clergyman was portrayed in novels and articles as susceptible to religious weakness and temptation. The biography and autobiography of the minister or priest becomes from the eighteenth century increasingly a portrayal of a life in constant struggle with demons, experiencing multiple religious conversions, and the need to keep seeking them, and – in the case of Protestant clergy – the need to find a good woman to save the minister or parson from himself. For the Catholic faith, the religious identity of the priest becomes increasingly problematic too. One of the features of the period from 1800 to 1960 was the increasing portrayal of the dissolute and immoral clergyman in need of constant challenge and supervision.[32]

By contrast, the ideal qualities of religiosity during most of the nineteenth and twentieth centuries became feminine. The woman was the angelic heart of the happy family and the happy nation. Woman was innately good, sensible and given to religiosity, rarely portrayed in stories or articles as in need of religious conversion or revelation, but merely needing careful nurturing along the already established route to marriage and motherhood. Motherhood became the ideal religious state in nineteenth- and early twentieth-century Europe. The mother was idealised as the one needing the protection, submission and adulation of men. A woman was the moral and religious heart of the household and the community, and to her men as husbands and sons owed fidelity and homage. The Woman's Column of the *British Messenger* told its readers in 1920: 'We women are called to be saints, here and now, during our earthly pilgrimage, amidst all the petty annoyances and disappointments of home or business life. Do you ask how? By our holy lives. And "holy" is simple another word for separation from the world.'[33] The novel and the magazine containing serialised stories became a very important means of broadcasting, circulating, enforcing and hybridising this gendered religious identity, making it adaptable, highly transportable between subcultures and transnational in modernity. As John Dwyer has noted, the novel was extremely important in Scottish moralising.[34] But it is important to note that it was also the ultimate female religious form, and women led their children to the novel to learn of the characters of the ideal female and the tempted man. The discourse was strong: that women were the religious solution, men were the problem.[35]

The Scots were not only great *consumers* of the print media in which the discourse on gendered Christian piety became so intensely hybridised in tracts, novels and magazines, but also the country became a specialist *producer* of them. The Scottish publishing industry of the nineteenth century developed a particular forte in religious and moral publishing – from the religious tracts of the largest producer in the English language, the Drummond Tract Enterprise of Stirling, through the scriptural publishing of William Collins of Glasgow, to the family, women's and children's magazines published by D. C. Thomson of Dundee. In biographical publishing, too, the Scottish Presbyterian tradition produced a wealth of clerical heroes who became prominent in England and the British Empire – notably the Rev. Dr Thomas Chalmers (1780–1847), who helped found the Free Church in 1843.

The nature of womanhood was represented as highly dependent on religious qualities, and made men's approach to religious authority highly problematic. Indeed, it is one of the great ironies of the Scottish churches from 1800 to 1960 that they were so male-controlled and apparently patriarchal when the popular conception of piety on which their cultural power had come to rest was heavily feminised. But this irony is no contradiction. It was the bedrock upon which Christian culture rested in that century and a half. Scottish churches were highly feminised spaces, with worship dominated by women in their finest clothes chaperoned by men in dull black. The Scottish Sunday remained highly protected (both by law and by custom), but it changed dramatically after 1800 into a woman's day – a day when women might parade to church or chapel in their finest clothes, lead the family on sedate Sunday walks, and preside over the family meal in the home, while men and boys found that their masculine games, pubs, sports and toys were forbidden. Women's sense of Sunday as 'their day' is overpowering in a reading of oral interviews of Scotswomen. Here, one woman from Stirling, born in 1914, provides a typical remembrance:

> Well, Sunday was my day because . . . on a Sunday morning I got dressed, you had a Sunday outfit you see. You only wore it on a Sunday; no other day except Sunday. Well, I went to my two pals; they went to the Catholic church. So I went with them to Mass on a Sunday morning so as I'd have my Sunday clothes on. When I got home I'd go to [Protestant] church with my mother. And then when I got home from that I kept on my clothes because I was going to the Sunday school and then we went to Bible class at night. And the reasons I went to all that was because I got wearing my Sunday clothes.[36]

Boys hated wearing their Sunday best dress, and remember Sundays as a suppression of their freedom. Men were demonised in moral media. A man from Springburn recalled the midweek entertainment to which children were exposed at the well-attended temperance youth movement:

> In Fountainwell Road there was a church where we used to go to, the Band of Hope – the 'Bandy' as we called it. And there you would get a bun and they would have lantern lectures showing the sins of drink – where the man just couldn't go past the pub when he got a bit of money – and where eventually he was able to go past the pub and become a teetotaller.[37]

This was typical and unavoidable fare in children's literature, reinforced for older age-groups in family and women's magazines. The sense of self-training, the imposition of self-discipline concerning the 'rules' of Christian culture, is emphasised in testimony. The patriarchal structures of power so common in accounts of the eighteenth and early nineteenth century became from the 1850s to the 1950s displaced by the more demanding power that individuals exerted upon themselves. Religious power had not only changed gender, its exertion had moved from church to the individual.

The rituals of piety became between 1800 and 1960 more and more the domain of women. Little research has been published on these rituals as it has in England, but examples of one of the most significant – churching, the ritual 'cleansing' of a woman after childbirth – was still practised in Scotland until at least the 1970s, suggesting that it may have been just as common north of the border in the eighteenth and nineteenth centuries as it was in England.[38] Rituals of Christian marriage and baptism became rituals dominated by women – feminised occasions organised and choreo-graphed according to women's sensibilities. Perhaps only funerals remained – certainly in the Presbyterian communities of the Highlands and Hebrides – rituals seemingly dominated by men and a dour masculinity. Church adherence and, even more, churchgoing were strongly female experiences. Hillis's analysis of the sex composition of Christian churches in Glasgow and Aberdeen between 1806 and 1923 shows women easily dominated in every denomination: 69 per cent of Catholic mass attenders, 63 per cent of Methodist members, 62 per cent of Congregational members, 64 per cent of Episcopalian confirmations, 67 per cent of Free Church communicants and 59 per cent of Church of Scotland communi-cants.[39] Going to church was key to the formation of female identity between 1800 and 1960. The church service had a strongly feminine atmosphere, with women in their most luxurious clothes. The Scottish Christian church was overwhelmingly women at prayer.

In a sense, this leaves more questions about men and religion. The paucity of research on masculinity in Scotland means that our under-standing of masculinity and religiosity is narrow. We know that female attributes of mothering, blessed by Christian discourse after 1800, were inversely linked to the demonisation of male temptation to sin, resulting in a deep distrust of fathering.[40] More has been researched on male-dominated religious sectarianism in Scotland and its links with sport, but this has not been theorised with the conceptual apparatus of gender history, and remains a lacuna for Scottish historians to fill. In these ways, there is as yet little material with which to construct a consideration of masculinity and religion in Scotland. But masculinity is crucial to this emerging story. The polarisation in representation of feminine piety versus masculine immorality textured dealings between the sexes and the law's treatment of domestic violence. The man who claimed 'he is come home a new man in the Lord Jesus' could leave a battered wife with little moral manoeuvre in either her community or the judicial process. Robert Anderson was let off by Lerwick sheriff court in 1887 from a charge of beating his wife Betsy when she withdrew her evidence upon accepting his claim to a Christian rebirth while in gaol. Still, the moral victory may in the end have been Betsy's. Her family life seems to have changed so much that she named her next and seventh child Harriet Beecher Stowe Anderson – adopting the names of America's Victorian feminist Christian icon who wrote *Uncle Tom's Cabin*. This seems a clear statement of a female evangelical victory against oppression.[41]

For many in Scotland until the 1950s, the power of this stark contrast between the female 'angel' and the male 'sinner-heathen' was the basis of an oppressive puritanism. And there, for complex reasons, it broke down. It was against this atmosphere that Marxists, liberals and feminists reacted with fury, including those historians of the 1960s and 1970s who wrote the new social histories of religion. From the 1960s, women themselves – especially young women and teenage girls – rejected the moral investment that Christian piety had been intent on putting into them. The sexual revolution lay at the root of a rejection of this construction of gendered Christianity; and, in the complex cultural revolution that followed, Scottish Christianity started to suffer a real problem – the disappearance of the perfect Christian. Neither man nor woman stood out in cultural representation as a Christian ideal.

SECULARISATION, MULTI-FAITH SOCIETY, FUNDAMENTALISM AND THE NEW AGE

The last quarter of the twentieth century unleashed profound changes in the religious character of Scotland. These were not in any way unique to Scotland, but were shared by most of Western Europe. The way in which this has been understood is increasingly the domain of the cultural historian, the sociologist and the anthropologist.

The decline of male Christian church attendance in Scotland started early in the twentieth century and was prolonged, while for women it started later and became severe only in the 1960s. In 1984, women made up 63 per cent of Scottish Christian churchgoers, and 61 per cent in 1994 and 60 per cent in 2002 – indicating in the context of rapid decline in church attendance that women's evacuation of the church in 1984–2002 was proceeding faster than that of men.[42] On top of that, it seems likely that the decline in the rate of women's religious participation had knock-on effects on male participation. Put crudely, if women stopped going to church, so did men. At the same time, the evidence already alluded to of the feminised nature of informal and unofficial religious culture seems to reveal quite clearly that this underpinned official Christian culture until the 1950s. The disappearances of the unofficial and the official religious cultures of Scotland seem to have been contemporaneous. In other words, just at the same time as women started to evacuate the churches and started to markedly secularise the rites of passage in the 1960s and 1970s (with dramatic declines of religious marriage and baptism), so the religious culture of women broke down as the passing of the liturgy from mother to daughter failed. Why this happened, and whether it was the mothers rather than the daughters who instigated this breakdown, still awaits research in Scotland.

Certainly, the sense of change among older Scots women interviewed in the 1980s and 1990s was profound. Here is a fairly typical example from a woman born in 1912:

> I don't know when it [religion] ceased to be quite as important. I'll tell you what I think is wrong nowadays. You see so much about science on these [television] programmes that that – I remember when my son was taking medicine, not one of these students believed in anything. He did join Greyfriars Church initially, but when he got further on and so steeped in science they would make you believe that you're just a chemical equation and that when you died it was just the chemical equation ceased working and that was it, you know. It used to depress me when I used to hear it because they could knock down every argument you had. And I'd say 'but the Bible', and my son would say the Bible was written by a man – a man writes a book, he doesn't always stick to fact. And so what could you say to that because I suppose it was written by a man and then I started to listen to programmes on there, scientific programmes, and I really – am torn in two. I can't decide now whether – I don't believe there's a hell, I think you make your own hell on earth . . . I can't believe that there's a heaven where there's angels fluttering about and all that. I can't believe that nowadays, but I'd like to think there's another life . . .[43]

The link between secularisation in the 1960s and the revolution in women's identities is the subject of increasing research in the western world. My own work on Britain has positioned Scotland in this – not because of any peculiarity to the Scottish experience, but because of the extremes of change from a religious to an irreligious nation, and because of the representativeness of what happened here within European experience. Quite suddenly, the feminised Christian religion that dominated the cultural representation of piety from around 1800 to the 1960s fell apart in the cauldron of reconstructing women's identities, the rise of sexual liberation, the liberation of sexualities and the end of the hegemonic puritan culture of Scotland. Though pockets of religious conservatism lingered, such as in the Western Isles, these too have felt the winds of secular change with increasing rapidity at the turn of the millennium. Women reconstructed their sense of their lives in very profound ways, often adopting new spiritual practices drawing on holistic notions of body and spirit (sometimes using eastern mystic sources), but usually without Christian practice or notions of religious redemption.[44]

What happened to the Scottish kirk in all this is as little understood as it is for the Church of England. The advance of women's interests in the Church of Scotland, with the ordination of elders and ministers from 1969, is well understood, but the cultural somersault that Christianity had to perform is not. The impact has been by no means confined to the Presbyterian church, but has spread to all Christian traditions to greater or lesser extents. Only in some of the non-Christian traditions has the revolution in gendered religious identities not been felt. For the bulk of Scots, though, at the beginning of the third millennium of the common era, there is a sense that religion is now marginal in public culture and is much less relevant to gender identities, and that Scotland belongs to a common European tradition (which may include Canada and Australasia) that is experiencing increasing isolation in a world in which all other continents remain deeply religious in public culture, confessional politics and formal religious ritual. European Christian religion has become androgynous at the same time as it has become marginal to our culture.

Secularisation of Scotland cannot be understood solely in terms of religious decline. The rise of the New Age since the 1960s has clearly been an important dimension to modern Scotland, as it has to multi-cultural societies generally. At Findhorn, as scholar Steve Sutcliffe has shown, Scotland has a particularly influential gateway to the evolution of New Age sensibilities – within which gods, spiritualities and the secular are mixed in a postmodernist brew which allows hegemony to no single conception of transcendence.[45] At the same time, the role of gender in the sectarianism of 'orange-and-green' bigotries, and in the racism towards blacks and Asians, remain largely uninvestigated. On another tack, gender dimensions seem bound up with the rise of religious militancy, conservativism or fundamentalism in all the main monotheistic religions (as well as some of the others). In the fundamentalist wings of Christianity and Islam in particular, there are gender issues of great importance. Yet, with only about 8 per cent of the Scottish population attending a Christian church, and less than 2 per cent more for other traditions, gender becomes less an issue of formal church connection than in the reconstruction of the secular self in postmodern society. As the secular condition of Scotland grows, gender is increasingly being constructed without benefit of religion.

FURTHER READING

Brown, C. G., *The Death of Christian Britain: Understanding Secularisation 1800–2000* (London: Routledge, 2001).

Brown, C. G. and J. Stephenson, ' "Sprouting wings?": Women and religion in Scotland c.1890–1950', in E. Breitenbach and E. Gordon (eds.), *Out of Bounds: Women in Scottish society 1800–1945* (Edinburgh: Edinburgh University Press, 1992).

Heelas, P. and L. Woodhead, *The Spiritual Revolution: Why Religion is Giving Way to Spirituality* (Oxford: Blackwell, 2005).

Larner, C., *Enemies of God: The Witch-hunt in Scotland* (London: Chatto & Windus, 1981).

Leneman, L. and R. Mitchison, *Sin in the City: Sexuality and Social Control in Urban Scotland 1660–1780* (Edinburgh: Scottish Cultural Press, 1998).

Mitchison, R. and L. Leneman, *Sexuality and Social Control: Scotland 1660–1780* (Oxford, Blackwell, 1989).

Mitchison, R. and L. Leneman, *Girls in Trouble: Sexuality and Social Control in Rural Scotland 1660–1780* (Edinburgh: Scottish Cultural Press, 1998).

Orr Macdonald, L., *A Unique and Glorious Mission: Women and Presbyterianism in Scotland 1830–1930* (Edinburgh: John Donald, 2000).

Williams, S. C., *Religious Belief and Popular Culture in Southwark c.1880–1939* (Oxford: Oxford University Press, 1999).

NOTES

1. The ratio of Scots men to women is 0.93 (that is, there are 93 men to every 100 women), but the ratio is 0.90 in the Church of Scotland, 0.89 in Catholicism, 0.84 in other Christian churches, 1.17 in Islam, 1.22 in Hinduism, 1.07 in Sikhism, and 0.96 in Judaism. Figures are calculated from data in Census (Scotland) 2001, table S203, obtained by online enquiry from the General Register Office for Scotland.
2. R. A. Mason (ed.), *John Knox: On Rebellion* (Cambridge: Cambridge University Press, 1994), pp. 23–4.
3. John Knox reported saying of the 'Blast' to Mary Stewart on 4 September 1561: 'for in very indeed, Madam, that book was written most especially against that wicked Jezebel of England'. Mason (ed.), *John Knox*, p. 177.
4. Ibid., p. 42.
5. A sense of the Kirk's intrusions into female sexuality is to be obtained from R. Mitchison and L. Leneman, *Sexuality and Social Control: Scotland 1660–1780* (Oxford: Blackwell, 1989).
6. Stirling Archive Services, Stirling General Associate Presbytery Minutes, 6 April, 7 June, 29 June 1773, 14 August 1781, CH3/286/1.
7. The parishes were Dundonald (1605), Belhelvie (1624) and Culross (1632). Figures calculated from data in W. R. Foster, *The Church before the*

Covenants: The Church of Scotland 1596–1638 (Edinburgh: Scottish Academic Press, 1975), pp. 75–6.

8. Figures calculated from a word-based search of transcribed kirk-session minute books of Sandwick Kirk Session, Shetland Archive, CH2/325/1 et seq.

9. J. G. Harrison, 'Women and the branks in Stirling, c.1600 to c.1730', *Scottish Economic and Social History* 18: 2 (1998), 114–31.

10. Shetland Archive, Sandwick Kirk Session, 20 June 1756, CH2/351/1.

11. A. L. Drummond and J. Bulloch, *The Scottish Church 1688–1843: The Age of the Moderates* (Edinburgh: Saint Andrew Press, 1973), p. 13.

12. S. Mechie, *The Church and Scottish Social Development 1780–1870* (London: Oxford University Press, 1960), p. ix.

13. Notably E. P. Thompson, *The Making of the English Working Class* (Harmondsworth: Penguin, 1963).

14. Nairn, quoted by Ian Jack, *Granta*, 11 January 2003.

15. A. A. MacLaren, *Religion and Social Class: The Disruption Years in Aberdeen* (London: RKP, 1974). MacLaren's work has since been widely critiqued, notably in P. Hillis, 'Presbyterianism and social class in mid-nineteenth-century Glasgow: a study of nine churches', *Journal of Ecclesiastical History* 32 (1981), 47–64.

16. For instance, I. Carter, *Farmlife in Northeast Scotland 1840–1914: The Poor Man's Country* (Edinburgh: John Donald, 1979); J. Hunter, *The Making of the Crofting Community* (Edinburgh: John Donald, 1977); and T. Dickson (ed.), *Scottish Capitalism* (London: Laurence & Wishart, 1980).

17. C. Larner, *Enemies of God: The Witch-hunt in Scotland* (London: Chatto & Windus, 1981), p. 92.

18. See my marginalisation of women's history in C. G. Brown, *The Social History of Religion in Scotland since 1733* (London: Methuen, 1987), esp. pp. 94–6, 250–2.

19. R. Mitchison and L. Leneman, *Girls in Trouble: Sexuality and Social Control in Rural Scotland 1660–1780* (Edinburgh: Scottish Cultural Press, 1998), pp. 119–24.

20. M. F. Graham, 'Women and the church courts in Reformation-era Scotland', in E. Ewan and M. M. Meikle (eds), *Women in Scotland c.1100–c.1750* (East Linton: Tuckwell, 1999), p. 187.

21. D. A. Symonds, *Weep Not for Me: Women, Ballads and Infanticide in Early Modern Scotland* (University Park, PA: Pennsylvania State University Press, 1997), p. 163.

22. A. Clark, *The Struggle for the Breeches: Gender and the Making of the British Working Class* (London: Rivers Oram Press, 1995); Hillis, 'Presbyterianism and social class'.

23. L. Abrams, 'From demon to victim: the infanticidal mother in Shetland 1699–1899', in Y. G. Brown and R. Ferguson (eds), *Twisted Sisters: Women, Crime and Deviance in Scotland since 1400* (East Linton: Tuckwell, 2002), pp. 180–203.

24. Shetland Archive, AD 22/2/1/55.

25. C. G. Brown, *Postmodernism for Historians* (London: Pearson Longman, 2005), p. 64.

26. Quoted in *Dictionary of Scottish Church History and Theology* (Edinburgh: T. & T. Clark, 1993), pp. 108–9.

27. L. Orr Macdonald, *A Unique and Glorious Mission: Women and Presbyterianism in Scotland 1830–1930* (Edinburgh: John Donald, 2000), p. 167. The remainder of this section relies heavily on Orr's book. See also Neil T. R. Dickson, *Brethren in Scotland 1838–2000* (London: Paternoster Press, 2002).

28. And incidentally the first lay person since the era of the Reformation.

29. This paragraph draws upon *inter alia* P. Crawford, *Women and Religion in England 1500–1720* (London: RKP, 1993); P. Ranft, *Women and Spiritual Equality in Christian Tradition* (New York: St Martin's, 2000); M. R. Miles, *Carnal Knowledge: Female Nakedness and Religious Meaning in the Christian West* (New York: Vintage, 1991); D. Cressy, *Birth, Marriage and Death: Ritual, Religion and the Life-Cycle in Tudor and Stuart England* (Oxford: Oxford University Press, 1997), esp. pp. 475–82; and J. Gregory, 'Homo Religiosus: masculinity and religion in the long eighteenth century', in T. Hitchcock and M. Cohen (eds), *English Masculinities 1660–1800* (London: Longman, 1999).

30. J. Dwyer, *Virtuous Discourse: Sensibility and Community in Late Eighteenth-century Scotland* (Edinburgh: John Donald, 1987), esp. pp. 117–37.

31. *British Messenger*, January 1878 and February 1878.

32. I tackle these issues in C. G. Brown, *The Death of Christian Britain: Understanding Secularisation 1800–2000* (London: Routledge, 2001), pp. 88–114.

33. *British Messenger*, February 1920.

34. Dwyer, *Virtuous Discourse*, pp. 141–64.

35. Brown, *Death of Christian Britain*, pp. 58–87.

36. Quoted in C. G. Brown and J. Stephenson, ' "Sprouting wings?" Women and religion in Scotland c.1890–1950', in E. Breitenbach and E. Gordon (eds), *Out of Bounds: Women in Scottish Society 1800–1945* (Edinburgh: Edinburgh University Press, 1992), pp. 103–4.

37. Quoted in Brown, *Death of Christian Britain*, p. 115.

38. On churching in twentieth-century London, see S. C. Williams, *Religious Belief and Popular Culture in Southwark c.1880–1939* (Oxford: Oxford University Press, 1999).

39. P. Hillis, 'Church and society in Aberdeen and Glasgow, c.1800-c.2000', *Journal of Ecclesiastical History* 53 (2002), 707–34, p. 731.

40. L. Abrams, ' "There was nobody like my Daddy": fathers, the family and the marginalisation of men in modern Scotland', *Scottish Historical Review* 78: 2 (1999), 219–42.

41. This case is examined in detail in C. G. Brown, 'The unconverted and the conversion: gender relations in the salvation narrative in Britain 1800–1960', in W. J. van Bekkum, J. N. Bremmer and A. L. Molendijk (eds), *Conversion in Modern Times* (Leuven: Peeter, 2005), 183–99.
42. P. Brierley and F. Macdonald, *Prospects for Scotland 2000* (London and Edinburgh: Christian Research/NBSS, 1995), pp. 24–5. Website www. christian-research.co.uk accessed 16 March 2005.
43. Scottish Oral History Centre Archive, University of Strathclyde, respondent 006/Mrs C.2 (b. 1912), pp. 22–3.
44. P. Heelas and L. Woodhead, *The Spiritual Revolution: Why Religion is Giving Way to Spirituality* (Oxford: Blackwell, 2005).
45. S. J. Sutcliffe, *Children of the New Age: A History of Spiritual Practices* (London: Routledge, 2003).

5

Education and Learning

Lindy Moore

INTRODUCTION

Education was, and arguably still is, one of the core institutions through which the Scottish national identity has been defined. Incorporating a national framework established in the seventeenth century when Scotland was an independent country, education was associated with a common culture and various supposed qualities of the Scottish character such as individualism, social ambition and a respect for talent above birth.[1] The iconography of the 'lad of parts' – the boy who rose from humble beginnings with the aid of the local parish schoolmaster (the dominie) – was embedded in a wider generic assumption of egalitarianism, defined in terms of social class. This was, however, a masculine ideology. The definition of the 'democratic tradition' of education in terms of access to university entry and social mobility excluded girls and women; the universities were closed to them, and individuality, ambition and talent were not considered desirable feminine qualities. The seeming inclusiveness of the concept hid fundamental gender differences and inequalities by foregrounding the masculine as the norm. Thus, in contemporary discourse, educational provision was discussed in terms of girls' admission to or exclusion from the educational system. For example, in 1868 the Argyll Commission supported the principle of mixed-sex schools on the grounds that 'if the separation of boys and girls is insisted upon, it will be difficult to supply the latter with the same educational advantages which they now enjoy'.[2]

As Helen Corr has shown, this gendered version has been incorporated into educational histories, perpetuating the masculine narrative.[3] Recent research recovering the educational histories of girls and women or analysing gender differentiation is still very uneven in its coverage; the eighteenth and mid-twentieth centuries, in particular, await investigation, and any comments made here must be tentative. General educational histories vary in the extent to which they incorporate the information that has become available; and, even in the case of more gender-aware writers, the masculine institutional system is still embedded as the frame of reference: 'Entry to university was open to anyone (but not women or girls)'.[4] Yet, despite this masculinist historiographical tradition, the very positive developments in academic standards that have occurred since 1700 have actually affected women more powerfully than men. In the eighteenth century, women were probably poorer at reading and certainly far less skilled at writing than men. They were barred, even as learners, from the academic secondary schools and the universities and formed only a small proportion of schoolteachers. At the end of the twentieth century, all these educational institutions were open to them, and, despite the overall rise in academic standards, girls were achieving better examination results than boys, and women formed the majority of higher-education students and of schoolteachers and were established as academics and educational administrators. Rather than just providing a chronology of this progress, in which female achievements are measured against the masculine criteria of the lad of parts and university success, this chapter will also explore some of the issues highlighted by a gendered analysis, such as the influence of the learning environment – formal and informal – within the school, the role and experiences of teachers and academics, the impact of national policies and administrative structures and the differing responses made by men and women to formal and informal learning opportunities.

ACCESS TO SCHOOLING

In the eighteenth and early nineteenth centuries, school education usually began after infancy and, particularly for males, might continue intermittently well into adulthood, depending upon individual opportunity and motivation. Only for the very poorest children in the parish was education provided free. Most middle-class and working-class girls and boys (or rather, their parents) selected and paid for one or more 'classes' (subjects) from those offered by a teacher or school. Subjects were usually learnt sequentially; and, when a number of subjects were being studied simultaneously (most often by middle-class children in the towns), the pupils often attended several different teachers or schools. Apart from the few pupils who boarded at school, it was the exception for either working-class or middle-class children to be taught daily over a period of several years in one specific educational institution. This 'cafeteria' form of education, based on parental choice of school, subject and timing, enabled learning to be fitted in with domestic needs and the agricultural or employment seasons for working-class families, and with business arrangements, family holidays or travel in the middle classes, but it makes gender or social-class comparisons of individual learning opportunities and take-up more difficult.

There were regional variations; and, as Robert Anderson and Jane McDermid have shown, attendance was differentially influenced for the sexes by isolation, industrialisation, religion and tradition.[5] Comparative figures for the eighteenth century are scarce, but those available for a few schools of the Society in Scotland for Propagating Christian Knowledge (SSPCK) in the 1720s showed a ratio of four boys for every girl in rural Aberdeenshire and three to one in Shetland. In the 1830s, there were a little over half as many girls as boys attending any Scottish school (parochial, endowed, subscription, charitable or private) in many areas, especially the Highlands and the North-East, and overall there were 70 per cent as many girls at school as boys. By 1851, girls' overall attendance had increased to 80 per cent of that of boys. There were more girls than boys at private schools (which included schools for both the wealthiest and the poorest) and at Roman Catholic schools (which were among the poorest). The lowest percentage of girls occurred in the two types of school most closely associated with the traditional Scottish educational system – parochial schools (39 per cent) and burgh schools (29 per cent). The attendance of the older pupils reflected the pull of local industry; in textile towns, where there was employment for girls, the boys stayed on at school, while in the heavy-industry or mining towns, girls stayed on longer. Until the Second World War, half of the pupils receiving a post-elementary education were still being taught in the advanced departments of the public elementary schools.[6]

By the 1880s, the upper tier of the secondary schools consisted of the larger endowed and higher class schools.[7] These were predominantly single-sex, although they also included some of the best-known of the old co-educational burgh schools. More affordable academic opportunities for the majority of pupils came from the development of the pupil-teacher system (1846–1906) and the network of almost 200 designated 'higher grade' schools created after 1899. Girls took full advantage of these schemes and by 1920 formed a slight majority of the pupils at both inter-mediate (three-year) and full five-year grant-aided secondary schools.

Up to the 1890s, the public examinations taken by middle-class pupils were effectively gendered, with boys sitting an assortment of government, professional and university bursary examinations while girls took various university local examinations.[8] In 1888, the Scotch (from 1918 'Scottish') Education Department (SED) introduced the Leaving Certificate, and this rapidly became the single most important school examination in Scotland. By 1894, girls constituted 41 per cent of the candidates even though pupil teachers (where girls were the large majority) were only admitted to the examinations for the first time the following year.[9] Throughout the twentieth century, there was greater pressure on boys to stay on longer at school and do well academically, and they were given greater financial support. However, many working-class boys found school confining and wanted to leave for the independence and status of earning, while girls often preferred staying on at school to the confining unpaid drudgery of helping in the home. Concerns about underperforming boys surfaced in the 1940s when tests found girls in the senior secondary schools to be more intelligent and higher achievers than the boys. In the mid-1980s, girls were achieving higher qualifications than boys in both the Standard Grade and Higher examinations; and, by the end of the century, girls of all social classes were outperforming boys of the same social class. Between the 1960s and the 1980s,

> The female advantage grew, it should be noted, in a system that was in the process of abandoning most of the little single-sex provision it made, that had no public educational programme of positive discrimination in favour of girls, and that was neglectful of gender equality in matters of curriculum.[10]

THE CURRICULUM

The Presbyterian church of the reformers wanted a godly commonwealth, whose members knew their religious duties from close knowledge of the Bible, a theology that required a literate public of both sexes. Schooling was 'serious, earnest, harsh, utilitarian, ordered, dominated by a desire first to bring all to personal eternal salvation through instruction in reading'.[11] By the seventeenth century, the core curriculum, which was expected to take about two years of study, consisted of learning to read and spell from the Bible and the memorising of psalms, prayers, graces and the catechism. Whether learnt at home or school, this was similar for all classes, and for both girls and boys. Where parents tried to avoid or shorten this schooling (most often for girls), the authorities attempted to enforce attendance. It therefore seems likely that in the eighteenth century almost as many girls as boys were taught to read, but probable that a higher proportion of women became only semi-literate, as there were more objections to women reading non-religious works, and men had more frequent opportunities to use their reading skills.[12] The Gaelic and Scots languages created linguistic barriers, and religious denomination was an important variable. Not only were both male and female Scottish

Catholics far less literate than any of the Protestant denominations, but also in the mid-nineteenth century the gender difference in literacy (measured by signing one's own name) was much greater for Catholics than Protestants.[13] The percentage of Scots able to sign increased faster for women than for men, and by 1900 illiteracy had effectively disappeared.

In the eighteenth century, gender differentiation in learning began when children were aged between six and ten, and was vocationally oriented. Boys might be sent on to learn writing, arithmetic and possibly Latin at the parochial or burgh school, while most girls went to (or remained at) schools taught by women, to learn needlework and knitting. In the nineteenth century, sewing schools were often intended specifically for the poor, but in the eighteenth century they were also extremely important for girls from the middle class and even the landed gentry. Few girls learnt writing, which was a sharply gendered skill throughout the eighteenth and early nineteenth centuries. It has been estimated that, in mid-eighteenth-century Scotland, 85 per cent of women compared with 35 per cent of men could not even sign their own name.[14] Individuals of either sex might never be taught to write because it was considered unlikely to be of any economic value to them, but it was only females who might have their training blocked on religious or moral grounds.

The Union with England in 1707 enhanced Scotland's commercial activities, but it also aroused in the middle-class elite an ambiguous sense of social inferiority. As a result, new vocational and cultural subjects appeared in the curriculum, such as navigation, mathematics, geography, book-keeping and surveying for boys and men. For girls and women, there were new needlework, cookery, laundry, domestic management and child-rearing skills to learn, and new fashions in dress, music, dancing and interior decoration to study.[15] While the studies of middle-class boys were based around book-learning, those of most girls employed a practical pedagogy. When, in 1743, the rector of Dalkeith Academy regretted that so much education was spent on boys and so little on girls, he was making a value judgement on the type as well as the quantity of teaching given to boys and girls respectively.[16]

As the written medium came to be seen as an indicator of European sophistication, upper middle-class girls began studying it, but even more influential was the contemporary discourse on femininity initiated by the Scottish Enlightenment literati, who introduced new concepts of civic humanism and communal cohesion, the value of private life and the domestic circle, and a new role for women as reformers of society through their influence as companionate wives and intelligent mothers.[17]

There was increasing public discussion about female education and the cultivation of the feminine intellect and rationality, with a radical minority even advocating higher education for women.[18] As a consequence, the second half of the eighteenth century saw a great improvement in the education of middle-class girls. By 1800, writing had become a standard competency, and their studies normally also included spelling, arithmetic, grammar, French, geography and 'the globes' (terrestrial and astronomical). This change in their curriculum had a long-term consequence for the relative status of male and female teachers. Male teachers were considered to have the academic learning and pedagogical methods appropriate for literacy-based work, and they were able to take on the academic education of middle-class girls in both private and public classes and to open large, influential secondary day schools for girls in Edinburgh and Glasgow in the 1830s and 1840s with a broad curriculum and a particular emphasis on science.[19]

When, however, unfavourable comparisons were made about the lifestyle and standards of Scottish working-class households compared with those of the English, there was a patriotic opportunity for middle-class Scottish women to make a space for themselves within the male-dominated educational system by establishing separate schools with a separate curriculum for working-class girls, taught by women of approved moral standards and publicly managed by themselves.[20] The explicit curriculum remained similar to that of the earlier 'woman' or 'dame' schools – Bible and catechism study, reading and possibly writing in addition to basic sewing, but it was now centred on an implicit curriculum aimed at the inculcation of domestic skills and middle-class religious, moral and work-ethic habits.

A new secular 'national' curriculum was effectively introduced when state grants towards school buildings and pupil teachers began, accompanied by school inspection, in the 1840s, although initially this applied to only a few schools. Through the encouragement of equal school attendance (compulsory from 1872) and standardised attainments in basic reading and writing for both sexes, this curriculum encouraged greater gender equality than had previously occurred through parental choice. But the acceptance of a lower (although compulsory) level of arithmetic and the introduction of compulsory needlework for girls in the 1860s also formalised a gender differentiation which remained in place officially until the Sex Discrimination Act of 1975. Sewing was not only made compulsory for girls, but became prohibited to boys, even though they sometimes sewed or knitted at home to earn money. During the late nineteenth and the early twentieth century, additional girls-only subjects were added to the curriculum: cookery, laundry-work, home-craft, hygiene and sex education. Insufficient resources for teaching these subjects meant that they were not always compulsory, but their generic title of 'domestic economy' indicated their objective. Boys were specifically excluded from those subjects, and those wishing to become chefs or tailors had to learn their trades elsewhere. Suggestions that parts of the domestic-economy syllabus, such as health, cleanliness, budgeting or parenthood, were relevant to both sexes were never taken up, reflecting the extent to which the curriculum was being used by the state to establish a differentiation of gender roles in working-class family life and to define domesticity and motherhood as a patriotic ideal for all girls.

In the local communities, there was considerable resistance to the introduction of practical lessons for girls into the mixed-sex elementary schools, as the time spent on needlework squeezed out other subjects or left girls struggling to achieve similar academic levels to boys. The idea that girls were being educated for the 'woman's sphere' was no less prevalent than previously, but by the mid-nineteenth century the incorporation of girls into the democratic tradition of Scottish education meant that academic instruction was seen as an essential part of the process, and it was considered a cause for pride that an increasing number of girls were learning French, Latin and mathematics alongside the boys.[21] Attempts by educational conservatives to introduce a practical syllabus for working-class boys were largely unsuccessful, as they failed to overcome the academic ideology of the 'lad of parts', but in the twentieth century the SED used its power to impose social-class differentiation (albeit defined in terms of ability) in education. Handicrafts for boys, usually woodwork and later metalwork, were systematically introduced. By the 1920s, the SED's policy was that most boys and girls should be doing quite different practical courses and that the other subjects in pupils' curricula should be influenced by their vocational objectives. Thus schools were often sites of conflict where pupils, teachers and even school boards manoeuvred to manipulate or evade the regulations of the education authorities.

Apart from the differentiation in technical subjects for boys and girls, gender in the curriculum was generally ignored as an issue by policy-makers, yet a gender bias was deeply embedded in assumptions by parents, teachers and pupils about the respective abilities of boys and girls and the appropriate subjects for them to learn, by school timetabling permutations, by the sex of the subject teachers, by the allocation of value or compulsion to certain subjects, by gender-specific content in the curriculum and textbooks with strongly gendered messages and even by the barring of one or other sex from taking certain examinations or being awarded certain prizes or bursaries. As the example of literacy illustrates, gender-differentiated subject preference is class- and time-specific. A brief examination of two curriculum subjects, science and physical education, will illustrate just some of the interesting and subtle changes and influences that await further research.

Science was not invariably considered a 'male' subject. In America in the late eighteenth to the early nineteenth century, it was studied more by girls than boys. In Scotland, too, middle-class girls and women were attending popular science lectures and classes in subjects such as astronomy, physical geography and chemistry. But, by 1905, the development of a 'strange prejudice' against teaching girls science had been noted.[22] Various factors contributed to this change in attitude. In the eighteenth century, science was seen in a theological and philosophical sense as illustrative of God and his powers, and was therefore appropriate for religious women to learn about. There was emphasis on the value of science in correcting 'old wives' tales', thus ensuring that mothers gave their children accurate information. It was argued also that the new scientific knowledge, applied to the domestic environment, would reduce infant mortality and improve domestic health and the home environment. Together, these views encouraged the concept of science as being relevant to females. Contrary trends were also evident in the eighteenth century, changing the definition of science and its applicability. Subjects such as gravitation, mechanics, optics, navigation and astronomy were being taught to boys as vocational subjects. Women's knowledge, learnt verbally and by experience in the home, or passed down in letters and receipt (recipe) books, became superseded by formal male scientific methodology. Medical professors began teaching new midwifery techniques. By the mid-nineteenth century, the emphasis was on the usefulness of science for promoting the economy and technology, and as such there were various campaigns to introduce it into the school curriculum of boys in the second half of the century.[23] Science became seen as irrelevant and incomprehensible to women, and attempts were made to introduce a science curriculum relevant to girls by relating it to domestic economy. By 1919, science was the most popular boys' subject and the least popular with girls.[24] In 1970, three-quarters, of male pupils, but only half of all female pupils, took a science subject. Twenty years later, almost all boys and girls studied science, although there was still considerable gender differentiation between specific science subjects. This considerable shift was in part a result of the Sex Discrimination Act of 1975, but even more influential was the introduction of a standard national curriculum in 1983, although there had been virtually no consideration of the implications for gender equality at the time of its introduction.[25]

Physical education brought with it awareness of body movement and body contact, which were especially contentious issues particularly with respect to the sex of the teacher. These were usually men, teaching dancing, deportment and fencing in the eighteenth century and callisthenics, drill, gymnastics, athletics and later field sports in the nineteenth century. In the second half of the nineteenth century, male specialists, often ex-army men, established themselves. Then came the introduction of Swedish exercises, specially trained female teachers from England and the opening of the co-educational Scottish College of Hygiene and Physical Training at Dunfermline in 1905. When the lower-paid female students were appointed to teach boys as well as girls, male students from the college had difficulty finding employment, and complaints by male teachers included a vitriolic attack entitled 'Is our race to become effeminate?'[26] Training in masculinity for working-class boys was perceived as a matter of national interest following the South African War, when there was strong pressure for compulsory military drill to be introduced into the elementary schools as part of a 'national efficiency' campaign. But after Scottish doctors emphasised instead the importance of environmental factors for children's health, the emphasis moved from drill to nutrition and from masculinity to femininity, as the school curriculum shifted from preparing young men to fight to a greater emphasis on training working-class women to provide better meals and home environment.[27]

For both sexes, physical education was also a means of confirming class differentiation. The Victorian concept of masculinity had been introduced into the corporate ethos of boys' secondary schools through team sports and games, and J. A. Mangan has explored the role this played in assimilating Scottish boys into a British middle-class cultural identity suitable for the Empire.[28] But the way in which Scottish females were incorporated into this imperial culture remains to be examined, as does the question of how female pupils experienced the introduction of team sports and the corporate ethic into girls' secondary schools; in this context, they were clearly not intended to invoke masculinity. Later in the twentieth century, a new gendered debate about curriculum content arose out of the division of the teacher-training of physical education into two single-sex colleges, as this resulted in two different styles of teaching. From the 1950s to the 1970s, female teachers favoured an aesthetic/expressive form of physical education based on 'human movement' while men taught a skill-centred, scientific approach; but, as men held most of the senior posts in the state schools, women found it difficult to get their approach incorporated into school syllabuses.[29]

As this discussion of physical education illustrates, the formally pre-scribed curriculum was not the only thing pupils learnt at school or college. Various cultural mores, including those regulating gender behav-iour and gender expectations, were incorporated into the ethos and organ-isation of schools and colleges, both implicitly and explicitly. Women may have been more aware than men of these gendered pressures: a teenager who preferred climbing trees complained about being expected to play at 'hoosies wi' auld tay pots wi' the young quinies', and a middle-class woman noted ironically: 'the woman's point of view, as the men who have conducted my education from the time when I was eight years old until now have never allowed me to forget, is essentially different from man's'.[30] This 'hidden' curriculum was articulated in a variety of ways including the spatial organisation of pupils by sex, the application of discipline through supervision or corporal punishment, and the school ethos.

Proponents of the democratic tradition pointed to the prevalence of co-education as proof of gender equality in the history of Scottish edu-cation. There were, indeed, seventeenth- and eighteenth-century refer-ences to girls and boys attending various kinds of schools together; but, although it was seen as the responsibility of the community to make edu-cational provision for all children, this did not mean that all educational needs within the community were seen as similar; class and gender differentiation was taken for granted. The cafeteria system of taking classes, and access by girls and boys to what were often effectively multi-departmental or 'omnibus' schools in the towns, did not necessarily mean equality of access to all departments or teachers, or that the same subjects would be either wanted by, or available to, both girls and boys. Nineteenth-century Scots used the more accurate term 'mixed schools' rather than 'co-educational' schools'. David Stow's positive and there-fore rather different concept of co-education was based on the ideal of the family and home, a patriarchal model where the man had absolute authority, where adult roles were sharply gendered and access, use and decoration of space was also gendered. Stow, an early nineteenth-century pioneer of teacher-training, and his followers were not in favour of indis-criminate 'mingling' – on the contrary, they wanted spatial use carefully supervised. Strategies used in Scottish schools and other academic insti-tutions such as the teacher-training colleges and universities to manage the gendering of space included separation by time and by physical divi-sion within classes, as well as the demarcation of sex-segregated areas within the school. Such arrangements were dependent on pupils' age and social class, whether they attended daily or as boarders, the design of the building, the extent of overcrowding, the curriculum subject and the personal preferences of teachers. A supporter of co-education argued that it helped to destroy the consciousness of sex on which separatism was based, and which segregation therefore kept consciously before the minds of both sexes.[31] In practice, educational management and policies concerning physical boundaries, gender-differentiated curricula, pedagogical methods, gendered discourse within the school, clothing codes, discipline, movement and staff role models often had the overall effect of reinforcing gender differentiation.

The lady superintendent, appointed to supervise girls, was the only member of staff in secondary schools with an explicitly gendered remit. The first posts, in private schools, were followed from the 1860s by burgh schools trying to attract middle-class girls. The lady superintendent had an especial interest in controlling female pupils' movement and body language; thus girls were not to run, cross their legs in the presence of a master, or mix with boys outside the school. The later post of 'woman adviser' was introduced by legislation between 1950 and 1972 for schools with over 200 girls where the head teacher was male, the change in title reflecting the shift of emphasis. There were no comparable supervisors for boys; in the nineteenth century, the job was done, if by anyone, by the janitor, yet it was boys who were generally the more aggressive and active, who took up more space, both in the school and in public spaces, and whose behaviour was perceived as more problematic and a potential issue for school discipline and occasionally even civil disorder.

The stern ethos of Scottish Calvinism carried over into education, and it was widely accepted that physical punishment was the path to knowledge, even in Bible classes. This ethos was exacerbated by pressure to pass school inspections and maintain discipline in large classes, resulting in the widespread use of the leather tawse. A Stoic acceptance of punishment was linked to the middle-class English public-school concept of manliness – so its use was prevalent among all social classes of boys, but it was largely class-differentiated for girls. The common use of corporal punishment in mixed-sex secondary schools may have been one of the reasons for many middle-class girls being sent instead to private schools, and for the creation of separate departments for girls in co-educational schools, where female behaviour and female disciplinary issues were placed under the management of the lady superintendent. Nevertheless, substantial numbers of both sexes continued to be beaten, and corporal punishment was not abolished throughout Scotland until 1986.[32]

Darling and Glendinning suggest that even in the 1990s the head teacher, especially in a secondary school, was expected to act 'not just as an educational leader, but also as an authority figure who is ultimately responsible for the effective control of young people's behaviour'.[33] So long as this authority was backed up by corporal punishment, ambitious male teachers had to conform to a particular model of masculinity, and the appointment of women as head teachers, especially in mixed-sex secondary schools, was unlikely.

In the nineteenth-century burgh schools, there was an intensely intellectual and competitive atmosphere within the classroom but little moral or corporate life outside it. This combination has been described as creating a 'moral neutrality', which encouraged the admission of girls to these secondary schools on equal terms.[34] But it is a question not only how 'equal' girls were, but also whether the intense academic ethos that permeated many secondary and elementary schools was in fact gender-neutral, since the employment of male teachers introduced masculine pedagogies and academic values to the female pupils. One writer used the phrase 'boy culture' to describe the emphasis on the masculine-orientated curriculum of classics and mathematics, the competitive examinations and interest in the success of old boys at university prevalent throughout his co-educational elementary school.[35] It was only in the private and proprietary single-sex girls' schools, where the middle-class pupils were not intending to follow a career and where an emphasis on academic study was therefore seen as unnecessary, that there was an opportunity to develop instead a feminine cultural ethos. In those schools, the curriculum could be as flexible as required, subject selection was often broader than that in secondary schools for boys; and, given the smaller numbers involved, it could be pupil-centred with a cultural emphasis, from theatre visits to acting out French plays, from botanical excursions to jujitsu. Intelligent women looking back with hindsight questioned whether, even academically, the formal learn-by-rote pedagogy of the government-inspected schools was really an improvement. Meanwhile, reforming women educationalists such as the founders of St Leonard's School in St Andrews (1877) and St George's School, Edinburgh (1888) attempted the even trickier task of combining a feminine school culture with a high standard of academic study. The cultural capital available in private schools for upper middle-class girls was matched in secondary middle-class boys' schools by access to the classical world and the development of a corporate ethos through sporting activities; but it was largely absent from the state schools, where clever boys and girls studied single-mindedly for the Leaving Certificate for university or teacher-training college entrance.

TEACHERS

Although 'woman' schools were in evidence by at least the mid-seventeenth century, most teachers in eighteenth-century Scotland, unlike England, were male.[36] Edinburgh, which became well known for its private schools for middle-class girls in the second half of the eighteenth century, was exceptional, and at that time almost 20 per cent of the teachers there may have been women.[37] Elsewhere, town councils and kirk sessions permitted and sometimes actually supported private-adventure schools taught by women when they perceived a need in the locality for the teaching of the catechism, psalms and basic reading skills to infants and girls. But the assumption that women lacked an intellectual education and training in teaching methods meant that they were only officially appointed to burgh schools to teach feminine skills such as needlework or 'paistrie', or, from the late eighteenth century, 'the accomplishments'.[38] Women had to promote specifically gendered objectives, pedagogies and management skills to gain an entry into general public schoolteaching: a master 'can neither perceive nor understand what the judging critical eye of a female catches with a single glance'.[39] The ensuing movement towards separate schools or departments for working-class girls meant that by 1838 about a fifth of all Scottish schoolteachers were female; but this was still a sharp contrast with England, where over two-thirds of teachers were female in 1841. By the 1860s, Scottish schoolmistresses were being employed more often in mixed-sex elementary schools, although it was not until the Education Act of 1861 that they were legally permitted to teach in the parochial schools, and then only for elementary subjects and sewing.[40] By 1871, women formed almost half of the workforce, and the female percentage continued to rise thereafter; women were 70 per cent of teachers in 1911 and, in 1994, 92 per cent of primary schoolteachers and 50 per cent in state secondary schools.[41]

Using a nominal analysis, this changing sex ratio of Scottish teachers is often referred to as the 'feminisation' of the profession; but sex and gender are not synonymous, and even a majority of one sex or the other in an organisation or a profession may not be sufficient to alter public perception of the ideal gender model. Moreover, such perceptions are influenced by time, place and context, and what may be seen as a masculine skill or institution in one context may be seen as feminine in another. The early nineteenth-century Scottish pioneers of infant-school education envisaged the ideal trained infant-teacher as male, possibly assisted by a female; but this became an area where females soon became accepted as the experts (rationalised in terms of their innate maternal sympathy), and it later became the only promoted post in state schools which women teachers had a realistic chance of obtaining.[42] Nevertheless, the school management structure meant that, in the ubiquitous all-age schools of the 1880s, most of the teachers in charge of infants were male. This was criticised by a school inspector on the grounds that men were 'obviously quite unsuited for such a charge'.[43] Although male infant-teachers were still the majority, the role had become feminised. In contrast, the ideal type of elementary teacher, caught in the iconic myth of the dominie, remained male, even though the sex ratio of the elementary teaching profession changed and women became the majority. The high percentage of female teachers found throughout the English educational system had previously been characteristic in Scotland only of the minority Catholic sector, and the increasing proportion of women in the Presbyterian educational system was seen as indicative of a crisis of national identity.[44] In the nineteenth century, the fast-growing Catholic education sector struggled with few resources. The schools were heavily dependent on female teachers, low-paid and mostly unqualified (certificated teachers had to be imported from England), but gaining status from their position as intermediaries between the clergy and the Catholic laity.

Gendered inequality was built into the teaching profession at all levels.[45] Existing gender inequalities in salary were institutionalised as an integral part of state educational policy after the 1872 Education (Scotland) Act, when two distinct pay scales were introduced, keeping women's pay at just under half that for men. Women also received less financial assistance with their training; indeed, the predominantly middle-class female teacher-training students financially supported the male students. Moreover, a higher percentage of women than men were refused admission to the teacher-training colleges even though the female candidates were generally the more highly qualified. By gendering the teaching profession, the changing demands of the labour market could be met through the introduction of short-term restrictions or relaxations aimed only at women. Between 1874 and 1914, an 'age bar' (at 25) for provisionally certificated teachers affected women especially, since a higher proportion of women were refused places at the training colleges and therefore could not obtain their full certificate, and between 1915 and 1945 many of the educational authorities operated a marriage bar for women, while at the end of the twentieth century a high proportion of women teachers were on temporary contracts.[46] Lower expectations of women teachers were formalised from 1926 to the 1960s, during which time virtually all the men, including primary teachers, had to have a university degree. By 1971,

> selection and socialization processes were playing a major part in channelling able teenage girls into a secondary school track characterised by academic under-achievement and the discontinuation of mathematics and science studies. This . . . led on to non-graduating, liberal-arts courses in the colleges of education and thence to primary school teaching.[47]

Institutionalised sexism in schools' attitudes to teachers and in the administrative hierarchy formed part of the hidden curriculum of schools. As a headmistress commented wryly, 'In a patriarchal country like Scotland, it was natural enough that a certain aura of unconscious superiority should surround the men's staff-room'.[48] The message transmitted to the next generation was that working with the younger children was women's work and that men would 'naturally' hold positions of responsibility in a school; and, for most of the period between 1700 and 2000, this message accurately reflected the attitudes of Scottish society.[49] As Mary Clarke, first headmistress (1914–24) of the endowed Edinburgh Ladies College (now The Mary Erskine School), noted, there were few opportunities for promotion in co-educational schools, and the relative absence of single-sex schools restricted the educational opportunities for professional women in comparison with those to be found in England.[50] Only from the 1960s did sex discrimination come under debate, criticism and finally legislation, and only in the 1990s were equal-opportunity policies introduced into schools. During this period, however, structural bias in the teaching hierarchy was increased by the introduction of a more formal promotion ladder which left women who took time out for children at a greater disadvantage.[51] Consequently, schools were attempting to foster a critical awareness of inequalities in society, while themselves exhibiting an unequal distribution of professional positions.

GENDERED GOVERNANCE

Acts of 1616, 1633 and 1696 effectively established a national and public system of education by setting a tax on the local landowning parishioners (heritors), making school provision a legal responsibility of the whole parochial community and introducing an administrative structure in partnership with the Presbyterian Church.[52] In essence, this remained the framework of educational provision until 1872, although it became supplemented by an increasing range of voluntary, denominational and private educational provision. While the national and public nature of this educational framework is generally emphasised, its gendered nature is not. It may be self-evident, but it is never explicitly stated that the legislation, policy, funding and management of these parochial and denominational schools was controlled by men. In addition, unlike England, where schools of the Society for Promoting Christian Knowledge (SPCK) were established in towns as well as rural areas in the eighteenth century and were under local funding and local management which sometimes included women, in Scotland SSPCK schools were set up only in rural areas, mainly in the Highlands and Islands, and were under the close and efficient managerial control of the all-male central committee. In the cities and towns, grammar (Latin), English and occasionally charity schools were established under the control of the civic authorities, some of whom also supported burgh schoolmistresses; and the kirk sessions and town councils attempted to regulate, or at least inspect, all the adventure (private) teachers and schools within their locality. In the early nineteenth century, public provision in the towns was supplemented by sessional and district schools under the management of local lay churchmen and ministers. Men also controlled the universities and most of the further-education institutions established in the nineteenth century.[53]

This pattern of control organised through formal, structured male hierarchies provided few opportunities for women to become actively involved in educational management. Some women landowners were involved in setting up schools for the tenants on their estates or promoting spinning schools to encourage economic development in the locality, but it would seem that it was only at the very end of the eighteenth century that middle-class women found a sphere of influence and activity for themselves within the new voluntary societies.[54] At that time, genuine concern about the conditions of the poor, especially of women and children, became interwoven with a religiously based evangelising fervour which provided women with the personal motivation and the moral authority to move into the public arena in support of philanthropic associations, especially religious or educational societies supporting the new infant, charity and Sunday schools. Women began visiting and sometimes managing such schools, inspecting especially the school environment, tidiness, clothing and pupil behaviour. In her examination of similar schools in England between 1800 and 1861, Joyce Goodman draws on van Drenth's concept of 'care', arguing that this close supervision formed part of the pedagogical strategies of surveillance which lay at the heart of 'care', a new disciplinary force which characterised evangelical work.[55]

Under the 1872 Education (Scotland) Act, the old administrative framework of landowners and church was replaced by a system of 986 elected school boards covering the entire country. For the first time, women were officially admitted to the governance of the national educational system; they could both vote for, and be elected to, the school boards.[56] Although this set an important precedent, in practice, upper middle-class women and female members of the landed gentry probably had less influence under the school-boards system, based on political and economic power, than previously when they could point to social class and gender as their qualifications for establishing and managing separate charity and subscription schools for girls and the poor. Far fewer women than men were eligible to vote for school boards, and school-board membership was almost entirely male with a high proportion of church representatives. The small group of exceptional women who were elected to the school boards in Edinburgh and Glasgow were important as agents and role models, but give a misleading impression of the presence and influence of women in Scottish local educational governance in general.[57] When the school boards were converted into thirty-eight county and burgh education authorities in 1918, men formed 95 per cent of the elected members.[58] Not all women stood for election from an identification with gender issues. Class and religious interests and, in the twentieth century, political and welfare issues were of more concern to many women, but they were perceived and grouped in terms of gender and allocated responsibilities accordingly. In view of the philanthropic evangelical role that many women had previously undertaken, it was not surprising that women generally were seen as useful advisers on the moral environment of schools, girls' education and their domestic-economy curriculum.

As secular control of the educational system developed from the 1840s onwards, the popular predisposition towards a national system of education allowed the SED, established in 1872, to gain greater power and influence over education than its equivalent in England. This also had gendered implications for governance, since it enabled the Oxbridge-educated Scottish civil servants to ignore women's pressure groups and left relatively fewer alternative educational opportunities for independent female involvement. Women had especial difficulties penetrating the administrative hierarchy itself, and the earliest women were appointed, like their male colleagues, through the old boys' network. The first official woman inspector was appointed in 1902, and she and her successors were assigned to deal almost entirely with female domestic subjects.[59] Not until 1930 was a woman appointed to the rank of His Majesty's Inspector; and women remained a small minority. As in the civil service and teaching, salaries were a signifier of unequal status. The first two women HMIs had first-class honours degrees and did the same work as men, but their salary scale ended where men's of the 'same' rank began. In England, the Secretary to the Board of Education set up a separate parallel section for women within the inspectorate (1905 to the mid-1930s) which boosted female numbers, though women inspectors complained of their lower status. This was a less obvious solution in Scotland, where there were few single-sex girls' schools or female teacher-training colleges for the women to inspect, a factor which also impacted on opportunities for women to obtain appointments as school governors.

Dana Britton has suggested that all bureaucratic institutions are inherently gendered in a masculine sense, in that they have rules, a hierarchy and an impersonalised system of working.[60] Furthermore, they are supported and influenced by a network of external cultural, political and administrative structures which themselves will be gendered. One definition of a gendered institution is number-dependent. In terms of right of access, even one individual can be important, hence there are frequent references in gender histories to the 'first' person of the opposite sex to become a member or student of a single-sex institution, or holder of a particular post or occupation, as a signifier that thereafter access was theoretically open to both sexes.[61] In a broader cultural context, it can be argued that a critical mass is necessary to change the ethos of an institution in a psychological and social sense, to provide a culture within which people feel comfortable learning, researching, creating, arguing and debating, rather than always doing so as both a minority, and therefore a representative, of their sex. There is also an issue of power relations, in that there is a need for enough people of the minority sex to get their issues on the agenda. Studies of Scottish educational policy have illustrated how little influence women have had, although this evidence has often been provided implicitly rather than explicitly.[62] Overlapping membership of educational bodies resulted in a male 'policy community', maintained by a system of appointment and patronage, in which women were disadvantaged by structural and systematic exclusion.[63] The minority of women in senior posts in schools, further and higher educational institutions, policy-making bodies or administrative posts experienced these gendered power relationships throughout the nineteenth and twentieth centuries.[64]

INFORMAL LEARNING

Formal education was not the only kind of learning experience available, although it is emphasised in educational histories because it more clearly embodies the national identity, much of it was provided or controlled by legislation and it was given prominence in contemporary middle-class educational discourse. But equally important, if not more important, for most individuals were the learning opportunities available through home reading or correspondence courses, public lectures or libraries, private tuition or evening classes, commercial crammers or vocational colleges, learned societies or mechanics' institutes and philanthropic or political associations. In the eighteenth century, the church sermon was an important learning experience for women. Men could broaden their experience and learning by travel or by meeting others with mutual interests, but women were generally hindered from doing this by practical considerations of domestic management and children and by opposition to their free association with whomever they pleased or to activities which took them outside their domestic sphere: 'hence a taste for reading becomes to females of still greater importance than it is of to men'.[65] The growth of a secular ideology, combined with the development of the publishing industry and private-subscription and circulating libraries, increased access to reading – although there was also an ambivalence about this where women were concerned that did not apply to men, and women were often advised to keep their reading and learning secret. The frequent prescriptions about the appropriate subject matter for women's reading were never applied in a similar fashion to men as a sex. Excluded or marginalised from much formal and semi-formal institutional education, women developed alternative strategies for making use of the learning opportunities available. They attended a variety of public and private lectures and classes both for self-education and specifically to train as governesses or teachers, despite objections that the subject matter was unsuitable or irrelevant to their domestic duties or that the presence of both sexes made them 'improper and dangerous'. In the early nineteenth century, a small group of middle-class Edinburgh women gained some access to the literary salons, and women made increasing use of periodicals and the press as didactic sites, adapting the masculine discourse to their own interests.[66]

Sabbath or Sunday schools were important sources of informal educational provision for both boys and girls. Originally established in the late eighteenth century to counter the vandalism and misbehaviour perpetrated by youths, they quickly became more important for girls than boys and, by the mid-nineteenth century, were increasingly staffed by women rather than men. The schools were attended regularly by 60 to 70 per cent of all girls in the early twentieth century and remained important learning environments for girls into the 1930s.[67] As Sabbath schools moved into evangelical instruction, evening classes took over some of the basic skills education for pupils who worked during the day; but, unlike Sabbath schools, where girls overtook boys in both enrolment and attendance, girls were much less likely than boys to attend evening classes. In Scotland, unlike England, statutory powers for adult education were retained in the hands of the SED and the local-authority sector, which restricted their remit to vocational evening classes for young workers, a category in which women's position was ambivalent. The classes were always segregated, and the narrower range of subjects offered to females (usually limited to reading, writing, arithmetic, needlework and cookery) and the timing of the classes, which made them difficult for women with children to attend, may have contributed to their lesser appeal.

In more informal environments, it was women who were the more enthusiastic about taking up such educational opportunities as were available or making their own educational provision, yet they remain peripheral figures in histories of adult education. Nineteenth-century efforts to widen university access through extra-mural classes or university local examinations were countered by the argument that the universities were already accessible to any who might wish to attend. Since only men were admitted as matriculated students, it was evident that this debate was being conducted within male terms of reference. The SED used the same argument in the twentieth century as a reason for not giving funds to the Workers' Educational Association (WEA). Again, when courses were provided, it was women who made greatest use of them; there were almost twice as many women as men attending Edinburgh WEA classes in the 1930s and the 1960s.[68] The adult-education courses for women run by co-operative associations were also more successful than those aimed at men, and one of the most successful of all the 'self-help' educational institutions was the Scottish Women's Rural Institute, which began, despite considerable opposition, in 1917. Women's higher participation in community education has continued. In the 1990s, 81 per cent of adult students learning in schools were female, and women formed 70 per cent of the learners participating in community education provided by Lothian Region.[69]

HIGHER EDUCATION

In the eighteenth and the early nineteenth century, when only a minority of university students actually graduated, the definition of 'higher education' was fluid. Women attended midwifery and various popular lecture courses given by university professors, and in 1796 the endowed

Anderson's Institution opened in Glasgow with classes open to women, followed briefly in 1842 by the ambitious, single-sex Queen's College, Glasgow.[70] From the 1860s, women and sympathetic male colleagues began campaigning for the admission of women to the universities, organised extra-mural courses taught by university staff and opened medical schools for women as well as promoting improvements in the secondary education of girls and opening new proprietary schools.[71] By the 1880s, the four old universities all offered degree-level examinations for women, the most popular being the St Andrews LLA (Lady Literate in Arts), which many students studied for by distance learning. In 1892, women were legally admitted to the Scottish universities, and by the 1920s they formed a third of the students; but they were hit harder by the reduction in schoolteaching during the 1930s' Depression, and numbers declined. A later retrenchment in schoolteacher recruitment in the 1960s again affected women particularly, but an unexpected development this time was a consequent increase in the proportion of women entering higher education, a change largely attributable to new attitudes and confidence among young women.[72] By 1999, women formed the majority of entrants to both full-time and part-time higher education, and there was a fresh wave of concern about underachieving males. While there has been little historical research into the gendered experiences of Scottish school pupils, there are a number of studies on the experiences of university students.[73] Conversely, while the gendered experiences of Scottish teachers in the past have received attention, there is little research on the experiences of academics and administrators in further and higher education; but it seems likely that, as in the school system, the co-educational arrangements generally in place in universities and further-education colleges in Scotland increased women's opportunities as students but restricted their opportunities to participate as creators and disseminators of knowledge, administrators or policy-makers.[74]

CONCLUSION

The hierarchical and centralised administrative structures created by the civic, ecclesiastical and state authorities formed considerable obstacles to women becoming involved in education. Scotland is revealed as a chauvinistic, patriarchal society where women had little influence. And yet this is not the whole story. The conceptual chasm between the Scots and the English as to what constituted an appropriate public education was demonstrated especially clearly in the case of women. The Scottish tradition equated egalitarian opportunity with access to academic learning while the English view was instrumental, based on social-class differentiation. Judged in terms of its academic tradition, Scotland had much to be proud of despite legislative, administrative and financial obstacles introduced by the English and Anglo-Scottish policy-makers. At the end of the eighteenth century, attempts were made to provide higher-education facilities for women, and in the 1830s and 1840s private schoolmasters pioneered the prototype of secondary schools for girls. In the mid-nineteenth century, Scottish women had a higher literacy rate than both English women and English men, a higher proportion of Scottish elementary schools were providing French, Latin and mathematics teaching for girls, and Church of Scotland representatives were pressing the government to permit a more academic training for female teachers.[75]

Given the historical gender bias of both research and researchers in educational history, these and many other aspects await further examination. One approach would be to turn the focus onto the educational experience of Scottish girls and women, a move which would foreground different institutions and new forms of learning. It would look at women's campaigns to introduce their own agenda outside the formal educational structure, through informal and family networks, ladies' educational associations and adult-education classes. Women gave particular support to English literature, modern languages and cultural activities in the school and university curriculum, and they used unconventional pedagogies and media to obtain learning and to propagandise their knowledge. They introduced health and social-welfare issues to the educational agenda, and they pioneered twentieth-century nursery and infant schooling and vocational training for infant and secondary-school teaching, housekeeping, nursing and social work. As *The Biographical Dictionary of Scottish Women* illustrates, there have been many exceptional women of influence in Scottish education.

But, as this chapter shows, gendering the history of education involves more than simply 'adding women on'. Throughout the last 300 years, the agenda of the Scottish educational system has been driven by considerations of the national interest. This has been interpreted by historians in terms of educational provision for the male population, yet in practice the education of females was even more specifically and comprehensively influenced and often curtailed by the perceived needs of the Scottish national identity and national economy. In addition to intentionally gendered policies, many other political and managerial decisions have had an unintentional or unpredicted impact on gender differentiation and equality in education. Thus, when the state began introducing a national framework to measure the efficiency and effectiveness of its grant aid, an unintentional consequence was to bring girls and boys into greater parity in terms of access, attendance and academic standards. Policies intended to reduce social-class inequalities, such as extra-mural university teaching or the creation of the comprehensive school system, had a greater, unforeseen impact in reducing gender inequality, a reflection both of the intractability of social-class inequality and the embedded cultural assumptions regarding gender inequality. In the 1990s, the potential impact of educational innovations on gender equality was appreciated and examined in a contemporary context.[76] The impact of many historical educational innovations still awaits research.

FURTHER READING

Anderson, R. D., *Education and the Scottish People: 1750–1918* (Oxford: Clarendon Press, 1995).

Corr, H., 'An exploration into Scottish education', in W. H. Fraser and R. J. Morris (eds), *People and Society in Scotland, vol. 2, 1830–1914* (Edinburgh: John Donald, 1990), pp. 290–309.

Darling, J. and A. Glendinning, *Gender Matters in Schools: Pupils and Teachers* (London: Cassell, 1996).

Fewell, J. and F. M. S. Paterson (eds), *Girls in their Prime: Scottish Education Revisited* (Edinburgh: Scottish Academic Press, 1990).

McDermid, J., *The Schooling of Working-Class Girls in Victorian Scotland: Gender, Education and Identity* (London: Routledge, 2005).

Paterson, L., *Scottish Education in the Twentieth Century* (Edinburgh: Edinburgh University Press, 2003).

Riddell, S., 'Gender and Scottish education', in T. G. K. Bryce and W. M. Hume (eds), *Scottish Education* (Edinburgh: Edinburgh University Press, 1999), pp. 857–68.

NOTES

1. D. McCrone, 'Culture, nationalism and Scottish education: homogeneity and diversity', in T. G. K. Bryce and W. M. Humes (eds), *Scottish Education* (Edinburgh: Edinburgh University Press, 1999), pp. 235–43.
2. Quoted in L. Moore, 'Invisible scholars: girls learning Latin and mathematics in the elementary public schools of Scotland before 1872', *History of Education* 13:2 (1984), 121–37, here p. 121.
3. H. Corr, 'Dominies and domination: schoolteachers, masculinity and women in 19th-century Scotland', *History Workshop Journal* 40 (1995), 151–64.

4. H. M. Paterson, 'Secondary education', in H. Holmes (ed.), *Scottish Life and Society: Institutions of Scotland, vol. 11: Education* (East Linton: Tuckwell Press, 2000), pp. 136–53.

5. R. D. Anderson, *Education and the Scottish People: 1750–1918* (Oxford: Clarendon Press, 1995), pp. 107–42; J. H. McDermid, 'The Schooling of Working-Class Girls in Nineteenth-Century Scotland: The Interaction of Nationality, Class and Gender', Ph.D. thesis, Institute of London, August 2000.

6. In Scotland, unlike England, a public school was one under the management of an educational authority.

7. 'Higher class' was a classification, not a reference to social class, although higher-class school pupils were predominately middle-class.

8. L. Moore, 'The Aberdeen University local examinations 1880–1911', *Northern Scotland* 15 (1995), 45–61.

9. Royal Commission on Secondary Education, *Minutes of Evidence*, vol. 6, *P.P.*, 1895, para. 14271.

10. A. McPherson and J. D. Willms, 'Equalisation and improvement: some effects of comprehensive reorganisation in Scotland', *Sociology* 21:4 (1987), 509–39, here p. 530.

11. A. Bain, *Patterns of Error: The Teacher and External Authority in Central Scotland, 1581–1861* (Edinburgh: Moubray House Publishing, 1989), p. 26.

12. A contested point. There is a considerable literature emphasising the gender difference in literacy rates, chiefly based on the writing of signatures (signing), which was arguably a different skill (L. Williams, 'Scottish literacy', in Holmes (ed.), *Scottish Life and Society*, pp. 344–59).

13. Anderson, *Education and the Scottish People*, pp. 109, 118. In 1869, 54 per cent of Catholic men but only 38 per cent of women could sign their names at marriage (compared with Protestant results of over 90 and 80 per cent respectively).

14. R. Houston, 'The literacy myth?: illiteracy in Scotland 1630–1760', *Past and Present* 96 (August 1982), 81–102.

15. D. J. Withrington, 'Education and society in the eighteenth century', in N. T. Phillipson and R. Mitchison (eds), *Scotland in the Age of Improvement: Essays in Scottish History in the Eighteenth Century* (Edinburgh: Edinburgh University Press, 1970), pp. 225–44; E. C. Sanderson, *Women and Work in Eighteenth-century Edinburgh* (Basingstoke: Macmillan, 1996), pp. 74–107.

16. J. Barclay, *A Treatise on Education: or, an Easy Method of Acquiring Language . . .* (London: P. Vaillant, 1749), pp. 235–8.

17. J. Dwyer, *Virtuous Discourse: Sensibility and Community in Late Eighteenth-century Scotland* (Edinburgh: John Donald, 1987).

18. S. J. Smith, 'Retaking the register: women's higher education in Glasgow and beyond, c. 1796–1845', *Gender and History* 12:2 (July 2000), 310–35.

19. L. Moore, 'Young ladies' institutions: the development of secondary schools for girls in Scotland, 1833–c.1870', *History of Education* 32:3 (May 2003), 249–72.

20. This topic awaits research; but see A. J. Dalgleish, 'Voluntary Associations and the Middle Class in Edinburgh, 1780–1820', Ph.D. thesis, University of Edinburgh, 1991, pp. 157, 208; 'Female schools for cleanliness, morals, and decorum', *Scots Magazine*, March 1804, pp. 198-202, April 1804, pp. 249–53, May 1804, pp. 329-33; J. Goodman, 'Undermining or building up the nation? Elizabeth Hamilton (1758–1816), national identities and an authoritative role for women educationalists', *History of Education* 28:3 (September 1999), 279–96; L. Orr MacDonald, *A Unique and Glorious Mission: Women and Presbyterianism in Scotland 1830–1930* (Edinburgh: John Donald, 2000), pp. 41–62; L. Moore, 'Educating for the "woman's sphere": domestic training versus intellectual discipline', in E. Breitenbach and E. Gordon (eds), *Out of Bounds: Women in Scottish Society 1800–1945* (Edinburgh: Edinburgh University Press, 1992), pp. 10–41; R. Russell, 'Women of the Scottish Enlightenment: Their Importance in the History of Scottish Education', Ph.D. thesis, University of Glasgow, 1988.

21. Moore, 'Invisible scholars'.

22. SED, *Secondary Education (Scotland) Report for the Year 1905 by J. Struthers* (HMSO, Cd 2793), p. 249.

23. J. Stocks, 'Technical schools and the teaching of science in Scotland', in Holmes (ed.), *Scottish Life and Society*, pp. 218–36.

24. National Archives of Scotland [NAS], ED7/1/26, 'Secondary curricula'.

25. L. Croxford, 'Gender and national curriculum', in J. Salisbury and S. Riddell (eds), *Gender, Policy and Educational Change: Shifting Agendas in the UK and Europe* (London and New York: Routledge, 2000), pp. 115–33.

26. Letters, *Educational News*, 26 April, 17 and 31 May, 21 June 1912, pp. 374, 454, 514, 592–3.

27. I. Thomson, 'The origins of physical education in state schools', *Scottish Educational Review* 10:2 (November 1978), 15–24.

28. P. Bilsborough, 'School sport for boys in Glasgow, 1866–1914', *Physical Education Review* 11:2 (Autumn 1988), 97–105; J. A. Mangan, 'Missionaries to the middle classes', in Holmes (ed.), *Scottish Life and Society*, pp. 415–34.

29. I. Thomson, 'Power, control and status in physical education', *Scottish Educational Review* 35:1 (May 2003), 48–59.

30. W. Watson, *Glimpses o' Auld Lang Syne* (Aberdeen: Aberdeen University Press, 1905), p. 71; J. A. Norrie, *Memories of the Old High School (1880–1889): Some of the Grand Old Masters* (Dundee: William Kidd and Sons, 1924), p. v.

31. W. Jolly, *The Public School: Its Organization, Management and Teaching: Being Suggestions to School Boards bearing on the Efficiency of Common Schools* (Edinburgh: T. Laurie, 1874), pp. 19–20.

32. L. Paterson, *Scottish Education in the Twentieth Century* (Edinburgh: Edinburgh University Press, 2003), pp. 122, 142.

33. J. Darling and A. Glendinning, *Gender Matters in Schools: Pupils and Teachers* (London: Cassell, 1996), p. 74.

34. R. D. Anderson, 'Secondary schools and Scottish society in the nineteenth century', *Past and Present* 109 (1985), 176–203.

35. J. Allardyce, *Bygone Days in Aberdeenshire: Being a History of the County from a Standpoint Different from that of Previously Published Works* (Aberdeen: The Central Press, 1913), p. 149.

36. R. T. D. Glaister, 'Rural private teachers in 18th-century Scotland', *Journal of Educational Administration and History* 3:2 (1991), 49–61.

37. Data extracted from A. Law, 'Teachers in Edinburgh in the eighteenth century', *Book of the Old Edinburgh Club* 32 (1966), 108–57.

38. J. Grant, *History of the Burgh Schools of Scotland* (London and Glasgow: William Collins, 1876), pp. 527–31.

39. 'Female schools for cleanliness, morals, and decorum', p. 249.

40. The 1851 Educational Census returns listed fifty-eight schoolmistresses and fifty-nine unpaid female teachers and pupil teachers working alongside 1,270 male teachers and pupil teachers – an example of how official policy might be circumvented.

41. *Answers Made by Schoolmasters in Scotland to Queries Circulated in 1838, by Order of the Select Committee on Education in Scotland*, 2 vols (1841), P.P. 1841, xix; H. Corr, 'An exploration into Scottish education', in W. H. Fraser and R. J. Morris (eds), *People and Society in Scotland, vol. 2, 1830–1914* (Edinburgh: John Donald, 1990), pp. 290–309; L. Paterson, *Scottish Education in the Twentieth Century*, pp. 123, 147.

42. H. Corr, 'The sexual division of labour in the Scottish teaching profession 1872–1914', in W. M. Humes and H. M. Paterson (eds), *Scottish Culture and Scottish Education 1800–1980* (Edinburgh: John Donald, 1983), pp. 137–50; J. Scotland, *The History of Scottish Education, vol. I* (London: University of London Press, 1969), pp. 279–85.

43. Quoted in A. Roberts, 'Scotland and infant education in the nineteenth century', *Scottish Educational Studies* 4 (1972), 39–45, here p. 43.

44. J. McDermid, 'Catholic working-class girls' education in lowland Scotland, 1872–1900', *The Innes Review* 47:1 (Spring 1996), 69–80, and her ' "Intellectual instruction is best left to a man": the feminisation of the Scottish teaching profession in the second half of the nineteenth century', *Women's History Review* 6:1 (1997), 95–114. In 1851, women were 35 per cent of Scottish teachers and 62 per cent of English teachers.

45. Corr, 'Dominies and domination'; Corr, 'The sexual division of labour'; J. Fewell and F. M. S. Paterson (eds), *Girls in their Prime: Scottish Education Revisited* (Edinburgh: Scottish Academic Press, 1990); M. Cruickshank, *A History of the Training of Teachers in Scotland* (London: University of London, 1970).

46. Corr, 'The sexual division of labour'; C. Adams, 'Divide and rule: the marriage ban 1918–1945', in Fewell and Paterson (eds), *Girls in their Prime*, pp. 89–108.

47. P. Burnhill and A. McPherson, 'Careers and gender: the expectations of able Scottish school-leavers in 1971 and 1981', in S. Acker and D. W. Piper (eds), *Is Higher Education Fair to Women?* (Guildford: SRHE and NFER-Nelson, 1984), pp. 83–115, here p. 84.

48. M. G. Clarke, *A Short Life of Ninety Years* (London: A. and M. Huggins, 1973), p. 34.

49. Darling and Glendinning, *Gender Matters in Schools*, p. 44.

50. Clarke, *A Short Life of Ninety Years*, p. 39; Corr, 'Dominies and domination'. In 1920, 96 per cent of grant-aided intermediate schools (offering a three-year secondary course) and 85 per cent of grant-aided full secondary schools were mixed-sex.

51. Darling and Glendinning, *Gender Matters in Schools*, pp. 44, 54–75.

52. D. Withrington, 'Church and state in Scottish education before 1872', in Holmes (ed.), *Scottish Life and Society*, pp. 47–64.

53. L. Moore, 'Women in education', in Holmes (ed.), *Scottish Life and Society*, pp. 316–43. The domestic-science colleges established in the 1870s and 1880s were an exception.

54. See note 20 above.

55. J. Goodman, 'Women governors and the management of working-class schools, 1800–1861', in J. Goodman and S. Harrop (eds), *Women, Educational Policy-Making and Administration in England: Authoritative Women since 1880* (London and New York: Routledge, 2000), pp. 15–35.

56. Anderson, *Education and the Scottish People*, pp. 165–73; A. Bain, *Towards Democracy in Scottish Education: The Social Composition of Popularly Elected School Boards in Fife (1873–1918)* (Auchterderran: Fife Council Education Service, 1998).

57. H. Corr, ' "Home rule in Scotland": the teaching of housework in Scottish schools 1872–1914', in Fewell and Paterson (eds), *Girls in their Prime*, pp. 38–53; M. Smitley, 'Women in Victorian and Edwardian politics: female electors and representatives in Scotland 1881–1914', paper read at 'Re-Presenting the British Past: Women, Gender and History in the British Isles' conference, University of Glamorgan, 2–4 April 2004.

58. Calculated from *The Scottish Educational Directory and Year-Book for 1920* (Aberdeen: Aberdeen Free Press Office, [1920]).

59. T. R. Bone, *School Inspection in Scotland, 1840–1966* (London: London University Press, 1968); NAS, ED7/4/16, 'Women Inspectors'.

60. D. M. Britton, 'The epistemology of the gendered organization', *Gender and Society*, 14:3 (June 2000), 418–34.

61. In practice, as the debacle of the female medical students at the University of Edinburgh in the 1870s illustrated, right of access did not always remain constant.

62. For example, R. D. Anderson, *Education and Opportunity in Victorian Scotland: Schools and Universities* (Oxford: Clarendon Press, 1983); A. McPherson and C. D. Raab, *Governing Education: A Sociology of Policy since 1945* (Edinburgh: Edinburgh University Press, 1988).

63. M. Macintosh, 'The gender imbalance in Scottish education', *Scottish Affairs* 5 (Autumn 1993), 118–23; Fewell and Paterson (eds), *Girls in their Prime*. W. M. Humes, *The Leadership Class in Scottish Education* (Edinburgh: John Donald, 1986) provides a detailed analysis of the 'policy community' in the 1980s but generally ignores the gender bias.

64. C. Dyhouse, *No Distinction of Sex? Women in British Universities, 1870–1939* (London: UCL Press, 1995); Moore, 'Women in education'.

65. E. Benger, *Memoirs of the Late Elizabeth Hamilton with a Selection from her Correspondence and other Unpublished Writings* (London: Longman, Hurst, Rees, Orme and Brown, 1818), vol. 2, pp. 141–2.

66. J. Rendall, 'Bluestockings and reviewers: gender, power and knowledge in Edinburgh, c. 1800–1830', paper read at 'Culture, Gender, Power' conference, Glasgow, 11–13 October 2002.

67. C. G. Brown and J. D. Stephenson, ' "Sprouting wings": women and religion in Scotland c. 1890–1950', in Breitenbach and Gordon, *Out of Bounds*, pp. 95–120.

68. J. B. Barclay, 'Adult Education in South-East Scotland: The Development and Techniques of Adult Education with Special Reference to South-East Scotland', Ph.D. thesis, University of Edinburgh, 1960, pp. 371–6.

69. L. Tett, 'Where have all the men gone? Adult participation in community education', *Scottish Journal of Adult and Continuing Education* 1:2 (Autumn 1994), 41–8.

70. Smith, 'Retaking the register'; Moore, 'Young ladies' institutions'.

71. S. Hamilton, 'The first generation of university women 1869–1930', in G. Donaldson (ed.), *Four Centuries: Edinburgh University Life* (Edinburgh: University of Edinburgh, 1983), pp. 99–115; Moore, 'Women in education'; L. Moore, 'The Scottish universities and women students, 1862–1892', in J. Carter and D. Withrington (eds), *Scottish Universities: Distinctiveness and Diversity* (Edinburgh: John Donald, 1992), pp. 138–46; L. Moore, *Bajanellas and Semilinas: Aberdeen University and the Education of Women 1860–1920* (Aberdeen: Aberdeen University Press, 1991); C. D. Myers, 'The Glasgow Association for the Higher Education of Women, 1878–1883', *The Historian* 63 (Winter 2001), 357–71.

72. Burnhill and McPherson, 'Careers and gender'.

73. For women students, see the bibliography in Moore, 'Women in education', and theses by C. Logan, C. Myers and J. Wakeling on the University of Glasgow and M. Penman on the University of St Andrews.

74. For university academics before 1920, see Dyhouse, *No Distinction of Sex?* and Moore, *Bajanellas and Semilinas*, pp. 48–53. See also M. B. Gauld, 'One hundred years of women: the quest for equality', *Aberdeen University Review* 55:4, no. 192 (Autumn 1994), 370–6.

75. Moore, 'Educating for the "woman's sphere" ', pp. 18–19.

76. E. Turner, S. Riddell and S. Brown, *Gender Equality in Scottish Schools: The Impact of Recent Educational Reforms* (Manchester: EOC, 1995); S. Riddell, 'Gender and Scottish education', in Bryce and Humes (eds), *Scottish Education*, pp. 857–68.

6

Medicine, Science and the Body

Eileen Janes Yeo

The development of Scottish science and medicine has often been presented as a great success story. And rightly so, in many ways. The Scottish Enlightenment gave birth to the modern social sciences, first to a sociological (conjectural) history and later to the sciences of political economy and government. Scottish medicine can boast a parade of firsts, among them breakthroughs in obstetrics, anaesthetics and antisepsis, and a cluster of first-rate training institutions that turned out practitioners who then worked round the world. As David Hamilton proclaimed, 'Scots doctors were the pace-setters in the medical services of England, the Empire and the armed forces', a verdict that was endorsed by Derek Dow: 'Scottish medical schools have for more than two centuries played a role in global healthcare out of all proportion to the size of our country or its population'.[1] Indeed, Scotland can even claim the first battles fought by women for entry into British medical schools, led by the redoubtable Sophia Jex-Blake.

This chapter will refocus the story, highlighting the importance of constructions of gender. Science and medicine are key discourses of modernity, that is, important systems of knowledge which become embedded in cultural institutions, like medical, educational and media institutions, where experts with cultural authority, like doctors and teachers, exert power in people's lives. This knowledge contains understandings of male and female human nature and potential, and has been influential in determining what social roles men and women have been encouraged to play. This chapter will explore the developing 'scientific' knowledge about gender and human nature by monitoring demarcation disputes around sensitive boundary lines where gender issues featured. The chapter will treat medicine as a paradigm case, and patrol contested boundaries in chronological order, between woman and man midwives, licensed and complementary practitioners, male and female doctors, and between men and women in other health professions, like nursing and health visiting. Finally, the chapter will place medicine in a wider scientific context, also inflected by gender.

MAN AND WOMAN MIDWIVES: AN EIGHTEENTH-CENTURY STORY

The conventional narrative about eighteenth-century Scottish medicine is about heroic institutional and individual pioneers. It stresses the establishment of university and extra-mural teaching (especially but not exclusively in Edinburgh and later in Glasgow); it profiles the individuals who stood out, like the Monro dynasty. It tracks the development of gate-keeping colleges which licensed practitioners, even if sometimes rather casually by offering mail-order surgical diplomas.[2] All of these institutions were exclusively for men, with one exception. Women could get the same training in midwifery as male medical students in Edinburgh, Aberdeen and Glasgow, and become licensed both in Edinburgh and the West of Scotland.[3] Otherwise, in the usual historiography, women have been pushed to the margins of modernity, as traditional healers in the countryside and in the private sphere of the family.

This interpretation can conceal episodes of contention, like the controversy about the legitimacy of men versus women midwives that raged in the mid-eighteenth century. Although men had been active in complicated deliveries earlier,[4] a trio of Scottish man midwives set up their practices and training establishments in London and created the medical speciality which came to be called obstetrics and gynaecology. William Smellie, James Douglas and his more famous pupil William Hunter, who became the royal accoucheur, rested their expertise on their scientific approach.[5] It is always important to ask what people meant by science. In this case, science meant training with visual aids and technology (instruments) to assist performance. Man midwives attended courses in which pictures of the pregnant body and the process of birth were important, as were mechanical models of women, for practising the use especially of Smellie's various models of forceps. To establish their scientific legitimacy, the man midwives railed at the mismatch of women with science ('the province of a man').[6]

Of course, 'scientific' man-midwifery was challenged, by traditional midwives as well as by professional and protective men. Elizabeth Nihell quickly entered the fray with *A Treatise on the Art of Midwifery* (1760). Targeting Smellie, the grounds of her objections were threefold: first, the theoretical and thus useless nature of his training. Nihell asked what analogy there could be 'between a mere machine and a body, sensible delicate, animated and well organised?'[7] For her, knowledge was tactile rather than visual: 'the touch then, is the most nice and essential point of the art of midwifery'. As appropriate training, 'our great practice, or lying-in hospitals, where there is full liberty for the young female practitioners to make observations, can render it familiar to the learner. I presume I may take for granted', she continued, raising the issue of sexualised touching, 'that such a practical study is not extremely decent, not proper for young lads.'[8]

Second, she attacked their instruments ('especially their forceps, whether Flemish, Dutch, Irish, French or English, bare or covered, long or short, straight or crooked, windowed or not windowed are totally useless or rather worse than good for nothing, being never but dangerous and destructive'). 'Nature', Nihell insisted, 'if her expulsive efforts are but, in due time, and when required, gently and skilfully, seconded by the hands alone, will do more, and with less pain than all the art of the instrumentarians with their whole armory of deadly weapons'.[9] Ironically, she considered the instruments to be blind in their operations despite the man midwives putting such an emphasis on visualisation rather than touch in their training.

Finally, Nihell attacked the unsavoury types of men who presented themselves for training: 'broken barbers, tailors, even pork butchers, for I know myself one of this last trade, who after passing half his life in stuffing sausages, is turned an intrepid physician and man-midwife'.[10] Her argument, that women were the only proper persons to handle the intimate parts of other women, was reinforced by the supposed fulminations of irate husbands who equated medical with sexual touching. The anonymous *Petition of the Unborn Babes to the Censors of the Royal College of Physicians* (1751) objected to accoucheurs, who were permitted 'to treat our wives in such a manner as frequently ends in their destruction, and to have such intercourse with our women, as easily shifts itself into indecency, from indecency into debauchery'. Smellie was attacked for his indecent digital manipulations; Hunter was cited for his shady collusion with secret childbirths.[11]

Whether Scottish women midwives vented such spleen is unclear. The doctors who gave lectures in midwifery to medical students and women, like Glasgow University's father and son Professors Thomas and William Hamilton, tended to train in London under Hunter and Smellie. Their students were taught in the London way, using the midwifery machine and 'leather child' before being allowed to do live deliveries on the poor either in infirmaries or at home. The Scottish man midwives were seeking, unlike some of their English counterparts, 'to educate, rather than eradicate' women practitioners.[12] But the majority of Scottish women midwives never sought these qualifications, and licensing died out in 1826 although lectures continued into the 1830s.

Hunter and Smellie invoked 'science' to try to rebuff accusations of lascivious touching. The illustrations used in Hunter's classroom are especially worth further scrutiny. As Ludmilla Jordanova has observed,[13] the earlier representation of the pregnant body had usually shown the foetus as a miniature adult floating in the space of the womb, which was depicted as only a small part of a full woman. The drawings that convey Hunter's understanding of the baby *in utero* are quite shocking to the modern eye (see Fig. 6.1 overleaf). The woman resembles butchered meat; only a small section of her body is shown, and, where the cross-section ends, the rest of the body is simply sawn off, making the depicted part look more like leg of mutton than leg of mother! The vagina and pudenda are also sliced through, giving the impression of a gaping hole. By contrast, the images in midwifery training manuals, whether Smellie's of 1752 or that used by Prof. Munro Kerr in the early twentieth century at the University of Glasgow, represented the mother more 'respectfully' by either draping the figure or representing the whole woman, even if sketchily.

Hunter, who also pioneered schools of anatomy and dissection as a part of medical training, wished to portray what was indisputably natural and therefore scientific. But he ended up conveying a kind of hyper-materiality in which the woman was reduced to an animalistic birth machine without other attributes. In 1776, he even supervised the first successful artificial insemination, a procedure possible because he held an emerging 'modern' view of women's role in conception. Hunter no longer saw women as contributing seed that needed to be heated by passion and pleasure to achieve fertilisation. Rather, he saw women more as passive receptacles to be impregnated.[14] But of course he was not the only culprit.

His work was part of the scientific underpinning of tendencies coming from elsewhere in the culture to re-view women as primarily maternal and passionless, full of soft sensibility rather than teeming with sexuality. In Hunter's images, as Jordanova has pointed out, there was a suffocating intimacy between mother and child that again fortified the maternal dimension of womanliness which became the dominant nineteenth-century understanding of femininity. Other influential Scottish doctors reinforced this important role for women. William Buchan, whose best-selling *Domestic Medicine* (1769) went through some 142 English-language editions, proclaimed that 'nothing can be more preposterous than a mother who thinks it below her to take care of her own child' or who is 'so ignorant as not to know what is proper'.[15] Significantly, the medical establishment of Edinburgh pilloried Dr Buchan for trying to democratise health-consciousness in this way.[16]

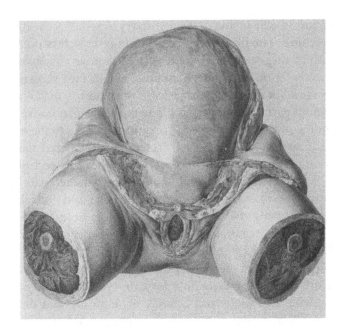

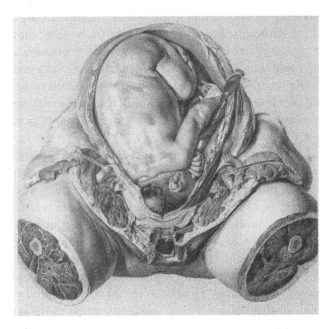

Figure 6.1 (a) and (b):   *From William Hunter,* The Anatomy of the Human Gravid Uterus *(Birmingham: John Baskerville, 1774).*
Permission to reproduce from Glasgow University Library, special collections (Hunterian)

PROFESSIONALISATION AND EXCLUSION: ERECTING THE BORDERLINE BETWEEN SCIENCE AND QUACKERY

Although the attempt to establish scientific and professionalised medicine was well under way in Scotland in the eighteenth century, conventional accounts in the history of medicine spotlight the early nineteenth century as the critical formative period. Not only did courses of training proliferate, but also medical periodicals, especially the *Lancet*, edited from 1823 by Dr Thomas Wakley, engaged in aggressive medical politics to support 'scientific' practice, to dismantle the hierarchy based on social status and to discredit complementary therapies, or what was called 'quackery' at the time. Medical societies, banding together as the British and Provincial Medical Association in 1832, and medico-ethical societies, which spread nationwide in the late 1840s, not only established codes of conduct but also policed them, sometimes in quite brutal ways.[17]

The Manchester Medico-Ethical Society expelled its own vice president for having unknowingly consulted with a homeopathist, while Dr John Elliotson, the esteemed Professor of Medicine at University College in London, who introduced the stethoscope into medical practice, was forced to resign from his post after being attacked in the *Lancet* for giving public demonstrations of mesmerism. The Association for the Protection of Homeopathic Students and Practitioners was a response to the Edinburgh University Medical Faculty's refusal to award an MD to Alfred Pope, who refused to swear *never* to practise homeopathy.[18] Although Edinburgh and Glasgow could boast Colleges of Physicians and Surgeons that were already licensing practitioners in the eighteenth century, the nationalisation of the process culminated in the 1858 Medical Act, which established criteria for degrees and licences, and created a Medical Register of practitioners holding approved qualifications. As important for the policing of medical outlaws, an 1878 amendment to the Act made it possible to prosecute unregistered practitioners who called themselves doctors or charged for their healing services.

All of these developments had gender implications. The therapies which medical gatekeepers targeted as illegitimate were all more accessible in terms of gender and class as well as founded on more democratic epistemologies. The emerging medical establishment was an early target for working-class radicals. The *True Scotsman*, the Edinburgh Chartist paper, launched constant attacks on monopolists of knowledge, published articles on how to be your own doctor, and welcomed advertisements from women healers like Mrs Lee, who described her treatments as so mild that they did not 'prevent any from their daily occupation'.[19]

In Scotland, however, there was no clear dividing line between trained medics and complementary therapists. Despite unremitting attacks from the *Lancet*, a significant number of trained doctors, who accepted orthodox theories of disease, nonetheless rejected therapeutics like surgery and chemical drugs and opted instead for gentler treatments like hydropathy's water baths and wraps.[20] Although hydropathy now has its historians,[21] much of the terrain of Scottish complementary medicine and its gender dimensions remains to be mapped.

In the hydropathic world, as the *Aberdeen Sanitary Reformer* reported in 1862, women were acknowledged professionals, especially in the United States, where the New York Hygeio-Therapeutic College boasted a woman professor of obstetrics and published a list of 100 licensed practitioners, of whom twenty were women.[22] In Scottish and English spas, female practitioners administered treatments to women and children; and some, like Mrs John Smedley, achieved considerable eminence, not least with her best-selling *Manual of Practical Hydropathy for Ladies and Children*.[23] Similarly, Mary Sergeant Gove Nichols, who lived and practised in Glasgow for several years, wrote *A Woman's Work in Water Cure and Sanitary Education* (1869). She recounted how, after several of her babies had died, she educated herself in medicine using her attending physician's library and observed that, despite corporate prejudice, individual 'scientific men have assisted me in the attainment of knowledge and rejoiced in my usefulness, though they could give me no diploma'. Although nervous about stepping into the public spotlight, she then gave lectures on anatomy, physiology and on the prevention and cure of disease to 'prepare women for the better performance of the duties of their proper sphere as wives and mothers'.[24]

Nichols was also a spiritualist. Alex Owen's study of spiritualism has begun to take stock of the world of complementary healing in mid-nineteenth-century London, an inventory which now needs to be extended to Scotland. What is striking is that more than half of the London practitioners who advertised themselves in the spiritualist press, and who would also have employed other complementary healing techniques, were women.[25] This prominence was not surprising, as the world of complementary healing prized some of the qualities culturally assigned to women. Most of the fringe therapies treated the whole patient, relied on mobilising invisible energy and spiritual power and used natural and gentle remedies. Women, with their supposedly larger endowment of spiritual and psychic power, their gentleness and closer relationship to nature, could easily enter this therapeutic world. Thus, for example, Mrs Olive, who healed while in trance, was famous for curing tumours.

One of her satisfied patients urged others to avoid being 'tortured' by medics who administered 'remedies worse than the disease' and instead to take 'advantage of her 'painless and more certain means of cure'.[26] Scottish hydropathists railed against medicalised childbirth, where 'hundreds of the loveliest in the land are from year to year martyred, and thousands more are frightfully tortured'; and testimonials from Scottish mothers (including vicars' wives) insisted that hydropathic childbirth was 'like a *pleasant dream*', 'as if nothing had occurred'.[27]

A continuing feature of complementary medicine was that it gave an active role to mothers in the healing process and tried to facilitate home ministration, of course profiting along the way. Rev. Alexander Munro of Aberdeen proposed a kind of sexual division of healing where 'members of the medical profession' would manage public hygiene while domestic and individual hygiene would be the responsibility of trained mothers and nurses, who would literally become the doctors in the house.[28] A rash of homeopathic manuals appeared – Nicolls has traced at least forty titles by the 1870s – which could be bought from homeopathic chemists along with medicine chests 'for Professional or Domestic Use'.[29] Hydropathic magazines and manuals were filled with do-it-yourself instructions; and pieces of apparatus, like sitz baths, were available for purchase. In 1875, Mary Nichols's husband began the Co-operative Sanitary Company, which marketed health products including the 'Turco-Russian or Hot Air and Vapour Bath, Food of Health, Wheaten Groats, Bean Bags, Pocket Swimming Life Preserver, Fair Air Pillow'.[30]

Hydropaths were also keen supporters of more formal medical training for women, whose special mission would be to treat other women and children, indeed who had a 'natural superiority to men for work of this kind'.[31] Partly, proponents hoped to slip hydropathic training into medical schools, tied to the women's apron-strings, so to speak. Alexander Munro was an incessant advocate, and even urged women to sidestep diplomas in the meantime and let free trade rather than monopoly dictate their fate and protect the public against quackery, since an incompetent hydropathist 'cannot succeed in establishing a remunerative practice'.[32] Perhaps this was special pleading, as Munro himself was being attacked as unqualified, to which he replied that he had taken courses in all the conventional medical subjects 'that I might occupy no false or dubious position', but did not present himself for examination because he thought that the examiners would fail him, knowing him to be a practising hydropathist.[33] The very presence of women in fringe medicine and the emphasis on home cure acted as a red rag to the professional medical bull, who saw them as evidence of ignorance and backwardness.

MEN AND WOMEN IN MEDICINE, 1869 ONWARDS

The debate about the proper place of men and women in the medical field reached apoplectic proportions from 1869 onwards, when Sophia Jex-Blake and her female colleagues presented themselves for medical training at the University of Edinburgh. They chose Scotland because of its reputation for 'enlightened views' and Edinburgh for its 'freedom from ecclesiastical and other trammels'.[34] The ensuing controversy not only split the medical faculty, the university and the city but also resonated nationwide. The protracted struggle has received token mention in histories of Scottish medicine, although it has loomed larger in research about women's access to higher education and the medical profession.[35] This section will not trace every step forward and back in the campaign for medical education and registration for women. However, it is worth noting that the pathway was full of obstacles and ambushes, epitomised by the last-ditch attempt of the women in 1876 to sit a midwifery examination which would qualify them for the Medical Register. On that occasion, not only did Dr Andrew Wood pronounce that obstetrics 'was just the branch of practice for which women were *least* fitted', but also the examiners resigned *en masse*, making it impossible for the examination to take place.[36] Rather, this section will highlight how the arguments on both sides of the battle revolved around the supposedly 'natural' division of labour between the sexes, the consequent way in which they should work together in the medical world and a correlative issue, the question of what offended the delicacy and sensibility 'natural' to women.

Even the opponents of women doctors did not argue that woman's place was only in the home. By the mid-nineteenth century, the sexual communion of labour was the talking point, namely how men and women with their masculine and feminine qualities could best work together in the public world.[37] The emergent nursing profession under the leadership of Florence Nightingale had used this communion formula to establish their legitimacy, positioning the doctor as the father-curer and the qualified nurse-mother as the moral and sanitary healer. Even the medical journal, the *Lancet*, agreed that women's sanitary visiting to spread the laws of health to the homes of the poor would give a human and loving face to public health and would 'proselytise in quarters where masculine and rougher apostles could scarcely gain a hearing'.[38]

In 1878, however, the *Lancet* made one of the clearest statements of how gender difference and sexual communion endorsed women nurses but not women doctors. At the point where the British Medical Association refused to admit some of the Edinburgh-trained women into membership, the *Lancet* argued that women were destined by God and nature to play the role of helpmeets to men, not leaders, and that everything followed from this essential point:

> In the economy of nature – whether expounded by the Oracular utterance, or evolved by experience – the ministry of woman is one of help and sympathy . . . The moment she affects the first or leading *rôle* in any vocation she is out of place, and the secondary, but essential part of helpmeet cannot be filled.[39]

The editorial went on to claim that, in many ways, men would be better nurses as they had greater strength than women, steadier hands, equally gentle touch and ample tact; but men were simply unsuited to obedience! 'Man's nature', announced the *Lancet*, 'rebels against the complete surrender of his own judgment and that implicit obedience in spirit, as well as letter, which are the first essentials of a good nurse.' The obedience of nurses was perhaps more ideology than reality: the aptly named Rebecca Strong, matron of the Glasgow infirmary, even resigned when she did not get her way; and matrons were usually of higher social status than the doctors with whom they worked.[40] According to the sexual division proposed by the *Lancet*, nursing alone coincided with another contemporary female identity used to authorise women's public work, that of social mothers.[41] Patients were depicted as children:

> it is woman's prerogative to nurse, whether the helpless being at her mercy be an infant, or an adult reduced to the level of childhood by disease. Women cannot desert the position of nurses of the sick unless they also abandon the rearing and tending of the young.

The supporters of women doctors also subscribed to the idea that human nature was divided by gender. Like all participants in the debate, they managed to dress custom up as nature and to project onto nature all kinds of social conventions that gained authority from the transfer. Jex-Blake insisted that women had been the natural healers in the family and in many cultures from time immemorial, and, most importantly, that women were the most appropriate practitioners to treat other women. The essential delicacy and purity of nature dictated that women should treat women and men minister to men as 'the *natural* course',[42] although she hastily added that she did not think it 'morally wrong for men to be the medical attendants of women'.

Unfortunately, in their eagerness to prove their suitability for medicine, women doctors tended to demote the sister profession of nursing, which their opponents held out as the permitted line of advance. Jex-Blake argued that, since 'women are *naturally* inclined and fitted for medical practice', why should they 'be limited to merely the mechanical details and wearisome routine of nursing while to men is reserved all intelligent knowledge of disease, and all study of the laws by which health may be preserved or restored'?[43] In another way, however, nursing suited their tactical purposes. Continuing the earlier story where man midwives were accused of groping, now the issue of women's seeing and touching, especially in the dissecting room and the hospital ward, became the problem. The opponents of the Edinburgh students, like correspondents of the *Medical Times and Gazette*, painted lurid pictures of sexual trespass:

> by dissecting the human genital organs with *sang froid* which surely must be assumed in the presence of males, the female students have unsexed themselves in the eyes of the young men and thereby have denuded themselves of the privileges of their sex. It is sheer clap-trap to say that the holy pursuit of science, or the Professional succour of women warrants this.[44]

The proponents of women doctors argued that, since there was nothing indelicate about women nurses witnessing and treating nude male patients, why the fuss about women doctors? Jex-Blake was struck by the 'curious inconsistency', that Nightingale and her nurses were praised for 'going among the foulest sights and most painful scenes to succour, not their own sex, but the other'.[45] Supportive medical men made the same arguments. At a meeting of the Edinburgh Royal Infirmary in 1871, to consider allowing women to have clinical teaching there, Dr Sir James Coxe asked: 'are the nurses in the wards not females, and are they not present during the medical visits, without proving a restraint either on freedom of speech *or* freedom of action?'[46] A letter attacking both the Infirmary and the *Medical Times* argued that 'hundreds of elderly men had their ailments carefully attended to by female nurses, whom they usually preferred for their care and gentleness', and delivered the *coup de grâce* by citing a country surgeon who had been forced 'to teach a daughter to pass the catheter on her own father' with 'no demoralising result'.[47] Ministers of religion, like the Rev. Dr Charteris, also rallied to the women's side, enlarging on Jex-Blake's favourite mottos: 'to the pure, all things are pure' and '*honi soit qui mal y pense*'. A companion argument was that science was moral and that, therefore, there was nothing unseemly in women studying anything scientific.

And yet, medical science was moving away from women at the very moment they tried to nail their colours to its mast. An early pointer was the scandal about Edith Pechey, one of Jex-Blake's cohort. She came third in a chemistry examination but was denied the Hope Prize reserved for the top four candidates. The explanation was that, as she did not attend the chemistry class with the men, she did not attend the class at all – an argument which rightly offended the sense of justice of even some opponents of women doctors. The Hope Prize entitled the winners to laboratory privileges. Writing about the early 'Women in Medicine', Elaine Thomson makes the interesting argument that medical science was becoming more laboratory-based, more engaged with vivisection and ultimately more concerned with pathogens and drugs. Many women remained in an older tradition of physiology, partly because of the difficulties of laboratory access and partly because they were attracted to a gentler mode of treatment, which stressed physiological balance as the key to health, to be achieved by healthy diet, exercise, lots of fresh air and a minimum of drugs.[48] However, women doctors were not always professionally friendly to the army of women practitioners making their living through complementary healing, which even more fervently endorsed gentleness.

The vexed issue of mixed teaching rumbled on into the twentieth century. The way that women students finally gained entry to the Edinburgh Royal Infirmary was by the Scottish Association for the Medical Education of Women endowing two wards there. Dr Louise Eichoff recalled training in 1936, when women were still debarred from the Infirmary's Surgical Outpatients Department. She and some colleagues tried to enter 'inconspicuously'. The tutor, spotting them, threatened that he would withhold their diplomas. But

> undeterred, we attended regularly, worked assiduously, carefully maintaining our position at the back of the men at all times . . . We did extra duties in the Outpatients, giving ourselves most valuable practice, and at all times were quietly obedient and willing, deferring to any gentleman wanting a go. No banners and fights for women's rights for us!

Their reward was that 'our D. P. s were laid out along with the gentlemen's', and women were admitted thereafter.[49]

Yet on one occasion they did wave banners. In first-year anatomy in 1932, they still had a separate dissecting room, and in second year they were asked to stay away from certain lectures; but, after making representations, they received parallel lectures in an 'expurgated edition'. In the physiology class, the women students were relegated to a gallery where they could discreetly prepare some unusual visual aids for the final lecture. The lecturer and male students looked up to see 'a gas-filled balloon, a large stork carrying a baby and the caption "Physiology of Reproduction Simplified: The Stork Theory" '.[50] It is important to note that these women appreciated being able to 'retain our sensitivity and sensibility', and Eichoff expressed her 'deep appreciation of the tutors of that era who showed such fine feeling and understanding about women students' needs'.

By contrast, the St Andrews Medical School, located in Dundee, opened in 1898 and ran mixed classes from the start without incident. One of the first students, Elizabeth Bryson, recalled it as

> a Medical School that never knew what it was NOT to have women in lectures and hospitals. We were friends from the start and remained friends with our fellow students until the end, and never did I hear an unseemly word or an offensive joke.

Indeed, the first encounter with the dissecting room, which proved a traumatic right of passage in other medical schools, where male colleagues deliberately aggravated the ordeal, soon changed from an initially 'bewildering' experience into 'a fascinating voyage of discovery into an unknown country'. The journey also became so comfortable that men and women students often took their tea together among the cadavers.[51] Bryson met the man she eventually married on this medical-school journey.

WOMEN'S MEDICAL PROGRESS: TWO STEPS FORWARD, ONE STEP BACK?

Bryson was concerned to retain the 'ethereal essence' of femininity within her medical work. The terms on which women negotiated their entry and were also allowed into the medical profession were restrictive as well as expansive. New professional opportunities were opened, but the avenues of advance ran only in certain directions. The insistence of the pioneers that they had a special mission to attend to the bodies of women and children meant an ongoing limitation of professional opportunities. Bryson was a case in point. Not only did she graduate both as a BA and a MB from St Andrews, but also she qualified by research for an MD degree (in 1907) and had earned the highest references. Nonetheless, no resident position in an ordinary hospital was open at the time (even the Nottingham Children's Hospital 'could not appoint a woman').

Fortunately or unfortunately for her, a tailor-made advertisement appeared for 'a woman doctor, preferably Scottish, to go to New Zealand as an assistant for a term of three years in a large general practice'. After her mother had met and approved the head doctor and his wife, Bryson took the job and was 'treated as a daughter in their home'. Two younger brothers followed the same training route into Scottish medical careers without anyone treating them as putative children. It was a contradictory situation that, of course, involved gains as well as limitations. How far women had come can be measured by the starting point of Prof. Lister declaiming that 'not a single medical man would send a daughter to study in a mixed class'; such an action 'would be utterly revolting to all idea of maiden modesty', a sentiment shared by Sir Robert Christison, perhaps the most strident opponent of the women students. But, by 1921, his granddaughter, Irene V. E. Christison, was a leading light in the Edinburgh Women's Medical Society and was training to become a doctor.[52]

Work in the missionary field or in other capacities in the Empire or Commonwealth was an important option for medical women.[53] Sometimes this led to fascinating careers, as was the case with Glasgow-trained Dr Lydia Torrance Allen, who graduated in 1923 and went abroad to work in her father's hospital in Palestine and then to appointments in India, finally ending up back in Britain working as a consultant in Woolwich, having married an army major and picked up a competence in French, German, Arabic, Yiddish and Hindustani along the way.[54] Honoria S. Keer, another Glasgow graduate (1910), had a less happy experience when appointed in 1925 as a Lady Medical Officer in Nigeria. Her conditions of service stated bluntly that a marriage bar existed and that ladies 'are not eligible for the higher administrative medical appointments'. By 1931, she was being badgered to resign because of her growing deafness, and then ordered to leave and accept a small pension.[55]

At home, the job openings were predictable. The turn-of-the-twentieth-century eugenic panic about the efficiency of the British race further ratified the women's chosen place in medicine. Their declared special competence to treat mothers and children seemed even more vital now that national and imperial survival were at stake. In a lecture to the Edinburgh Women's Medical Society in 1916, Dr Haig Fergus, in upbeat mood, spoke of

> visions of great possibilities ahead of women doctors, as Health Visitors, as Teachers of Young Mothers, as Lecturers at Baby Clinics, we saw them settling such problems as the Domestic Training of Girls at School, the Feeding of poor mothers without thereby pauperising them, the Establishment and right use of Maternity Hospitals, wherever required, the rearing of a race of supermen, and finally, we saw them admitted by a grateful country to the sacred precincts of a future Ministry of Health.[56]

Women doctors felt strongly that the area of reproductive biology should be their province, not least because of their understanding of the emotional issues that were important for patients. While undoubtedly true, the idea that women were more emotionally responsive was yet another example of mobilising 'nature' in choosing the work appropriate for women. Elizabeth Bryson let the men 'have all the surgery they want – all the broken bones and hernias and obscure abdominal exploratory operations – even a lot of midwifery! – but the women must conquer in the field of Gynaecology'.[57] Dr Isabel Hutton was also sensitive to the psychological dimensions of well-being, and wrote pioneering sex manuals (*The Hygiene of Marriage* went through numerous editions), books on mental illness and on the menopause.[58]

Of course, some women tried to break beyond the barriers and dismantle the taboos (which were partly of their own making). The issue of handling male bodies was the most radioactive boundary. Anne Crowther has noted that the only women permitted to touch men's bodies were mothers, nurses, wives and prostitutes![59] Jex-Blake had been invited to set up a field hospital in Sarajevo during the Balkan risings of the 1870s, but refused because she worried that, by treating men, she would damage the professional chances of all medical women.[60] The First World War occasioned a repeat of the opportunity, with a different outcome. A formidable battler, Elsie Inglis[61] offered the British army field hospitals entirely staffed by women, an offer which they were happy to refuse. However, both the French and Serbian governments accepted her Scottish Women's Hospitals, and by 1916 her work had made its mark. The British War Office invited women doctors to volunteer. According to Moberly Bell, only one patient asked to be transferred because of being treated by women, and his decision was overruled by his mother![62] After the war experience, the hysteria about women doctors handling men's bodies died away.

Nonetheless, the war was no triumphant watershed for women in science or medicine. Carol Dyhouse and others writing about the inter-war period have called attention to the profound need of men to re-establish their masculinity in the wake of their experience of wartime carnage, involving the wholesale mutilation of male bodies and minds. Unfortunately, in London, medical men tried to rebuild their battered masculinity by expelling women from some of the hard-won training space as well as by creating a male-only culture of rugby matches and masonic rites. Whether this rhythm of one step forward and two steps back was also the Scottish movement still needs research. But articles in the *Edinburgh University Magazine*, however ironically they lampooned women students for being swots, also suggested the existence of a male-bonding culture which women probably could not join. A piece from

1929 entitled 'I don't like women' asked whether the woman medical student has

> ever revelled in the fun of a torch-light procession, and braved the subsequent letters of 'Shocked Parent' and of 'Anxious Father' in the *Despatch*? Has she ever thrown her dignity to the winds and pleaded with the callow youth of Edinburgh to risk its penny and its reputation in the . . . Waverley Carnival? Has she ever held up an affluent-looking gentleman and denuded him of petty cash, all in the name of the Infirmary? Has she been severely hacked about the shins while playing hockey for her 'Varsity'? By these will she be judged in after-life.[63]

The gender hierarchy re-cemented in this period is still proving hard to dismantle.

GENDER TENSIONS IN THE HEALTH-CARE PROFESSIONS: A LATE TWENTIETH-CENTURY STORY

Whatever their difficulties with advancement in the medical profession, women in the early twentieth century established a near-monopoly over a range of other health professions including nursing, health visiting and midwifery. A deep sense of national crisis, understood not only in economic and imperial terms but also eugenically in terms of the possible decline and fall of the British race, gave a tremendous impetus to women's occupations in the health field. After the South African War, which exposed the poor physical state of army recruits, the 1904 *Report* of the Interdepartmental Committee on Physical Deterioration helped put health, especially of mothers and children, at the centre of the national agenda. The welfare state was born partly out of statutory measures to address the issue of the quantity and quality of the British race. The Midwives (Scotland) Act of 1915, like the Midwives Act of 1902 for England and Wales, regulated the training, examining and licensing of midwives. Incidentally, the new requirements changed the social profile of the profession over time from older working-class mothers to younger middle-class single women, although Scottish 'howdies' still preserved the older mould.[64] From 1907 onwards, municipalities established health-visiting services as well as school feeding and medical examination, opening yet more job opportunities for women doctors and nurses.[65] Nursing became a full-fledged profession in 1919.

This safe zone of women's professions was breached in the 1960s by the entry of men, especially into health visiting and nursing. Until that time, traditionalists had thought of the health visitor as a 'well-baby nurse'; she was definitively gendered as female in all relevant legislation, so that a new name 'male health visiting officer' had to be coined for the newcomers. Issues about dealing with sexed bodies (and gender roles) of clients again surfaced in the debate about men's entry. In Aberdeen, both the Director of the Training School, D. Joan Lamont, and the Medical Officer of Health, Dr Ian MacQueen, argued that men were especially suited to dealing with older men, who could speak to them more freely about intimate problems, and to giving sex education lessons to teenage boys. Indeed, teams of men and women health visitors were invited to act as a kind of putative family, giving adequate support both to men and women in their family roles, aiming 'to strengthen the special attributes of each sex'![66]

The ingress of men has created new hierarchies which have undermined equal opportunities yet again but in a complex way. Progressive steps from one point of view entailed backsliding from another. The old-style health professional had been a single woman devoting herself totally, even sacrificially, to her vocation on the social motherhood model which had been developed in the 1850s. In the 1950s half the Scottish district nurses studied by Rona Ferguson were still unmarried and childless.[67] But, with the marriage bar breaking down in many occupations after the Second World War and in the context of labour shortage in the developing welfare state, it became possible for married women and mothers to contemplate a professional career. Part-time working was not only attractive to them but has also become the solution in the health and medical fields for retaining skilled staff and, theoretically, for facilitating career progression. The Royal College of Nursing's 1999 initiative to secure 'Gender equality in career progression' supported this solution.[68]

Unfortunately, it seems that women taking the part-time route are considered less committed, less reliable and less capable of high-level responsibility. Part-time nurses 'are caught in a "tender trap", getting left behind in terms of career progress'.[69] From the moment men entered these health professions, the fact that they would have fewer career breaks and provide 'a useful element of stability' was considered a recommendation.[70] And, even now, little has happened to counteract the conclusion in 2001 that, although nursing is predominantly a female profession, 'the gender profile is similar to that of other professions in so far as, the higher the level of management, the lower the proportion of women'.[71]

CONCLUSIONS AND WIDER REFLECTIONS

This chapter tells no Whiggish tale of scientific progress. Rather, the stories here are riddled with contest and contradiction. Every phase in the medical saga was part of a larger cultural context which contained additional reinforcing discourses, not least from the physical and social sciences. Taken together, these powerfully shaped understandings of men and women's human nature and their correlative places in scientific work. Some women actively negotiated these cultural pressures, exploiting contradictions and finding room and roles for themselves that were not originally intended. In midwifery, women tried to retain their own expertise and defend their medical epistemology. The eighteenth-century Scottish university, where attendance at lectures was more important than graduation, was paradoxically more open to women, who could and did show up for lectures.[72]

Historians are now drawing attention to Enlightenment ideas about the role of women in the progress of 'society' (as social formation and polite culture). But the Enlightenment was itself a contested development. Dr John Gregory, in his best-selling *A Father's Legacy to his Daughters* (1774), like Lord Kames, John Millar and others, regarded women as the softening agent who would bring gentleness and moral tone to civil society and would civilise strong male minds. The treatment of women would also be a litmus test of the stage that civilisation had reached.[73] Although a key agent and marker, women were still considered embedded in nature, their nurturing and child-bearing role essential but unchanging, whereas men were capable of historical development.

Gregory, like Millar, supported women's education, but also fenced it round with the idea that its aim was to equip women to carry out their maternal duties. The power of vital religion (see Chapter 4) was also hardening prescriptive ideas of gender division and confining women, in theory, to maternal duties in the home. This was not an ideological framework which invited women into public scientific or professional work. Nonetheless, women took advantage of any opportunities for study, formal and informal. They also made a place for themselves in public writing, even if their position was legitimised only when they wrote fiction or wrote on the public sciences, like political economy, in the form of tales for children or workers.[74]

There was also a radical fringe to the Scottish Enlightenment which championed a more democratic intellect and proposed widening educational opportunity to previously excluded women and working men. Sarah Smith has shown how John Anderson's Institution (ultimately the University of Strathclyde) opened in 1796 and appointed a succession of professors friendly to women's education who ran courses of lectures on natural philosophy, mathematics, geography and chemistry which attracted large audiences, of whom half were women right into the 1840s.

In 1842, a Queen's College for women opened in Glasgow, boasting considerable local support and poaching some of the Andersonian staff.[75] Smith suggests that both initiatives seemed to disappear by the late 1840s because of the growing power of separate-spheres ideology and because of university reforms which more stringently regulated access.

As ideas of gender difference sharpened, so women increasingly mobilised their assigned sensibility and maternal mission to move beyond the home and moralise the public sphere. By the mid-nineteenth century, women had created a feminist version of the communion of labour that insisted on the need to combine masculine and feminine principles in public action. The National Association for the Promotion of Social Science (NAPSS, 1857–84), which embodied key understandings of mid-century social science, welcomed the communion of labour formula and became one of the first arenas for women's public speech. It appointed G. W. Hastings as its secretary and Scotswoman Isa Craig as its assistant secretary. But other sciences ranged themselves on the opposite side of the fence, where some medics argued that energy channelled into mental pursuits depleted reproductive power, while positivist sociology idealised women but placed them firmly in the home.[76]

Women who excelled in mathematics and the natural sciences often tended to work within a variant of the communion formula by becoming part of a family scientific enterprise,[77] as sisters (Caroline Herschel), daughters (Agnes Syme, later Lady Lister) or wives (Lady Kelvin). Although virulently opposed to women in medical school, Lister welcomed his wife's help in their home-based laboratory, where she even tested for safe doses of chloroform by breathing the gas herself. There was one exceptional female star, Mary Somerville (1780–1872), born in Jedburgh and later admitted into the Astronomical Society (but only as an honorary and not a full member) and dubbed the Queen of Science. She achieved fame with *On the Connexion of the Physical Sciences* (1834), and in her eighty-ninth year saw her *Molecular and Microscopic Science published*. Helped in a chivalrous but never patronising way by many scientific luminaries, Somerville was nonetheless conscious of her self-presentation, and stressed her small physical stature, her shyness and her commitment to wifehood and motherhood so as not to appear transgressive.[78]

Local women added national scientific associations to their established culture of lecture-going. When the British Association for the Advancement of Science refused to issue women's tickets, Edinburgh women simply forced their way into lectures in 1834, a situation rectified by the 1840 Glasgow meeting, when a substantial income came from women who 'sat out even the driest discussion of the Sections'. Ladies' tickets for the NAPSS meeting in Glasgow in 1860 sold out within days, and 'not a few ladies thereafter joined on the ordinary terms of associates'.[79] This usually unnoticed activity paved the way for women to enter scientific societies – sometimes smoothly, as in the case of the Edinburgh Field Naturalists and Microscopical Society, which admitted women members from its first year (1869), and sometimes roughly, as when the persistent Marian Farquharson was blackballed from the Linnean Society even as fifteen other women were accepted as fellows in 1904.[80] Research is needed on how such women might have been active, from the late 1860s onwards, in Ladies' Education Associations, which ran classes including in the sciences and pushed university doors open for their daughters.[81]

At the turn of the twentieth century, with evolutionary and eugenic paradigms dominant, the communion formula was biologised, but in an ambiguous way. Biologists Patrick Geddes and his co-author J. Arthur Thomson, Professor of Natural History at Aberdeen, were key agents in this metamorphosis. As well as holding the Chair in Biology at Dundee, Geddes also developed his civic sociology in his Outlook Tower in Edinburgh and, in 1903, helped to found the Sociological Society, the first British learned society in that discipline. Geddes and Thomson repudiated struggle and competition as engines of evolutionary development, and insisted on a law of co-operation and love being paramount throughout the organic and social worlds. They detected an anabolic tendency towards constructive nurturing which was complemented by a catabolic metabolism that actively consumed energy. Regarding 'woman as the relatively more anabolic, man as the relatively more katabolic', they insisted that both were necessary in the public sphere of modern life, and gave the 'civic matriarch' important roles.[82]

At first, they made the notorious proclamation that sex differences 'decided among the prehistoric Protozoa cannot be annulled by Act of Parliament'.[83] But then they learned from feminists like Olive Schreiner, whose *Women and Labour* (1911) they praised as being 'full of power and insight'. By 1914, they began to insist that the full nature of sex difference was not yet known, and they transformed the feminist argument about gender being socially constructed into biological language, calling for a distinction between what was due to nature and to 'nurture'.[84] They thus repudiated the view, which had been dominant at least since the Enlightenment and embedded in canonical sociological theory, that 'man is more variable than woman, that the raw materials of evolution make their appearance in greatest abundance in man'. Rather, the real possibilities for development could only be discovered by experiment – carried out by women: 'social evolution is an experimental art. And one quite unworkable plan is that man should prescribe what the lines of woman's evolution are henceforth to be.'

Geddes and Thomson thus joined a larger intellectual current which was questioning and undermining 'scientific' ideas about women's smaller brain size and inferior intellectual capacity.[85] Together with widening access to university education and trends towards standardising school curricula for both sexes, especially after the Second World War, these initiatives opened the way for expanding opportunities in scientific fields, although often still shaped by gender stereotyping. Thus women chemistry graduates often went into food chemistry (part of domestic science) before the First World War, and into cosmetics chemistry between the wars. Energised by the women's liberation movement of the 1960s and 1970s, feminist scholars put their subjects under the microscope and analysed equity issues in their professions and epistemology and methodology in their disciplines. But even now, forty years further on, there is no clear success story to tell. In all the fields so far explored, equal advancement has not been achieved, and now women's family responsibilities are being held against them.

Both the Royal Colleges of Glasgow and Edinburgh showed their concern about the disproportion of women who reach the upper levels of the medical professions in Scotland by joining a working group to review the measures needed to support female staff during their child-rearing years. Recent statistics reflect a slow movement in the direction of equity at the top. Thus the number of female consultants moved from 19 per cent in 1997 to 23 per cent in 2003. Nonetheless, the statistics still tell an unequal tale, with women clustering at the lower rungs of the professional ladder despite the fact that by the 1990s they formed some 50 per cent of Scottish medical graduates, and the percentage has been growing since then.[86] Unfortunately, the usual solution, part-time work, has not dramatically aided career progress for women in any profession.

In science and engineering, the scenario is more bleak still. The percentages of women studying these subjects have been rising, but some 75 per cent of UK graduates do not go on to do research or take up employment for which they are qualified.[87] Energetic initiatives were launched in the mid-1990s to attract more women into science. For example, the Scottish branch of the Association of Women in Science and Engineering runs an attractive website which contains profiles of individuals engaged in fascinating careers. Nonetheless, the 'recent news' section has featured remarks by President Summers of Harvard University, who suggested that 'innate differences' between men and women help explain the absence of top-level female professionals in scientific fields.[88] It is disappointing that such powerful gatekeepers are still thumping an essentialist drum. The twenty-first century has not, so far, seen the resolution of epistemology or equity issues in the sciences and medicine. These transmute into different forms but remain alive and kicking nonetheless.

FURTHER READING

Bryson, E., *Look Back in Wonder* (Dundee: David Winter & Sons, 1966).

Crowther, A., 'Why women should be nurses and not doctors', 2002, http://www.ukchnm.org/seminars01.html

Eagle-Russett, C., *Sexual Science: The Victorian Construction of Womanhood* (Cambridge, MA: Harvard University Press, 1989).

Geddes, P., and J. A. Thomson, *Sex* (London: Williams and Norgate, 1914).

Jex-Blake, S., *Medical Women: A Thesis and a History* (Edinburgh: Oliphant, Anderson & Ferrier, 1886).

Newton, J., 'Engendering history for the middle class: sex and political economy in the *Edinburgh Review*', in L. Shires (ed.), *Rewriting the Victorians* (London: Routledge, 1992).

Owen, A., *The Darkened Room: Women, Power and Spiritualism in Late Victorian England* (London: Virago, 1989).

Phillips, P., *The Scientific Lady: A Social History of Women's Scientific Interests 1520–1918* (London: Weidenfeld & Nicolson, 1990).

Witz, A., *Professions and Patriarchy* (London: Routledge, 1992).

Yeo, E. Janes, *The Contest for Social Science: Relations and Representations of Gender and Class* (London: Rivers Oram, 1996).

NOTES

I would like to express my gratitude to Dr Marguerite Dupree and Dr Anne Cameron for reading the manuscript in whole or part, and thank them, Prof. Anne Crowther and Dr Lesley Diack for generous bibliographical help. I would also like to thank Lynn Sinclair for helping me research women in science. I must exonerate them all from the views expressed in the chapter, which are entirely my own.

1. D. O. Dow (ed.), *The Influence of Scottish Medicine: A Historical Assessment of its International Impact* (Park Ridge, NJ: Parthenon, 1988), pp. xi–xii; D. Hamilton, *The Healers: A History of Medicine in Scotland* (Edinburgh: Canongate, 1981), pp. xi, 126; also H. Dingwall, *A History*

of Scottish Medicine (Edinburgh: Edinburgh University Press, 2003), pp. 5, 181.

2. Hamilton, *Healers*, p. 43, ch. 3; Dingwall, *History*, ch. 6.

3. A. Cameron, 'From Ritual to Regulation: The Development of Midwifery in Glasgow and the West of Scotland, c.1740–1840', Ph.D. thesis, University of Glasgow, 2003, p. 7 for work by L. Reid and H. Diack on Edinburgh and Aberdeen; A. Cameron, 'A unique source for the history of midwifery in Scotland: the Minutes of the Faculty of Physicians and Surgeons of Glasgow', *Scottish Archives*, 11 (2005); J. D. Comrie, *History of Scottish Medicine* (London: Wellcome History of Medicine Museum, 1932), vol. 2, p. 435.

4. A. Wilson, 'Varieties of man midwifery', in W. F. Bynum and R. Porter (eds), *William Hunter and the Eighteenth-century Medical World* (Cambridge: Cambridge University Press, 1985), p. 346.

5. Willocks, 'Scottish man-midwives in eighteenth-century London', in Dow, *Influence*, pp. 46–57 for a progressivist view; for a gender analysis, J. Donnison *Midwives and Medical Men: A History of the Struggle for the Control of Childbirth* (New Barnett, Herts: Historical Publications, 1988); A. Wilson, *The Making of Man-Midwifery: Childbirth in England 1660–1770* (London: UCL Press, 1995).

6. E. Nihell, *A Treatise on the Art of Midwifery: Setting forth Various Abuses therein, especially as to the Practice with Instruments: the Whole Serving to put all Rational Inquirers in a fair way of very Safely Forming their own Judgment upon the Question: What it is Best to Employ, in cases of Pregnancy and Lying-in, a Man-midwife or, a Midwife* (London: A. Morley, 1760), p. 32.

7. Ibid., p. 50.

8. Ibid., p. 311; pp. 310ff. is a long section on 'Touching and how the skill can be used to assist complicated labours', compared with only one page in W. Smellie, *A Treatise on the Theory and Practice of Midwifery* (London: D. Wilson, 1752), p. 180.

9. Nihell, *Treatise on Midwifery*, p. 454.

10. Quoted in Willocks, 'Scottish man-midwives', pp. 47–8.

11. Frank Nicholls' Petition, quoted in R. Porter, *Bodies Politic: Disease, Death and Doctors in Britain, 1650–1900* (London: Reaktion Books, 2001), pp. 224–7; R. Porter, 'A touch of danger: the man-midwife as sexual predator', in G. S. Rousseau and R. Porter (eds), *Sexual Underworlds of the Enlightenment* (Manchester: Manchester University Press, 1988), pp.206–32.

12. Cameron, 'From ritual to regulation', pp. 111, 140, 147, 150–5, 218.

13. L. J. Jordanova, 'Gender, generation and science: William Hunter's Obstetrical Atlas', in Bynum and Porter (eds), *William Hunter*, pp. 404–9, 387–8.

14. See A. McLaren, 'The pleasures of procreation: traditional and biomedical theories of conception', in ibid., pp. 325–8, 331–2, 337–9.

15. W. Buchan, *Domestic Medicine; or, a Treatise on the Prevention and Cure of Diseases* (Edinburgh: J. Balfour and W. Creech, 1797 edn), p. 2.

16. Ibid., Introduction.

17. See E. Janes Yeo, *The Contest for Social Science: Relations and Representations of Gender and Class* (London: Rivers Oram, 1996), pp. 102–3.

18. For disciplining, see Manchester Medico-Ethical Association, *Eighteenth Annual Report*, 1865–6, pp. 5, 15–16; T. Parssinen, 'Professional deviants and the history of medicine: medical mesmerists in Victorian Britain', in R. Wallis (ed.), *On the Margins of Science: The Social Construction of Rejected Knowledge*, Sociological Review Monograph 27 (March 1979), 106, 113; A. Winter, *Mesmerized: The Powers of Mind in Victorian Britain* (Chicago, IL: University of Chicago Press, 1998); P. Nicolls, 'The social construction and organisation of medical marginality: the case of homoeopathy in mid-nineteenth-century Britain' in R. Jütte et al. (eds), *Historical Aspects of Unconventional Medicine,* (Sheffield: European Association for the History of Medicine and Health, 2001), p. 177.

19. *True Scotsman*, 20 and 27 October 1838. The topic of Scottish health radicals is under-researched. Women were active in phrenology, a popular science of the mind. Of the handful of women public lecturers listed by R. Cooter, two were Scots – Mrs Aitken of Dumfries, whose husband was her demonstrator, and Mrs Hamilton of Paisley, who was robustly defended by the socialists. See R. Cooter, *The Cultural Meaning of Popular Science: Phrenology and the Organization of Consent in Nineteenth-century Britain* (Cambridge: Cambridge University Press, 1984), pp. 157, 273, 284.

20. J. Bradley and M. Dupree, 'Opportunity on the edge of orthodoxy: medically qualified hydropathists in the era of reform, 1840–60', *Social History of Medicine*, 14:3 (2001), 419, 421; J. Bradley and M. Dupree, 'A shadow of orthodoxy?: an epistemology of British hydropathy, 1840–1858', *Medical History* 47 (2003), 180.

21. J. Bradley, M. Dupree and A. Durie, 'Taking the waters: the development of hydropathic establishments in Scotland 1840–1940', *Business and Economic History* 26:2 (1997), 426–37.

22. Rev. Alexander Munro (ed.), *Aberdeen Sanitary Reformer and Family Guide to Health* (Aberdeen: G. Cornwall and Sons, 1861), pp. 280–1.

23. See the glowing review, ibid., pp. 167–8; also John Smedley, *Practical Hydropathy*, 4th edn (London, 1869), p. 12, and advertisements for Matlock Bank establishments.

24. M. S. Gove Nichols, *A Woman's Work in Water Cure and Sanitary Education* (London: Longmans, Green, 1869), pp. 1, 4–5; B. Aspinwall, entry on Mary and Thomas Nichols in the *New Oxford Dictionary of National Biography*.

25. Alex Owen, *The Darkened Room: Women, Power and Spiritualism in Late Victorian England* (London: Virago, 1989), pp. 112, 115–21.

26. As quoted in ibid., p. 119.

27. Rev. Alexander Munro, *Aberdeen Water-Cure Journal* (London: Partridge, 1859), pp. 189, 186–7.

28. *Aberdeen Sanitary Reformer* (1861), p. 26; also A. Hunter, *Hydropathy: its Principles and Practice for Home Use, chiefly intended for Mothers and families* (Edinburgh and Glasgow: John Menzies, 1878), pp. 311, 318. Hunter ran establishments in Gilmorehill, Glasgow, then in Bridge of Allan.

29. Nicolls, 'Social construction', pp. 173–4.

30. *Herald of Health*, January 1876, p. 107; *Oxford DNB* entry on M. and T. Nichols.

31. *Aberdeen Sanitary Reformer* (1862), p. 96.

32. *Aberdeen Water-Cure Journal* (1859), p. 184.

33. *Aberdeen Sanitary Reformer* (1861), p. 171.

34. S. Jex-Blake, *Medical Women: A Thesis and a History* (Edinburgh: Oliphant, Anderson & Ferrier, 1886), p. 71; M. A. Elston, 'Edinburgh Seven (act. 1869–73)', *Oxford DNB*; S. Roberts, *Sophia Jex-Blake* (London: Routledge, 1993).

35. For professionalisation and access issues, see A. Crowther, 'Why women should be nurses and not doctors', 2002, http://www.ukchnm.org/seminars01.html; A. Witz, *Professions and Patriarchy* (London: Routledge, 1992); S. Walby et al., *Medicine and Nursing: Professions in a Changing Health Service* (London: Sage, 1994); J. Geyer-Kordesch and R. Ferguson, *Blue Stockings, Black Gowns, White Coats: A Brief History of Women Entering Higher Education and the Medical Profession in Scotland* (Glasgow: University of Glasgow, Wellcome Unit for the History of Medicine, [1994]); W. Alexander, 'Early Glasgow women medical graduates', in E. Gordon and E. Breitenbach (eds), *The World is Ill-Divided: Women's Work in Scotland in the Nineteenth and Early Twentieth Centuries* (Edinburgh: Edinburgh University Press, 1990); S. Hamilton, 'The first generations of university women 1869–1930', in G. Donaldson (ed.), *Four Centuries: Edinburgh University Life 1583–1983* (Edinburgh: Edinburgh University Press, 1983), pp. 99–115. Heroine narratives include E. Moberly Bell, *Storming the Citadel: The Rise of the Woman Doctor* (London: Constable, 1953); C. Blake, *The Charge of the Parasols: Women's Entry into the Medical Profession* (London: Women's Press, 1990). For more complex analysis, see C. Dyhouse, 'Driving ambitions: women in pursuit of a medical education, 1890–1939', *Women's History Review* 7:3 (1998), 322–43. Important unpublished studies include M. A. Elston, 'Women Doctors in the British Health Services: A Sociological Study of their Careers and Opportunities', Ph.D. thesis, University of Leeds, 1986, some of which appears in her ' "Run by women, (mainly) for women": medical women's hospitals in Britain, 1866–1948', in L. Conrad and A. Hardy (eds), *Women and Modern Medicine* (Amsterdam: Rodopi, 2001), pp. 73–108;

E. Thomson, 'Women in Medicine in Late Nineteenth- and Early Twentieth-century Edinburgh', Ph.D. thesis, University of Edinburgh, 1998.

36. Jex-Blake, *Medical Women*, pp. 196–7.

37. Yeo, *Contest*, pp. 127–8, 133–4 for points in this paragraph; A.-M. Rafferty, *The Politics of Nursing Knowledge* (London: Routledge, 1996), pp. 31, 40.

38. *Lancet*, 19 April 1862; Aberdeen Central Library has the Aberdeen Ladies Sanitary Association papers (1859–81).

39. *Lancet*, 17 August 1878, p. 227 for quotes in this paragraph.

40. S. McGann, *The Battle of the Nurses: A Study of Eight Women who Influenced the Development of Professional Nursing, 1880–1930* (London: Scutari, 1992), p. 109. For home nursing, see B. Mortimer, 'Independent women: domiciliary nurses in mid-nineteenth-century Edinburgh', in A.-M. Rafferty et al. (eds), *Nursing History and the Politics of Welfare* (London: Routledge, 1997), pp. 133–49; also B. Mortimer, 'The Nurse in Edinburgh c.1760–1860: The Impact of Commerce and Professionalisation', Ph.D. thesis, University of Edinburgh, 2002.

41. Yeo, *Contest*, pp. 122–6.

42. Jex-Blake, *Medical Women*, p. 7.

43. Ibid., p. 6.

44. *Medical Times and Gazette*, 26 November and 5 November 1870; *Edinburgh University Magazine* 11 (1 February 1871).

45. Jex-Blake, *Medical Women*, pp. 40–1.

46. Coxe quoted in ibid., p. 100.

47. *Medical Times and Gazette*, 26 November 1870.

48. E. Thomson, 'Women in Medicine', p. 95.

49. L. Eichoff, typescript 'Women medical students, 1832–37, "THE LADIES" ', University of Edinburgh Archives, Information on First Women Graduates of Edinburgh University.

50. Ibid.

51. E. Bryson, *Look Back in Wonder* (Dundee: David Winter & Sons, Dundee, 1966), pp. 163, 179, 109, 217, 220, 222. For dissecting-room trauma, see Dyhouse, 'Driving ambitions', p. 327. Alexander, 'Early Glasgow women' shows how women doctors were able to combine medical practice and marriage, pp. 75–6.

52. Edinburgh University Women's Medical Society, Minutes, 9 December 1921, University of Edinburgh Archives, Da67; her father was Sir Archibald Christison, son of Sir Robert.

53. See, for example, ibid., 10 December 1920; Queen Margaret College Medical Club, Minutes, 20 October 1920 for opportunities in the Empire; also A. Witz, ' "Colonising women": female medical practice in colonial India', *Clio Medica* 61 (2000), 23–52.

54. Obituaries in *Medical Woman: Bulletin of the Medical Women's Federation*, *British Medical Journal* 293 (19 July 1986), University of Glasgow Archives, DC 317.

55. J. A. Calder to H. S. Keer, Letter of Appointment, dated 6 July 1925; Director of Medical and Sanitary Service to Dr Kerr, dated 16 October 1928, Special Condition of Service Applicable to Lady Medical Officers; A. Fiddian to Dr Keer, Letters dated 18 September 1931, 11 December 1933; Dr Keer to A. Fiddian, Letter dated 22 September 1931, University of Glasgow Archives, DC 171.

56. Edinburgh Women's Medical Society, Minutes, 22 January 1916.

57. Bryson, *Look Back*, p. 202.

58. I. Hutton, *Memories of a Doctor in War and Peace* (London: Heinemann, 1960), pp. 214ff.; also her *Last of the Taboos: Mental Disorders in Modern Life* (London: Heinemann, 1934) and *Hygiene of the Change in Women – the Climacteric* (London: Heinemann, 1936).

59. Crowther, 'Why women should be nurses', p. 7.

60. M. Todd, *Life of Sophia Jex-Blake* (London: Macmillan: 1919), pp. 479–80.

61. M. Lawrence, *Shadow of Swords: A Biography of Elsie Inglis* (London: Michael Joseph, 1971), pp. 53ff. tells how Inglis, infuriated by Jex-Blake's authoritarianism, launched a project for a rival Medical College for Women and forced Jex-Blake's School to close in 1898. Biographies of Inglis include E. Shaw McLaren (her sister), *Elsie Inglis: The Woman with a Torch* (London: SPCK, 1920); E. Crofton, *The Women of Royaumont: A Scottish Women's Hospital on the Western Front* (East Linton: Tuckwell Press, 1997); L. Leneman, *In Search of Life: The Story of Elsie Inglis and the Scottish Women's Hospitals* (Edinburgh: Mercat Press, 1994).

62. Moberly Bell, *Storming the Citadel*, p. 153.

63. Boanerges, 'I don't like women', *Edinburgh University Magazine*, 29 October 1929. See too D. J. Clark, 'The Royal Medical Society today', *Synapse* 9 (1959), 61–2, for 'fear of the destruction' of the 'atmosphere of a club' until 1964; Dyhouse, 'Driving ambitions', 332–3.

64. L. Reid, *Scottish Midwives: Twentieth-century Voices* (East Linton: Tuckwell Press, 2000), pp. 1–2; Yeo, *Contest*, pp. 222–3.

65. See Jane Lewis, *The Politics of Motherhood: Child and Maternal Welfare in England, 1900–1930* (London: Croom Helm, 1980).

66. My thanks to Lesley Diack, who has generously shared her source material: D. J. Lamont, 'Is there a place for men in health visiting?', Royal Society of Health Congress, *Papers*, 1966, pp. 2–3; I. A. G. MacQueen, 'Male health visitors – the present position', *The Medical Officer*, 21 October 1966, p. 223.

67. R. Ferguson, 'Recollections of life "on the district" in Scotland, 1940–70', in J. Bornat et al. (eds), *Oral History Health and Welfare* (London: Routledge, 1999); see www.arts.gla.ac.uk/History/Medicine/Dougall.html for her other work.

68. H. Kay, *Women and Men in the Professions in Scotland* (Scottish Executive Central Research Unit, 2001), ch. 5, conclusion; available at www.scotland.gov.uk/cru/kd01/red/men11.htm

69. M. Whittock et al., ' "The tender trap": gender, part-time nursing and the effects of "family-friendly" policies on career advancement', *Sociology of Health and Illness* 24:3 (May 2002), 305, which is London-based research with findings replicated nationwide.

70. MacQueen, 'Male health visitors', p. 223.

71. Kay, *Women and Men*, ch. 5, 'Nursing'.

72. S. Smith, 'Retaking the register: women's higher education in Glasgow and beyond, c. 1796–1845, *Gender and History* 12:2 (July 2000), 310–35, here pp. 312–14; P. Phillips, *The Scientific Lady: A Social History of Women's Scientific Interests 1520–1918* (London: Weidenfeld & Nicolson, 1990), pp. 79, 122–33.

73. M. Moran, ' "The commerce of the sexes": gender and the social sphere in Scottish Enlightenment accounts of civil society', in F. Trentmann (ed.), *Paradoxes of Civil Society: New Perspectives on Modern German and British History*, rev. 2nd edn (New York: Berghahn Books, 2003), pp. 68–71; also her 'Between the savage and the civil: Dr John Gregory's natural history of femininity', in S. Knott and B. Taylor (eds), *Women, Gender, and Enlightenment, 1650–1850* (New York: Palgrave Macmillan, 2005); J. Gregory, 'A father's legacy to his daughters', in J. Todd (ed.), *Female Education in the Age of Enlightenment* (London: William Pickering, 1996). See too the recent work of J. Rendall, including 'Feminising the Enlightenment: the problem of sensibility', in M. Fitzpatrick et al. (eds), *The Enlightenment World* (London: Taylor and Francis, 2004); 'Women and the public sphere', *Gender and History* 11:3 (1999), 475–88; 'Clio, Mars and Minerva: the Scottish Enlightenment and the writing of women's history', in T. Devine and J. Young (eds), *Eighteenth-century Scotland: New Perspectives* (East Linton: Tuckwell Press, 1998). Also R. Olson, 'Sex and status in Scottish Enlightenment social science: John Millar and the sociology of gender roles', *History of the Human Sciences* 11 (1998), 73–100; M. Burstein, *Narrating Women's History in Britain, 1779–1902* (Aldershot: Ashgate, 2004), ch. 1.

74. J. Newton, 'Engendering history for the middle class: sex and political economy in the *Edinburgh Review*', in L. Shires (ed.), *Rewriting the Victorians* (London: Routledge, 1992), p. 8; [W. Empson,] 'Illustrations of political economy: Mrs Marcet – Miss Martineau', *Edinburgh Review* 57 (1833), 3; Yeo, *Contest*, pp. 22–3.

75. Smith, 'Retaking the register', pp. 317–24.

76. Yeo, *Contest*, p. 337 n. 4; C. Eagle-Russett, *Sexual Science: The Victorian Construction of Womanhood* (Cambridge, MA: Harvard University Press, 1989), pp. 40–2, 93, 149.

77. See A. Shteir, 'Botany in the breakfast room: women and early nineteenth-century British plant study', in P. Abir-Am and D. Outram (eds), *Uneasy Careers and Intimate Lives: Women in Science 1789–1979* (New Brunswick, NJ: Rutgers University Press, 1987), pp. 31–44; A. Shteir, *Cultivating*

Women, Cultivating Science: Flora's Daughter and Botany in England, 1760–1860 (Baltimore, MD: Johns Hopkins University Press, 1996); R. Fisher, *Joseph Lister 1827–1912* (London: Macdonald and Janes, 1977), pp. 78, 84; A. King (niece), *Kelvin the Man* (London, Hodder and Stoughton, 1925), pp. 33, 96.

78. D. McMillan (ed.), *Queen of Science: Personal Recollections of Mary Somerville* (Edinburgh: Canongate, 2001), pp. xxiii–xxv, xxxi–xxxvi; E. Gordon and G. Nair, *Public Lives: Women, Family and Society in Victorian Britain* (New Haven, CT: Yale University Press, 2003), pp. 91–7.

79. Phillips, *Scientific Lady*, p. 204; *Glasgow Herald*, 28 September 1840, 19 September 1855; NAPSS, Minutes of the General Local Committee, 8 November 1860, Glasgow City Council Archives, DTC14.2.33, Mitchell Library.

80. Edinburgh Field Naturalists and Microscopical Society, Minutes, 30 November 1869, 16 April 1870, National Archives of Scotland, GD434/1/1; A. Gage and W. Stearn, *A Bicentenary History of the Linnean Society of London* (London: Academic Press, 1988), pp. 89–91.

81. For example, L. Moore, *Bajanellas and Semilinas: Aberdeen University and the Education of Women, 1860–1920* (Aberdeen: Aberdeen University Press, 1991), pp. 6–10; C. Dyhouse, *No Distinction of Sex? Women in British Universities, 1870–1939* (London: UCL Press, 1995), p. 15.

82. P. Geddes and J. A. Thomson, *Sex* (London: Williams and Norgate, 1914), pp. 208, 244.

83. P. Geddes and J. A. Thomson, *The Evolution of Sex* (London: Williams and Norgate, 1889 [1901]), pp. 267, [286].

84. Geddes and Thomson, *Sex*, pp. 213, 208, 251, 239, 258 for quotes in this paragraph. For Geddes, see my 'Feminising the citizen: British sociology's sleight of hand?', in B. Marshall and A. Witz (eds), *Engendering the Social: Feminist Encounters with Sociological Theory* (Maidenhead: Open University Press, 2004), ch. 5, and also ch. 1 for canonical social theory; H. Meller, *Patrick Geddes: Social Evolutionist and City Planner* (London: Routledge, 1990).

85. Eagle-Russett, *Sexual Science*, pp. 158, 164–5.

86. For statistics, see Kay, *Women and Men*, table 5.4; NHS Scotland, *Workforce Statistics*, table B3; Working Party of the Federation of Royal Colleges of Physicians, *Women in Hospital Medicine: Career Choices and Opportunities* (June 2001). All these sources are available online.

87. BBC News, 17 September 2004, http://news.bbc.co.uk/1/hi/sci/tech/3665898.stm

88. M. O'Rourke, 'Don't let Larry Summers off the hook yet: why the Harvard president's tactless social science was a bad idea', AWiSE SET News, 28 January 2005; V. Valian, 'Raise your hand if you're a woman in science',

reprinted from *Washington Post Outlook*, 30 January 2005. L. Segal, *Why Feminism? Gender, Psychology, Politics* (Cambridge: Polity 1999) critically examines the resurgence of ideas of genetically based sex differences in socio-biology.

7

Gender, the Arts and Culture

Siân Reynolds

> But first
> she wants to strip the willow
> she desires the keys
> to the National Library
>
> Kathleen Jamie, 'The Queen of Sheba'

The air is full of noises about Scottish culture. Some noises drown out others. Over the last twenty years or so, a number of controversies have been aired about whether or not Scottish culture was diverted, encouraged or suppressed after the Act of Union of 1707: whether the Enlightenment was marked by anglicisation, or whether it had deeper roots in Scotland; whether Presbyterianism has been a force suppressing creativity or, on the contrary, encouraging clear thinking; whether Scotland was a 'hotbed of genius' or a cultural backwater; whether the Kailyard, the drunk man looking at the thistle, *Braveheart*, *Trainspotting*, or the hard man of Glasgow most authentically represented the nation's culture – and so on.[1] Some voices were pessimistic, others more positive or nuanced. As a sort of counterpoint to these debates, the question of gender, at first occasionally, later with some insistence, started to be raised. It is fair to say that there was little sign of this until the feminist revolution of the post-1970s. An early example of a wake-up call was an article by Carol Anderson and Glenda Norquay in *Cencrastus* in 1984, opening with the statement that 'even a cursory glance over past issues of this magazine, and most others with similar concerns, will reveal the male monopoly on Scottish culture'. They argued that it was dominated not only by men but also by certain ideas about masculinity and virility; what was needed was 'a collective effort to uncover the social and *cultural* history of women in Scotland' (my italics).[2]

This strongly worded appeal was understandable in context; and that history is still needed. Since then, however, many voices, including male writers on Scottish culture, have continued to echo this theme, enthusiastically agreeing that 'one of the main features of Scottish culture in the twentieth century is . . . that it has been male-dominated, arguably to a greater extent than most modern societies';[3] 'Scotland was a male-dominated culture';[4] 'the overwhelmingly male-dominated nature of Scottish society';[5] '[there are ways in which] Scottish history and culture have been crudely phallocentric';[6] and so on. The problem with such statements – especially if found in writings otherwise largely devoted to men – is that they all too often go unquestioned and unexamined. Is it really the case that Scotland is (or was) more male-dominated than elsewhere? Than England, Wales, Ireland, France? A moment's thought tells us that if one looks at the intellectual and cultural history of all these countries, one finds that the universities, the law, the churches, art and music training, theatre management and the publishing world as a whole (except perhaps the novel) have been virtually no-go areas for women for centuries, barring a few breakthroughs and exceptions. Only in the late nineteenth to the twentieth century, and only with real force in the last twenty or thirty years or so, have the gatekeeping mechanisms formally excluding women from access to valued cultural arenas seriously given way. Scotland is surely not so very different from other countries in this respect. That doesn't mean that women have not been *present* as distinctive cultural forces in Scottish history. Throughout all that time, women are recorded – somewhere – as audiences for, performers of and indeed creators of imaginative work, though the records are patchy and have often been lost by the gatekeepers, and the genres where women were numerous are not always highly prized by historians.

This chapter suggests that if we are to take seriously complaints that Scotland is, or was, male-dominated, we need to look carefully, and in a historical context, at the cultural narratives we have inherited. The existing literature attempting this is uneven. Some approaches virtually ignore gender. A collective book, published in 1993, was intended to 'mark the start of a new subject in its own right, Scotland as a great creative force in European civilization'.[7] It is in many ways a useful and informative collection by specialists; but, as the signs on French level crossings say, 'Be careful: one train can hide another'. In this case, a nationalist agenda, directed against 'cultural cringe', seems to have masked the gender-blindness of the collection. Its jacket lists thirty-three cultural heroes, from Duns Scotus to John Grierson and Sorley MacLean, by way of Burns, Hogg, Telford, Kelvin, Stevenson, MacDiarmid and others, to enforce the claim that 'No nation of its size has contributed so much to world culture'.[8] It is indeed an impressive list for a small nation with a history of emigration. On inspection, the names are virtually all from the past: they are all canonical, that is, well known in their fields, which are mostly literary or learned ones. The list gives a broadly accepted, if unintended, picture of Scotland's culture as being particularly productive of trained thought, writing and enquiry (rather than fine art or music, for example). Lastly, all the names are those of men (and even the book's long index contains hardly any women's names). It does rather obviously conform to the accusation, often heard in the 1990s, of only listing 'dead white men' in cultural history. There is no shortage of books open to the same objection. So, is the often-quoted male domination a matter of perception rather than reality?

One response has been 'the return of the repressed', an alternative cultural history, consisting of anthologies or monographs about Scottish women as creators. These would include collections such as Catherine Kerrigan's *Anthology of Scottish Women Poets* (1991) and Douglas Gifford and Dorothy McMillan's *The History of Scottish Women's Writing* (1997). An example from fine art was the exhibition and book on the 'Glasgow Girls', women artists trained at the Glasgow School of Art in the late nineteenth century.[9] These books fit an established pattern in women's history: the rediscovery and re-evaluation of neglected or forgotten voices. So one could, with little difficulty, construct an 'alternative' female pantheon calling out for recognition, including past names such as Joanna Baillie, Jane Welsh Carlyle, Nan Shepherd, Jessie King and Phoebe Traquair, all of whom have recently received much critical attention, and ending with such well-recognised contemporary figures as Elizabeth Blackadder, Liz Lochhead, Muriel Spark and Evelyn Glennie. Such 'pantheonisation' can take the form of an exhibition, such as 'Modern Women', held in the Scottish National Portrait Gallery in 2004–5, and helpfully raises neglected profiles. *The Biographical Dictionary of Scottish Women* (forthcoming 2006) is similarly designed to provide more knowledge about named individuals than was readily available at the start of the twenty-first century. In cultural history, initiatives like this are established procedure, and do not of course only concern women. The writer James Hogg, for example, now firmly in the pantheon, was marginalised in the later nineteenth century, only to see a stunning revival of his fortunes in the twentieth century; the same could be said to some extent of Robert Fergusson.

Finally, some writers have tackled head-on the question of gender and Scottish culture. In 1993, Alexandra Howson published a hard-hitting essay arguing that, in current Scottish cultural debate, 'women are marginalised and femininity is selectively deployed as a symbolic category'.[10] Shortly afterwards, Christopher Whyte edited a collection, *Gendering the Nation* (1995), with articles from male and female writers seeking to disprove the proposition that 'Nationalism is always bad news for women', and which considered sexuality as well as gender. Both these analyses offer a good starting point for an approach to gendering Scottish culture more generally. Unsurprisingly, their focus is largely on writing, since literary specialists are responsible for much recent scholarship and analysis in this area. And they are also more concerned with contemporary culture, without much historical perspective. So we do have a number of partial responses to a perceived absence, but little in the way of overall synthesis.

How best to take this debate further, without simply arguing about who should, or should not, be in the Scottish pantheon? It is generally a good idea to define one's terms. What exactly is Scottish culture? Of the supposed gulf between 'high' and 'popular culture', Angus Calder has written that it takes little knowledge 'to expose the fact that forms supposed to be high have been modified by "popular" influences, and in most cases even originated in the "popular" arena'.[11] Calder goes on to suggest that in Scotland the gulf between 'high' and 'popular' culture is less gaping than elsewhere – that 'artists in various media are closer to popular life in Scotland than is common south of the border . . . perhaps we owe it to Burns that poetry in Scotland isn't always associated with pure elocution, strenuous intellectualism and genteel boredom'.[12]

There may be some truth in this, especially in the earlier period; but, in a short chapter, it is impossible to discuss in detail every kind of Scottish culture. So, this chapter is largely concerned with the production first of Scottish traditional culture(s), and then with the rather 'high culture' topics of literature, philosophy and the arts, rather than with modern urban popular culture. To engage properly with the latter would mean bringing a gender perspective to bear on television and radio, popular music, dance and sport – in short, to write a history of everyday life. (Calder again: 'Unfortunately, the broader alternative is so capacious that it includes everything'!)[13] But we can accommodate the idea behind Calder's claims by trying to map some of the elements of the Scottish 'cultural field' in the sense of the term used by Pierre Bourdieu: that is, an overall context in which some activities and players carry more status or power than others. 'The cultural field is a structured space of relations . . . New entrants to the field [are] necessarily situated within the network of competing positions.'[14] Such relationships change all the time, so we need to bring a historical dimension to the field while examining it from the specific point of view of gender, that is, with an awareness of both femininity and masculinity, rather than Bourdieu's more usual approach via social class. It means looking at the means of entry to given spaces in the cultural field, the kinds of activity and genres which have commanded most attention or respect, and the shifts over time. This is an agenda for a book, not a chapter; so each century is here used as the framework for a few case studies, to try to outline a provisional analysis. Ideally, this could lead to the further research that is needed.

THE EIGHTEENTH-CENTURY FIELD (1): THE ORAL TRADITION

What is remarkable about Scotland in the eighteenth century is that it was a high point both for awareness of traditional culture, Gaelic and Scots (ballads, songs and poetry), and for learned and urban culture (the Enlightenment). The standing of these cultures within the overall field of prestige, attention and power has varied over time. For eighteenth-century contemporaries, Gaelic culture was the most self-contained, despite its international vogue, given a boost by the so-called Ossian fragments: the actual culture of the Gàidhealtachd 'flourished in relative isolation and obscurity'.[15] The Scottish Enlightenment, by contrast, although not yet called by this name (popularised in the twentieth century), was recognised at the time as a high-profile phenomenon, carrying great prestige, and being linked by patronage to high society and the middle classes. Meantime, the collection of Lowland Scottish ballads and lore, while popular with urban society, was less confidently appre-ciated. There was some dismay, for example, that Burns chose to spend so much of his last years on Johnson's *Scots Musical Museum*. Retrospectively, cultural commentators have reconstructed the field rather differently. Gaelic culture has been celebrated, and to some extent restored to life, by scholars and campaigners, though it remains a minor-ity phenomenon.[16] The Scottish Enlightenment remains an undeniably striking moment in cultural history, and is regularly re-celebrated, yet it has also been reassessed and criticised in some quarters as being both socially and politically conservative and exclusive, compared to its con-tinental equivalents, and indeed as less 'Scottish' than it might be.[17] The vernacular Scots culture, on the other hand, has seen its stock rise strik-ingly. It is sometimes argued that it served a form of nationalism at a time when the political Union made more explicit challenges to London more dangerous.[18] And Edwin Muir could write that while 'the greatest poetry of most countries has been written by the educated middle and upper classes; the greatest poetry of Scotland has come from the people'.[19]

How do these fields respond to a gendered analysis? Gaelic culture came from an unequivocally patriarchal society, based on the clan and dynastic marriages, marked by a martial context, and associated with various taboos on women's activities. Its leading forms of cultural expression were poetry and song, originally dominated by a bardic elite, 'a privileged caste of formidable erudition'[20] using classical common Gaelic, an artificial literary language taught in bardic schools. Official bards were male, as they were too in Wales and Ireland. Women were originally unlikely to have training in the principal form of poetry, the panegyric, 'the domain of bards . . . [I]t was frowned on for women to . . . follow their example . . . [T]hey were restricted to work-songs, cradle-songs and laments.'[21] Yet the same tradition can be viewed from a different angle: 'from its earliest appearance, Gaelic folksong has contained a strong element of women's composition, exemplified by the distinctive waulking songs, communal work songs for shrinking the wool tweed and performed in Scotland by women only'.[22] In other words, the separation of genres can be seen as distinctiveness or exclusion, strength or weakness, depending on how highly each genre is prized. Today, ironically, the 'waulking songs' are seen as particularly authentic. John MacInnes writes that these anonymous songs which probably accompanied various communal tasks are 'intensely lyrical, intimate, passionate and vivid', depicting the whole order of 'Gaelic society through women's eyes'.[23]

There were also, despite the bardic tradition, 'an unusual number' of individual women poets: Martin Martin wrote of his native Skye that 'several of both sexes have a quick vein of poesy'.[24] By the eighteenth century, in fact, the bardic tradition was in decline, and new poetry combining classical and vernacular language came into existence, which seems to have opened up opportunities for women. Poets who bridged the gap between the two traditions include Sileas na Ceapaich (c.1660–1729), who wrote laments, and Màiri Nighean Alasdair Ruaidh (a.k.a. Mary MacLeod, c.1615–1707), whose work was transmitted orally and first written down in 1776; unusually for a woman, she wrote praise-poems.[25] Women remained a minority among Gaelic poets, yet a figure could later emerge like Màiri Mhòr nan Òran (Mary MacPherson, 1821–98), who wrote passionately about the Clearances and whose lyrical qualities made her 'still one of Gaeldom's best-loved poets and songmakers'.[26] In the twentieth-century Gaelic revival, both sexes have taken part, from Sorley MacLean and Iain Crichton Smith to younger poets like Meg Bateman and Anne Frater.[27] A provisional conclusion has to be that Gaelic culture has a particular chronology, broadly patriarchal, but that it has been far from a male monopoly.

The parallels with the oral tradition in Scots are clear; but the gender situation is slightly different. Margaret Laidlaw, mother of James Hogg, famously rebuked Walter Scott for 'improving' the ballads she had provided for him: 'there was never ane o my sangs till ye prentit them yoursel, and ye hae spoilt them awthegither. They were made for singing and no for reading.'[28] She was one of many women providing the sung ballads, written down, with or without music, by Scott and other collectors. As Emily Lyle writes, 'wherever we are given the names of singers from whom the songs were drawn, . . . women feature very prominently. Although the world of ballads and songs was by no means an exclusively female domain, the situation is quite often one of a male collector and a woman who was . . . his star singer.'[29] It is this tradition (rather than the Gaelic one) which is referred to as the 'remarkable song culture [of Scotland] in which higher and lower ranks of society participated'[30] and which has long been regarded as distinctive of Scottish society.[31]

Learned and popular culture came together in the person of Anna Gordon, a.k.a. Mrs Brown of Falkland (1747–1810), daughter of an Aberdeen professor. Francis James Child, editor of *English and Scottish Popular Ballads* (1882–98), thought 'no Scottish ballads . . . superior in kind' to those she supplied. Anna Gordon's repertory came from her mother, from a family servant, and especially from her aunt Anne Forbes Farquharson. Mrs Brown sang but did not publish, and Scott published in his *Minstrelsy* some of her ballads he had not composed. It has been claimed that hers 'are framed from an explicitly female indeed even feminist perspective', telling of the troubles in wait for women, including childbirth, infanticide and cruel treatment, as well as love. The odd, individual nature of her songs, which she may have changed in performance, unsettled the view of tradition as unchanging and repetitive, while her belonging to 'polite society' unsettled views of the 'popular'.[32] The pattern of female performance and male collecting continued: William Motherwell was provided with material by Agnes Lyle in the 1820s, and Andrew Crawfurd by Mary McQueen. In the twentieth century, Hamish Henderson recorded the songs of traveller-singer Jeannie Robertson (1908–75), 'the finest modern exponent of traditional ballad-singing'.[33] This kind of partnership (male collector/female singer) was not invariable, however: already at the turn of the nineteenth to the twentieth century, female collectors Frances Tolmie and Marjory Kennedy-Fraser both recorded songs from the Western Isles, and they have had successors in the twentieth century.

If one were to agree with Muir, then, that the 'greatest poetry' in Scotland came from the 'people', then it is clear that in both the Gaelic and the Scots traditions we have a story of the people's culture, well recognised by specialists, which is *not* massively male-dominated. It includes separate forms of cultural production which may have been exclusive to one or other sex, and it also has great areas of uncertainty. The authorship of traditional poems and songs is not always clear; what does emerge is that their performance and memorising appear to have been to a large extent in the hands of women, who are in some sense seen as 'authentic' bearers of folk culture, while the educated men, and occasionally women, who wrote down their messages were generally in a different world. Both were necessary to construct and preserve a cultural field specific to Scotland.

THE EIGHTEENTH-CENTURY FIELD (2): THE ENLIGHTENMENT

The relations between the Scottish Enlightenment and the vernacular and largely oral traditions described above were not simple: in their writing, educated men like David Hume sought to eradicate 'Scotticisms' yet admired the old traditions. Fletcher of Saltoun had earlier written: 'I knew a very wise man . . . [who] believed if a man were permitted to make all the ballads, he need not care who should make the laws of a nation'.[34] But this was the age when women's 'position as purveyors of oral culture was being undermined by a growing emphasis on literate forms'.[35] Once education was being highly valued, literacy became the key to being taken seriously in cultural terms, despite Fletcher's sally.

R. A. Houston has looked sceptically at the more extreme claims for Scotland's precocious and widespread male literacy, indicating that it can reasonably be compared to other countries of Northern Europe. But one constant remains throughout all the incomplete statistics of the eighteenth and nineteenth centuries: on average, female literacy remained far behind men's. In Lowland Scotland in 1750, in the early days of the Scottish Enlightenment, 65 per cent of men could read and write, but only about 15 to 30 per cent of women.[36] In general terms, until the midnineteenth century, 'women were usually much less literate than men', indeed being 'systematically discriminated against'.[37] There are nuances to be introduced: not being able to write did not mean that one could not read.[38] Class was obviously important, and the most literate women were to be found in the higher echelons of society. The daughters and future wives of the many professional men, academics and lawyers of the university cities of Scotland sometimes received quite a good education. However, they were often discouraged from displaying learning, and even gentlewomen 'were ignorant of grammar, mathematics, the classical . . . and the rudiments of spelling'.[39] Writer Elizabeth Hamilton (1758–1816) was advised by her aunt 'to avoid any display of superior knowledge'.[40] John Gregory, Professor of Medicine, counselled his daughters: 'If you happen to have any learning, keep it a profound secret especially from the men, who generally look with a jealous and malignant eye on a woman of great pairts and cultivated understanding'.[41] Small wonder that he was one of Mary Wollstonecraft's targets in 1792. There are examples of educated women on the fringes of the Enlightenment, especially in later years, more literary than philosophical perhaps: Edinburgh philanthropist and hostess Eliza Fletcher (1770–1858) in her autobiography identified the close connections between a network of literary women, including Elizabeth Hamilton, Anne Grant, Joanna Baillie, Margaret Cullen and Mary Brunton, some of whom were daughters of, or connected to, male intellectuals. Margaret Cullen's sister Robina had married John Craig Millar, radical son of Enlightenment philosopher John Millar, and founded a community on the banks of the Susquehanna in 1795. Both sisters inspired the early interest of Frances Wright in the politics of the American republic. Only recently has much research centred on such figures, whose writings were sometimes anonymous or fell into that vast category of women's writing: correspondence and unpublished journals and memoirs.[42]

But a gendered history of the Scottish Enlightenment – which remains to be written – would all the same have to start from the proposition that an intellectual movement centred on the universities, academies and informal watering holes, such as taverns, was inevitably conducted *very largely* in the absence of women, and indeed deliberately excluded them from its key centres. A recent description of Edinburgh as 'capital of the mind' describes it as a 'bachelor society', yet claims that it required 'a peculiar social environment' in which 'educated folk, sometimes women as well as men' met to discuss issues of knowledge and philosophy.[43] While informal contacts were of course possible, most serious intellectual intercourse took place in carefully demarcated all-male spaces – sometimes university lecture-halls (to the back of which women sometimes crept, though Colin McLaurin 'took no notice of their being there'). More often, it meant repairing to taverns and coffee-houses where respectable women could not follow – such as the Poker Club.[44] There were also exclusively male clubs, such as the Select Society of Edinburgh (1754–64).[45]

Numerous hostesses did entertain the poets, academics and lawyers in Glasgow and Edinburgh; but offering tea did not amount to keeping a salon in the French style (the latter in any case a space where women were numerically in a tiny minority). That did not mean that the writers of the Enlightenment did not 'enjoy the company of intelligent women',[46] or that they did not write about them in their works on civil society.

William Alexander, in his *History of Women* (1781), wrote that 'the rank and condition in which we find women in any country, marks out to us with the greatest precision, the exact point in the scale of civil society to which the people of such country have arrived' (a remark often made in later years by other men, and usually from a similar position of unjustified complacency). But their approach was in any case largely concerned with politeness and the 'civilizing influence' of women, and had little to do with the intellect (indeed, women's influence is often thought to have inhibited intellectual liberty), nor did it connect with plans to provide more education for women.[47]

The inevitable conclusion of seeking to historicise the Scottish Enlightenment, a time when an Englishman claimed he could 'take fifty men of genius and learning by the hand'[48] at an Edinburgh crossroads, is that in its heyday it was a specifically masculine culture, rather than a universal one. In this, it is at once similar to and different from the French Enlightenment. Whereas there, too, the leading figures were educated men, their world was less institutionally regulated than that of Scotland. The world of the *Encyclopédie* extended a little further into mixed society, reaching not simply the salons but also bourgeois gatherings where men and women were present. It has been argued by Carla Hesse, with a little exaggeration perhaps, that there was 'another enlightenment' in France, illustrated by the many women who were reading and publishing works in a variety of genres in the late eighteenth century.[49] In Scotland, while there are individual examples of educated women, the institutions and in particular the universities were formidable mechanisms for keeping women away from *public* connection with advanced thought.

For larger-scale participation by Scottish women in progressive thinking, we would probably have to look forward to later female intellectual networks. These were still numerically very small, and had not yet acquired much critical mass. Scotswoman Marion Reid's *Plea for Woman* (1843) was probably the first work in Britain or America to give priority to achieving civil and political rights for women, and was particularly influential in the USA. The debates about women's rights in the nineteenth century are in their way the equivalents of the Men's Enlightenment. In terms of democracy, to campaign for women's rights was an inclusive and extended form of democratic thinking, rather than an exclusive and restrictive one. Yet it rarely receives consideration as an *intellectual* movement, no doubt because it was associated with the ups and downs of a political movement, often reduced by historians to the fight for suffrage, but also because it required the backing of its own 'organic intellectuals', who were still in short supply.

In no way comparable in intellectual depth with the Select Society of Edinburgh, but a forum for independent thought nonetheless, was the city's Ladies' Debating Society, started by Sarah Siddons Mair in 1865 and frequented at first by very young women of genteel Edinburgh society.[50] One of its aims was to campaign for women's higher education, in order precisely to acquire intellectual depth, a cause that took many more years to accomplish. It could be argued that while the Men's Scottish Enlightenment was accomplished in the eighteenth century, preparing the way for the scientific and philosophical thought of the nineteenth, the Women's Scottish Enlightenment took place only much later and more gradually. It too was linked to the ancient universities – but this time the link was conflictual, since the universities long resisted attempts by women to graduate. Contemporary with similar movements all over Europe and America, this was not a specifically Scottish movement, but it had its own flavour. The battles to be admitted to medical school in the 1870s, most fiercely and publicly waged by Sophia Jex-Blake and the 'Edinburgh seven', as described by Eileen Janes Yeo in Chapter 6, the debates in the 1890s over whether women's education should be distinctive (i.e. including domestic subjects), and the struggle to allow women to graduate, linked networks of women, united in a common purpose in both Glasgow and Edinburgh and other university cities.[51]

THE FIELD IN THE NINETEENTH CENTURY: WRITING, SCIENCE AND FINE ART

During the nineteenth century, a number of developments affected Scottish culture as the Enlightenment years apparently faded to a remembered golden glow. The most significant was population change, embodied both in emigration and the move to the cities that accompanied industrialisation. Depopulation meant that oral traditions were lapsing or surviving only in remoter areas like the Western Isles. The literary scene appeared to decline too. Sir Walter Scott died in 1832, and many Scottish publishers moved to London, although Edinburgh remained a centre for book-printing. There is a conventional narrative describing some 'loss of nerve' in nineteenth-century Scottish culture, because industrialisation did not produce its Dickens or Mrs Gaskell to write about Glasgow. The story moves very quickly from Scott and Galt to a disparaging account of 'the Kailyard', the kind of popular and undemanding fiction which looked nostalgically back to a small-town society without ambition or challenge, ignoring the realities of Scottish urban society. Although the so-called Kailyard authors, except Annie S. Swan, were mostly men (Barrie, Crockett), there is some tendency to associate undemanding literature with women readers. However, this narrative, which views the period as the lost years when Scotland's 'Scottishness' was undistinguished, has also been challenged from various directions.

Cairns Craig has approached it by pointing to major Scottish writers who emigrated, taking Scottish consciousness south (Carlyle, Mill, James Frazer) or abroad (Robert Louis Stevenson), and to the confusion over the Kailyard. He calls criticism of it 'a category mistake': the Kailyard should be viewed instead as a Scottish example of popular tastes in reading which could be seen anywhere in Europe with the spread of literacy.[52] From another direction, the 'feminist retrieval' approach to nineteenth-century literature has sought to revive the fortunes of Scottish women writers of this period, well known in their day, less well known since, but rescued by republication. They would include novelist Susan Ferrier (1782–1854) and in particular Margaret Oliphant (1828–97). The latter has seen a spectacular rise both in her critical visibility and in critical appreciation. She was in the past cited as a writer of talent whose work suffered since she had to maintain her financially disaster-prone family, but it has been reassessed much more positively.[53] Another writer highly valued today is Jane Welsh Carlyle (1801–66), formerly in the shadow of her famous husband, now ensconced as 'one of the best letter-writers in the English language'.[54] Significantly perhaps, both the latter lived largely south of the border, not necessarily from choice. And autobiography, memoirs, journals and letters, which today tend to be regarded as a separate genre, 'life-writing', constitute a form of literature until recently less valued within the 'cultural field' than the classic triad of poetry, drama and fiction. Although by no means confined to women, life-writing opens the door much more widely to their recognition as writers – the popularity of such minor but interesting figures as Elizabeth Grant of Rothiemurchus (1797–1885) dates from the republication by Canongate of her *Memoirs of a Highland Lady* in the 1990s. Late twentieth-century publishing policy, dictated in part by increased awareness of a large female readership, has played a considerable part in reviving the fortunes of women writers.

But nineteenth-century Scotland also had particular achievements in the fields of science and, to a lesser extent perhaps, the visual arts. Unlike literature, for which the only initial qualification required was literacy and book-learning, both of these fields were particularly hard to enter as amateurs. Scotland is justly celebrated for its 'two great ages of science, the mid-eighteenth and mid-nineteenth century'.[55] If one looks at the early lives of William Thomson (later Lord Kelvin; 1824–1907) and

James Clerk Maxwell (1831–79), both outstandingly talented men, one finds that both were also fortunate in their family connections and their education. Thomson's father was professor of mathematics at Glasgow University. Educated at home and informally at the university, where he showed remarkable promise, William enrolled at 18 at Cambridge, where he received 'the best mathematical training available anywhere in Britain'. Three years later, he was a fellow of Peterhouse and was editing the *Mathematical Journal*. Married twice, he had no children. James Clerk Maxwell, son of a well-connected landowner, studied at Edinburgh Academy, was taken to meetings of the Royal Society of Edinburgh and entered the university aged 16, eventually going in turn to Cambridge, where he became a member of the select Apostles group, presenting papers on the philosophy of science. He too had a childless marriage. There is little need to labour the point that these trajectories were simply not possible for a woman, however talented.[56]

The case of Mary Somerville (1780–1872) contrasts in almost every particular with that of the two men of science. Born Mary Fairfax in Jedburgh, brought up in Burntisland, daughter of a naval lieutenant, she had one year at Miss Primrose's boarding school, but mainly taught herself from the family library. Obliged to indulge her precocious taste for mathematics in secret because of her father's disapproval, at 24 she married, moved to London and continued to study, without encouragement from her first husband, who died young leaving her with two children. Only the status afforded by widowhood enabled her to gain access to Edinburgh's intellectual circles, where she at last met informal encouragement and tuition and became familiar with the latest thought in mathematics. After her second marriage, to the army doctor William Somerville, the couple became well known in London's scientific circles; but it was only at the age of 51 that she published her translation of Laplace's *Mécanique céleste*, which required specialist knowledge. It was a recommended text at Cambridge by 1837, before our two scientists arrived there. Mary Somerville is best remembered as a writer on science and an expositor of other people's original research, as she remarked herself. Yet, as a philosopher of science, she wrote the classic *On the Connexion of the Physical Sciences* (1834), which ran into many editions and inspired many scientists. The fact that we call them scientists at all is partly because William Whewell coined the term after reading *The Connexion*: 'how valuable a boon it is to the mass of readers, when persons of real science, like Mrs Somerville, condescend to write for the wider public'.[57] Mary Somerville had a total of six children, three of whom died in infancy, and she had to travel constantly because of her husband's health. Given the obstacles with which this scientist *manquée* had to contend, the wonder is not that there was only one of her, but that she contrived any of this at all, let alone being hailed by contemporaries as 'the queen of science'. It does show, however, that there was some openness in the scientific academic community to a woman writer. The story of would-be women doctors in Edinburgh, by contrast, became a saga resolved only after much struggle, because of the practical threat to the male profession.[58]

In the fine arts, the gatekeeping mechanisms were breached piecemeal at first, but then collectively and with some success. Women of the middle classes were often offered some tuition in drawing and painting, but it rarely went beyond amateur status. However, they were admissible to art schools at various dates. The most striking example shows what a difference both institutional and private encouragement could make. Glasgow's growing prosperity led to the appearance of private patrons and funding for the art training of both men and women. In the 1880s, a group of male painters, some of whom exhibited in the Glasgow Institute of Fine Arts in 1885, decided to call themselves 'the Glasgow Boys'. Reacting in part against the stranglehold of the Royal Scottish Academy in Edinburgh, they shared some characteristics, such as their dislike of academic historical painters ('the Gluepots') and their admiration of Whistler and contemporary French naturalists. They had also shown how being a group could be good for one's artistic fortunes, and constituted a major peak of the nineteenth-century Scottish artistic landscape. Overlapping with this phenomenon, and carrying on afterwards, was an explosion of art and crafts by the first generation of women students at the Glasgow School of Art. When Francis (Fra) Newbery (1853–1946) became head of the School in 1889, his term of office saw a remarkable expansion of the numbers of talented women who enrolled. At the time, they received little attention from the art-critical community, and for years they appear to have been completely forgotten, apart from those associated with Charles Rennie Mackintosh (another victim of neglect by his contemporaries). The fact that we know about them at all is thanks to feminist intervention, via an exhibition in 1988, followed by a book.[59] These artists, many of whom travelled to study abroad and lived the independent lives of the 'new woman', included the two Macdonald sisters, Frances and Margaret, Jessie King, Bessie McNicol and others. Although never a group in their lifetime, they now, remarkably, have an entry under 'Glasgow Girls' in the *Oxford Dictionary of National Biography* (2004), alongside that of the Glasgow Boys. The case shows that, in order to be recognised, a group identity, even manufactured posthumously, is often helpful, and is more frequent among men than women (cf. 'The Scottish Colourists'). The case also raises the question of genre. Many women artists worked in the 'non-heroic' genres of illustration, embroidery, furniture design, enamelling and ceramics, often described as crafts (and in the ascendant in this period with the Arts and Crafts movement). The same was true of Phoebe Traquair, and of several women associated with the Edinburgh circle of Patrick Geddes at about the same time (the Old Edinburgh Art school).[60] Within the crafts, too, there was to some degree a pecking order, with 'harder' genres like woodwork, metalwork and enamelling being taken more seriously outside specialist circles than embroidery and textiles, in an obvious reflection of discourses about masculine and feminine.

A conclusion one might draw from these brief case studies is that, during the nineteenth century, the gender-configuration of the cultural field in Scotland conformed fairly closely to the general European pattern. Most cultural establishments remained the preserve of men; but increasingly individual women, often privileged either by education or social status, or by personal proximity to creative circles, started to make a mark on the field. Scotland had its 'new women' of the 1890s and 1900s, though they were often more concerned with fighting for civil and political rights than with making a cultural mark. Some, like Inverness-born Marion Dunlop (1864–1942), did combine the two, by bringing their artistic training to suffrage-campaign artefacts and pageants, though these brought no rewards in terms of their careers. Institutions like universities and art schools gradually opened their doors.[61] But women creators were often swallows who did not yet foretell a summer, fading from memory until deliberately rediscovered in later years, since they were often in practice isolated, even eccentric. Official histories of the cultural field tend to concentrate on movements, influences and groups. In this respect, Scotland was probably no more or less male-dominated than other countries.

THE TWENTIETH-CENTURY FIELD FROM 1914: SCOTTISH DISTINCTIVENESS?

Twentieth-century Scotland offers us a paradox in terms of gender, though again it is not peculiar to Scotland. With the changes in the status of women across most countries in Europe – civil, legal, property and political rights, formal policies of equal education and training, equal pay and anti-discrimination laws – one would expect to find a steadier growth of their participation in the arts and cultural activites than is the case. Cultural creators tend to come from among people who have at least some cultural capital, whether education or parental example. As in the past, many educated men in the twentieth century had cultural ambitions, while the newly educated women often enthusiastically became teachers, librarians, nurses and clerks, careers only gradually opened to them – but which they often had to leave on marriage. Creativity ought to have been a possibility, and some talents must have gone unobserved. Chronologically, however, the breakthrough of Scottish women of talent to recognition in the twentieth century has been gradual, uneven and individual, with a massive increase in the years since 1970.

The cultural field in the twentieth century was configured very differently from that of previous centuries. While there were still some legal and institutional hangovers, by and large the opposition to women's entry into any areas of the creative and performing arts was no longer blocked by rules. There had been fewer formal obstacles in some fields in any case: once mass literacy was achieved, it was theoretically possible for women to become writers, although both higher education and the world of publishing were male-dominated. And women had always been present and necessary as performers: actresses, singers, dancers, musicians. This continued: many Scottish actresses became well known in the twentieth century. But while there was no *formal* prohibition on their becoming film directors, orchestral conductors, publishers, theatre directors, playwrights or TV producers, or on receiving training in art schools or musical conservatoires, the number of Scotswomen who actually became noted creative players on the newly open and expanding cultural field remained small for much of the century. Among the few examples of success by Scottish women in the art world are Joan Eardley (1921–63) and Anne Redpath (1895–1965), though neither achieved instant fame. Eardley's reputation was largely posthumous, and arguably neither is as well known outside Scotland as one would expect. Literature has proved something of an exception, but analysis of literary movements helps illustrate something about the field more generally.

If we look briefly at two examples of Scotland's 'literary moments' in the twentieth century, it becomes clear that there was no ban on women joining them, but they offered little attraction to women to do so. The 'Scottish Renaissance Movement' of the 1920s and 1930s offers one kind of field, with its most powerful pole of attraction being its central figure, Hugh MacDiarmid/Christopher Grieve, who sought to 'encompass modern Scottish experience in a new national language and in a poetic style informed by . . . modernist practice'.[62] The writers of the 1920s and

1930s, while very different from each other, and not necessarily agreeing with MacDiarmid, fraternised intellectually around small short-lived magazines, in a world from which women were not excluded, but where to be a 'Scot', according to MacDiarmid, was to be 'dominated by the conception of infinity, of the unattainable, and hence ever questioning, never satisfied, rationalistic in religion and politics, romantic in art and literature'.[63] It was not impossible for women to think these thoughts (although in practice Scotswomen sufficiently educated, liberated and acquainted with advanced literary circles to do so were not all that numerous, even in the 1920s), but above all women were not envisaged as thinking them by the *men* who thought them. It is arguable that, as Christopher Harvie has written, some of these men, particularly Lewis Grassic Gibbon, wrote 'with sensitivity about women, while their pub society . . . kept women on the sidelines'.[64] They were certainly 'rarely given credit as contributors'.[65] Margery Palmer McCulloch has collected a set of source documents on the Scottish Renaissance Movement, culled from the periodicals of the time. But, despite her positive desire to give full prominence to associated women writers, such as Naomi Mitchison, Willa Muir and Catherine Carswell (who all wrote and/or translated extensively, and were determined characters), we find her saying reluctantly that 'in the early studies of the period, the Scottish renaissance was defined by its male creators alone . . . Women . . . did not on the whole take a public part in the literary and social/political debates of the time.' She was obliged to be satisfied with rather patchy documentary evidence of their writing in this context.[66] Other writers have been fiercer, about the misogyny of Hugh MacDiarmid in particular, arguing that the influential Scottish Renaissance was not just constructed without women but was *contrasted with* them. As Aileen Christianson has put it, *A Drunk Man Looks at the Thistle* 'irritates a woman reader by a sense of exclusion':

> You're the moon, the muse, the beautiful other, the threatening other, the child bearer. But you're not part of the centre, you're not in there thinking along with MacDiarmid, grappling with rage at misplaced patriotism, life, death, eternity. He's got you firmly placed elsewhere. Man's role is at the centre, your role is out there somewhere else.[67]

A later constellation of writers, the poets of mid-twentieth-century Scotland, have been enshrined in a famous painting by Alexander Moffat, *Poets' Pub* (1980), frequently reproduced on book jackets and in studies of Scottish culture. The problem here has nothing to do with the quality of the men represented, poets whose contribution to Scottish literature is generally well recognised: they include MacDiarmid in old age, alongside Norman MacCaig, Edwin Morgan, Sorley MacLean and others. The problem is one of perception: that the pub is the explicit centre of fraternity. United in the painting around a pint, though few of them are actually drinking, these men represent creativity in its most male, collective and exclusive expression. In case the message isn't clear enough, the periphery of the picture contains references to male views of women – a Gauguin Tahitian, Delacroix's *Liberty*, both bare-breasted, and a woman of the night in the shadows.[68]

Rather surprisingly, this picture dates from 1980, a time when feminist cultural analysis was newly available. Certainly earlier in the century, hardly anyone was likely to criticise any intellectual movement or group for its 'masculinity'. What emerges with some clarity, looking back with hindsight, is that feminist thought from the 1970s on, with its particular focus on cultural patriarchy, has made it possible to read back into earlier ages their gender imbalance, while at the same time making it possible to accept without complexes 'masculine' forms of culture as precisely that – masculine, instead of assuming that they stand for the whole of Scotland. Nowadays, for example, Christopher Whyte can argue, against Christianson, that in *A Drunk Man* MacDiarmid was articulating a very specific Scottish masculine angst, not claiming to be universal.[69] Awareness of the existence of a troubled masculinity in Scottish culture has only really been possible in recent years, thanks to new approaches, specifically more gender-conscious ones, in literary commentary. Both Whyte and Christianson seem to me to be right about the poem – it does exclude women from higher thought and centrality, and it is concerned with masculine angst. The difference is that in post-1980 Scotland this can seem obvious to us in a way it never was at the time.

The same approach can today be taken to other apparently dominant male groups as well, whether writers such as William McIlvanney and James Kelman, who have written about and through the voice of the Glasgow male working class, and who are often bracketed together (misleadingly, no doubt, but it happens), or through the group of 1980s 'masculinist' painters, like Ken Currie and Peter Howson. If we can agree, for example, that Spark's *The Prime of Miss Jean Brodie* (1961) described a virtually all-female and socially restricted world, we can also see that Welsh's *Trainspotting* (1993) also described virtually all-male and socially restricted worlds. The 'hard man', the marginalised drug-user, and the posh schoolgirl can all be seen as representing some group in Scottish society: no one today is going to mistake a single voice as universal. In most critical writing about Scottish literature in the last ten years, there has been a deliberate effort to apply a gendered analysis.[70]

It is true that such ideas are not universally shared: outside Scotland, what appear to be male stereotypes of Scottish culture (the hard man, Robert Burns as Jack the Lad, even the Tartan Army) have a good deal of currency as representing the nation. As A. L. Kennedy remarks, 'There's still an idea that the Scottish product will be grim and gritty and male'.[71] There is a sort of critical mass behind such assumptions, although it would be inaccurate to describe such writers as Alasdair Gray, say, or Iain Banks, let alone poets like Matthew Fitt and Don Paterson, in these terms. Viewed historically, however, there have been far more Scottish women writers published in recent years. While Naomi Mitchison, Elspeth Davie and to some extent even Muriel Spark were isolated, somewhat maverick figures, outside any movement, today there is a degree of critical mass for women too. For a long while, Liz Lochhead had to bear the burden of being a lone female voice, almost a token presence in Scotland; but she has been acknowledged as an important role model. Without Scottish women writers constituting a group, what has changed is that there is no longer exclusion of voices coming from women's consciousness. The younger generation contains a range of women's voices, providing their own context and implicit if not explicit support: Janice Galloway, A. L. Kennedy, Ali Smith, Kathleen Jamie, Jackie Kay and others.[72]

The foregoing paragraphs largely refer to literature for two reasons: firstly because, despite problems of access to publishers and reception by the public, it has always been *comparatively* easier for women to break into the literary world; secondly, because literary scholars have been working at gender analysis for longer than most historians, whose chapters on culture are often the section of their work least sensitive to gender.[73] If one surveys non-literary aspects of the cultural field in twentieth-century Scotland, one finds a patchier picture, although the chronology is roughly similar. Most of the arts establishments – theatre, cinema, broadcasting, fine art, periodicals, museums and galleries, the press, opera, the symphony orchestras – were overwhelmingly and rather surprisingly male in staffing, creative work and leadership, for most of the twentieth century. Such changes as there have been – and they are not negligible – have taken place only relatively recently, so much so as hardly to be 'historical'. However, we do have sufficient data to suggest that they represent an irreversible if not always rapid move towards greater participation by women in the cultural professions.

Figures available from the 1991 census show the distribution of the sexes in cultural occupations in Scotland. Overall, there were 27,600 individuals in Scotland in these occupations, of whom women represented 35 per cent, men 65 per cent. The detailed figures now available for this data enable us to see profiles of particular sectors. Women accounted for 90 per cent of clothing designers, 70 per cent of librarians and 56 per cent of archivists and curators. In all other professions, they were in the minority, though they came close in industrial design (43 per cent), the performing arts (42 per cent) and visual artists, including commercial artists (41 per cent). Surprisingly perhaps, women made up only 35 per cent of 'authors, writers and journalists' (partly because of the statistical dominance of journalism) and were clearly a minority in music (22 per cent), photography, film and video operation (22 per cent) and architects (9 per cent).[74] Nevertheless, these figures indicate that, already by 1991, women were entering these professions in larger numbers than in the past. The provisional figures for the 2001 census, which have not yet been fully analysed, show that this overall trend is continuing. Using differently based figures relating to employment (rather than named profession) for 2001, women constituted 49 per cent of employees in the narrow or 'everyday' definition of cultural jobs, that is, what most people would mean by the arts, while they were in a majority in the cultural sector more broadly defined (which includes tourism, heritage and sport).[75]

Within these overall figures, clearly women are over-represented in some areas (librarianship) and under-represented in others, like architecture, for reasons which remain speculative but can be guessed at. However, it is also the case that within most sectors they are rarely in key positions. Although for some time now the majority of students studying creative arts in higher education in Scotland (up to two-thirds by 2002–3) have been women, this presence has not yet been reflected in later career paths. A report on the arts in 1997 found that 'women are highly visible in most organisations and throughout education, and yet absent from positions of real influence in decision-making and presentation and creation of work'.[76] While present at employee level, they constituted for example only 28 per cent of artistic directors. In [classical] music, men 'composed and conducted 99% of works . . . 85 per cent of the writers and directors of drama productions were male and just under 60 per cent of artists featured in solo exhibitions . . . were male'. The same balance was true of applications for Scottish Arts Council grants. The most recent figures (2002–3) for teaching staff at the Royal Scottish Academy of Music and Drama indicated that 63 per cent were men, whereas the student body was over 60 per cent female, and similar figures applied to the art colleges in the two major cities. These figures were roughly comparable to both the rest of the UK and Europe, with music and cinema being, predictably perhaps, given their historical profiles, areas where women are rarely present at the top. So it is not yet the case that the cultural field is a level playing field.[77]

Nevertheless, the arts establishment in Scotland has also seen some changes towards greater gender balance. To take a few random examples, the Spring 2005 programme for the Traverse Theatre, Edinburgh, which specialises in new Scottish writing, advertised ten plays in full production written by men and five by women (plus two readings); twelve male directors, and four female directors are named. Hardly gender equality, perhaps, but a difference from twenty or even ten years ago. Playwriting has been a sphere in which women have generally been a tiny minority; but that appears to have changed.[78] It is probably too soon to expect there to be many women film-makers, given their rarity everywhere except in television.[79] But Lynn Ramsay's *Ratcatcher* (1999) has been one of Scotland's most exported films in recent years. The founding of the Scottish Poetry Library in 1984 was, according to Christopher Harvie, 'as significant in its way as the founding of the Irish literary theatre in the 1900s'.[80] Its founder and first director was poet Tessa Ransford, who has also edited *Lines Review*. The magazine *Chapman* has been edited by Joy Hendry for many years, and both women have been constant fighters for greater gender balance in Scottish arts. Elspeth King has been a prominent figure in museum curatorship, though a lone one: virtually all Scotland's major galleries and museums have always had men at their heads. Women have been appointed to some leading positions in the arts in Scotland (Minister of Culture, Director of the Scottish Arts Council, newspaper columnists, Principal of the Glasgow School of Art). Some of these developments have accompanied, or followed, the ferment about devolution, but there is no obvious causal link.

CONCLUSION

At the end of this brief survey, then, our conclusions about the Scottish cultural landscape are that there has not been some timeless gender divide in which creative forces were all male, with women always playing supporting roles or consuming culture as patronesses, readers and audiences. On the other hand, neither has there been steady 'progress' over time, with women gradually taking their place as full participants in cultural affairs and creative arts. The story is a more complicated one. In pre-industrial Scotland, some forms of traditional culture, despite a generally patriarchal society, were marked by a high rate of participation by women, which perhaps needs more research than it has yet received. As that society declined, a more urban and institutional culture replaced these forms, drawing on a different kind of past. From earliest times, the advanced sectors of Scottish culture, as in the rest of Europe, drew on the all-male institutions first of the Church, then of Scotland's early-established universities. Scholarship was confined to men. If 'a fair case, in terms of its culture, can be made that the second language of Scotland was Latin until the 1720s',[81] we can be sure who was excluded from it. Enlightenment changed life massively for educated Scotsmen: as Michael Lynch reminds us, 'by 1750, the Edinburgh medical school . . . had established a reputation second to none, in Britain and Europe', while over the next 100 years Scotland's universities educated some 10,000 doctors to Oxford and Cambridge's 500.[82] As the institutional world enlarged for men, it actually became even further out of reach for women, who were systematically excluded from centres of learning and were left to amateur status in the arts. They lacked the range of education and, on the whole, travel, which sustained cultural initiatives. That did not prevent original, determined, gifted, and usually privileged, women from making a breakthrough, and in larger numbers than is generally recognised; but the 'lass of pairts' was not encouraged.

Things began to change in the later nineteenth century, though only when pressure from women met agreement from sympathetic men (like Fra Newbery). Institutional barriers crumbled. But it took longer for habits and mindsets to change, in both sexes. Virtually all the cultural role models of the past were men, and the men of the present had informal ways of excluding women. It has taken the renewed and determined form of feminism of the late twentieth century, a slow burn in Scotland perhaps, but eventually recognised within the male cultural establishment and public opinion, to see really major change. This is a blink of the eye in historical terms, and it is still in progress.[83] One indication is the clearly deliberate attempt to include women writers in the '100 best Scottish books of all time', a list published, no doubt to stir up controversy, by the magazine *The List* in 2005. Twenty-four books by women were included in the top 100 titles, with another twenty-seven in the next 100. It is worth noting, however, that the vast majority of the women writers mentioned there are living today, and not a few are still comparative beginners; only a dozen are from previous generations of writers.[84]

'It is perhaps only in this present generation that a more inclusive vision of Scottish culture has begun to be formulated', Lynch wrote in 1993.[85] I am not entirely sure that he had gender in mind; but this view would fit with hopes for a new inclusive pluralism in Scottish culture. This short chapter has only been able to scratch the surface of the subject of gender and Scottish culture. It has not tackled sexuality, a major aspect of gender, and it has not attempted to combine the topic with the question of ethnicity in Scotland – whether immigration from Ireland in the nineteenth century, the place within Scottish culture of expatriates from England and Wales in the twentieth century, or the increasing numbers of new Scots from much further afield in recent years. In an optimistic view, Scotland would be able to move on from some rather one-dimensional stereotypes towards the 'polyphonic' culture that Robert Crawford wishfully imagines, with many voices (differing in region, ethnic origin, language, sex, class and religion).[86] But one step in that direction which historians could take would be to use the keys to the National Library in order to study Scotland's cultural past in a far more inclusive way.

FURTHER READING

See the books cited in the notes and also:

Craig, C. (ed.), *The History of Scottish Literature*, vols 2–4 (Aberdeen: Aberdeen University Press, 1987–8).

McMillan, D. and M. Byrne (eds), *Modern Scottish Women Poets* (Edinburgh: Canongate, 2003).

Normand, T., *The Modern Scot: Modernism and Nationalism in Scottish Art* (Aldershot: Ashgate, 2000).

Whyte, C., *Modern Scottish Poetry* (Edinburgh: Edinburgh University Press, 2004).

NOTES

I would like to thank Christopher Whyte for his helpful reading of this chapter.

1. T. Nairn, *The Break-up of Britain* (London: New Left Books, 1977); C. McArthur, *Scotch Reels* (London: BFI, 1982); C. Beveridge and R. Turnbull, *The Eclipse of Scottish Culture: Inferiorism and the Intellectuals* (Edinburgh: Polygon, 1989); C. Craig, *Out of History* (Edinburgh: Polygon, 1996); D. McCrone, *Understanding Scotland: The Sociology of a Nation* (London: Routledge, 1992; 2nd edn 2001); T. M. Devine, *The Scottish Nation* (London: Penguin, 1999), esp. ch. 13; and many other books. See Chapter 1 in this collection.

2. Carol Anderson and Glenda Norquay, 'Superiorism', *Cencrastus* 15 (1984), 8–10.

3. R. J. Finlay, 'Culture. 21', in M. Lynch (ed.), *Oxford Companion to Scottish History* (Oxford: Oxford University Press, 2001), p. 152.

4. R. J. Morris, 'Introduction', in W. H. Fraser and R. J. Morris (eds), *People and Society in Scotland, vol. 2, 1830–1914* (Edinburgh: John Donald, 1990), p. 2.

5. R. Watson, 'Dialectics of voice and place: literature in Scots and English from 1700', in P. H. Scott (ed.), *Scotland: A Concise Cultural History* (Edinburgh: Mainstream, 1993), p. 118.

6. R. Crawford, 'Dedefining Scotland', in S. Bassnett (ed.), *Studying British Cultures* (London: Routledge, 1997), p. 93.

7. Scott (ed.), *Scotland: A Concise Cultural History*; see n. 5 above.

8. Ibid., jacket.

9. J. Burkhauser (ed.), *Glasgow Girls: Women in Art and Design 1880–1920* (Edinburgh: Canongate, 1990); cf. J. Helland, *Professional Women Painters in Nineteenth-century Scotland* (Aldershot: Ashgate, 2000).

10. 'No Gods and precious few women: gender and cultural identity', *Scottish Affairs* (November 1992), 48; the reference is to C. Harvie, *No Gods and Precious Few Heroes* (London: Arnold, 1981).

11. A. Calder, *Revolving Culture* (London: Tauris, 1994), p. 235.

12. Ibid., p. 242; the same, *pace* Calder, would be true of Wales.

13. Ibid., p. 235. Perhaps this has yet to be done. There are some useful historical studies of popular culture, though they tend to concentrate disproportionately on masculine pursuits like football and drinking. See T. C. Smout, *A Century of the Scottish People 1830–1950* (ch. 6); Harvie, *No Gods* (ch. 5); W. H. Fraser, 'Developments in leisure', in Fraser and Morris (eds), *People and Society*, pp. 236–64. Calder in *Revolving Culture*, p. 239, writes that 'ballet does not necessarily represent something intrinsically finer than football', with which one can agree – though the opposite is also true.

14. J. Lane, *Pierre Bourdieu: A Critical Introduction* (London: Pluto, 2000), p. 73.

15. D. S. Thomson, 'Gaelic Scotland', in D. Glen (ed.), *Whither Scotland: A Prejudiced Look at the Future of a Nation* (London: Gollancz, 1971), p. 134.

16. See the articles on Gaelic language and culture in Lynch (ed.), *Oxford Companion*, p. 332.

17. For example, '[P]redominantly clerical and in political terms conservative', B. P. Lenman, 'From the union of 1701 to the Franchise reform of 1832', in R. A. Houston and W. W. J. Knox (eds), *The Penguin History of Scotland* (London: Penguin, 2001), p. 342. Among other estimates and re-estimates of the Enlightenment, see A. Calder, 'The Enlightenment', in I. Donnachie and C. Whatley (eds), *The Manufacture of Scottish History* (Edinburgh: Polygon, 1992), pp. 31–50; T. Devine, *The Scottish Nation* (London: Penguin, 1999), chs 4, 6.

18. Cf. D. Daiches, *The Paradox of Scottish Culture* (Oxford: Oxford University Press, 1964).

19. Quoted in C. MacDougall, *Writing Scotland: How Scotland's Writers Shaped the Nation* (Edinburgh: Polygon, 2004), p. 156 (and many other places).

20. J. MacInnes, 'The bard through history', in T. Neat with J. MacInnes, *The Voice of the Bard: Living Poets and Ancient Tradition in the Highlands and Islands of Scotland* (Edinburgh: Canongate, 1999), p. 325.

21. A. Frater, 'The Gaelic tradition up to 1750', in D. Gifford and D. McMillan (eds), *A History of Scottish Women's Writing* (Edinburgh: Polygon, 1997), p. 3; and her 'Women of the Gàidhealtachd and their songs to 1750', in E. Ewan and M. Meikle (eds), *Women in Scotland: c.1100-c.1750* (East Linton: Tuckwell, 1999), pp. 67–82.

22. J. Shaw in Lynch (ed.), *Oxford Companion*, p. 466.

23. J. MacInnes, 'Gaelic folksong', in D. Daiches (ed.), *A New Companion to Scottish Culture* (Edinburgh: Polygon, 1993), p. 115; see also D. U. Stiùbhart, 'Women and gender in the early modern western Gàidhealtachd', in Ewan and Meikle (eds), *Women in Scotland*, p. 238.

24. Frater, 'The Gaelic tradition', p. 1; Neat with MacInnes, *Voice of the Bard*, p. 339ff.

25. J. MacDonald, 'Gaelic literature', in Lynch (ed.), *Oxford Companion*, pp. 255–6.

26. Ibid., p. 256; also Neat with MacInnes, *Voice of the Bard*, p. 340: 'she could read her own poetry in print but not write it'; it was taken down from her recitation.

27. C. Kerrigan, *An Anthology of Scottish Women Poets* (Edinburgh: Edinburgh University Press, 1991). See also Derick Thomson', 'Gaelic literature', in Scott (ed.), *Scotland: A Concise Cultural History*, pp. 127–44; and D. Thomson, *An Introduction to Gaelic Poetry* (London: Gollancz, 1974).

28. Daiches (ed.), *New Companion*, p. 16.

29. Lynch (ed.), *Oxford Companion*, p. 587.

30. A. Calder, 'The Enlightenment', in Donnachie and Whatley (eds), *The Manufacture of Scottish History*, p. 49; see also Joy Hendry, 'Snug in the asylum of taciturnity: women's history in Scotland' in the same collection.

31. Cf. MacDougall, *Writing Scotland*.

32. William Donaldson, entry on Anna Gordon Brown, in the *Oxford Dictionary of National Biography* (Oxford: Oxford University Press, 2004), hereafter *ODNB*; D. A. Symonds, *Weep Not for Me: Women, Ballads, and Infanticide in Early Modern Scotland* (University Park, PA: Pennsylvania State University Press, 1997); H. Henderson in Daiches (ed.), *New Companion*, p. 18–9.

33. Henderson in Daiches (ed.), *New Companion*, p. 17.

34. Quoted as epigraph for Scott (ed.), *Scotland: A Concise Cultural History*.

35. R. A. Houston, *Scottish Literacy and the Scottish Identity* (Cambridge: Cambridge University Press, 1985), p. 65.

36. Houston, quoted in R. D. Anderson, *Education and the Scottish People* (Oxford: Oxford University Press, 1995), p. 15.

37. Houston, *Scottish Literacy*, pp. 57, 67.

38. Dugald Stewart: 'There is scarcely a person of either sex to be met with [in Edinburgh] who is not able to read', quoted in Anderson, *Education*, p. 20.

39. J. Buchan, *Edinburgh, Capital of the Mind* (London: Murray, 2003), p. 248.

40. Miss [E. Ogilvy] Benger, *Memoirs of the Late Mrs Elizabeth Hamilton* (1818), vol. 1, p. 50.

41. *A Father's Legacy to his Daughters* (1774), quoted in Buchan, *Capital of the Mind*, p. 259.

42. See J. Rendall, 'Clio, Mars and Minerva', in T. M. Devine and J. R. Young (eds), *Eighteenth-century Scotland* (East Linton: Tuckwell, 1999); J. Rendall, ' "Friends of liberty and virtue": women radicals and transatlantic correspondence, 1789–1848', in C. Bland and M. Cross (eds), *Gender and Politics in the Age of Letter-Writing, 1750–2000* (Aldershot: Ashgate, 2004), pp. 77–92; and J. Rendall's entries on these women in *The Biographical Dictionary of Scottish Women* (forthcoming, Edinburgh University Press, 2006), hereafter *BDSW*.

43. Buchan, *Capital of the Mind*, p. 248.

44. Minute book reproduced in D. Daiches, J. Jones and P. Jones, *A Hotbed of Genius* (Edinburgh: Edinburgh University Press, 1986), p. 155. Hume, Smith, Robertson and Black were among its members in 1776; on McLaurin, see Buchan, *Capital of the Mind*, p. 248.

45. Very early in the century, a female debating club, the Fair Intellect club in Edinburgh, was started by a small number of well-born young Edinburgh ladies. At least it shows that the idea was thinkable. Houston and Knox (eds), *Penguin History of Scotland*, p. 329; cf. Lynch (ed.), *Oxford Companion*, p. 135.

46. Daiches et al., *Hotbed*, p. 93.

47. Alexander, quoted in Rendall, 'Clio, Mars and Minerva', p. 137; and see n. 50 below.

48. Quoted in Daiches et al., *Hotbed*, p. 1.

49. C. Hesse, *The Other Enlightenment: How French Women Became Modern* (Princeton, NJ: Princeton University Press, 2001). Germany too had prominent groups of women intellectuals in the early nineteenth century. Oddly enough, as a footnote to this discussion of inequality of opportunity, the cultural dominance of the kirk, at least according to T. C. Smout, may also have diverted 'the *lad* of pairts' away from independent thought more than his French equivalent: 'the middle class gave many of its best brains to the ministry which would in later times have been spread more widely', *A History of the Scottish People 1560–1830* (London: Fontana edn, 1981), p. 480.

50. L. M. Rae, *Ladies in Debate, Being a History of the Ladies' Edinburgh Debating Society 1865–1935* (Edinburgh: Oliver & Boyd, 1936); *ODNB* (2004) entry on S. Mair; and S. Innes, entry on Mair in *BDSW*. On attempts to construct a dichotomous intellectual field in the early nineteenth century, where expertise would be viewed as masculine while women of letters were

granted some practical and moral authority, see Judith Newton, 'Engendering history for the middle class: sex and political economy in the *Edinburgh Review*', in Linda Shires (ed.), *Rewriting the Victorians: Theory, History and the Politics of Gender* (London: Routledge, 1992), pp. 1–17. Note p. 9: 'there are some things women do better than men; of these perhaps novel-writing is one', quoted from the *Edinburgh Review* 51, p. 446.

51. See, for example, L. Moore, *Bajanellas and Semilinas: Aberdeen University and the Education of Women 1860–1920* (Aberdeen: Aberdeen University Press, 1991), and Chapter 5 in this volume.

52. Craig, *Out of History*, p. 107; this argument is also made by T. M. Devine in *The Scottish Nation*, ch. 13; see also M. Lynch, 'Scottish culture in historical perspective', in Scott (ed.), *Scotland: A Concise Cultural History*, pp. 15–46.

53. P. Davis, *The Victorians*, vol. 8 in the *Oxford English Literary History 1830–1880* (Oxford: Oxford University Press, 2002), pp. 197–201 and 147–53. See also the major contribution to rescuing writers from neglect by the Canongate Classics series, general editor Rory Watson.

54. She is so described both in M. Drabble (ed.), *The Oxford Companion to English Literature* (Oxford: Oxford University Press, 2000 edn) and in the article on Jane Welsh Carlyle in the *ODNB* (2004) by K. Fielding and D. Sorensen.

55. J. Lenihan, 'Mathematics and science', in Scott (ed.), *Scotland: A Concise Cultural History*, p. 291. No reference is made in that chapter to Mary Somerville; see below.

56. Information from the *ODNB* articles on both men and from Leniman, 'Mathematics and science'.

57. See *Nature,* 401 (26 April 2001), 1,031.

58. D. McMillan (ed.), *Queen of Science: The Personal Recollections of Mary Somerville* (Edinburgh: Canongate, 2001); cf. Chapter 6 in this collection.

59. Burkhauser (ed.), *Glasgow Girls*; cf. n. 9 above.

60. E. Cumming, ' "A gleam of Renaissance hope": Edinburgh at the turn of the century', in W. Kaplan (ed.), *Scotland Creates: 5,000 Years of Art and Design* (Glasgow: Glasgow Museums and Art Galleries, 1990), pp. 149–61; E. Cumming, *Phoebe Anna Traquair 1852–1936* (Edinburgh: Scottish National Portrait Gallery, 1993).

61. A note on classical music. Although traditional and folk music thrived in Scotland, 'art' or classical music did not, after the Reformation: there were no conservatoires, and, although Edinburgh and later Glasgow became fully functioning if minor European musical centres in terms of concerts and performances, it was not until the 1890s, and the rise of several Scottish composers (all men) and the foundation of what is now the Royal Scottish Academy of Music and Drama, that there were the beginnings of a national 'serious music' culture. Within these limits, Scotland provided several women performers and instrumentalists in the nineteenth century, such as

opera singer Mary Garden (1874–1967); but they generally trained abroad. Orchestras, as elsewhere, were almost all male, though chamber groups contained women players.

62. C. Craig, 'Culture. 24', in Lynch (ed.), *Oxford Companion*, p. 156.

63. Quoted in R. Watson, *The Literature of Scotland* (London: Macmillan, 1984), p. 352.

64. Harvie, *No Gods*, p. 134.

65. Craig, 'Culture. 25', in Lynch(ed.), *Oxford Companion*, p. 158.

66. M. P. McCulloch (ed.), *Modernism and Nationalism: Literature and Society in Scotland 1918–1939, Source Documents for the Scottish Renaissance* (Glasgow: Association for Scottish Literary Studies, 2004); this is a rich source of material, giving as full a place to women in these circles as possible. It appears from the documents cited here that they too often saw women's destinies as shaped largely by domestic responsibilities; see introduction, p. xvii. Cf. J. Foster, 'The twentieth century 1914–1979', in Houston and Knox (eds), *Penguin History of Scotland*: 'Scottish patriarchalism', he writes, 'survived alive and well into the second half of the 20th century including the early 1960s, which saw younger marriages and more children before the arrival of the contraceptive pill. Then, in common with the rest of Britain, there began a major shift in family and social life', p. 437.

67. A. Christianson, 'Flyting with "a Drunk Man" ', *Scottish Affairs* 5 (1993), pp. 126–35.

68. The picture is in the Scottish National Portrait Gallery in Edinburgh; to be fair, the same artist has done a striking portrait of Muriel Spark. But compare the more recent, mixed, group portrait by Calum Colvin of several Glasgow writers.

69. C. Whyte, 'Gender and sexuality in the *Drunk Man*', *Scottish Affairs* 5 (Autumn 1993), 136–46.

70. A recent example, aimed at the popular market, was the book and TV series *Scottish Writing*, by Carl MacDougall (see n. 31 above), which includes a chapter on women's writing (perhaps inevitably called 'Lost voices') and makes a serious effort to refer to women's writing in other chapters. On the other hand, the cover illustration for MacDougall's book, by Sandy Moffatt, again identifies Scottish writing with men, in this case Robert Burns and Irvine Welsh.

71. MacDougall, *Scottish Writing*, p. 179.

72. A. Christianson and A. Lumsden (eds), *Contemporary Scottish Women Writers*, (Edinburgh: Edinburgh University Press, 2000), introduction.

73. Christopher Harvie's chapter on culture in *No Gods* (1991) was more suggestive and open to gender analysis than many, but this seems to have rather waned in his contribution to the *Penguin History of Scotland* (2001).

74. Figures from 1991 from S. Galloway, *Cultural Occupations*, a CCPR briefing paper (Glasgow: Centre for Cultural Policy Research, August 2004), consulted on www.culturalpolicy.arts.gla.ac.uk Thanks go to the CCPR for

help in locating these data. Definitions of 'cultural professions' vary; see the briefing papers in question for detailed explanations. We need more historical research than is yet available on women in the cultural professions.

75. Figures for 2001 from S. Galloway, *Employment in Scotland's Cultural Sector 1998–2001*, a CCPR briefing paper (Glasgow: Centre for Cultural Policy Research, December 2003) consulted on www.culturalpolicy. arts.gla.ac.uk

76. S. Coleman, 'Arts', in *Engender, Gender Audit* (Edinburgh: Engender, 1997), pp. 72–9.

77. Galloway, *Cultural Occupations*, pp. 20–3.

78. Successful Scottish women playwrights of recent years include Sharman Macdonald, Liz Lochhead and Sue Glover. And contemporary male playwrights like John Byrne and John Clifford cannot be called patriarchal.

79. On cinema, see a half-hearted (because unexamined) reference to the lack of women directors in C. McArthur (ed.), *Scotch Reels: Scotland in Cinema and Television* (London: BFI, 1982), pp. 67–8. See also D. Petrie, *Screening Scotland* (London: British Film Institute, 2000), introduction – a useful collection. F. Hardy, 'The cinema', in Scott (ed.), *Scotland: A Concise Cultural History*, mentions no women at all, despite the contribution to the Scottish documentary tradition from, among others, Ruby Grierson, Jenny Gilbertson and Margaret Tait.

80. C. Harvie, 'Scotland after 1978', in Houston and Knox (eds), *Penguin History of Scotland*, p. 521 – a nice accolade which does not, however, mention Tessa Ransford by name.

81. M. Lynch, 'Scottish culture', in Scott (ed.), *Scotland*, p. 39.

82. Ibid., p. 40.

83. 'It has been a slow process getting women [film] directors through . . . If you suggest a female road movie or a movie with two female leads, you are always shot down with "Oh we've had *Thelma and Louise*". Can you imagine how many road movies there are about men?', *The Scotsman*, 20 January 2005, quoting a woman producer based in Edinburgh. The article was, however, largely about 'Scotland's most senior female TV exec', Agnes Wilkie, head of features at STV, who was more optimistic. Television has been more woman-friendly than the cinema, in Scotland and everywhere else.

84. *100 Best Scottish Books of All Time*, introduction by Willy Maley (Edinburgh: The List, 2005).

85. Lynch, in Scott (ed.), *Scotland*, p. 37.

86. Crawford, 'Dedefining Scotland', p. 93.

8

Work, Trade and Commerce

Deborah Simonton

INTRODUCTION

Throughout the modern period, workplaces were gendered spaces, whether farm, workshop, factories, shops, offices or institutions. The character of gender boundaries and constructions varied – both by time and by place. The culture of the Highland croft, the Aberdeen bakery, the Edinburgh bank, the Glasgow shipyard, the Bo'ness ironworks and the Dundee mill were different, but in all cases gender was at work. Men and women operated within a variety of work cultures that reflected shifting relationships between workers and masters and between the sexes. At the same time, the gendered aspect of the workplace became modified to accommodate ideological shifts. Many changes reflected those of the wider British, European and, ultimately, western world. Others were specifically Scottish, located in the culture and custom of Scotland. So, in some trades and occupations, a clear gendered division of labour operated, while some occupations and workplaces became gender-specific, based variously on arguments couched in discourses of skill, the family economy, status, education, strength, honour, domesticity or simply masculinity and femininity. And always there are exceptions to the dominant narrative: men might be seen as weavers, but women wove. Men were the 'workers', while women were 'working women'.

This chapter will address the character of the workplace and workplace culture, looking at experiences of work, trade and commerce with a particular focus on the gendered relationships within those physical and ideological spaces. It will explore factors that shaped the workforce and how that workforce negotiated the activities and space within which it operated. This chapter is not a history of the industrial revolution in Scotland or of the economy generally; also it is not a narration of the labour movement. Notably, given the tendency to bemoan the lack of basic research in Scottish women's history, this chapter is also testament to the range and depth of research that exists, giving historians a base on which to build. If some of this is 'sex'-aware but not 'gender'-aware, it is because women and men are discussed but the relationship is not always analysed; but gender is becoming more fully thought through, for example by Anna Clark and Eleanor Gordon on textile workers, and Arthur McIvor and Ronnie Johnston on Scottish coalmining.[1]

Work took place in the context of a fluid social and economic structure. The start of our period was one of economic expansion in industry and agriculture, which was part and parcel of an increasing commercial marketplace at home and abroad. Effectively, few barriers separated town from country, industry and trade from farming or industrial workers from agricultural labourers. The countryside produced much of the labour for the towns, particularly women, and there was a constant movement of people between them; many early industries were located in rural areas, while industry and trade relied on agricultural products. While the timing, and indeed the pattern, of change varied regionally, these developments contributed to shaping the meaning of work for both men and women. The most obvious changes were that work was increasingly defined as waged labour, that the location of work changed for many and that the structure and use of time altered. In conjunction with these shifts, the meaning of work changed so that skill and status took on new connotations, and the gendered parameters of work were redefined.

Many historians have located work in the home, referring to the family or household economy; and hiring patterns in agriculture and rural industry reflected contemporary perceptions that the family was a work unit. These practices had long-term implications in the ways that patriarchal structures and ideas permeated discourses about gender and work. Importantly, the idea of family economy tends to imply a coherent, negotiated, collaborative and unified household – a rural idyll, destroyed by industrialisation. But, as Pam Sharpe commented, 'there are more indications of conflictual than consensual relationships'.[2] Power relationships were not neutral, since position gained through age, gender and economic control shaped how units worked – or did not. The patriarchal notion of 'men in charge' by virtue of gender and recognition as heads of households certainly shaped household, workshop, mine and industrial relations. But other male and female workers negotiated their own space through consensus and contest.

THE AGRARIAN WORLD

Until after 1851, most people lived and worked in the countryside. Over time, men became more clearly identified with farming, marking a shift

from a largely family enterprise, while women became more clearly identified as casual, part-time workers, or left altogether. 'Improvement' and
commercialisation influenced the kinds of work each sex did, but gender
and skill shaped the context, so that women's 'natural' abilities meant
they were more likely to be engaged in 'fiddly' work while men claimed
the tools and practices that could be associated with skill and standing.

The ideal was the couple working their own land, whether farm,
tenancy, plot or croft, usually dividing roles and tasks in customary divisions of labour, which were age- and gender-specific. Thus men worked
primarily in fields and with livestock while women ran the 'barnyard'
including the house and its contiguous land, looking after small animals
and usually a vegetable plot, and marketing surpluses for important cash
income. It was common to combine work on one's own plot with waged
labour on another's farm or in rural industries. So ploughmen or hinds in
the Lothians worked for a 'gudeman', a substantial tenant, and received
wages or payment in kind. Waged labour was rare in the Highlands, and
subtenants worked a small strip of land, paying rent by unpaid labour on
the land.[3]

Research in France is suggestive of the gendered allocation of space.
Lucienne Roubin argues that females controlled the peasant household,
especially the kitchen, which 'represented an organic complex minutely
compartmentalized into a maze of storerooms . . . fully known only to
the *maîtresse* of the house and manager of the domestic economy'. Female
space extended beyond the house to encompass gardens supplying the
household with fresh food. Fields were male space, where women went
only when men needed help, such as during harvests.[4] While Scottish
women clearly worked in fields, there is an important psychological truth
to this gendered space where each had areas in which they were 'in
charge'. In some regions, women customarily stood while men ate, or ate
separately from them. It might have been simply a practical and customary division of labour, though it could be interpreted as evidence of
supremely patriarchal behaviour. Johansson's research on Sweden offers
a different reading, linking to Roubin's 'female space', in that women
were not subserviently 'standing at meals' but were in control of their
work and their space.[5]

The gendered context is reflected in the fact that men comprised the
bulk of regularly hired labour and women represented temporary labour,
especially at harvest, which always required extra hands. Irish and
Highland women contributed most of the incomers, while seasonal
female labour was supplied by family hiring. Cottages were let to hinds,
ploughmen, or widows with daughters, in return for day labour. It was

often essential for an adult male worker to bring a woman with him, as Midlothian ploughman Andrew Corsbie explained: 'he could not be in service without marriage'.[6] This evolved into the bondager system, whereby a male was expected to provide one female for up to forty days' work without wages, and another who received modest wages. In Midlothian and Berwickshire, 'wives of hinds are generally bound to shear in the harvest without wages [as rent payment], but with full harvest food, and must work at all outdoor labour especially sowing and hay harvest for the customary wages of the country'.[7]

Nevertheless, many people did not work in their own family, particularly single young men and women day labourers or servants. Farm service, and particularly married farm service, continued to be a feature throughout the eighteenth and much of the nineteenth century, unlike England but more like continental Europe. Farmers paid married servants in kind but housed, fed and paid unmarried men and women.[8] Female servants were less common on large farms, but were more important on small and medium-sized holdings, where as 'in and out girls' they did housework, worked with cows and joined in fieldwork. By the 1860s, more attractive jobs in towns made it difficult to keep servants or daughters on farms; so, as the bondager system declined, Lothian farmers boarded servant girls from Ireland or the Highlands to meet labour needs.[9]

In improved agriculture, new crops, like the soft-fruit industry in Clydeside and the Carse of Gowrie, and growing urban demand provided commercial farmwork for female day labourers. In the south-east, turnips and potatoes replaced summer fallow and led to a significant increase in farm labour. For example, an additional 100 workers were needed on a farm in Haddington, East Lothian, with a resident workforce of 150.[10] Henry Stephens pointed out that 'Field workers consist mainly of young women in Scotland but mainly of men and boys in England'.[11] George Culley, agricultural reporter for south-east Scotland, confirmed the resilience of female field labour in 1870: 'The Scotch practice differs from the English in the much more extensive employment of women. Throughout the whole of my district women are employed in all the lighter and in not a few of the heavier operations of farm labour.'[12] Commercial farming, together with the disappearance of commons and many smallholdings, caused many women to turn to day labour.

Agricultural work, and specifically fieldwork, retained locally specific but enduring gendered characteristics. Men claimed work with horses or large implements on the grounds of their special skills and superior strength. They were also better paid. Thus specialist horsemen operating the two-horse plough assumed higher status in a job from which women were excluded.[13] In fieldwork, women were considered particularly adept at hand weeding; and 'a woman, though not so strong is more alert, and generally, more neat in picking the young turnips with her fingers, when they are so close that the hoe cannot separate them'.[14] This so-called natural skill was fostered by early expectations and training. Yet, in 1823, Hugh Miller described the Highland division of labour as:

> It is the part of the husband to turn up the land and sow it; the wife conveys the manure to it in a square creel with a slip bottom, tends the corn, reaps it, hoes the potatoes, digs them up, and carries the whole home on her back. When bearing the creel she is also engaged in spinning with the distaff and spindle.[15]

Thus, while there were specified gender roles, clearly women also did heavy work; this account testifies to the 'multi-tasking' character of women's work that echoes across the economy.

The most notable shift in gendered practices was the gradual change in mowing. Increased use of the scythe instead of the sickle, especially for corn, meant that men, who 'were physically better equipped to wield the heavier instrument', gradually replaced women reapers.[16] Women had long been reapers, with one modern commentator noting that because stalks were cut low down, the sickle 'was especially used by women, who are said to be physiologically better adapted to bending than men'.[17] Because the sickle retained advantages, the transition from one to the other was slow. Women's displacement from mowing depended on crops, size of the workforce, and requirements of speed and care in cutting. Nevertheless, the move from the sickle or heuk, used by women, to the two-handed, heavier scythe, long associated with male strength, forced women out of work where they had been considered 'our neatest cutters' according to an Elgin farmer. The scythe was introduced in grain areas of Banffshire, Aberdeenshire and the Lothians by the 1840s, but at the same time these areas adopted the scythe-hook, a sickle used as often by women as men.[18] As mowing took over, fewer women had an opportunity of higher cutters' wages, though less well-paid work of gathering, binding and stacking demanded more women. Nevertheless, women substituted for men as needed. Thus farmers used women as temporary elastic labour during peak seasons; they also used them to depress wages, since they were almost always cheaper than men. The effect was to widen the differential between male and female wages as reapers. This coincided with a noticeable increase in wages of domestic servants, and contributed to shifting women's employment from fields to service.

The income from butter- and cheesemaking on family farms had long been the perquisite of the farmer's wife; and Scottish women invariably tended cows. In Ayrshire, 'unlike England, every process connected with the milk, the butter, or the cheese is conducted by women, and rightly too'.[19] Their skill was acknowledged by better wages than in the rest of agriculture, while farmers as far apart as Aberdeenshire and Dumfries engaged men on condition that wives milked. 'This in many cases necessitates a second class man to be taken, on account of his supplying one or two good milkers'.[20] Dairying was permanent, and could not be handled by casual labour. On small commercial farms in Kyle and Cunninghame, wives and daughters formed the labour force, while larger farms hired extra workers, though wives still made most of the cheese. General opinion agreed that 'They work, and work very hard'.[21] The pressures of commercial dairying challenged the bucolic ideal. A dairymaid explained:

> We can't complain of our work; we start at 5am, and then we milk till 7 . . .
> In the house we start at once to work after meal . . . Dinner is at 12; start as
> soon as finished to go and feed the cows; we work away with straw, turnips
> and other jobs till 4 . . . Then feed cows again; rest from 5:30 to 7, then milk
> to 8, then fodder cows, which takes half an hour.[22]

Women in upland areas rose early to get milk to trains for town delivery, while those nearer did so to ensure that milk arrived warm, catering for contemporary preferences. The increasing difficulty of finding girls willing to be dairymaids is suggestive of women's desire to leave it behind, and the shortage was universally bemoaned by 1890: 'the cry of the dairying districts is loud, that dairy-women were difficult to get at all and fully qualified dairy-women are very rare indeed'.[23] As women withdrew from the work, they also lost control of the skill, while John Spier believed that the dearth of dairymaids caused the adoption of milking machines.[24]

By the 1890s, the days of cheap female labour were over; daughters of hinds found better pay and conditions in domestic service. Although there may have been less work available, the flight of young women from the countryside was often a positive decision sometimes due to the lack of real opportunities in important and valuable work. Women's contribution continued to be important until at least the twentieth century, for example on Border farms and Highland crofts. However, the Second World War marked women's disappearance from active participation in agriculture. Firstly, the process of mechanisation accelerated rapidly, transforming horse to tractor power, so that 'by the early 1950s the traditional Border farm scene of men with horses (and attendant women workers) was giving way to a lonelier picture of one-man with machine'. Secondly, Land Army 'girls' broke down rural isolation, bringing with them new ideas. Many remained after the war, marrying into the community.[25]

The time-honoured fishing industry involved the whole family, but was shaped by gender: men went out in boats; women dealt with the catch. The notion of 'going to sea' was as much about masculinity and rites of passage as it was about work. 'They go to sea as boys at 14 . . . become men at 18 and marry soon after'.[26] On the east coast, 'becoming a man' was linked with taking a full share in a boat, which with marriage gained youths the fullest possible standing in the community.[27] The only Scottish women on boats migrated from station to station to handle the catch; when fetching mussels involved a boat trip, it became men's work, although women collected mussels by hand locally. Women had a special niche marketing catches, primarily before merchants began to control the industry. Newhaven fishwives were well known in Edinburgh, marked out by their distinctive dress and apron. Women took great pride in their role, and accounts from Embo on the Dornoch Firth are testimony to the respect these women commanded in the family and community.[28] Herring-fishing depended on women as gutters, packers and smokehouse workers. Fishing girls, following the fleet around the coasts to the Western Isles and down to Yarmouth, earned relatively well; they received a signing-on fee (arles), a living allowance and wages. With their room and board paid, they could bring home a tidy sum. A woman from Embo remembered:

> Sometimes the fish, the herring would be very scarce, an' we would have nothin' to do, an' we would be browned off. 'Cause it was all piecework; an' then, no money, you see? So all we did was knit all the time . . . An' then, maybe the fishing would come good. An' there would be a glut. And we had to be up at six in the morning . . . An' we would come in that station at 12 o'clock.[29]

One recalled: 'it was a free and easy time, you weren't restricted – like you know, in a factory where there were bosses'.[30] Local women also awaited the catch, processing and packing as quickly as possible. One observer timed women at Wick gutting twenty-six herring per minute, commenting that such 'bloody' work damaged the young girls.[31]

Fishing shifted to commercial organisation from the 1830s, when gutting, packing and net-making were centralised and more men sailed on merchants' boats rather than shared crew ownership. So, while some women's work disappeared, commercial operations created jobs, particularly if they could follow the trade. In the twentieth century, the emergence of canning and packing factories took some work into the unseen sector, and continued commercialisation changed familial participation. Women became wage-earners at an early stage, not having been involved in share schemes, and played an important role in strikes at the beginning of the twentieth century. Aberdeen female fishworkers struck for increased wages in 1913, setting off a wave of strikes across the industry.[32]

URBANISATION AND COMMERCIALISATION

Commercial activity characterised the mid-eighteenth century, arising from increased internal and international trade; the urban community began to open up, so that there was more freedom to trade. However, the corporate community and its regulatory practices showed great resilience, so that the urban scene varied from community to community. Corporate regulation helped protect trades, maintain quality and regulate the workplace and through it the community, linking economic, social and political roles in explicit and implicit ways with important ramifications for rank, status and gender. In Aberdeen, the Dean of Guild, Merchant-councillors and Trades-councillors were elected positions, and such men came exclusively from the very tiny commercial elite.[33] These same men were central to the vigorous growth of trade, commerce and industry that influenced the development of towns across Scotland; and rules about admittance to the guildry relaxed, admitting men of the new breed.

Commerce became more overtly men's work, as the world of business became decisively reconstructed as a masculine realm, where men, disciplined in habit, controlled the flow of commerce.[34] Commentators couched the concept of tradesman firmly in a male idiom. Adam Smith explained: 'It would be necessary that almost every man should be a man of business, or engage in some sort of trade'.[35] The language of business defined the tradesman as restrained, non-emotional and self-disciplined. In admonishing him to be diligent, Smith advised him to learn the business: 'The man, however, must . . . live by [business] suitably to the qualifications which it requires . . . He must have all the knowledge, in short, that is necessary for a great merchant, which nothing hinders him from becoming but the want of a sufficient capital.'[36] Business reputation or 'credit' was central to business: 'There is a particular nicety in the credit of a tradesman . . . [he] has but two sorts of enemies to encounter with, namely, thieves breaking open his shop, and ill neighbours blackening and blasting his reputation; and the latter are the worst thieves of the two'.[37] Business reputation was also important to women, and the vulnerability of the female trader and her ability to navigate the male world of trade required a consciousness of the terrain she was travelling.

The legacy of guild and corporate structures maintained much of their significance, though new working practices undercut their solidarity. Guild regulation of the workplace and access to it through apprenticeship and mastership helped to embed masculinity into artisanal work and to claim work that was perceived as skilled. Such rules and corporate structures existed to maintain standards of production, hold up prices and prevent unskilled labour from undermining guildsmen's position. As pressures grew from merchants putting work out to unincorporated areas, from new unregulated trades, from governmental laissez-faire attitudes, and from shifts in the economic structure which threatened to undermine many older trades, guild members became ever more assiduous in asserting their right to control labour and production. Significantly, to maintain their status, guilds more explicitly defined work practices with respect to masculinity.

Guilds operated as male structures that paralleled the male life cycle, validating manhood and citizenship. They were the protectors of skilled labour, which saw itself as opposed to domestic industry or proto-industrial work. They drew distinctions between workshop and home, linking females with the latter and men with the former. Whereas guild work was considered to be *honourable* by guildsmen, other types of work, and therefore other workers, were *dishonourable*. Pressure from 'untrained', 'unskilled' and 'dishonourable' labour clearly challenged the rules, regulations and standing of guildsmen. The status attached to work roles was masculine, particularly in corporate communities where economic status was closely linked to political power and standing. The notion that status attaches to the workers and not the work is explicit in the identity of male workers, and implicit in reworking notions of skill when gender is at stake. Thus, 'skilled' work in guild shops was increasingly defined as men's work and craft mysteries as something not to be shared with women. These concepts were deeply embedded into male workers' identity, and reverberated throughout workplace discourses.

Along with a sense of industrial improvement and growing prosperity, social aspirations governed the actions of wide sections of eighteenth-century society. There was a 'dizzy sense of opportunity' with the growth of trade and new prospects for men, with spin-offs for others like lawyers and doctors who serviced the trading community.[38] Distinctions between labourer and artisan were blurred by increasing employment of waged labour instead of journeymen qualified by apprenticeship. There was relatively little tension at the lower rungs of the middle classes, where employers and employed were of a similar number; but it mattered when men had little opportunity to become masters. The scale of rapid change fostered not only social mobility but also social tensions, which had implications for gender. When prevented from attaining masterships, men could become obsessed with the 'symbolic capital of honour'.

Entrenched and gendered divisions of labour, together with the political and economic structures of many towns, inhibited women's access to certain trades and occupations. Nonetheless, within town economies, women managed to install themselves in numerous activities, sometimes using the corporate structure, other times working in unregulated activities, or in tolerated or 'female' work. The urban economy represented both opportunity and danger, with the risk of destitution, prostitution and other hazards, even for 'unprotected' middle-class women. There was a steadily rising female-to-male sex ratio in Scottish towns; for example, Aberdeen was 61 per cent female, and 'the temptations of cheap commodious houses, of easy access to fuel, and to all the necessaries and comforts of life from our vicinity to the port and the market of Aberdeen and of the high probability of finding employment from some of the many manufactories carried on in our neighbourhood' drew many women into town.[39] Their economic role was acknowledged, and their status as traders widely recognised, yet they could rarely claim rights of their own. For women, like men, economic and social roles were closely linked; and, in the fluidity characteristic of commercial towns, women actively claimed commercial identities.

Across the urban landscape, men and women worked jointly. Complex networks of family connections fostered business, and many brides had commercial experience and skills that they brought to marital partnerships.[40] Wives appear regularly with husbands in legal documents such as apprenticeship indentures, especially for girls. Legal documents and port books contain wives signing for consignments and women trading in their own right.[41] When Robert Cumming, Deacon of Edinburgh Fletchers, came to court in 1735, it was noted 'that the defender's deceased spouse managed and directed his whole affairs except that of buying and selling his fleshes the last of which she very often did too'.[42] Often wives were the most important person in the shop, responsible for its smooth running: providing food, keeping accounts, selling products, collecting debts, purchasing raw materials and running errands. An Edinburgh court case observed: 'there is nothing more common than for married women to be praeapositura in either assisting their husband in carrying out his business or carrying on in business separately from their husbands'.[43] Thus, guild regulations often specified that masters were to be married. James Cheape's indenture to a Leith cooper required the artisan's wife to retain him if her husband died during the apprenticeship term.[44]

Women often worked side by side with husbands and substituted for them in the short or long term, indicating that some work was interchangeable. Women certainly learned many of the same tasks as men, and did them if required. However, if work was interchangeable, ideas about it were not; a wife temporarily took on *men's* work, assisting him in 'his business'. When he was available, she was to get on with *her* work.[45] Much of the critique of women was directed at 'masterless' women, who appeared to challenge the rights and privileges of the corporate community. The Merchant Company of Edinburgh, for example, complained about the numerous female shopkeepers, since 'they have no title to the privilege of trade in this city, which is hurtfull to the trading burgesses, who bear the public burdens of the place'.[46]

Of course, a substantial population of single and widowed females worked in their own right, and wives often worked in separate trades from their husbands. Usually, wives' and daughters' right to a trade was not formally recognised. In Edinburgh, however, in an apparent attempt to control the market, both men and women were compelled to enter the Merchant Company, paying entry fees or buying licences. Some women had a right to trade through relationships to fathers and husbands; others had served an apprenticeship, while others appear to have been admitted to trade, as Sanderson speculates, because the Company was low on funds.[47] So, while this right to trade did not earn them political power, they used the corporate system to entitle them to engage in business.

As widows, they were permitted to continue as relicts of their husbands precisely because authorities preferred that they worked rather than receive public charity. They frequently kept their husbands' trades, using their knowledge and experience and hiring workers for tasks that they could not perform either through lack of ability and knowledge or because of customary taboos and restrictions. Margaret Kennedy Morice shared her husband's bakery, centrally located on Castle Street, Aberdeen, managing it for twenty-seven years after his death in 1770. She traded as 'Margaret Morice and Co.', deliberately keeping her married name to retain the prestige and commercial identity developed when the partnership had built up a substantial and respected business. She took apprentices from families of good standing, collecting premiums comparable to those of male bakers. A well-regarded business, it was not artificially propped up by the guild, and demonstrates the potential for women to continue substantial businesses themselves.[48] In some cases, widows gained greater economic status than other women and a certain amount of independence. Yet, coping with difficulties attendant on women operating alone, as masterless persons, meant that many were unable to maintain their livelihood. Many remarried, particularly younger ones, since they offered husbands entry to the ranks of burgesses. Networks of friends, family or trade colleagues could give widows advantages over spinsters operating in the urban economy.

Women consciously situated themselves in the trading milieu. In 1764, Margaret Craig advertised that she would continue as a merchant, claiming that business 'will be carried on as formerly', retaining the goodwill of her husband's customers: 'they may depend on being well and readily served', and she would 'carefully obey' commissions from the country.[49] She literally set out her stall as a competent and reliable businesswoman, using wording typical of men's advertisements to establish her place in the commercial community, not a 'feminine' discourse; nor did she trade on femininity. She certainly was not unique: numerous other women placed advertisements employing similar language. So, by the use of language and the creation of a business persona, women established themselves in the commercial and corporate community of Aberdeen. The operation of a 'civil business' with a good reputation gained them credit in the community.

Many married women worked independently from their husbands, and single women populated town businesses. Needle trades were especially important; women were milliners, mantua-makers and seamstresses making all sorts of goods including underwear, children's clothes and gravecloths, as well as the high-class millinery which growing fashion demanded – activities which could and did bring them into competition and conflict with tailors. Millinery was a good trade where women made names for themselves in the mercantile community. Importantly, 'such trades contained the potential for independence because *they were skilled trades and had to be learned*'.[50] Apprenticeship records show that partnerships were important to milliners and mantua-makers, and 'better' firms regularly apprenticed new girls and appeared conscientiously run, successful enough to employ at least two women and two apprentices.[51] In Aberdeen, milliners Misses Ramsay and McKenzie worked in a partnership upstairs from Miss Forbes, also a milliner.[52] Records also emphasise the overwhelmingly female character of these trades, suggesting that these women operated independently or in a roughly equal partnership with tailor husbands.

Partnerships were a time-honoured way for couples to operate, and female partnerships shared many of the same advantages. In Edinburgh, at least 140 single women ran businesses, often in female partnerships.[53] Partnerships halved rent, servants and other costs connected with managing a concern. Especially relatives, often sisters, lived together sharing expenses. Sanderson has drawn out women's perspectives on partnerships in Edinburgh. Cissy Murray looked back on her partnership with Janet Muschet, a milliner: 'I am sartin never was 2 more happy than we were, . . . I never think on the years we spent thegether but with regrate'.[54] It is certain that some women strove for and valued independence; and Cissy's cousin, Ann Buchanan, wrote to Muschet in 1758: 'my most sincere thanks for your ready Agreeing in taking me in partners with you and [Cissy]; Oh how happy will I be with you both . . . they were told att home that it was Lady Polmaise that first made the proposal of taking me in with you; So . . . Dont say Anything that it was myself, I long for the time when I shall be with you'.[55] She saw it as an equal partnership, later objecting to being treated like a servant by Muschet. While the expectations of the two cousins were different – Cicely needed an income while Ann was secure in a landed family – both valued the partnership. Their decision-making processes comprised complex considerations including emotional, moral and economic ones.

Yet, around this commercial activity, a contemporary discourse antipathetic to businesswomen was developing.[56] There was also a tension with the emerging ideology in which women were increasingly defined in terms of and restricted to domestic pursuits. They were rarely perceived as 'independent'; and married women and widows often used their marital association, however obliquely, to bolster their claims in the corporate world. Single women were even more vulnerable. Women in commerce had not only to obtain credit but also to stay in credit. They had to retain their reputations as traders who could be trusted and whose characters were seen to be above reproach. Reputation was both a private and a public attribute. It was effectively a political commodity, which was not only worth owning and demonstrating but also worth protecting and publicising. They also used family connections, networks and patronage to further their standing. Thus, women gained an identity in the community by utilising the language of the corporate world, and claimed a place in that world by exploiting the mechanisms of commerce in a world of growing trade and consumerism.

INDUSTRIAL CHANGE

Co-existence was a key feature of industrial development, and a recurring theme was the variety of organisational patterns that operated, sometimes in competition, sometimes complementarily. With each system came different interpersonal relationships between co-workers, managers, masters and owners. Manufacturing embraced a number of different patterns: handicrafts, domestic industry, mechanised and centralised work, for example factories, and outwork. Frequently, these elide into one another but represent different workplace structures, sometimes locations, work discipline and the value placed on industrial time. In each, a gendered division of labour operated, gaining its purchase from arguments about the construction of gender, skill and status.

Few in the rural population held adequate amounts of land to gain their living directly from their own holding; so, in addition to working for others, households turned to domestic industry. This was part of survival strategies often orchestrated by wives, including apprenticeship or sending children to service. In many areas, there was little other paid work for women. In Lowland Scotland, women were more vulnerable to seasonal underemployment in agriculture, and they commonly turned to stocking-knitting, linen and wool-spinning and straw-plaiting while their husbands took waged work. In the Highlands, the north-east Lowlands and Orkney, women took up commercial spinning while men fished or farmed.[57] A Buchan observer noted: 'There was little produce to sell off such a croft, and the great source of revenue was the money earned by the women spinning lint'.[58] Thus, a sexual division of labour was reinforced, even where only some members engaged in domestic industry. Linen relied on female labour in Bute, Kintyre, Argyll, western and Highland Perthshire and the east of Scotland, as did handloom weaving of Paisley shawls and Harris tweeds and woollens in the Borders. High women's wages in late eighteenth-century Aberdeenshire were attributed 'to the extensive manufactory of stockings at Aberdeen, which has taught all of them to knit; and so industrious are they, that, in travelling the high road, they knit as busily as at home'; hand knitters could be found in pockets throughout the country into the 1870s, and this continued as an essential part of life in Shetland still longer.[59] Women also kept busy in cloth centres like Dundee, Glasgow, Perth, Paisley and Aberdeen. 'All over Scotland, every housewife and family spin; has the yarn wove, dyed, etc. etc., at her own expense; having clothed her family she sells the surplus.'[60] Notably, in this instance, women organised it. The flexibility of female labour was one factor that attracted entrepreneurs to the countryside. It was work that could be fitted in, and, like much of women's work, was largely task-orientated. The Minister at Keith Hall believed a woman could knit 'and do some little things about her house at the same time. Or she can work at her stocking while feeding her cows.'[61] The connection with the land remained the backdrop for domestic industries, and male association with land meant that even when domestic industries brought in greater income, they remained identified primarily as women's work, casual and supplementary.

Of course, both men and women worked in the classic division of labour of women spinning and men weaving. Women's work was pivotal, as Adam Smith indicated:

> To say nothing of the industry of the flax-growers and flax-dressers, three or four spinners, at least, are necessary in order to keep one weaver in constant employment; . . . It is not by the sale of their work, but by that of the complete work of the weavers, that our great master manufacturers make their profits.[62]

The pay for spinning did not match the scarcity of the yarn, because custom kept prices down; since it was women's work, it was invariably cheaper. And, as Smith noted, the work of weavers was the visible product of the industry, ultimately allowing them to claim the wage and the work. After the mid-eighteenth century, commercial spinning spread beyond the main weaving areas largely because better-paid opportunities enticed women from spinning into muslin embroidery, bleachfields and ultimately factories.[63]

Men claimed handloom weaving as a skilled artisanal trade, although many women wove part-time, and small masters hired daughters and wives. Nevertheless, women usually wove on smaller and less complicated looms and on lighter and cheaper cloths.[64] As factory spinning shifted pressure from spinning to weaving, the male handloom weaver's position as an artisan solidified, partly because of his scarcity. The demand for weavers, however, allowed former female spinners to move to weaving. So, by 1800, women and children comprised a third of weavers in the linen industry in the south of Scotland.[65] Weavers tried to enforce statutory minimum wages and apprenticeship regulations to protect the trade; using traditional artisan rhetoric, they claimed that because they had served an apprenticeship, they 'deserved their just reward', situating their trade in guild traditions. Instead of incorporating women, they tried to bar them from apprenticeships. But tensions between men who hired family members and journeymen who saw women as competition meant that they failed to reconcile the male bonding of artisanal traditions with family working. When weavers in Paisley and Dalmarnock attacked powerlooms, pointedly women did not join in. Clark suggests that 'perhaps the masculine, artisanal rhetoric employed by the weavers alienated women'.[66]

Gender relations in textile factories echoed relationships in domestic industries. Tenters used skill and artisanal rituals, initiation fees and male posturing to create a position of exclusivity, but earned female power-loom weavers' support in disputes with employers. Mule spinners, in contrast, brought artisanal traditions into the factories with them, and utilised the association of strength with skill to help retain their status and exclusive control of heavier mules. They also positioned themselves in opposition to women, whom employers put onto smaller and lighter mules, as at Ballingdoch in Stirlingshire and Catrine near Glasgow.[67] Early in the nineteenth century, as a cost-cutting measure during a period of falling profits and workplace conflict, Glasgow cotton employers put women onto 250–300-spindle mules, precisely those originally deemed too heavy.[68] In response, 'several unemployed mule spinners planned to "assist in maltreating some of the Broomward Female Spinners"' ultimately wounding several and killing one.[69] Importantly, they did not object to women working – it was competition for men's jobs they resented. The high level of female employment, especially married women, in Dundee jute factories conferred a degree of economic independence, freedom from direct patriarchal control, and a public role that arguably undermined the material basis of male dominance.[70] But, as in many factories, gendered division of labour remained: women wove and men gained 'skilled' jobs as beamers, dressers and in maintenance work – positions of authority and better paid.[71]

Conceptualisation of the family wage, that is, a wage high enough to support a family, was central to gender-stereotyping and to defining women's work as secondary. It was primarily a bargaining tool situated in the struggle over male wages and status, and largely ignored the fact that many people did not live, or work, in 'families'. It is significant that the main group of workers for whom the family wage was an issue were skilled men, inheritors of the artisan, who constituted the first trade unions. These men believed that a family wage, by which they meant *their* wage, would reduce women's participation in the labour markets leading to less competition for jobs. It was important to remove women from areas where they did the same work or worked in the same industries as men, since they undercut men's wages, status and control. Similarly, it was necessary to ensure that women's work remained less well paid and inferior to men's. Men and their unions believed that men's position would then be enhanced absolutely and in relation to employers. This argument is reminiscent of claims for protection of skill and status deriving from guilds and artisan craftwork. On the one hand, it was not about women but about protecting male craft position and independence *vis-à-vis* the capitalist who wished to control labour supply. On the other hand, it clearly was about gender, because the targets were women. It was firmly attached to the image of a breadwinning male supporting a dependent wife. Having a non-working wife was a measure of masculinity as well as a building block in working-class notions of respectability. Women's work thus also came to be defined as 'appropriate'. 'Appropriate' meant work that men did not want, but also work that suited the feminine frame and delicacy and was situated in an appropriate space, usually home.

Attitudes of the hiring classes could be ambivalent. Some factory owners refused to hire married women; others did not hire mothers, like the manager of Cowan's paper mill in Penicuik, in 1865: 'With a view to prevent the neglect of children in their homes, we do not employ the mothers of young children in our works'. He made an exception for 'widows or women deserted by their husbands, or having husbands unable to earn a living'.[72] Gordon shows that Dundee employers, though not especially philanthropic, felt a need to reconcile their employment of large numbers of women, especially married women and mothers, with the 'prevailing ideology of domesticity'. Thus they organised domestic-economy classes and contributed towards crèches in the city.[73]

A significant feature of the Scottish division of labour was the growth of heavy industries, primarily in the west of Scotland and across the central belt, and granite-quarrying around Aberdeen. Largely male, they marked a shift in men's work from textiles to heavy industry. While the work was hard, indeed soul-destroying, men had a sense of job satisfaction and pride that was situated in their male identity and the masculine culture of the workplace. McIvor and Johnston's research on miners underlines this construction of masculinity. The 'hard man' discourse was central to their identity. 'The breadwinner status, high-risk *machismo* culture and sacrifice at work had provided pivotal moral justifications for male empowerment in the home and family . . . Manliness was forged in the pits through exposure to life-threatening risks underground', and was posited against the female domestic sphere.[74] Heavy industries thus contained a paradox: the high-paid, dangerous work that forged men's masculinity also created the conditions to disable them, and to disable not only their body but also their sense of self, their identity, their masculinity.[75] Aspects of the artisan tradition remained for colliers and steelworkers in the sense of skill that 'strength and judgement demanded of their work, and the engineer took satisfaction in his expertise as long as he was left with a modicum of initiative'.[76] Their job satisfaction cannot be separated from their sense of solidarity in a male workshop where rites of passage controlled the hierarchies of worker status, and custom and control shaped the ways workers operated on the shop floor. Class antagonism may have begun to play a part, but gender was deeply embedded in the system.

Mining illustrates the contradictions about strength and gender. Before 1842, women carried, pulled or pushed baskets of coal, stone and ores from the face to the surface, and around the site or into markets. Scottish women reported carrying loads of three hundredweight; a basket of 170 pounds required two men to lift it onto their backs. One commented that 'lads are no fit to stand the work like women'. Rarely did women hew or 'get' the coals, which was clearly coded as men's skilled work, but exceptionally they substituted for men or assisted husbands. When the Mines Act banned them from the face, many would have agreed with 53-year-old Isabel Hogg: 'You must tell the Queen Victoria that we are guid loyal subjects; women people here don't mind work, but they object to horse-work'.[77] The motivation behind the Act owed not a little to the domestic construction of femininity, but many male colliers wanted women removed because they worked for lower wages than men.

The geographic specificity of heavy industries created pockets of men's work while leaving a dearth of work for women in many areas (a feature that operated in reverse in Dundee). Many women turned to sewing and other outwork to meet household needs. Outwork based on the manufacturers' factory or large workshop combined with a network of agents was a common way to put work out to women in dispersed rural communities and towns. Scottish merchants set up industrial schools and urban warehouses from which they controlled training and homework. Glasgow merchants put out flowering to thousands of seamstresses in Ayrshire; 20,000 to 30,000 worked for MacDonald's at the height of the trade.[78] Yet the system put women in a particularly vulnerable position, since the employer dictated pay and dates of completion. As in domestic industry, fines were levied for 'unsatisfactory' work, and seamstresses had little recourse. Despite the prominence of sewing, the range and quality of outwork was vast: dressmakers, shirtmakers, seamers, tailors, milliners, umbrella, parasol and stick-makers, staymakers, paper, box and bag-makers.[79] In Glasgow, the 1911 census reported that 34.9 per cent of married women workers were homeworkers; two earlier surveys demonstrated that 8 per cent were married, 84.3 per cent widowed in 1900, and in 1907, 45.4 per cent were married and 26.7 per cent widowed.[80] Such high proportions of married and widowed women underline their need for income and the probability that they had dependants. Nevertheless, one Glasgow clothier commented disparagingly: 'the outside workers who do our shirts are generally the wives of artisan and other workmen, who have nothing to do at home in the absences of their husbands, and is so much money earned when otherwise they would have gone idle'. A corrective came from the Scottish Council of Women's Trades, pointing out that the numbers working for 'pin money' were 'so small as to be absolutely negligible'.[81] In fact, men were subject to irregular employment and seasonal or cyclical unemployment, so that women had to work, frequently becoming central to the family income. Homework was stagnating in Glasgow, but the signs of decline across homeworking were apparent. In 1901, there were 3,642 employed female homeworkers and by 1911 only 2,640, most in garment trades.[82] This was mirrored in the decline in textiles across Britain, including Dundee jute; the depressions of the 1920s and 1930s hit the trades hard, and cotton never recovered from the loss of markets to overseas competitors and competition from synthetics.

New industries, together with new manufacturing processes, mark the period from about 1880. The First World War introduced women to engineering; and, despite their virtual exclusion with demobilisation, the experience built their confidence and opened their eyes to different kinds of work.[83] They were likely candidates for light industries using assembly-line techniques, which played on 'natural' female dexterity. Men took the lion's share of the new jobs, and these industries did not develop rapidly enough to replace jobs lost in older manufactures. Nonetheless, chemicals, electronics, food-processing, pharmaceuticals, electrical equipment, household furnishing, optics and precision engineering relied heavily on women. Primarily industries with an established female workforce augmented it, especially those that adopted new production methods and assembly lines first, since it was logical to expand with a proven workforce. The permanent disappearance of the marriage bar after the Second World War played a crucial role in changing the shape of the workforce in instrument-making and electrical engineering. In the early 1930s, women comprised 20 per cent of the workforce; in the 1970s they had become almost 50 per cent.[84] Women became less likely to be restricted to a narrow range of work, were no longer marginalised in 'female' industries and were less at risk from economic fluctuations and decline in single industries. Electrical component assembly, inspecting and packing goods, electronic office equipment and 'teleworking' also created new homework taken up by women.

Yet gendered difference continued, usually around what was constructed as skill difference, in that men had an intrinsic right to skilled work, defined by long-standing craft traditions, while females remained subsumed in ideas of what they could and should do. For example, in printing, 'there was no such thing as a timeserved journeywoman'. Reynolds's account of Scottish typesetters shows how girls were not apprentices but 'learners', 'indicating that they were not really acquiring a skill, just "learning on the job", which was standard for most semi-skilled occupations'. 'Learning' lasted two to four years, shorter than the traditional seven years still served by boys. Only in 1923, after the introduction of new machinery and processes and the dispute of 1910, did women gain the right to be admitted to keyboard training classes at Heriot-Watt College.[85] Thus, women were most restricted in those areas where men could still claim a craft component of the work, which allowed them to align it with masculine notions of skill, custom and control. Male solidarity also colluded to prevent women from gaining access to the knowledge. In one sense, it did not matter if women had 'skill' or ability; it was assumed that they did not. For example, male compositors in Edinburgh 'were adamant . . . that women were *not* skilled workers'.[86] Gendered division of labour was situated in women's special (unrecognised) skills of dexterity, speed and ability to withstand monotony and handle simple, light work, and men's particular ability to handle heavy, difficult, dirty or even 'real' skilled work. This was a protective mechanism – protective of a male preserve which they mystified and continued to control. In this sense, it speaks not only of maleness but also of men's place in the hierarchy and their patriarchal right to command power and authority in the workplace as well as home. Effectively, women became assemblers rather than 'makers', and, within the male-constructed world of manufacturing work, remained casual and frequently part-time workers. For example, between 1951 and 1981, the numbers of Scottish females working part-time rose from 5 per cent to 41 per cent; in 1981, only 7 per cent of men worked part-time.[87]

WHITE-COLLARS AND WHITE-BLOUSES

From the mid-nineteenth century, towns reflected a more masculine approach to commerce, while domesticity and the reconstruction of bourgeois masculinity and femininity contributed to gendered notions of the workplace. New opportunities for men and women emerged in the 'white-collar' sector, and mid-century marked signs of change in female educational opportunities with a more evident women's movement claiming work for middle-class women. White-collar work, or white-bloused work as Jane Lewis labelled it, was particularly significant.

By 1851, women had come to outnumber men in the population: as many as a third of women never married in nineteenth-century Scotland. In addition to needing work, many single middle-class women wanted to 'do something' with their lives, and pro-actively carved out niches in white-bloused work. For working-class men and women, the sector provided social mobility, a 'better' kind of work with higher status. Because the work was 'new' in the way it was organised and understood, both men and women had to stake their claim to it, and different accommodations to gender emerged as a result. Thus, the story of white-collar/ white-bloused work is one of each sex claiming its place, often with a tension between what was seen as male work and female work. The story is a highly nuanced one embedded in issues of gender, custom and control.

Family businesses became more visibly identified with males and more firmly embedded in legal and financial practices, yet women continued to be shopkeepers and street sellers, cabaret proprietors and landladies of lodgings and inns. They worked in family shops and ran their own businesses. Stana Nenadic estimates that women owned and operated about a fifth of nineteenth-century British firms.[88] Many women, largely spinsters, populated the business world; most worked in garment trades, often as dressmakers and milliners with lifelong careers. Through acquisition of skills and acumen, they could position themselves as businesswomen and proprietors. Using partnerships, or 'dovetailed' approaches where a few related enterprises, often built on family connections, reinforced and supplemented one another, women ran successful businesses. Yet, as Nenadic shows, their relative invisibility resulted from accommodating customer expectations, de-commercialising their product. As business became more overtly masculinised, aggressive business practices and unrestricted competition marked the successful businessman. In this context, the businesswoman had to tread a careful course between 'business' and sensibility. To maintain her respectability and business, reputation was credit, and the dominant discourse of domesticity shaped the way these businesswomen constructed their business identities.[89]

Domestic service reflected the dominance of bourgeois ideology, becoming 'a *sine qua non* of social distinction' in the nineteenth century.[90] A predominant route for many girls, it replaced farm service and domestic industry, and in 1851 a third of women workers were servants.[91] Numbers rose until the twentieth century but, unlike most of Europe, rose again after the First World War with the lack of other opportunities and the poverty of the interwar years. The cult of domesticity and feminisation of the household were significant factors together with changes in occupational opportunities, particularly as discourses came to more sharply define household work as particularly suited to women and women as particularly suited to domestic tasks. Domestic service was highly gendered, and became even more so towards the end of the nineteenth century, as men migrated to work with an association with masculinity and status, even if that status was also under challenge. To a former male servant, service was 'something like that of a bird shut up in a cage. The bird is well housed and well fed but deprived of liberty.'[92] Subservience and independence were not only male issues, but there is little doubt that they contributed to driving men to take up other work.

Through much of the nineteenth century, service paid better than other work for young women when the advantages of room and board were factored in.[93] It was often preferable to the hard and 'dirty' work of the farm, and, in the life stories of women, might be an option that was juggled with other work. But service *was* hard work with long hours, a need to be at the 'beck and call' of patrons and the sheer drudgery of cleaning. As a servant in Dunblane said, 'About the back of seven in the morning you would be shouted to and you would be at their beck and call 'til about eight or nine at night . . . I didnae wait very long, I don't mind telling you'.[94] Most servants were the 'maids of all work', that is, the only servant in the household, and thus drew the worst jobs and the heaviest work. They were highly mobile, frequently moving jobs to gain advancement, better pay or just different situations. Some made a career of it, but for most it was a life-cycle position. Young women's views of service were variable, of course. Some gained a sense of status working in a 'good house', as one young woman who found a place as the fourth housemaid in a large house in Helensburgh said: 'that was me started on the ladder up'.[95] Others moved on quickly, particularly as other opportunities such as shop and clerical work opened up: 'I didnae like it [service] much so I moved on – to better things I hope. I went to the grocer shop as a message girl, that was ten shillings a week.'[96]

Male clerks increased in number as a more commercial society placed value on literate skills, thus creating a good job for working- and middle-class men with the ability to write in a fair hand, do accounts and so on. Indeed, for many Victorian clerks, the potential existed for rapid advancement into management and even into ownership. 'This apparent path to "the top" was one of the foundations of the "middle-class" identity of clerical work that survived into the twentieth century.'[97] James McBey described his feelings and sense of status as he embarked on a banking job in the mid-nineteenth century: 'My new toggery lay on the chest beside my bed. The long trousers were the symbol of manhood;

the hard black hat, the dickey and cuffs were the livery of respectability.'[98] Not only was clerking respectable, it offered the opportunity to advance in what was clearly seen as a male culture. Glasgow businessman William Jacks, the son of a shepherd, who rose to business tycoon 'via the counting house', told clerks 'what all clerks ought to be, capital businessmen'.[99] But, as R. Guerriero Wilson argues, the entrenchment of an elite blocked the way to the top of the 'ladder of success'. Opportunities for rapid advancement, with potential to become bosses, declined, and clerical work became a permanent occupation based on serving and supporting others, making office work less attractive for men.[100]

From a male occupation, clerical work became a largely female job. Feminisation implies that men owned the work and the workplace. Much of the work was new, although offices operated around a particularly male culture. Men owned the old work, such as administration and copying, and possessed the status (or lack of it) that went with it. With new work, women were able to identify and claim their own spaces, using the inventions of telephones, telegraph and most obviously the typewriter to argue for work which was peculiarly theirs: 'the typewriter, like other technological inventions, was one part of complex structural developments . . . that changed the face of the office and the sex of the worker'.[101] They were hired for work at the lower end of the scale in banks, insurance companies, shipping firms and large merchant houses from the 1870s. Hiring lower-paid women for menial work saved money and preserved the male career structure, and more interesting and better-paid work became men's property. Employers assumed that women were more tractable, less likely to seek promotion, would leave on marriage, be content with lower wages and not demand promotion.[102] Thus, the clerical hierarchy created a profile of segregation and higher-status jobs for men. In the private sector, especially large companies, the 'executive' was almost always a man.

The association of men with technology is reflected in the introduction of computers in the office, a discussion that notably did not accompany the typewriter. Cockburn's comment that 'women may push the buttons but they may not meddle with the works' provides an apt description of gender relations in the computerised office. Male control of technology and by implication their control of 'skill' has been an essential element in analysing the gendered nature of white-collar work.[103] Gender relations were hierarchical in that initially men designed and controlled computer production processes, while women entered data or performed clerical tasks. However, the increasing use of computers, especially microcomputers instead of centralised computer systems, led to a change in gender relations, overturning the view that the supervisor knew how to handle software while the 'non-technical' secretary did not.[104] Two paradigms remain. One is the persistence of an association of men with technical know-how, whether justified or not, and a sense of control and increased status. The other is the growing confidence and practical experience of female office workers with computerised technology, which gives them a certain amount of control over the work itself.

There are parallels in the retail sector. As larger stores joined the high street, and as the retail sector grew and changed from small, often family-run, stores to larger diversified department stores after about the 1880s, it was progressively more difficult for young men to become shopkeepers, providing a disincentive for them to continue in the trade. Those who did usually managed to retain or gain supervisory positions, or sell expensive or high-status items. Young women, on the other hand, saw these jobs as new opportunities, a step up from domestic service, and a popular first job. The wage was up to twice what a maid earned, they didn't have to buy uniforms, hours were shorter, there was more time off and they felt less 'ordered about'.[105] Large stores and small shops differed, and by the 1880s many large stores closed by 7pm; but 8pm or 10pm closing was perfectly feasible, with small shops far likelier to close late and open early.[106] Living arrangements for many shop employees (and nurses) mirrored the pattern for domestic servants and reflected living-in arrangements of some nineteenth-century industrial workers, when owners had felt compelled to provide accommodation. Partly the system echoed society's demand for supervision of young females away from home, although living-in arrangements were often made for men as well. Living-in gradually disappeared for shopworkers, however, and by 1900 only Jenner's in Edinburgh continued to provide accommodation in Scotland.[107]

What is clear from testimony from the beginning of the twentieth century is that young women made choices, deciding between full- and part-time work, between service, shops and factories, and valuing the experiences differently. For example, one saw Woolworth's as bringing them status – 'we must have thought we were toffs' – while another saw Woolies as a step down from skilled work in the mill, 'an intricate job at the designs'.[108] In contrast to clerical work, retail was more likely to draw working-class girls in larger numbers. For many, it remained a temporary job, either as a first step to something better or as a job before marriage. But it also had the potential of a 'career'. A sales assistant said of her first job in a paint and wallpaper shop: 'I liked it alright, but when I got something better that was the main thing'. A year later, she was offered an assistant's post in a baker's, but on a day holiday was offered a position in a grocer's at Kippen: 'So, I just jumped at this and told the other company that I wouldn't be, that I had found something more suitable. So I was there forty years. I loved my job.'[109]

Like the rest of the tertiary sector, professions underwent important changes. More fields claimed professional status, and numbers within professions increased as other occupations succeeded in protecting access and creating special preserves. Stearns describes the older liberal professions as 'the most persistently aggrieved segment of the middle class'. They fell behind the new upper class in status and income, while the numbers of professionals outpaced the jobs available, blocking their own advancement or the chance to ensure sons a place.[110] The importance of social status continued to be a crucial measure of success, especially in professional families, and erosion of their position and standing was keenly felt.

Professions have a long feminine history. For example, healing, nursing and midwifery have ancient origins, 'dame schools' were highly visible if largely unrecorded, and philanthropy and charity work have long been considered the province of 'ladies bountiful'. Thus, women's professional role became formalised around the same time as other white-collar work expanded. It would be foolish, however, to ignore the strong male craft traditions in surgery, and the intellectual traditions that allowed men to dominate senior administrative and educational positions. Education combined with growing feminism contributed to pushing the boundaries of medical and legal professions, while some women gradually made their way into the higher echelons of administrative and managerial careers. The need to preserve exclusivity contributed to restrictions on women entering many professional fields. By their very character, professional fields operated by segregated, stratified and exclusive access routes; and education, status and cultural tradition acted as gatekeepers. So did gender. Broadly speaking, women's interface with professions took two routes between those that always had a large female component and those that were male-dominated and controlled. Nursing, teaching and social work fall into the former category; law, medicine, pharmacy, clergy and managerial work into the latter. Changes within male professions also focused on the gendered division of labour. Professions such as accountancy and management were very young, needing to claim their position. Shifts in clerical work created significant distinctions between secretaries and administrators, while developments in medicine, hospitals, university education and discoveries sharpened divisions in health care.[111] Despite nursing gaining professional status, they became positioned separately from doctors, being seen as 'his' assistant. Thus, as women fought to gain the right to study and practise as doctors, they had to position themselves against the female nurse; and, even when they had achieved educational rights, most faced continued and endemic resistance, especially from male doctors.[112] Vertical segregation existed from the outset in teaching, with men initially gaining greater access to training and certification and to better pay and higher-status positions. In addition, there was overt discrimination in hiring practices, such as in Glasgow between the wars, when 'most male applicants were offered appointments and only a proportion of female applicants were considered'.[113] In higher education, the differential was even more pronounced. At the University of Aberdeen, the first lecturer in her own right was appointed in 1918, and the first woman professor in 1964.[114]

CONCLUSION

Gender has been an enduring feature of the workplace over the last 300 years. It shaped constructions of the workplace, the work and the workers. Gender is, however, not timeless in the way it is understood, and a number of factors contributed to its reconstruction across the period. These included the location of work and the spaces it occupied, the ways that skill and expertise were reconstructed to fit changing situations, and concomitantly the application of and meanings associated with tools, machines and technology. Similarly, gender was endemic in workplace hierarchies and the character of occupational segregation. Ultimately, gender was integral to defining the workers – the men and women who worked.

Men's and women's association with the home and the configuration of their household roles were central to how gender related to work. Long-standing association of women with upkeep of the home and child care linked them physically to the home as workplace more firmly than men. Agriculture, domestic industry and industrial homework continued to associate women with house and home. It was a place they could claim as their own female space, a place where they were in charge. Such associations relied on the wife and mother as model, although most of the female workforce were single. Thus, ideas about married women's roles carried over into understandings of all women's work and contributed to defining their femininity. Men, in contrast, did not retain a close psychological association with the space of the home; their work was seen as properly in the fields or the workshop, and ultimately the idea of 'going out to work' was more clearly associated with them. They contributed to household sustenance through their work, and as paterfamilias held a philosophical and legal responsibility for it. The claim for a family wage was based explicitly on this responsibility and situated in perceptions of their masculinity. The significance of this role for men cannot be underrated – it is still difficult for some men to 'allow' their wives to work, seeing it as challenging their masculinity. McIvor and Johnston's work on disabled miners points up how closely tied these men were to the hard-working breadwinner image.

Factors which contributed to the gendered character of the workplace, such as mechanisation, skill, status and division of labour, were situated in relationships between men, and between men and women, in the workplace. As work and the workplace changed, men negotiated their place in the new relationships that emerged. They vigorously maintained their claim for work that was perceived as skilled and which underpinned their sense of masculinity. 'Skill' is essentially a linguistic device to claim work that could be associated with status and standing. It was variously constructed out of a range of materials: location, training, complexity, strength and control, for example. But, importantly, it was tautologically defined as male – in other words, in different settings, skill was reconstructed to reflect traits that were defined as masculine. In constructing skill and claiming skilled work, men distanced themselves from work that was based in the home – defining homework and domestic industry as dishonourable work, and the workers as without honour. Thus they increasingly associated domestic industries with unskilled, untrained and inferior work, positioning women and unapprenticed men as inferior workers. Artisanal traditions of apprenticeship, rites of passage, exclusivity and the notion of becoming 'masters' were deeply embedded in men's 'property of skill'. Thus artisans, merchants, mule spinners, male clerks and doctors built on these traditions, reconstructing skill in new situations. They describe the dignity and status that men derive from work, which contributes to their construction of gender.

Women were most restricted in those areas where men could claim a craft component for the work, which allowed them to align it with masculine notions of skill, custom and control. Men were adamant that women did not have skill. This appears contradictory in that women sewed, set type, spun, used sickles and repaired threads on spinning machines. Yet female abilities, usually learned informally, and associated with dexterity and fiddly work, were seen as natural attributes, not skills. Male ownership of skill excluded women from recognised training routes – apprenticeships, training on mules and education including professional training. Not only did the lack of training opportunities reflect the masculine character of skill and the notion of a closed shop, it also epitomised the view that women's work required little training, and women workers were temporary and interchangeable. The perception that women did not have 'careers' was itself a reason for not giving training.

In claiming skill, men also claimed the machines, particularly those that they could associate with status. Mechanisation can be linked to increased division of labour and de-skilling, especially when women are put on the machine; however, machines and tools are often associated with men and their property in skill, especially if it can be argued that the machine is 'too complex' for women to understand – sometimes code for 'heavy', requiring strength. Women became associated with assemblage, while men made, supervised and repaired machines. Thus, power-loom weavers were female, and tenters who repaired the machines were male. 'The designation of some occupations as mere "machine minding" concealed the elements of genuine skill required to perform the task and often reflected the inflated claims of manufacturers regarding the efficiency of a machine as well as the interests and capacity of employers to label work as unskilled or semi-skilled in order to cheapen the cost of labour.'[115] Instead, women's 'natural' abilities with nimble fingers helped inscribe some machines and tasks as female. So the typewriter was the female tool par excellence – and typing on the computer carried this notion into the modern office. The female machine and task thus was inferior, poorer paid and lower in status. The converse was true of men's machines and tasks. Manual tasks also had a duality, in that sometimes women were allocated laborious fiddly hand work; other times, hand work was coded as craftwork and claimed for men.

Status shaped relationships across the workplace. Skill, tools and the male breadwinner head of household all contributed to assigning men control in the workplace. Thus, hierarchies throughout occupations assigned men roles as overseers, supervisors and managers. Not only were these among the best-paid jobs, but also they were seen to reflect men's natural patriarchal position. Women, however, were seen as needing to be controlled, supervised and watched over. References to masterless women illustrate the concerns of the male community – an anxiety about disorderly women. Such unease was evident in the description of Dundee factory women as 'over-dressed, loud, bold-eyed girls'.[116] They did not conform to the self-effacing Victorian ideal, and were out of control. The importance of controlling women and of maintaining male status were significant factors in determining how culture defined men and women in relation to the workplace.

The late twentieth century saw some erosion of these constructions, but vertical and horizontal segregation still shaped the workplace. Men could still be seen as natural breadwinners and women as tractable, casual and flexible workers, working for 'pin money' or 'extras' for the family. Looking back to 1700, almost all women worked. Domestic tasks, unpaid charitable work, waged work and businesses made up aspects of their lives. As work became waged, more structured and identified in a way that it was recorded and seen, married women seemed to disappear, only to resurface as censuses became more sensitive. By 2000, work was defined differently, but even statistics show that women were clearly workers. In Scotland, 60.4 per cent of Scottish married women, 39.6 per cent of single women and 39.6 per cent of widowed and divorced women worked in statistically recognised occupations; the bulk of these clustered in 'intermediate non-manual' (20.1 per cent) and 'junior non-manual' (35.6 per cent) work, with only 10.8 per cent in 'top jobs', though this last figure more than doubled since 1961.[117] Formal part-time work was the creation of the twentieth century, and large numbers of women turned to it, though in many cases with no job security, pensions or benefits. Only with 'job-share' where a 'real' job was shared were such workers guaranteed a semblance of equality with other workers, while European directives provide some statutory security for all workers.

Women's skills and status acquired through their work had particular meanings for them. The Scottish fishwife gained respect, both from her community and from her family, for her strength, skills and reputation as a worker, as well as her marketing ability in preparing and selling the catch. They were considered prodigious workers and admired throughout their village.[118] Likewise, the dairywoman was respected for her practical skills in dairying, milking and preparing butter and cheese. They also saw this skill and special role gaining them a measure of independence, much as the herring girls of north-east Scotland did. Scottish women between the wars recollected their factory work with affection, citing job satisfaction, pride in the work and an identity with one's machine.[119] Businesswomen of the eighteenth, nineteenth and twentieth centuries carved out niches for themselves, and shopworkers often loved their jobs. Within the gendered constructions of the workplace, men and women created their identities and negotiated their spaces, using work for a range of purposes from the simply instrumental need to earn a living to fulfilling psychosocial needs above and beyond simply working.

FURTHER READING

Abrams, L., *Myth and Materiality in a Woman's World: Shetland, 1800–2000* (Manchester: Manchester University Press, 2005), ch. 4.

Clark, A., *The Struggle for the Breeches: Gender and the Making of the British Working Class* (Berkeley, CA: University of California Press, 1995).

Devine, T. M. (ed.), *Farm Servants and Labour in Lowland Scotland, 1770–1914* (Edinburgh: John Donald, 1984).

Gordon, E., 'Women, work and collective action: Dundee jute workers, 1870–1906', *Journal of Social History* 21: 1 (1987), 27–47.

Gordon, E., 'Women's spheres', in W. H. Fraser and R. J. Morris (eds), *People and Society in Scotland, vol. 2, 1830–1914* (Edinburgh: John Donald, 1990), pp. 206–35.

Gordon, E., *Women and the Labour Movement in Scotland* (Oxford: Clarendon Press, 1991).

Gordon, E. and E. Breitenbach (eds), *The World is Ill Divided: Women's Work in Scotland in the Nineteenth and Early Twentieth Centuries* (Edinburgh: Edinburgh University Press, 1990).

Houston, R. A., 'Women in the economy and society', in R. A. Houston and I. D. Whyte (eds), *Scottish Society 1500–1800* (Cambridge: Cambridge University Press, 1989), pp. 118–47.

McIvor, A., 'Women and work in twentieth-century Scotland', in A. Dickson and J. H. Treble (eds), *People and Society in Scotland, vol. 3, 1914–1990* (Edinburgh: John Donald, 1992), pp. 138–73.

Reynolds, S., *Britannica's Typesetters: Women Compositors in Edwardian Edinburgh* (Edinburgh: Edinburgh University Press, 1989).

Sanderson, E., *Women and Work in Eighteenth-century Edinburgh* (London: Macmillan Press, 1996).

Simonton, D., *A History of European Women's Work, 1700 to the Present* (London: Routledge, 1998).

Smout, T. C., *History of the Scottish People 1560–1830* (London: Collins, 1969).

Smout, T. C., *A Century of the Scottish People 1830–1950* (London: Collins, 1986).

Whatley, C. A., 'Women and the economic transformation of Scotland, c. 1740–1830', *Scottish Economic and Social History* 14 (1994), 19–40.

Whatley, C. A., *Scottish Society, 1707–1830: Beyond Jacobitism, Towards Industrialisation* (Manchester: Manchester University Press, 2000).

NOTES

1. E. Gordon, *Women the Labour Movement in Scotland, 1850–1914* (Oxford: Clarendon Press, 1991); A. Clark, *The Struggle for the Breeches: Gender and the Making of the British Working Class* (Berkeley, CA: University of California Press, 1995); A. McIvor and R. Johnston, 'Voices

from the pits: health and safety in Scottish coal mining since 1945', *Scottish Economic and Social History* 22 (2002), 111–33. Histories that integrate women include T. C. Smout, *History of the Scottish People 1560–1830* (London: Collins, 1969) and *A Century of the Scottish People, 1830–1950* (London: Collins, 1986); T. M. Devine (ed.), *Farm Servants and Labour in Lowland Scotland, 1770–1914* (Edinburgh: John Donald, 1984); W. Knox, *Industrial Nation: Work, Culture and Society in Scotland, 1800–Present* (Edinburgh: Edinburgh University Press, 1999); C. A. Whatley, *Scottish Society, 1707–1830: Beyond Jacobitism, Towards Industrialisation* (Manchester: Manchester University Press, 2000).

2. P. Sharpe, *Women's Work: The English Experience, 1650–1914* (London: Arnold, 1998), p. 8.

3. Smout, *History of the Scottish People*, pp. 304, 338.

4. L. Roubin, 'Male and female space in the Provençal community', in R. Forster and O. Ranum (eds), *Rural Society in France* (Baltimore, MD: The Johns Hopkins University Press, 1970), pp. 152–80, here pp. 158–9.

5. E. Johansson, 'Beautiful men, fine women and good workpeople: gender and skill in northern Sweden, 1850–1950', *Gender & History* 1: 2 (Summer 1989), 200–12, here p. 201.

6. Quoted in R. A. Houston, 'Women in the economy and society', in R. A. Houston and I. D. Whyte (eds), *Scottish Society 1500–1800* (Cambridge: Cambridge University Press, 1989), pp. 118–47, here p. 121.

7. Smout, *History of the Scottish People*, p. 298; M. Gray, 'Farm workers in north-east Scotland', in Devine (ed.), *Farm Servants and Labour*, pp. 10–28, here pp. 19, 21; R. Kerr, *General View of the Agriculture of the County of Berwickshire* (London, 1809), pp. 414–15.

8. See Devine, *Farm Servants and Labour*, pp. 1–4.

9. T. Devine, 'Women workers, 1850–1914', in Devine (ed.), *Farm Servants and Labour*, pp. 98–123, here pp. 106, 109.

10. Gray, 'Farm workers in north-east Scotland', pp. 11, 18; and A. Orr, 'Farm servants and farm labour in the Forth Valley and the south-east Lowlands', in Devine (ed.), *Farm Servants and Labour*, pp. 29–54, here p. 39.

11. H. Stephen, *The Book of the Farm* (Edinburgh, 1844), vol. 1, p. 227.

12. Quoted in Devine, 'Women workers, 1850–1914', p. 98.

13. Houston, 'Women in the economy and society', p. 121; Devine, 'Women workers, 1850–1914', pp. 99–100.

14. G. Skene Smith, *A General View of the Agriculture of Aberdeenshire* (Aberdeen, 1811), p. 521.

15. Quoted in E. Richards, 'Women in the British economy since about 1700', *History*, 59, no. 197 (1974), 337–57, here p. 341.

16. Houston, 'Women in the economy and society', p. 121.

17. A. Fenton, *Scottish Country Life* (Edinburgh: John Donald, 1977), p. 54.

18. W. Howatson, 'Grain harvesting and harvesters', in Devine (ed.), *Farm Servants and Labour*, pp. 124–54, here pp. 126–8.

19. A. Sturrock, 'Report of the agriculture of Ayrshire', *Prize Essays and Transactions of the Highland Society of Scotland*, 4th series, I (1866–7), p. 89.

20. Quoted in R. H. Campbell, 'Agricultural labour in the south-west', in Devine (ed.), *Farm Servants and Labour*, pp. 55–70, here p. 66.

21. Quoted in ibid., p. 62.

22. GB Parliamentary Papers, Royal Commission on Labour, 1893, pt I, p. 68.

23. Ibid., p. 52.

24. Campbell, 'Agricultural labour in the south-west', p. 66.

25. B. W. Robertson, 'In bondage: the female farmworker in south-east Scotland', in E. Gordon and E. Breitenbach (eds), *The World is Ill-Divided: Women's Work in Scotland in the Nineteenth and Early Twentieth Centuries* (Edinburgh: Edinburgh University Press, 1990), pp. 117–35, here p. 132.

26. Sir J. Sinclair (ed.), *The Statistical Account of Scotland, 1791–1799*, ed. D. J. Withrington and I. R. Grant (Wakefield: EP Publishing, 1982), vol. 13, pp. 423–4.

27. M. Gray, *The Fishing Industries of Scotland, 1790–1914* (Oxford: Oxford University Press, 1978), p. 13.

28. P. Thompson, T. Wailey and T. Lummis, *Living the Fishing* (London: Routledge and Kegan Paul, 1983), p. 173; N. Dorian, *Tyranny of Tide* (Ann Arbor, MI: Karoma, 1985), pp. 33–7.

29. Dorian, *Tyranny of Tide*, p. 69.

30. Quoted in H. Bradley, *Men's Work, Women's Work* (Oxford: Polity Press, 1989), p. 99.

31. C. Weld, *Two Months in the Highlands* (1860), in T. C. Smout and S. Wood (eds), *Scottish Voices, 1745–1960* (London: Fontana Press, 1990), p. 88.

32. Thompson et al., *Living the Fishing*, pp. 168–73.

33. *Aberdeen Journal*, 3 October 1758; T. Devine, 'Social composition of the merchant class', in G. Gordon and B. Dicks (eds), *Scottish Urban History* (Aberdeen: Aberdeen University Press, 1983), pp. 92–111, here pp. 99, 100.

34. E. Kowaleski-Wallace, *Consuming Subjects: Women, Shopping, and Business in the Eighteenth Century* (New York: Columbia University Press, 1997), pp. 82, 87, 112.

35. A. Smith, *Wealth of Nations*, book 1, ch. 9, paragraph I.9.20.

36. Ibid., book 1, ch. 10, paragraph I.10.39.

37. D. Defoe, *The Complete English Tradesman* (London, 1726), p. 132.

38. Smout, *A History of the Scottish People*, pp. 339–40.

39. Sinclair, *The Statistical Account of Scotland*, vol. 14, pp. 285, 293–4.

40. See T. Donnelly, 'The economic activities of the members of the Aberdeen merchant guild', 1750–1799, *Scottish Social and Economic History* 1: 1 (1981), 25–40, on marital relationships in the creation of the Aberdeen power base.

41. GB Public Record Office (PRO), Board of Inland Revenue, *Apprenticeship Registers, 1710–1808*, vols 1, 2, 19–38, 41, 51–70; Houston, 'Women in the economy and society', p. 122.

42. Quoted in E. Sanderson, *Women and Work in Eighteenth-century Edinburgh* (London: Macmillan Press, 1996), p. 128.

43. Ibid., p. 125.

44. R. A. Houston, *Social Change in the Age of Enlightenment* (Oxford, Clarendon Press, 1994), p. 78.

45. See D. Simonton, *A History of European Women's Work, 1700 to the Present* (London: Routledge, 1998), pp. 30–6 and 76–83.

46. See Sanderson, *Women and Work*, p. 39.

47. Ibid., pp. 7–14.

48. E. Bain, *Merchant and Craft Guilds: A History of the Aberdeen Incorporated Trades* (Aberdeen, 1887), pp. 169, 171, 228; *Enactment Books, 5, Register of Indentures, 1622–1878*, City of Aberdeen Archives, pp. 164–219.

49. *Aberdeen Journal*, 11 June 1764. On the conflation of merchant and shop-keeper, see Sanderson, *Women and Work*, p. 5.

50. Sanderson, *Women and Work*, pp. 74–5.

51. PRO, *Apprenticeship Registers*, vols 1, 2, 19–38, 41, 51–70.

52. *Aberdeen Journal*, 22 June 1767.

53. Sanderson, *Women and Work*, pp. 184–94.

54. Quoted in ibid., p. 107.

55. Quoted in ibid., p. 95.

56. Kowaleski-Wallace, *Consuming Subjects*, pp. 82, 87, 112; and J. G. Turner, ' "News from the New Exchange": commodity, erotic fancy, and the female entrepreneur', in A. Bermingham and J. Brewer (eds), *The Consumption of Culture 1600–1800* (London: Routledge, 1995), pp. 419–39, here pp. 427–8.

57. Houston, 'Women in the economy and society', p. 121.

58. J. Milne, *The Making of a Buchan Farm* (Aberdeen: D. Wylie and Son, 1892), p. 16.

59. Quoted in I. Carter, *Farm Life in North-east Scotland, 1840–1914* (Edinburgh: Donald, 1979), p. 17; GB Parliamentary Papers, *Poor Laws*, 1834, xxiv, p. 217a; L. Abrams, *Myth and Materiality in a Woman's World: Shetland, 1800–2000* (Manchester: Manchester University Press, 2005), ch. 4.

60. *Annals of Agriculture* 10 (1793), p. 559.

61. Quoted in I. D. Whyte, 'Proto-industrialisation in Scotland', in P. Hudson (ed.), *Regions and Industries: A Perspective on the Industrial Revolution in Britain* (Cambridge: Cambridge University Press, 1989), pp. 228–51, here p. 247.

62. Smith, *Wealth of Nations*, book 4, ch. 8, paragraph IV.8.4.

63. Whyte, 'Proto-industrialisation in Scotland', p. 247; see also Houston, 'Women in the economy and society', p. 121, and C. A. Whatley, 'Women

and the economic transformation of Scotland, c.1740–1830', *Scottish Economic and Social History* 14 (1994), 19–40, here pp. 21–4.

64. I. Pinchbeck, *Women Workers and the Industrial Revolution, 1750–1850* (London: Virago, 1981), pp. 162–6.

65. M. Berg, 'Women's work, mechanisation and the early phases of industrialisation in England', in P. Joyce (ed.), *The Historical Meanings of Work* (Cambridge: Cambridge University Press, 1989), p. 82.

66. See Clark, *Struggle for the Breeches*, pp. 128–31.

67. Ibid., p. 133.

68. M. Freifeld, 'Technological change and the "self-acting" mule: a study of skill and the sexual division of labour', *Social History*, 11: 3 (1986), 319–43, here pp. 333–5.

69. Clark, *Struggle for the Breeches*, p. 135.

70. E. Gordon, 'Women, work and collective action: Dundee jute workers, 1870–1906', *Journal of Social History* 21: 1 (1987), 27–47, here pp. 28–9.

71. Ibid., p. 30.

72. Quoted in John Holley, 'The two family economies of industrialism: factory workers in Victorian Scotland', *Journal of Family History* 6 (1981), 64.

73. Gordon, 'Women, work and collective action', p. 31.

74. McIvor and Johnston, 'Voices from the pits', p. 129.

75. Ibid., p. 130.

76. Smout, *A Century of the Scottish People*, p. 108.

77. GB Parliamentary Papers, Royal Commission Reports on Children in the Mines (1842), xv, p. 30.

78. Smout, *A Century of the Scottish People*, p. 20.

79. A. J. Albert, 'Fit work for women: sweated home-workers in Glasgow, c. 1875–1914', in Gordon and Breitenbach (eds), *The World is Ill-Divided*, pp. 158–77, here p. 162.

80. Ibid., pp. 159, 163; J. H. Treble, 'The characteristics of the female unskilled labour market and the formation of the female casual labour market in Glasgow, 1891–1914', *Scottish Economic and Social History* 6 (1986), 33–46, here pp. 39, 46. See Gordon, *Women and the Labour Movement*, pp. 16–21, on the social construction of the census.

81. Treble, 'The characteristics of the female unskilled labour market', here p. 38.

82. Albert, 'Fit work for women', pp. 161–3.

83. See G. Clarsen, ' "A fine university for women engineers": a Scottish munitions factory in World War I', *Women's History Review* 12: 3 (2003), 333–56, describing a purpose-built factory that advertised 'to interest gentlewomen who intend adopting engineering as a profession' (p. 334).

84. A. McIvor, 'Women and work in twentieth-century Scotland', in A. Dickson and J. H. Treble (eds), *People and Society in Scotland, vol. 3, 1914–1990* (Edinburgh: John Donald, 1992), pp. 138–73, here p. 158.

85. S. Reynolds, *Britannica's Typesetters: Women Compositors in Edwardian*

Edinburgh (Edinburgh: Edinburgh University Press, 1989), pp. 51–2, 128, 137.

86. Ibid., p. 63.
87. McIvor, 'Women and work', p. 142.
88. S. Nenadic, 'The social shaping of business behaviour in the nineteenth-century women's garment trades', *Journal of Social History* 31: 3 (1998), 625–46, here p. 626.
89. Ibid.
90. C. Dauphin, 'Single women', in G. Fraisse and M. Perrot (eds), *A History of Women*, vol. 4, *Emerging Feminism from Revolution to World War* (Cambridge, MA: The Belknap Press of Harvard University Press, 1993), pp. 427–42, here p. 433.
91. Calculation based on data in C. H. Lee, *British Regional Employment Statistics, 1841–1971* (Cambridge: Cambridge University Press, 1979).
92. J. Burnett, *Useful Toil* (London: Allen Lane, 1974), p. 185.
93. See Simonton, *European Women's Work*, pp. 96–112, for service across Europe.
94. J. D. Stephenson and C. G. Brown, 'The view from the workplace: women's memories of work in Stirling c.1910–c.1950', in Gordon and Breitenbach (eds), *The World is Ill-Divided*, pp. 7–28, here p. 14.
95. Ibid., p. 15.
96. Ibid., p. 14.
97. R. Guerriero Wilson, 'Office workers, business elites and the disappearance of the "ladder of success" in Edwardian Glasgow', *Scottish Economic and Social History* 19: 1 (1999), 55–75, here p. 56.
98. Quoted in S. Dohrn, 'Pioneers in a dead-end profession: the first women clerks in banks and insurance companies', in G. Anderson (ed.), *The White-Blouse Revolution: Female Office Workers since 1870* (Manchester: Manchester University Press, 1988), pp. 48–66, here p. 50.
99. Wilson, 'Office workers', p. 58.
100. Ibid.
101. M. Davies, 'Women clerical workers and the typewriter: the writing machine', in C. Kramarae (ed.), *Technology and Women's Voices: Keeping in Touch* (London: Routledge, 1988), p. 31.
102. M. Zimmeck, ' "Get out and get under": the impact of demobilisation on the Civil Service, 1919–32', in Anderson (ed.), *The White-Blouse Revolution*, pp. 88–120, here p. 90.
103. C. Cockburn, *Machinery of Dominance: Women, Men and Technical Know-how* (London: Pluto Press, 1985), p. 12.
104. K. Tijdens, 'Behind the screens: the foreseen and unforeseen impact of computerization on female office workers' jobs', *Feminist Perspectives on Technology, Work and Ecology, 2nd European Feminist Research Conference, Graz, Austria* (1994), pp. 132–9, here p. 138.
105. Stephenson and Brown, 'The view from the workplace', p. 17.

106. McIvor, 'Women and work', p. 148.
107. Stephenson and Brown, 'The view from the workplace', pp. 17–18; M. Winstanley, *The Shopkeepers' World, 1830–1914* (Manchester: Manchester University Press, 1983), p. 69; McIvor, 'Women and work', p. 156.
108. Stephenson and Brown, 'The view from the workplace', p. 18.
109. Ibid., pp. 15–16.
110. P. Stearns, *European Society in Upheaval* (London: Collier Macmillan, 1975), pp. 218–19.
111. See Chapter 6 of this book.
112. See W. Alexander, 'Early Glasgow medical graduates', in Gordon and Breitenbach (eds), *The World is Ill-Divided*, pp. 70–94; and E. Russell, 'Women and medicine', in M. R. Masson and D. Simonton (eds), *Women and Higher Education: Past Present and Future* (Aberdeen: University of Aberdeen Press, 1996), pp. 295–6.
113. C. Adams, 'Public legislation, private decisions: the life of Miss Anywoman, Scottish teacher, born 1909', in Masson and Simonton (eds), *Women and Higher Education*, pp. 204–10, here p. 208; see also Chapter 5 of this book.
114. T. Blackstone, 'Education and careers: a rough road to the top', in Masson and Simonton (eds), *Women and Higher Education*, pp. 5–14, here pp. 10–11.
115. Gordon, *Labour Movement*, p. 35; on gender and machinery, see Simonton, *European Women's Work*, pp. 41–8.
116. Smout, *History of the Scottish People*, p. 88.
117. A. J. McIvor, 'Gender apartheid', in T. M. Devine and R. J. Finlay (eds), *Scotland in the Twentieth Century* (Edinburgh: Edinburgh University Press, 1999), pp. 188–209, here pp. 197, 201.
118. Dorian, *Tyranny of Tide*, p. 37.
119. McIvor, 'Women and work', p. 149.

9

The Family

Eleanor Gordon

INTRODUCTION

There is no dominant narrative of the history of the family in Scotland which can be deconstructed or challenged. Most accounts are either case studies, or fragmentary accounts which are often embedded in other histories. Therefore, this chapter will reassess the narrative which was entrenched in the history of the western family until relatively recently, in order to illustrate how this interpretation might be reshaped when reviewed through a gendered lens and applied to the Scottish experience. The key components of this dominant narrative are: since the pre-industrial era, the family/household has gradually shed its productive and economic role; industrial capitalism created an increasingly privatised family which was separated from the wider social world and from wider kin; companionate marriage became the norm and there was a sharpening of gender divisions within the family, with women increasingly associated with the role of wife and mother and men with the role of breadwinner.[1] The intention of this chapter is to draw on the insights of social and economic history, gender history and family history in order to break down this narrative and to illustrate the diversity of family life, of family forms and indeed of meanings of 'family'.

It has been remarked by a number of scholars that there is a good deal of common ground between those who are interested in family history and those who are interested in the history of gender.[2] They both share the premise that families and family relationships are deeply social and cannot be consigned to the biological or 'natural'. Both sorts of history also share the project of making visible and reclaiming the historical importance of individuals and areas of life which have been generally ignored while public life and events have been privileged in historical explanation. It is also true that family history and gender history have been concerned to demonstrate that the process of historical change is complex and that economic factors do not always have primacy in historical explanation.[3]

For all this common ground between historians of the family and gender historians, it is probably true that until the last couple of decades there has not been much overlap between the two approaches and that they have tended to plough different furrows. This has stemmed from different preoccupations. For all it sought to uncover the historical importance of everyday life and the 'private realm', family history as it developed in Britain was very much influenced by the traditional concepts in the social sciences such as modernisation and urbanisation. It was also concerned with meta-explanations and with using social-science methodologies of quantification and large-scale aggregate data. By contrast, in Europe, particularly in France, another stream of family history developed that took its inspiration from the Annales school and from anthropology, and which was interested in *mentalités* and combining demographic analysis with analysis of family patterns, sexuality and social and cultural variables.[4]

In Britain, the Cambridge Group for the History of Population and Social Structure became the leading centre for the study of the family, and its agenda dominated family history in Britain for two decades. These historical demographers were concerned with questions related to the relationship between families, modernisation and the fertility transition, and in large-group behaviour rather than individual or family experience. Indeed, one critic noted that one could easily conclude from the work of demographers that it was regions which had babies rather than people.[5] Although historical demography could not be chastised for ignoring women, it did take for granted assumptions about gender and gender relations rather than seeing them as requiring historical investigation. Even when the focus was on couples rather than women, usually the internal differences of power within families was ignored; it was assumed that decision-making was consensual and that the family was a single conflict-free unit.[6]

Whatever its limitations, historical demography has offered important insights into the family and has transformed our understanding of families in the past. We no longer view the pre-industrial family in Britain as a large, extended multi-generational unit and now know that by and large, since at least the early modern period, there has been a preference for nuclear units and that households typically consisted of fewer than five people. We also have a better understanding of the process of population growth in the 200 years or so from middle of the seventeenth century and of the central role of social factors in influencing these trends.[7] In Scotland, a rich seam of research into the fertility transition has provided some understanding of the social changes and social processes which underlay the decline in fertility in the second half of the nineteenth century, although all are underpinned by the assumptions that decision-making among couples is consensual and ignore the conflict and compromise which characterise decision-making.[8] Other approaches to the history of the family have been more concerned with family relationships and family dynamics than aggregate statistical data. These studies have questioned long-standing assumptions such as the view that industrialisation was a major watershed in the history of the family, and they have repositioned the family as an important agent of social change rather than as a passive unit which was shaped by economic forces.[9]

Therefore the work of historians of the family has led to significant revisions in the classical account of historians and of sociologists of family development and has provided us with a more complex picture of family forms, roles and relationships in the past. They have challenged notions of the family as timeless and 'natural' and made the topic more than a mere backcloth to 'real' historical action. They have shown how the family has changed in form and function and how family relationships have changed over time. However, family history has not generally been informed by a gendered approach which raises key questions of power, control, meaning, regulatory discourses and the role of the state in shaping families. This neglect has been as much the fault of gender historians as traditional family historians. Their focus, certainly in the early stages of women's history, was with making women visible in public arenas rather than exploring the areas which women were conventionally supposed to have occupied. Moreover, many feminist historians whose key influence was socialism were unsympathetic to the family, viewing it as the site of oppression for women and a prop of capitalism. The boundaries between family history and gender history have begun to dissolve, and it is instructive to explore how the closer relationship between the two has provided fresh insights into family history.

THE HOUSEHOLD ECONOMY

It has become a truism to argue that the pre-industrial family was a unit of production where all members contributed labour to a family-based enterprise which was usually home-based. In both rural and urban areas, there is a wealth of evidence illustrating the ways in which the family and the household were at the centre of productive activity. However, what is striking about the household economy on the eve of the agricultural revolution, industrialisation and the factory system is the variety of types of family-based production which existed. At the beginning of the eighteenth century, the archetypal peasant household economy where parents worked alongside their children on their own plot or strip of land, producing enough for their own needs, was probably not the most common way in which families subsisted. Although a number of families worked together in a unitary household economy, many families did not. We know that many men went out of the home to earn a wage; but, if we focus on women's work, it is clear that the household economy which we conventionally associate with the pre-industrial period was in fact far from being the dominant means by which families reproduced themselves.[10]

While many wives worked alongside their husbands, many more did not. Elizabeth Sanderson's study of eighteenth-century women's work in Edinburgh suggests that many wives worked independently from their husbands as milliners, shopkeepers, nurses, washers, schoolteachers and so on. Of 120 women roupers or auctioneers recorded in Edinburgh between 1730 and 1800, only two had the same occupation as their husbands.[11] When one also takes into account the extent of geographical mobility in early modern Scotland, the numbers of agricultural servants who migrated to towns and other rural areas for employment, many of whom were single women, and the numbers of apprentices who lived in the households of master craftsmen, the centrality to production of a simple family economy based in the household becomes even more questionable.[12]

While consideration of women's economic role is significant for understanding the means by which families reproduced themselves in the pre-industrial era, gender historians have also highlighted the fact that we need to focus on how this may have affected power relations within the family. Conventionally, it has been supposed that while all family members contributed to the pre-industrial family economy, work was supervised by the male head of household, who was invested with supreme authority. Indeed, the authority of the male head of household had legal, moral and religious sanction. Although marriage in Scots law was based on the mutual consent of the parties involved without the requirement of parental consent, and there was no double standard in the grounds for obtaining a divorce (adultery or desertion), in many other respects the law tipped the scales very much in the husband's favour. From the late seventeenth century, matrimonial property laws stated that upon marriage the husband assumed legal possession and control over all moveable property that his wife might have owned as a single woman, as well as any property and earnings that might come to her during marriage. Although Scottish wives had greater legal rights of inheritance and legal protection of their property than their English counterparts, the legal basis of marriage was based on a patriarchal model.[13] The law also sanctioned a degree of violence by husbands towards their wives. Until the nineteenth century, husbands had the right to chastise their wives physically: as long as the cruelty 'does not amount to gross personal violence, it is a valid defence to the husband that the wife's conduct was improper and deserving of punishment'.[14] The husband's legal authority was buttressed by religious and moral discourses, which vaunted male authority and counselled female obedience and subservience. The Exhortation given at the beginning of the marriage ceremony detailed the duties of the wife as 'to study to please and obey her husband, serving him only in all things that be godly and honest, for she is in subjection, and under the governance of her husband as long as they continue both alive'.[15]

Patriarchal authority was also manifested in myriad other ways: in some regions, it was customary for women to stand while the men ate, or for women to eat separately from the men; in other regions, men sat in armed chairs while other family members sat on benches or stools.

Yet, in practice, the ideology of patriarchy co-existed with a blurring of gender boundaries of authority and function. Women's contribution to the family's resources was clearly more than supplementary; it was indispensable, and this was often publicly or ceremonially recognised and often reflected in the power relations of the household. In Scotland, the classic example of this was among the fishing communities. In Auchnithie near Arbroath, the wives of fishermen were major contributors to family income: they baited the lines, prepared and sold the fish, would launch and beach the boats, and, in an act of supreme selflessness, would carry their menfolk on their backs to the boats so that they could begin their fishing trip dry. On the wedding night, a leather purse full of money was sent to the bride from her betrothed, a symbolic gesture which signified that she would have control of the family's resources.[16] It has been argued that women in fishing communities were often regarded as at least of equal status to men, and that in some families they were the dominant members of the household. Similar arguments have been made about the family economy of Lewis. Women were the mainstay of the household and took a heavier share of the work than the men, who were at times subjected to ridicule for being ineffectual. These women took such pride in their work that they felt ashamed if their menfolk had to perform any of the duties considered to be theirs.[17]

It has been suggested that, in the second half of the eighteenth century, increasing economic opportunities available to women as a consequence of proto-industrialisation and agricultural improvements may have eroded the traditional sexual division of labour and conferred more power and independence upon women. This probably exaggerates both the extent of women's subordination in the traditional household economy and the impact of economic factors alone on family dynamics and relationships. However, the degree of economic interdependence of spouses in the pre-industrial family probably required more mutuality and negotiation than implied by the starkly patriarchal nature of the law, even if it did not confer equality of prestige and power upon women. That and women's refusal to accept complete subordination to their husbands went some way to eroding and undermining patriarchal relations and gender inequalities on which the pre-industrial family was based. In early modern Scotland, the tradition of married women retaining their maiden name may not have implied women's independence from their spouses as some observers suggested; however, it may have been a symbol of women's resistance to the subordination of their husbands. Certainly, the evidence of separation cases suggests that there was a degree of reciprocity and mutuality in the pre-industrial marital relationship. Although the husband's cruelty was cited as the grounds for a judicial separation, wives such as Euphemia Vallance frequently referred to the fact that their husbands were profligate, idle, dissolute or drunken and could not fulfil their responsibilities as head of the household. Euphemia had endured her husband's physical violence for a number of years, but what roused her to seek a legal separation was his failure to be a reliable provider and to support the household economy. He had been 'in frequent practice of insulting and abusing the Customers who come into the Shop, whereby the business is likely to be utterly destroyed'.[18]

It was also recognised that marriage should be based on mutual affection and that the husband had duties as well as rights. One early eighteenth-century legal writer stated that, of the principal duties of the marriage contract, 'among the first are the conjugal love and affection between the married persons'.[19] The pre-industrial family was not merely an economic unit shorn of love and affection, and marriage was not simply an instrumental means of securing a livelihood. Choice of partner could involve considerations of the heart as well as the purse. Letters and autobiographies of this period are testimony to the strong emotional bonds between couples and the grief which was experienced at the loss of a partner. However, in the pre-modern family, the balance was tipped towards more practical considerations rather than romantic ones.

Whatever the impact of economic factors on gender relations, in the course of the eighteenth century changes in interpretations of the law indicate more censorious attitudes towards husbands' cruelty. Although provocation was enshrined in law as justification for cruelty, by the beginning of the nineteenth century it was rarely invoked by judges, who no longer subscribed to the idea that a quarrelsome wife deserved a beating.[20]

The conventional narrative locates key changes in the economic role of the family with the advent of industrial capitalism and the separation of home and work. Many historians have argued that the rise of industrial capitalism and the emergence of class society heralded a number of profound changes in social relationships and social institutions, including the family. Technological transformations which enlarged workplaces and separated them from home, combined with the emergence of an ideology which vaunted the domestic ideal, erected both physical and metaphorical barriers between home and work. These developments were said to have undermined an older family economy. Yet, as we have seen, the break-up of the family system of labour and household-based production long pre-dated industrialisation.

On the other hand, industrialisation did not completely disrupt the links between the household and work. The separation of home and work was a gradual process and did not always proceed in a linear fashion. The Post Office Directory for Glasgow of 1879–80 records scores of retailers and small businesses where the residential and business address were the same.[21] Even in the building trades, there were firms which continued to work from the home. Home could also be the site of work for many in the middle classes. Many general practitioners had consulting rooms attached to their homes well into the twentieth century. Some with modest practices had a shop and a pharmacy attached to the premises. William Walker, a general practitioner in Pollokshaws in the 1870s, had a practice where the shop was actually inside the house.[22] Indeed, these professions often resembled a family business, as wives and daughters were frequently called upon to act as unpaid secretaries or assistants. In Walker's case, his wife supervised the chemist shop, dispensed, and even prescribed for common ailments.

Even in households where the physical separation of home and work was complete, the world of work was not entirely sealed off from the enterprise. It was common for business meetings to be held in the home, or to have a study where business papers could be consulted. Conducting business required nurturing and maintaining social networks as well as demonstrating the sound basis of the enterprise. Therefore entertaining business associates in the home was common practice. Indeed, the dimensions of the middle-class nineteenth-century home, with its disproportionately large dining rooms with adjacent extensive larders, reflected the importance of business entertaining.[23] In many households, the idea of a boundary between a purely domestic realm and a business sphere was a fiction.

Feminist historians have long questioned the narrow definition of work as an activity based on a male norm of waged work outside the home. If we redefine work to include a much broader definition of economic activity than cash income derived from an officially recognised occupation, then we see that the household continued to be a locus of economic activity. For example, many working-class women and even lower middle-class women took in lodgers to supplement family income. In a study of Highland households in Glasgow's Broomielaw in 1851, half contained lodgers or boarders,[24] while in two of the lower middle-class streets of Glasgow's Claremont estate in 1891 sixteen couples took in boarders and lodgers.[25] None of these wives had a recorded occupation, yet in many instances the women managed the equivalent of small hotels or restaurants, albeit in a domestic setting. 'Self-provisioning' was a widespread practice among women in working-class communities. Knitting, sewing, converting old clothes into blankets, or fashioning makeshift furniture were all essential activities for families' subsistence. Working-class women had to be resourceful and deploy considerable initiative to keep the family solvent. It was common for women to wait until the shops were about to close before they bought provisions, knowing that items such as fish, meat and bread could be obtained at reduced prices.[26] The responsibility for 'making ends meet' was primarily a female one, and women frequently tapped into a network of sources of support and sometimes resorted to pawn shops, credit from local shopkeepers, Co-operative dividends and even local moneylenders to provide the essentials for their families. In one Glasgow working-class district in the 1930s, money would be borrowed from local small-time moneylenders 'lending five shillings and getting back seven', while pawning was done on a weekly basis with rings, suits and blankets pawned at the beginning of the week and 'lifted' on the Friday.[27]

It was not only the working classes who marshalled family resources and family members for economic survival. The middle classes had similar strategies in order to keep the business enterprise either solvent or prosperous. Family and kin were integral elements in the network of business and economic relationships throughout the nineteenth century and beyond, and intermarriage was common both within and between upper middle-class families. Cousin marriage may have reflected the frequency of contact between wider kin, but it was also a way of keeping property within the family. Liaisons between the children of business partners or prominent business families could ensure the economic survival of the firm in a competitive economic climate. The ship-owning dynasty of the Smith–Allan family is a good illustration of the importance of marriage and family in the continuation of a business enterprise. In this family, there are examples of cousin marriages, of two sisters marrying two brothers and, with the marriage of Robert Smith's daughter Jane to Alexander Allan of the Allan line, of a marital union which was crucial in uniting two shipping families. The Smith family tradition of marriage 'within the family' to cement business links continued into the early twentieth century and was replicated many times over among Scotland's business elite.[28]

Feminist economists and historians have long sought to dissolve the fictive division between production, reproduction and consumption and to highlight the vital role of domestic labour in the ways in which families maintain and reproduce themselves. Therefore they would question the notion that the family was ever only a unit of reproduction and consumption with productive functions consigned to a space outside of the home. Even if one accepts that the physical separation of home and work and the practice of leaving the home to earn an individual wage heralded the demise of the family as a unit of production, the persistence of household economic activity and the family system of labour into the early twentieth century suggests that, in historical terms, it is only relatively recently that we can characterise the family as primarily a unit of consumption. Indeed, it might also be the case that this status is temporary and short-lived. Recent changes in working practices and the growth of home-based business, of remote working and of flexible working have resurrected the household as locus of economic activity and may resurrect the notion of the family as a unit of production.

A PRIVATE HAVEN?

Related to the theme of the separation of production and consumption is the view that during the nineteenth century the family became an increasingly privatised and companionate unit focused on the nuclear unit of parents and children and which was isolated from wider kin and the wider social world or community. An ideology of domesticity combined with the increasing separation from work constructed the home as a spiritual enclave and a private retreat from the corruption of the material world of the market place. It is argued that these developments were matched by a differentiation in the roles of women and men, with women responsible for the maintenance of the home as a spiritual haven from the hostile public world, whereas men's role was to maintain the economic viability of the home. Although many of these changes were seen as incipient at the beginning of the nineteenth century and confined to the more affluent sections of society, by the early twentieth century the privatised nuclear family was assumed to have become pervasive and so well established that it became embedded as a dominant narrative in the history of the family.

There were certainly a number of changes in the nineteenth century which give credence to this view. These reflected and reinforced the private character of the home and underscored the role of the family as a haven and the repository of Christian morality. For example, changes in domestic architecture, particularly in upper- and middle-class homes, created a functional specialisation of rooms, in contrast to the pre-industrial period when people often ate, slept and entertained in the same room. By the end of the eighteenth century, we also see the innovation of corridors separating sleeping quarters from the main living areas. Changes in the interior decoration of the home reinforced the private and nest-like character. Previously, houses in the pre-industrial era had been simply if not austerely furnished. In the nineteenth century, domestic space, whether in grand houses or tenement flats, was crammed with furniture and ornaments. Colour schemes were rich and heavy, and furniture tended to be in mahogany or rosewood. The drawing room of Henry Houldsworth, a Glasgow manufacturer, is illustrative of the penchant the Victorians had for densely furnished homes. The inventory records that there were two sofas, twelve chairs, two easy chairs, four card tables, two teapoys, four stools, a sideboard, two pole firescreens, a Canterbury, another table, and a semigrand piano and stool. This was all in addition to mirrors, books, engravings, Chinese vases, mantelpiece ornaments, brass ornaments, clocks and ornaments under glass domes.[29] The amount and value of furnishings obviously varied from class to class, but by and large across the socio-economic scale the aim seemed to be to create an atmosphere of secluded retreat.

However, we should bear in mind that it was only a minority who had the financial means to acquire a well-appointed home with different rooms for eating, sleeping and living and where individual family members had the luxury of their own bedroom. By 1911, 62 per cent of Glasgow's residents lived in dwellings of one or two rooms, and in many working-class tenements several families shared a sink and a privy. Even in 1931, some 56 per cent of Glaswegians still lived in two rooms or fewer.[30] Rural accommodation could be even more primitive. One woman recalled how her grandparents' early twentieth-century house in the Western Isles housed the animals as well as the family and where 'privacy' was achieved by dint of putting a curtain round one's bed.[31]

Family rituals could also cement the idea of the home as a private haven and a refuge from the world. Family mealtimes became a ritual, with the symbolic significance underlining the unity of the family and its separate identity. The nineteenth century also witnessed the domestication of religion, which became no longer confined to churches and official places of worship. The practice of family prayers became commonplace, and Sunday worship and church usually took the form of a family outing. Family life and religion became intertwined, so that celebrations of religious holidays and rituals such as Christmas became essentially family celebrations. The emphasis on family privacy could also be seen in the expulsion of apprentices from the household and the rise of the family summer holiday.

The separation of the family household from work, more comfortable living arrangements, and even an ideology of domesticity which required a home-based wife, do not necessarily equate with an intensely privatised family which is an inward-looking haven and a retreat from wider social relationships. In the early modern period, the concept of 'family' was inclusive and flexible and was not defined by relationships of blood or marriage. Servants, apprentices and even friends could all qualify as family members.[32] By the nineteenth century, the meaning of 'family' may have shifted from its early modern meaning, to exclude apprentices and servants; but the category 'family' still remained a broad one, encompassing far more than the nuclear unit of children and parents. In some instances, 'family' embraced not only those related by blood or marriage but also those united by religious belief – what may be termed spiritual kin. In Scotland as in England, this was strongest in groups outside the established church. For example, the Glasgow family of Catherine Carswell, a journalist and novelist, regularly accommodated co-religionists of the Free Church and foreign missionaries in their home, often sharing beds and bedrooms with family members.[33] Although there was a clear demarcation between servants and 'family', occasionally servants were accorded symbolic membership of the household entity when included in rituals such as family prayers. In some instances, servants could be awarded quasi-familial status. Margaret Pinkerton's servants were recruited from the same families over several generations, and she maintained links with them over a long period and recognised those links in her will by leaving them significant amounts of money.[34] It was not uncommon for servants in one household to be related to each other, and in these cases we see 'parallel families' living and working side by side. As we have seen, boarders and lodgers, who were often relatives of the host family, were common in many working-class and some lower middle-class households. They often took their meals with the family, whether or not they were related to them, and were therefore in the ambivalent position of being *with* the family but not *of* the family. Like servants, lodgers could form 'parallel families', as many were related to each other. This was particularly common among lodgers in Glasgow's Highland community in the late nineteenth century.[35] This phenomenon of 'hidden' kin in households suggests that there was a complex web of family connections. In fact, the comings and goings of lodgers, servants and visitors, and their ambiguous status, reveals the household and the family as an ever-changing kaleidoscope of forms and meanings, rather than a static grouping or concept.

A number of historians have suggested that in fact extended families, which included wider kin within the household, became more prevalent in the nineteenth century.[36] Historians differ in their explanations for this higher incidence of extended family forms. Anderson suggests that it was the outcome of a strategy for maximising family resources, while Ruggles's argument is that the phenomenon can be attributed to the interaction of economic, demographic and cultural factors. For Ruggles, rising life expectancy, coupled with a cultural preference for living with extended kin, conjoined with economic factors to make the late nineteenth century a 'golden age' for extended-family structures. In other words, because people were living longer, there were more dependent relatives; there was an ideology which encouraged people to seek out kin for support; and rising incomes meant that families were in a better financial position to do so.

Extended living arrangements were therefore common in nineteenth- and early twentieth-century Scotland for both the working classes and the middle classes. In 1891 in one of Glasgow's middle-class districts, the incidence of extended family forms was just under 29 per cent, while among working-class Highland communities in the city the proportion of households containing extended kin in 1881 was about one quarter.[37] In fact, the percentage of households which conformed to the standard nuclear model with a male-headed unit was much smaller than suggested by these figures. Significant numbers of households which were classified as nuclear were actually one-parent units. In addition, large numbers of single-person households and other households were headed by women. In Glasgow's Claremont estate, the proportion of households that conformed to the stereotypical 'privatised' nuclear family was only half in 1851 and by 1891 had fallen to just over one third, a minority of all households.[38]

The high incidence of female-headed households is a noteworthy feature of household structure in nineteenth-century Scotland. There are a number of explanations for this, some of which are regionally and culturally specific: lower life expectancy among men, the availability of work for women in particular areas, and the fact that Scotland had had a high proportion of female celibacy since at least the eighteenth century. In 1861, around one in five Scottish women never married – higher than the English average.[39] The combination of these factors resulted in a high proportion of extended or complex households compared to simple or nuclear households. So, for example, in Dundee, which was often referred to as a 'woman's town', it has been estimated that about one-third of households were headed by women in 1904. In Shetland, the average percentage of female-headed households for all the different islands was 24 per cent in 1851, while in Glasgow's Claremont estate the proportion varied from one-third in 1851 to 40 per cent in 1891.[40] Indeed, in one Claremont street, there were more female- than male-headed households in 1891. Although these census statistics throw up interesting data which revise our image of the Victorian family as a social unit presided over a paterfamilias, the problem with them is that they provide only a snapshot of residential patterns and assume the family is a fixed unit rather than a process undergoing a life cycle. Household forms changed over the lifespan of the family, encompassing 'standard' nuclear, 'non-standard' nuclear and extended forms at various stages. The cyclical nature of household formation, with families experiencing different forms at different stages, makes it difficult to categorise families neatly into 'extended' or 'nuclear'. Nevertheless, the information which we have about household forms for nineteenth-century Scotland does much to undermine the conventional picture of the Victorian household as a nuclear unit organised around a male breadwinner and to question the hegemony of the privatised nuclear family.

Of course, 'family' is not co-terminous with 'household'; and, if we look at the network of connections between families and kin who do not co-reside, the notion of the family retreating to a nuclear core becomes even more difficult to sustain. Family networks continued to be of immense importance as sources of emotional, social and financial support. In urban working-class areas, they could be tapped as an employment and housing agency.[41] In some Dundee jute firms, family connections could facilitate recruitment if family members 'spoke for you'; and certainly in the skilled trades in the industry, family connections played an important role in the recruitment process.[42] Women were often the fulcrum of the network of kin relationships in working-class families, particularly in relation to child care. During the interwar Depression, many working-class families could not afford to look after their own children, who would often be boarded out to relatives. Similarly, during periods of illness, female relatives looked after relatives' children, an arrangement that could become permanent if death was the outcome.[43] It has even been suggested that the persistence of high illegitimacy rates in rural Banffshire in the nineteenth century was partly the product of grandparents' willingness and financial capacity to look after bastard children.[44] Among the middle classes, family was also an important source of financial support in business as well as personal matters. Small firms operating in a competitive market often looked to kin to bail them out of financial difficulties. Walter Paterson bought his house in Claremont Terrace in 1851, having borrowed the money from the trustees of the estate of his late father-in-law.[45]

For both the working classes and the middle classes, kinship networks continued to provide a cushion and a support for families in times of economic hardship or crisis. But 'family' could also mean a set of business connections, a marriage pool or a set of obligations and responsibilities. Relatives were often both friends and neighbours. Michael Anderson found in mid-nineteenth-century working-class Lancashire clusters of households of the same surname and originating from the same area.[46] In nineteenth-century Glasgow, there were similar clusters of families among the middle classes, with a great web of interconnections linking many of the families in adjacent streets.[47] Although Anderson explained this clustering in terms of working-class families' strategies to combat poverty and the hardships of industrialisation, the same reasons seem unlikely to apply to the middle classes. It is more likely that these residential patterns reflected the middle-class desire for social exclusivity and segregation from the lower classes as part of their quest to construct a coherent and stable middle-class identity and culture.

Historians have for some time argued that interaction with wider kin was relatively insignificant in the early modern period and that more distant kin were replaced by friends or self-selected relationships.[48] Even if there was a desire to keep in contact with kin, geographical mobility coupled with poor communications meant that it would have been difficult to maintain effective communication with kin who had moved away. Therefore, contrary to the view that the isolated nuclear family came to dominate in the course of the nineteenth century, kinship recognition may have been more significant in family life in the nineteenth and early twentieth centuries than in the pre-industrial period. 'Family' continued to be a flexible and fairly broadly defined term which defied any easy categorisation into extended or nuclear.

COMMUNITY

Although the nineteenth- and early twentieth-century family has been portrayed as a cosy haven which was cloistered from the public gaze in contrast to the open sociability of the early modern family, what is striking about the nineteenth-century family is its openness and porosity. Despite the claims about privacy, middle-class domestic life had to be paraded and ostentatiously displayed in order to vaunt its superiority and become a model for home life. Census enumerators' schedules, family papers and household inventories provide a rich source of information which reveal the middle-class home as a hive of sociability. Despite the supposed ubiquity of the calling card and prearranged 'at homes', the Victorian middle classes entertained a stream of casual visitors who included relatives, friends, business associates and fellow church members.[49] Visiting, which was primarily a female activity, could be a means of consolidating and nurturing social and professional networks; however, middle-class sociability encompassed much more than the orchestrated ritual of 'calling'. Victorian hospitality was abundant and took many forms, from dinners and soirées to large parties and balls. However, hospitality was not of the all-embracing kind which we associate with the early modern period.[50] It was exclusive in that it was offered to one's peers; indeed, it was a means of affirming who one's peers were. Entertaining in the home could serve a variety of purposes, and played an important role in constituting middle-class identity and culture and giving a public aspect to the middle-class home.

Working-class families would not have had the resources or the space to entertain on such a scale, although parties, sing-songs and entertaining were a common feature of working-class life. Their overcrowded accommodation and the legendary communality and neighbourliness of tenement life may not have made notions of 'privacy' redundant; but it would certainly have had different meanings from idealised conceptions of the privatised family cloistered in seclusion from the wider world.

It has often been suggested that industrialisation destroyed community life as well as disrupting kinship networks. While there may have been a decline in the importance of communal bonds and regulation in family life since the early modern period, community ties did not disappear with urbanisation and industrialisation. Families continued to be reliant on a wider network of support than could be gained from either immediate family or wider kin. The nineteenth-century middle classes were enmeshed in a network of communal activities, many of which were church-based or business-based. Common membership of a matrix of civic, philanthropic, professional and business-related organisations performed a variety of functions: it fostered friendships, greased the wheels of business transactions, advanced professional careers and acted as a marriage agency.[51] It was also crucial in the creation of a common middle-class identity and in constituting them as political, cultural and moral force.

Community and neighbourhood networks were vital to the economic and social welfare of the working classes in urban Scotland. Economic crises, the struggle for survival, the social and cultural dislocation which could be wrought by migration, and myriad other factors impelled the working classes to seek out and create structures and institutions of mutual interest and support. Among migrants, particularly those who originated from a particular ethnic group, there were strong communal and associational bonds. Irish, Highland and Jewish immigrants were particularly active in creating these networks of support.[52] Highlanders in Glasgow and Greenock formed their own churches, schools and charitable organisations, and in the second half of the nineteenth century the social and cultural organisations of the Highland community flourished. Jewish immigrants to Glasgow preferred assistance from their community to 'having to beg for help from philanthropic societies, or from the local Poor Law facilities'.[53] During the Depression in interwar Lanarkshire, the survival of the family, deprived of a male breadwinner, could be dependent on women's co-operative efforts in the community to make and even save money. Women organised the 'menage' system which involved a group of women contributing to a 'pot' each week, with each of them taking it in turns to receive all the money in the pot at set intervals.[54] They often worked collectively, pooling resources to keep each other's families out of crisis: as one working-class woman observed, 'You had to because you never knew what was round the corner'.[55] Mutual support took a variety of forms beyond economic reciprocity. For example, the practice of 'poinding', which involved the forced removal of furniture or household goods to pay for debts such as rent arrears, was commonplace in Scotland until relatively recently. In times of economic hardship, 'poindings' and evictions became particularly prevalent and were often fiercely resisted, particularly by the women of the local community.[56]

Crofting communities in the Western Isles required a strong communal basis for economic survival. Co-operative work lay at the heart of the crofting community, even to the extent of neighbours helping to build each other's houses.[57] According to one inhabitant who bemoaned the absence of this collective spirit after the Second World War:

> each crofter . . . they all helped each other out, shared their duties as best they could, gathering sheep for clipping, they all combined, clipped each other's sheep, helped each other at hay making. The corn was all cut by hand and hand sheafed, so they would club together for hand sheafing.[58]

In crofting communities, reciprocity and economic interdependence was much more highly developed than in urban life or even in other agricultural communities.[59] However, communal bonds, mutuality and collective action based on the neighbourhood were still vibrant across classes and regions into the twentieth century and were not supplanted by individual family strategies or state welfare agencies. The family may have been the primary locus of emotional and social support, but it was sustained in its endeavours by a dense network of community and neighbourhood organisations, institutions and practices. The boundaries between the 'family' and the community were permeable rather than sharply differentiated, and there seems to have been little attempt by the family to keep the outside world at a distance and to sever links with kin, community and neighbourhood.

GENDER RELATIONS

A parallel narrative to privatisation has been the ways in which the relations between husbands and wives have developed over the course of these changes. The rise of the privatised nuclear family is usually viewed as heralding a shift in the marital relationship to a more companionate form, with romantic love forming the basis of partner selection. At the same time, gender roles were said to have become more differentiated, with women's role focused almost exclusively on that of housewife and mother while men's role became more associated with that of provider and breadwinner. The concept of 'housewife' seems to have been a creation of the nineteenth century and was noted by one contemporary commentator in 1828:

> In the families in which all the members are so far advanced as to be fit for labour the aggregate amount of their earnings is very considerable, and is in general placed at the disposal of the eldest female whose sole employment consists in making purchases, and attending to the household duties.[60]

By the second half of the nineteenth century, a central plank of trade-union policy was the demand for a family wage, and a hallmark of working-class respectability became the family where the man was the financial provider who could afford to maintain a non-working wife. Definitions of work as a regular, full-time activity undertaken for a wage, usually outside the home and governed by market relations, came to dominate public discourses and official thinking and were reflected in census statistics, which tended to underestimate the extent of women's work.[61] By 1911, only 5 per cent of married women in Scotland were recorded as having an occupation. For many working-class families, men's poor wages and insecurity of employment meant that the family wage was an ideal to which they aspired rather a reality. Therefore there were significant variations in the participation rates of married women in the economy across classes and regions. Even the census records record fairly high levels of women's work in some areas. In Glasgow and Edinburgh, married women's work corresponded with national averages, while in Dundee and Shetland the figures were significantly higher.[62] Rather than viewing themselves as downtrodden drudges, working wives often proudly embraced their role. One Dundee woman referred disparagingly to Glasgow women as 'big fat lazy women', while an American journalist commented that 'in the Shetlands women are the best men'.[63] Although the ideology of domesticity discursively defined women's place as in the home, there were cultural variations in attitudes to married women working. In Glasgow's Jewish community, it was common for wives to contribute to the family business, or even have businesses in their own right, and this was a tradition which survived generations including transition to the suburbs.[64] In Shetland, women were not only prominent in the economy, they also dominated the islands numerically, visibly and discursively.[65] Therefore, if we take account of women's role in family strategies for survival and in 'self-provisioning', and the varied pattern of married women's work across region and class, it is by no means clear that a sharp demarcation of gender roles based on a male breadwinner and a non-working wife had become the established norm by the twentieth century.

What is clear is that women were primarily responsible for household duties and the nurturing and rearing of children. From the late eighteenth century, secular attitudes to the mother–child relationship emphasised the importance of childhood as a stage in the life cycle and conjoined with religious discourses which privileged female piety. The consequence was to exalt moral motherhood and to conceive of it primarily in relation to its moral and educative responsibilities to children. However, how the idealised role of motherhood was conceived, interpreted and experienced varied enormously. Among the working classes, economic constraints ensured that even if the ideology of domesticity and the attendant image of 'angel in the house' were well entrenched, full-time motherhood was not a practical reality for many working-class families. It is even questionable whether this model of motherhood encompassed the wider ideals and experiences across the middle classes, let alone the working classes. Indeed, some historians have suggested that it was not until the twentieth century that middle-class mothers placed children at the centre of their lives and experience, despite notions of 'angel in the house' occupying a central place in mythologies and discourses of nineteenth-century motherhood.[66]

According to the evidence of one study of children's experience of growing up in early twentieth-century Scotland, middle-class children did not spend much time with their mothers, who were more inclined to delegate child care to servants than cooking. One woman, born in 1902, recalled that she and her siblings 'spent a good deal of time with the maid . . . I really can't remember my mother ever, you know, taking me in her arms or anything like that'.[67] However, other middle-class mothers spent a good deal of time with their children and went to extraordinary lengths to entertain, amuse and educate them.[68] Working-class mothers had different priorities, and good housekeeping and the practicalities of child care were their preoccupations. Working-class children seemed to share the view that a good mother was defined in terms of their house-keeping abilities, and their memories revolved around their mothers' housekeeping skills. One woman brought up in interwar Lanarkshire extolled her mother's virtues:

> She was a perfect mother, you know. She could knit and sew. She could make a suit, she could bake, cook . . . My mother was clever in that way with her hands, and she looked after us very well but she didn't speak anything about her life.[69]

Despite prevailing views which stressed the morally redemptive and educative role of motherhood, competing models of motherhood, the mobility of meaning within the term and the disjuncture between the ideal and lived experience all point to the varied experiences of mother-hood even within the middle classes.

The dominance of the separate-spheres model of gender relations which has associated women with the home and family has to some extent obscured the family role of men. Until relatively recently, father-hood has not been seen as central to male identity. Either historians over-looked its importance, or conceptions of fatherhood were equated simply with the role of breadwinner. However, recently the domestic identity of men has been rehabilitated.[70] It has been argued that, for men, the public and private realms were permeable and interconnected; that both middle-class and working-class men saw themselves as much more than breadwinners, and that men could be more anxious and more caring – and even more involved in day-to-day child care – than was compatible with a conception of the father's role as that of a properly strict provider and little else. One Stirling woman who had thirteen siblings recalled of her father that, 'when my mother had the girls, when they were young he took over bath time and done our hair'.[71] There were, of course, many different ways of being a father, and diverse interpretations of the paternal role and the pressures of breadwinning could limit men's time with their families. Within these constraints, men were more than shadowy and marginal figures in Scottish family life and certainly more than the dour, aloof or drunken figure of the popular stereotypes.

From the late eighteenth century, cultural injunctions increasingly advocated ideals of romantic love and companionate union as the only basis for marriage. However, the legal basis of marriage remained resolutely patriarchal. Marriage laws in Scotland remained virtually untouched between the sixteenth century and the twentieth century. The only significant changes were the Married Women's Property Act 1881 and the 1938 and 1939 Acts which respectively extended the grounds of divorce to include cruelty and introduced civil marriage. Free consent remained central to the marital union to the extent that, although against the laws of the church and the state, 'irregular' marriage was still valid in Scotland until 1939, while Hardwicke's Act of 1753 meant the virtual disappearance of irregular marriage in England.

Love and affection had not been absent from the early modern marital relationship; but, from the late eighteenth century, it was expected that love should be the basis for marriage rather than a hoped-for outcome of it. However, popular beliefs and practice did not always coincide with these ideals, and the basis for matrimony was never a simple matter of personal choice based on romantic love. Neither was the choice a stark polarity between love and money. As before, usually elements of both these extremes came into play when choosing a marriage partner. For the working classes, a man's ability to be a good provider and a woman's domestic skills continued to be important considerations. Similarly, for the middle classes, rational calculation and romantic love were not necessarily mutually exclusive. The nineteenth-century bourgeoisie were noted for forming marital alliances that cemented business partnerships or prolonged political and economic dynasties, but it was rare for economic factors to be the sole reason for marriages.[72] The Victorian match saw romance and passion jockey with hard-headed calculation in the final decision. In terms of basis for the choice of partner and marriage relations, there was no sharp contrast between the early modern period and the nineteenth century. However, the balance shifted towards emphasising affection, companionship and love as essential ingredients for a successful marriage rather than seeing them as possible by-products.

Ideals of complementarity and companionship probably raised women's expectations of their husbands and the marital relationship. A. J. Hammerton has suggested that it was these rising expectations which partly generated the debate about marriage in the second half of the century, with women voicing criticism of husbands' abuse of their power and their unreasonable behaviour.[73] Yet, despite the availability of divorce for both men and women in Scotland, divorce rates were extremely low. It was only after the Married Women's Property Act of 1881, which restored to married women the right to own and control their own property, that there was any perceptible increase in divorce rates, suggesting that economic inequalities were the main obstacles to women seeking divorce or separation.[74] The law continued to be based on the principle of the husband's supreme authority, as indicated by Frederick Walton's adjudication in 1893: 'The husband as *dignior persona* is the head of the house. As his duty is to love and cherish his wife, so hers is to love and obey him.'[75] The law continued to be based on the principle of the husband's supreme authority. However, legal discourses indicate a shift in attitudes, as suggested by the comments of one legal authority in 1846 that

> Our ancient law gave the husband a right moderately to chastise his wife by corporeal punishment, and the doctrine has been so laid down even as the law at the present day. But this is so utterly inconsistent with modern manners, as not to be one which, it is at all probable that the court will sanction.[76]

Yet, as late as the 1830s, a Glasgow magistrate fined a man five pounds for slashing his wife's face and told him that 'If he had so beaten any other person, than his wife, he would have been punished most severely'. The same magistrate went on to fine a carter who had whipped his horse ten shillings and sixpence. Wife-beating continued to be common practice in nineteenth-century Scotland, with 95 per cent of domestic assault cases in Glasgow and Paisley between 1813 and 1838 involving men beating their wives. In a three-month period in 1824, fifty-six cases of wife-beating appeared before the Glasgow police court. Indeed, some men seemed to believe that they had a right to beat their wives, particularly if no weapon had been used. George Johnston, a travelling tinsmith, admitted murdering his wife but pled not guilty, claiming in his defence that 'I canna deny that I struck her, but with no weapon whatever'.[77]

Wife-beating continued to be prevalent in the first half of the twentieth century, and it has been suggested by some historians that a combination of factors multiplied male insecurities in the interwar period and may have contributed to the problem of male violence against women.[78] Although legal discourses seemed to be less tolerant of domestic violence, some courts still appeared to be equivocal about the legitimacy of provocation as grounds for cruelty. When, in 1932, Walter Parker was charged with stripping his wife naked and thrashing her with a belt, his justification was that she was of 'drunken habits'. The magistrate closely questioned her on her drinking habits and decided that he would imprison her husband only if she submitted to a medical examination, despite the fact that her daughter had witnessed the beating. She refused, and the charges against her husband were dropped.[79]

Of course, women did not always passively submit to either the constraints of the law or the violence of their husbands. Middle-class women used the device of marriage contracts to circumvent the law and to ensure that they retained control over their own property.[80] Women frequently retaliated against the physical abuse of their husbands, either in kind or by taking their violent husbands to court. Battered wives could also call on the support of the community. In the early modern period, communities used rituals known variously as 'ridings', 'rough music', 'skimmingtons' or 'charivari' to punish unacceptable behaviour, including excessive wife-beating. In more recent times, wives drew on female networks to provide witnesses or support if they had been beaten.[81]

Despite discourses that vaunted a family model based on a companionate conjugal unit supported by a male breadwinner, there was no unilinear movement towards one dominant family form from the nineteenth century through to the Second World War. The privatised family which was isolated from kin and community had by no means become consolidated in the nineteenth century, or even by the middle of the twentieth century. Rather, the diversity of family life is striking, as is the protean nature of the family. Families were flexible units, and a variety of strategies and forms were adopted to ensure their economic and emotional survival. The family was certainly not static or a stable unit between the nineteenth century and the Second World War. In the nineteenth century, death, disease and population mobility did much to destabilise families. In the first half of the twentieth century, suburbanisation, the increasing separation of home and work, greater geographical mobility and developments in popular culture and leisure, such as the cinema, all wrought changes on family life and gender roles.[82] However, continuities are as evident as change, and it was not until after the Second World War that we begin to see significant changes which ruptured the old family patterns and forms which had persisted for so long.

IDEALS AND DISCOURSES OF FAMILY LIFE

Edward Shorter has argued that the nuclear family was a state of mind as much as a particular structure or set of household arrangements.[83] In this sense, idealised notions of the family had an important impact on families and family life and on how people imagined and framed their lives. The day-to-day reality of family life and relationships was shaped by many factors, including cultural notions of the family, ideologies of gender and material circumstances. There were myriad ways in which idealised conceptions of family life and the discursively constructed family impinged on people's lives. Even in an overcrowded working-class tenement, women tried to construct family life around idealised conceptions of the home as a cosy and comfortable haven from the harsh realities of the world outside. The plethora of plants, ornaments, brass stands, crystals and antimacassars evident in working-class homes is indicative of the ways in which class-specific notions of respectability and gentility clearly influenced how working-class women furnished and decorated their homes.[84] Similarly, the ideology of domesticity and separate spheres, although originating in the middle classes, was shared by many within the working classes, even although it was probably only a minority of working-class families who could achieve the ideal.

Equally significantly, state policies, employers' policies and those of philanthropic organisations and churches were formulated in ways which reflected the cultural hegemony of the male-breadwinner nuclear family and which tried to mould working-class families in the image of this domestic ideal. Those who found themselves outside of this ideal suffered grim consequences. Women were expected to be economic dependants, therefore when they did work their wages were deemed to be supplementary even when they had no male wage to support them and might themselves have been providers. When legislation was introduced to curtail and regulate female and child labour in the nineteenth century, it was to a large extent motivated by a desire to foist the ideology of domesticity and separate spheres onto working-class families irrespective of their material circumstances.

Idealised conceptions of family life based around middle-class domestic ideology were also used to sanction intervention in working-class family life by voluntary and state agencies. In Scotland, the practice of boarding out children to foster parents was justified on the basis that these families were deemed to be failing to meet the standards of child care which accorded with middle-class ideals.[85] Similarly, Poor Law and welfare policies were informed by a familial ideal based on a male breadwinner. Under the Poor Law Act of 1845, outdoor relief was given on a discretionary basis which reflected and sought to reinforce prevailing moral codes and notions of a 'proper' family. Thus mothers of illegitimate children and widows who had fallen into 'immoral habits' were penalised by being denied outdoor relief.[86] The Beveridge Plan which formed the blueprint for Britain's postwar welfare society rested on a number of key assumptions, one of which was a gendered division of labour within the family. Once married, a woman traded any rights to insurance benefits which she had accrued in her own right for derived rights through her husband. These rights recognised the 'vital unpaid service' which women performed in 'ensuring the adequate continuance of the British race and of British ideals in the world'.[87] Although in theory the Plan was a comprehensive one which envisaged income maintenance for all from cradle to grave, in practice a woman's financial security was dependent on her husband's income. Thus the Plan served to institutionalise the male-breadwinner model of welfare and established a gendered notion of citizenship whereby on marriage women would draw on their spouses' contributions.

Discursive constructions of the family mediated people's experience of family life, informed local and central state policies and produced regulatory discourses which sought to eliminate aberrant behaviour by penalising those whose behaviour deviated from dominant cultural constructions of family life.

POST-SECOND WORLD WAR

If the 150 years or so from 1800 can be characterised by continuity rather than change in family life, then the period since the Second World War has been distinguished by the rapidity and profound nature of change, although many of the most significant changes did not take place until the 1970s. Some of the traits of family life which have been ascribed to the nineteenth-century model – emotional intimacy, marriage based on free choice, mutuality and understanding, child-centredness, privatised units of consumption – seem to be more apposite descriptions of the family in the second half of the twentieth century. On the other hand, the dramatic increase in divorce, cohabitation, the number of births outside marriage, and lower fertility make the contemporary family a very different proposition from any of its earlier incarnations.

If, as historical demographers have argued, the nuclear family has been statistically dominant over centuries, it may be the case that its ascendancy is over. Certainly, in 2001, most households contained only one family; but it was not the male-breadwinner conjugal ideal which had been so prominent in discourses for almost 200 years. In 2001, married couples with children made up 23.75 per cent of households, with those with no children adding another 12.58 per cent. Cohabiting couples made up 6.86 per cent of households, and 3 per cent of these had children. Lone-parent households numbered 10.5 per cent of all households and accounted for almost 22 per cent of households with children. About half of parents in single-parent households had never married. Almost one-third of households in Scotland were single-person, higher than the British average of 29 per cent, while in Glasgow one-person households outnumbered two-person households.[88] Women constituted 42 per cent of household heads. If it is borne in mind that many of these families are hybrid families composed of step-parents and step-children, and take account of the fact that about one-third of marriages end in divorce, a picture emerges of the modern family as more complex and varied than families of earlier generations. However, we should not lose sight of continuities in family form. As we have seen, low nuptuality, high illegitimate fertility and large numbers of lone-parent families have long been features of Scottish society.[89] Nor are broken families a contemporary phenomenon. Almost two centuries ago, the proportion of broken marriage was almost the same as it is today, but as a result of death rather than divorce. Fragmentation and instability have been perennial features of family life. The view that the 'traditional' family is disintegrating is based on the misconception that it ever existed.

One indisputable change has been the sharp decline in family size. In 1911, the average completed family size was almost six, in 1951 it was just under three and in 2001 it was 1.9. In general, women in Scotland are choosing to have fewer children and to have them later in life. In 2002, almost one-third of children were born to women in the 30–34 age-group compared with 14 per cent between 1971 and 1975. The mean age of marriage changed very little in the 100 years between 1850 and 1950. However, it has risen significantly in the last three decades, with the average age of marriage for women now around 32 and for men almost 35. Although this figure is partly a result of marrying for the first time at a later age, it is also due to the numbers who are remarrying, which inflates the average age of marriage. To a large extent, this shift can be attributed to changes in women's role, expectations and opportunities. Increasing employment and educational opportunities available to women since the 1960s, coupled with improved methods of contraception, have encouraged women to delay marriage and child-bearing.

The decline in the number of marriages, later age of marriage and the increase in the divorce rate does not necessarily mean a decline in partnership formation. The increasing numbers of divorcees who remarry, and the numbers cohabiting, indicate that people still seem willing to share their lives with someone else. What can these statistics and structural changes in the family tell us about the nature of the relationship between couples? It has been argued that in contemporary society people expect more emotional fulfilment and intimacy from marriage than in the past and that romantic love is viewed as the sole basis of marriage.[90] However, this companionate relationship based on equality, mutuality and shared intimacy is also more fragile and unstable because of the high expectations that couples have of each other. Secularisation and lack of religious commitment, coupled with the emphasis on personal fulfilment within marriage, mean that divorce is deemed to be no longer a moral issue but one of personal need. If this is indeed the basis for the modern couple relationship, then it would appear that it has taken 200 years for the nineteenth-century ideal of companionate marriage to take root and become part of the common language.

It is not entirely convincing that cultural expectations of a companionate relationship based on emotional intimacy necessarily translate into an equal partnership. Women's greater participation in paid work in the last few decades may mean that they have more economic independence; however, it is not clear that the gendered division of labour within the family has broken down. In fact, women's familial role to a large extent shapes their participation in the labour force, which is often organised around their child-care responsibilities. Many men are more involved in domestic tasks and in child care than their fathers were. However, there is no evidence that these tasks are equally shared with their partners. While the breadwinner role is no longer associated solely with the male partner, caring responsibilities have proved to be more resistant to change.

CONCLUSION

Common-sense conceptions of the family as an unchanging and 'natural' entity collapse in the face of the variety of forms, definitions and functions that can be associated with the family over the centuries. It is not even clear that we can compartmentalise the family into neat time periods characterised by a dominant family form, function, culture or morality. The flexibility of the family and its diversity are its most striking characteristics. The pre-industrial family certainly had more permeable boundaries than the contemporary family, and blood relations were less central to definitions of the 'family'. However, by redefining 'work' to encompass the many activities which women undertook to sustain the family's resources, we can see that the family's role as a productive unit spanned both pre-industrial and industrial society. The privatised nuclear family organised around a male-breadwinner model has dominated discursive constructions of the family for over two centuries, and yet as a material reality it has been relatively short-lived and was never universal. The high incidence of divorce, cohabitation, same-sex relationships, and births outside marriage, makes for a multiplicity of family forms in contemporary society, and yet the family is not so much breaking down as restructuring. Yet, arguably it is still the conjugal ideal which informs much of public policy and continues to be the touchstone for many people. In the course of their lifetime, individuals may experience marriage, single-parenthood and cohabitation, but the aim still seem to be for relationships based on longevity and commitment.

While there have been profound shifts in gender relations within the family since the early modern period, there has been no unilinear shift from resolutely patriarchal relations to ones of equality and mutuality. Patriarchal power in the pre-industrial family was based on law and ideology, but economic realities as well as individual force of personality allowed women to negotiate a more powerful place within this system. In the nineteenth-century, a companionate ideal was advocated; but it was framed by patriarchal legal and institutional discourses and thus did not promise equality for women within the marital relationship. In addition, the micro-politics of household power relations has always allowed a space for negotiation within these dominant discourses. Despite the myriad changes in women's role in the last three decades of the twentieth century, many would argue that women are still defined by their familial role and men by what they do outside of the family. Cultural expectations of an emotionally fulfilling relationship based on an equal partnership, and the blurring of the gender division of labour outside the home, may herald the breakdown of the gender division of labour in the contemporary family. However, given the enduring nature of these divisions and their entrenchment in social relations, this may be a pious hope.

FURTHER READING

Abrams, L., ' "There was nobody like my Daddy": fathers, the family and the marginalisation of men in modern Scotland', *Scottish Historical Review* 78:2 (1999), 219–42.

Abrams, L., 'Families of the imagination: Scottish family life in Scottish welfare policy', *Scottish Traditions* 28 (2003), 7–22.

Abrams, L., *Myth and Materiality in a Woman's World: Shetland 1800–2000* (Manchester: Manchester University Press, 2005).

Anderson, M., 'Population and family life', in A. Dickson and J. H. Treble (eds), *People and Society in Scotland Vol 3*, (Edinburgh: John Donald, 1992), pp. 12–47.

Anderson, M., 'Why was Scottish nuptiality depressed for so long?', in I. Devos and L. Kennedy (eds), *Marriage and Rural Economy: Western Europe since 1400* (Turnhout: Brepos, 1999), pp. 49–54.

Blaikie, A., 'A kind of loving: illegitimacy, grandparents and the rural economy of Northeast Scotland, 1750–1900', *Scottish Economic and Social History* 14 (1994), 41–57.

Gordon, E. and G. Nair, 'The myth of the Victorian patriarchal family', *History of the Family* 7 (2002), 125–38.

Gordon, E. and G. Nair, *Public Lives: Women, Family and Society in Victorian Britain* (New Haven, CT and London: Yale University Press, 2003).

Hughes, A., 'Domestic violence on Clydeside between the wars', *Labour History Review* 69:2 (2004), 169–84.

Jamieson, L. and C. Toynbee, *Country Bairns* (Edinburgh: Edinburgh University Press, 1992).

Leneman, L., ' "A tyrant and a tormentor": violence against wives in eighteenth- and early nineteenth-century Scotland', *Continuity and Change* 12:1 (1997), 31–54.

Leneman, L., *Alienated Affections: The Scottish Experience of Divorce and Separation, 1684–1830* (Edinburgh: Edinburgh University Press, 1998).

Leneman, L. and R. Mitchison, *Sexuality and Social Control: Scotland, 1660–1780* (Oxford: Blackwell, 1989).

McGuckin, A., 'Moving stories: working-class women', in E. Breitenbach and E. Gordon (eds), *Out of Bounds: Women in Scottish Society 1800–1945* (Edinburgh: Edinburgh University Press, 1992), pp. 197–217.

NOTES

I would like to thank Linda Fleming and Lynn Sinclair for allowing me to read sections of their forthcoming Ph.D.s, and Katie Barclay for her research on the postwar period.

   1. See T. Hareven, 'The history of the family and the complexity of social change', *American Historical Journal* 96 (1991), 95–124 for a discussion of

some of the grand theories which once dominated social-science disciplines on the history of the family.

2. Louise A. Tilly, 'Women's history and family history: fruitful collaboration or missed connection', *Journal of Family History* 12 (1987), 303–15, sets out the case for a closer collaboration between women's history and family history.

3. See M. Anderson, *Family Structure in Nineteenth-Century Lancashire* (Cambridge: Cambridge University Press, 1971) and L. Davidoff and C. Hall, *Family Fortunes: Men and Women of the English Middle Class 1780–1850* (London: Routledge, 1987).

4. For an example of this type of approach, see J. L. Flandrin, *Families in Former Times: Kinship, Household and Sexuality* (Cambridge: Cambridge University Press, 1976); A. Burgière, 'The formation of the couple', *Journal of Family History* 12 (1987), 39–53; R. Wheaton and T. K. Hareven (eds), *Family and Sexuality in French History* (Philadelphia, PA: University of Pennsylvania Press, 1980).

5. Alison MacKinnon, 'Were women present at the demographic transition? Questions from a feminist historian to historical demographers', *Gender & History* 7 (1995), 222–40.

6. See Wally Seccombe, *Weathering the Storm: Working-Class Families from the Industrial Revolution to the Fertility Decline* (London: Verso, 1993) for a discussion of the importance of gender power relations in explaining fertility patterns, particularly the fertility decline from the second half of the nineteenth century.

7. There is an extensive literature on this. See the following for a discussion of these revisions: E. A. Wrigley, 'Reflections on the history of the family', *Daedalus* 106 (1977), 71–85; P. Laslett, 'Characteristics of the Western family over time', in P. Laslett (ed.), *Family Life and Illicit Love in Earlier Generations* (Cambridge: Cambridge University Press, 1977), pp. 12–49.

8. D. J. Morse, 'The Decline of Fertility in Scotland', unpublished Ph.D. thesis, University of Edinburgh, 1987; A. Gilloran, 'Family Formation in Victorian Scotland', unpublished Ph.D. thesis, University of Edinburgh, 1985; S. P. Walker, 'Occupational Expansion, Fertility Decline and Recruitment to the Professions in Scotland 1850–1914', unpublished Ph.D. thesis, University of Edinburgh, 1986; Debbie Kemmer, 'The Marital Fertility of Edinburgh Professions in the later Nineteenth Century', unpublished Ph.D. thesis, University of Edinburgh, 1989.

9. In Britain, the work of Michael Anderson has been central in recovering the role of the family as an agent of social change and in demonstrating that industrialisation did not destroy the links between the family and wider kin.

10. See Chapter 8 in this volume.

11. Elizabeth C. Sanderson, *Women and Work in Eighteenth-Century Edinburgh* (Basingstoke: Macmillan, 1996), ch. 4.

12. See I. D. Whyte and K. A. Whyte, 'The geographical mobility of women in early modern Scotland', in L. Leneman (ed.), *Perspectives in Scottish Social History* (Aberdeen: Aberdeen University Press, 1988), pp. 83–106.
13. See Eleanor Gordon and Gwyneth Nair, *Public Lives: Women, Family and Society in Victorian Britain* (New Haven, CT and London: Yale University Press, 2003), pp. 161–3 for a discussion of married women's property rights.
14. Quoted in L. Leneman, ' "A tyrant and a tormentor": violence against wives in eighteenth- and early nineteenth-century Scotland', *Continuity and Change* 12:1 (1991), p. 48.
15. Quoted in K. Barclay, 'The law of marriage in Scotland', unpublished working paper, University of Glasgow.
16. M. H. King, 'A partnership of equals: women in Scottish east-coast fishing communities', *Folklife* 31 (1992–3), 17–35.
17. D. Macdonald, *Lewis: A History of the Island* (Edinburgh: Gordon Wright, 1978), p. 63.
18. Leneman, 'A tyrant and a tormentor', p. 42.
19. Quoted in Barclay, 'The law of marriage'.
20. Leneman, 'A tyrant and a tormentor', p. 49.
21. Gordon and Nair, *Public Lives*, p. 113.
22. Ibid., p. 110.
23. I. Gow, 'The dining room', in A. Carruthers (ed.), *The Scottish Home* (Edinburgh: National Museums of Scotland, 1996), pp. 125–54.
24. J. Mackenzie, 'The Highland Community in Glasgow in the Nineteenth Century', unpublished thesis, University of Stirling, 1987, p. 200.
25. Gordon and Nair, *Public Lives*, p. 45.
26. Lynn Sinclair, 'Silenced, Suppressed and Passive? A Refocused History of Lanarkshire Women, 1920–1939', unpublished thesis, University of Strathclyde, 2005.
27. A. McGuckin, 'Moving stories: working-class women', in E. Breitenbach and E. Gordon (eds), *Out of Bounds: Women in Scottish Society 1800–1945* (Edinburgh: Edinburgh University Press, 1992), pp. 197–217.
28. Gordon and Nair, *Public Lives*, pp. 48–50.
29. Ibid., pp. 20–1.
30. Linda Fleming, 'Jewish Women in Glasgow: Gender and the Immigrant Experience c.1880–1950', unpublished Ph.D. thesis, University of Glasgow, 2005.
31. L. Jamieson and C. Toynbee, *Country Bairns* (Edinburgh: Edinburgh University Press, 1992), p. 28.
32. N. Tadmor, *Family and Friends in Eighteenth-Century England* (Cambridge: Cambridge University Press, 2002).
33. Gordon and Nair, *Public Lives*, p. 127.
34. Ibid., p. 44.
35. Mackenzie, 'The Highland Community in Glasgow', ch. 5.

36. M. Anderson, *Family Structure in Nineteenth-Century Lancashire* (Cambridge: Cambridge University Press, 1971); S. Ruggles, *Prolonged Connections: The Rise of the Extended Family in Nineteenth-Century England and America* (Madison, WI: University of Wisconsin Press, 1987).

37. Mackenzie, 'The Highland Community in Glasgow', ch. 5.

38. Gordon and Nair, *Public Lives*, pp. 36–8.

39. M. Anderson, 'Why was Scottish nuptuality depressed for so long?', in I. Devos and L. Kennedy (eds), *Marriage and Rural Economy: Western Europe since 1400* (Turnhout: Brepos, 1999), pp. 49–54.

40. E. Gordon, *Women and the Labour Movement in Scotland, 1850–1914* (Oxford: Oxford University Press, 1991), p. 142; L. Abrams, *Myth and Materiality in a Woman's World: Shetland 1800–2000* (Manchester: Manchester University Press, 2005); E. Gordon and G. Nair, 'The myth of the Victorian patriarchal family', *History of the Family* 7 (2002), pp. 125–38.

41. Anderson, *Family Structure*.

42. Gordon, *Women and the Labour Movement*, p. 153.

43. Sinclair, 'Silenced, Suppressed and Passive?'.

44. A. Blaikie, 'A kind of loving: illegitimacy, grandparents and the rural economy of Northeast Scotland, 1750–1900', *Scottish Economic and Social History* 14 (1994), 41–57, here p. 55.

45. Gordon and Nair, *Public Lives*, p. 66.

46. Anderson, *Family Structure*.

47. Gordon and Nair, *Public Lives*, p. 47.

48. Gwyneth Nair, *Highley: The Development of a Community* (Oxford: Blackwell, 1988); Z. Razi, 'The myth of the immutable English family', *Past and Present* 140 (1993), 3–44; K. Wrightson and D. Levine, *Poverty and Piety in an English Village: Terling 1525–1700* (Oxford: Oxford University Press, 1979 and 1995).

49. Gordon and Nair, *Public Lives*, ch. 4.

50. F. Heal, *Hospitality in Early Modern England* (Oxford: Oxford University Press, 1990).

51. Gordon and Nair, *Public Lives*.

52. Fleming, 'Jewish Women in Glasgow'; J. Handley, *The Irish in Modern Scotland* (Cork: Cork University Press, 1947); R. D. Lobban, 'The Migration of Highlanders into Lowland Scotland', unpublished Ph.D. thesis, University of Edinburgh, 1969; J. Mackenzie, 'The Highland Community in Glasgow'.

53. Fleming, 'Jewish Women in Glasgow'.

54. Sinclair, 'Silenced, Suppressed and Passive?'.

55. McGuckin, 'Moving stories', p. 206.

56. See ibid. for examples of neighbourhood collective action.

57. Jamieson and Toynbee, *Country Bairns*, pp. 24–5.

58. Ibid., p. 24.

59. See Abrams, *Myth and Materiality* for female networks in Shetland.

60. Quoted in Gordon, *Women and the Labour Movement*, p. 76.

61. See Gordon, *Women and the Labour Movement*, pp. 16–21 for a discussion of the social construction of the census; and E. Higgs, *A Clearer Sense of the Census: Victorian Censuses and Historical Research* (London: HMSO, 1996).
62. Gordon, *Women and the Labour Movement*, pp. 20–1; Abrams, *Myth and Materiality*.
63. Gordon, ibid., p. 164; Abrams, ibid.
64. Fleming, 'Jewish Women in Glasgow'.
65. Abrams, *Myth and Materiality*.
66. A. Light, *Forever England: Femininity, Literature and Conservatism between the Wars* (London: Routledge, 1991).
67. L. Jamieson, 'Theories of family development and the experience of being brought up', *Sociology* 21:4 (1987), 591–601.
68. Gordon and Nair, *Public Lives*, ch. 5 for a discussion of middle-class motherhood.
69. Sinclair, 'Silenced, Suppressed and Passive?'.
70. L. Abrams, ' "There was nobody like my Daddy": fathers, the family and the marginalisation of men in modern Scotland', *Scottish Historical Review* 78:2 (1999), 219–42; S. M. Frank, *Life with Father: Parenthood and Masculinity in the Nineteenth-century North* (London and Baltimore, MD: Johns Hopkins University Press, 1998); S. Johansen, *Family Men: Middle-class Fatherhood in Industrializing America* (London: Routledge, 2001); J. Tosh, *A Man's Place: Masculinity and the Middle-class Home in Victorian England* (London and New Haven, CT: Yale University Press, 1999); Gordon and Nair, *Public Lives*.
71. Abrams, 'There was nobody like my Daddy', p. 232.
72. Gordon and Nair, *Public Lives*, ch. 3.
73. A. J. Hammerton, *Cruelty and Companionship: Conflict in Nineteenth-Century Married Life* (London: Routledge, 1995), p. 72.
74. Gordon and Nair, *Public Lives*, pp. 161–2.
75. Quoted in Gordon and Nair, *Public Lives*, p. 74.
76. Quoted in Leneman, 'A tyrant and a tormentor', p. 50.
77. A. Clark, *The Struggle for the Breeches: Gender and the Making of the British Working Class* (London: Rivers Oram Press, 1995), pp. 73–4.
78. See A. Hughes, 'Domestic violence on Clydeside between the wars', *Labour History Review* 69:2 (2004), 169–84 for a discussion of this debate.
79. Ibid., p. 179.
80. Gordon and Nair, *Public Lives*, pp. 162–5.
81. Leneman, 'A tyrant and a tormentor'; McGuckin, 'Moving stories'.
82. D. Gittins, *Fair Sex: Family Size and Structure 1900–1939* (London: Hutchinson, 1982).
83. E. Shorter, *The Making of the Modern Family* (London: Fontana, 1977), p. 205.
84. See Fleming, 'Jewish Women in Glasgow' for a discussion of the homes of working-class Jewish families in the Gorbals.

85. L. Abrams, 'Families of the imagination: Scottish family life in Scottish welfare policy', *Scottish Traditions* 28 (2003), 7–22.
86. T. Ferguson, *Scottish Social Welfare, 1864–1914* (Edinburgh, E. & S. Livingstone, 1958).
87. Quoted in R. Lister, ' "She has other duties": women, citizenship, and social security', in S. Baldwin and J. Falkingham (eds), *Social Security and Social Change: New Challenges to the Beveridge Model* (London: Harvester Wheatsheaf, 1994), pp. 31–44. I am grateful to Ailsa McKay for this reference.
88. All statistics are taken from the 2001 census.
89. M. Anderson, 'Population and family life', in A. Dickson and J. H. Treble (eds), *People and Society in Scotland, vol. 3* (Edinburgh: John Donald, 1992), pp. 12–47, here p. 42.
90. L. Jamieson, *Intimacy: Personal Relationships in Modern Society* (Cambridge: Polity, 1998).

Contributors

Lynn Abrams is Professor of Gender History at the University of Glasgow. Her research and publications are concentrated in modern European women's and gender history. Her books include *Gender Relations in German History* (1996) (co-edited with Elizabeth Harvey), *The Orphan Country: Children of Scotland's Broken Homes, 1845 to the Present* (1998), *The Making of Modern Woman: Europe 1789–1918* (2002) and *Myth and Materiality in a Woman's World: Shetland 1800–2000* (2005).

Esther Breitenbach is an Honorary Research Fellow in the School of Social and Political Studies, University of Edinburgh. She has written widely on the position of women in Scotland, has co-edited with Eleanor Gordon two volumes on Scottish women's history, and has co-edited with Fiona Mackay an anthology on women and contemporary Scottish politics. She has completed a Ph.D. on the topic of religion, empire and Scottish national identity in the nineteenth and early twentieth centuries.

Callum G. Brown is Professor of Religious and Cultural History at the University of Dundee. His books include *Religion and Society in Scotland since 1707* (1997), *Postmodernism for Historians* (2005), *The Death of Christian Britain* (2001) and *Up-helly-aa: Custom, Culture and Community in Shetland* (1998), and he is co-author of *The University Experience* (2004). He is currently working on a history of religion in twentieth-century Britain.

Eleanor Gordon is Professor of Gender and Social History at the University of Glasgow. She has written widely on nineteenth-century gender history, labour history and the history of the family, including *Women and the Labour Movement in Scotland, 1850–1914* (1991). Her most recent publication, co-written with Gwyneth Nair, is *Public Lives: Women, Family and Society in Victorian Britain* (2003).

Sue Innes had a first career in journalism, writing for the *Scotsman* and *Scotland on Sunday* among other newspapers. In 1998, she completed a Ph.D. at the University of Edinburgh on women and politics in inter-war Scotland, and went on to become a lecturer and research fellow at Edinburgh, Glasgow and Glasgow Caledonian Universities. She was also a co-ordinator and researcher for *Engender*. Her publications include *Making it Work: Women, Change and Challenge in the 1990s* (1995), *Engender* audits, and contributions to *Women and Contemporary Scottish Politics* (ed. Breitenbach and Mackay, 2001). She was also a co-editor of *The Biographical Dictionary of Scottish Women* (2006). Sue Innes died of a brain tumour in 2005.

Lindy Moore is Senior Assistant Librarian, Rhyl Library, Museum and Arts Centre, Denbighshire, Wales. As an independent researcher, she has written for twenty-five years on women's history and gender history in Scottish education, women's suffrage and public libraries. Publications include *Bajanellas and Semilinas: Aberdeen University and the Education of Women 1860–1920* (1991).

Jane Rendall is an Honorary Fellow in the History Department and the Centre for Eighteenth-Century Studies at the University of York. She is interested in eighteenth- and nineteenth-century British and comparative women's history, and particularly in Scottish women's history. Her publications include *The Origins of Modern Feminism* (1985), *Women in an Industrializing Society: England 1750–1880* (1990) and, with Catherine Hall and Keith McClelland, *Defining the Victorian Nation* (2000). She has also edited *Equal or Different: Women's Politics 1800–1914* (1987) and, jointly with Karen Offen and Ruth Roach Pierson, *Writing Women's History: International Perspectives* (1991). She is currently working on a study of the gendered legacies of the Enlightenment in Scotland.

Siân Reynolds is Emerita Professor of French at the University of Stirling. She has written widely on French and Scottish history. Books include *Britannica's Typesetters: Women Compositors in Edwardian Edinburgh* (1989), *France Between the Wars: Gender and Politics* (1996) and, co-edited with William Kidd, *Contemporary French Cultural Studies* (2000). She is a co-editor of *The Biographical Dictionary of Scottish Women* (2006). She is currently completing a book on Paris and Edinburgh during the belle époque.

Deborah Simonton is Associate Professor of British History at the University of Southern Denmark. Her publications include *The Routledge History of Women in Modern Europe* (2005) as editor, *A History of European Women's Work, 1700 to the Present* (1998), *Gendering Scottish History: An International Approach* co-edited (1999) with Oonagh Walsh and Terry Brotherstone, and *Women and Higher Education, Past Present and Future* (1996) with Mary Masson. Her research focuses on gender, childhood, education and work, especially in the eighteenth century, on which she has written widely. She is currently writing *Women in European Culture and Society* for Routledge.

Eileen Janes Yeo is Professor of Social and Cultural History at the University of Strathclyde and is Director of the Strathclyde Centre in Gender Studies. She is the author of *The Contest for Social Science: Relations and Representations of Gender and Class* (1996) and is currently writing a book on *Meanings of Motherhood in Europe and America*.

Index